KU-773-516

The
British
New Left

The British New Left

LIN CHUN

EDINBURGH
UNIVERSITY
PRESS

© Lin Chun, 1993
Edinburgh University Press Ltd
22 George Square, Edinburgh

Typeset in Linotron Ehrhardt
by Koinonia Ltd, Bury, and
printed and bound in the UK by
The University Press, Cambridge

A CIP record for this book is available from
the British Library

ISBN 0 7486 0422 7

FOR ROSA

Contents

Abbreviations

CCCS   The Centre for Contemporary Cultural Studies, Birmingham

CND   The Campaign for Nuclear Disarmament

CP(GB)   The Communist Party (of Great Britain)

CSE   Conference of Socialist Economists

END   The International Liaison Committee for European Nuclear Disarmament

HWJ   *History Workshop Journal*

IMG   The International Marxist Group

IS   International Socialists

IWC   The Institute for Workers' Control

LP   The Labour Party

MT   *Marxism Today*, London

NLB   New Left Books and Verso

NLR   *New Left Review*, London

NR   *The New Reasoner*, Halifax

RHR   *Radical History Review*, New York

SR   *Socialist Register*, London

ULR   *Universities and Left Review*, London

VSC   The Vietnam Solidarity Campaign

Preface

Without the support and help of many people, I could not have brought this work to fruition.

My deep appreciation goes to Gareth Stedman Jones for his trust and for enabling me to pursue an unfamiliar topic. I have learnt much from his guidance and criticism and should have learnt more.

I owe a special debt to Bernard Crick, Lionel Elvin, Anthony Giddens and Susan James. They all read entire or large parts of my doctoral dissertation, on which this book is based, and offered invaluable comments and suggestions. They also supported me in various other ways for which I am very grateful.

Janice and Wolfgang Stargardt have not only sustained me through the working on the book, but also taught me, by way of their friendship, what humanism and internationalism are. So have Robin Cohen, Nancy Fraser, Maurice Meisner, Sam Schweber, and Joan Scott, who helped me both intellectually and personally during difficult times while I was writing.

Allen Hunter and Leo Salingar were of great help in giving me useful references. My conversations with Michael Walzer were very enlightening. I respect him as a teacher and admire his tolerance towards my disagreements which sometimes must have seemed wilful. Tianyu Cao, Larry Epstein, Chinkeu Li, Saras Narsey, Funglin Ng, Benzhou Wang and David Wood, among other friends, involved themselves in this work in different ways, technical as well as substantial. My affection and gratitude go to them. And, I wish to express my heartfelt thanks to my editors for their warm encouragement and intelligent work, in particular Penny Clarke, Dilys Jones and Maureen Prior, and to Margaret Christie for compiling the index. On my return to China, Bernard Crick read the proofs for me. I thank him again from a distant land, with apologies.

I am also indebted to Michael Barratt Brown, Robin Blackburn, Ken Coates, Lawrence Daly, Stuart Hall, Margot Heinemann, Eric Hobsbawm, Ralph Miliband, Raphael Samuel, John and Constance Saville, Edward Thompson and Peter Worsley, for their concern, and the time and energy they spent in interviews, correspondence and making arrangements to allow me access to personal or institutional archives. At those points where I draw specifically on this material the source is stated in the text or notes.

Nick Stargardt's enthusiasm and generosity have always reminded me of my dear friends in China. He read the whole of the original thesis in its varied stages, made numerous critical suggestions and saved me from many mistakes both in its contents and language. I miss his intellectual seriousness and true comradeship.

I was most fortunate to have Robert Cohen's patient advice throughout the entire revising process for publication. Because of him, I have been able to make a real difference between the earlier and the present work. I profoundly appreciate him being an unfailing source of stimulus and criticism, and I came to rely on his kindness, wisdom and judgement.

Finally, I want to express my deep sadness at the sudden death of Martin Spencer, the former Secretary of the Edinburgh University Press. Indeed, feeling guilty about owing him too much made me press on with the book.

I am solely responsible for all errors on points of fact or interpretation that may remain.

L.C.

May 1992

Introduction

I found myself attracted by the New Left movement in Britain during the first year of my stay at Cambridge University as a graduate student. While I was working on a very different project, I learned a little about that movement from limited reading as well as from chatting with my supervisor, Gareth Stedman Jones, and soon I became irresistibly interested. Generally preoccupied as I was with questions posed by the deepening crisis of Marxist theories and socialist practices in the mid-1980s, what aroused my curiosity was the striking contrast between persistent socialist political culture in an advanced capitalist society (post-war Britain) on the one hand, and the rather confused attempt at a 'capitalist transformation' of a society under communism where I came from (post-Mao China) on the other. Moreover, this was sharpened by another odd contrast between developed and still growing Marxist scholarship in Britain and the low level of studies and rapidly declining faith in Marxism and socialism in China. The common separation between socialist rhetoric and politics took very different forms in the two countries between which I was naturally inclined to make comparisons. I found the British New Left a possible and maybe even advantageous starting point for pursuing my questions concerning the 'scientific' vitality and moral credibility of socialism with its most systematic and powerful theoretical expressions in various traditions of Marxism, especially because the superiority of the British system over our own seemed so evident in terms of both political democracy and social welfare. My questions were disturbing enough to lead me to choose a new research topic in the following year that required not only curiosity but also immense effort to think really hard about what my generation had experienced, growing up in largely isolated China in the period of the Cold War and the Sino-Soviet split, and inherited from the two revolutionary generations before us.

I am glad to have made a good choice – the specific history of the British New Left which I tried to explore taught me a great deal, and the long process of writing this book gradually led me to a better position from which I seek to clarify, if not yet to resolve, what has bothered me all these years in relation to the problems and retreat of socialism.

The term 'New Left' was not a British invention, but French.[1] It is often identified with the youth radicalism which swept over the advanced capitalist world in the late 1960s. This radicalism, combining with the anti-Vietnam protests, related attacks on higher education to the black revolt in the United States where the movements for civil rights and free speech had started earlier, in the late 1950s; to workers' strikes and factory occupations in France, Italy, Germany, as well as England; and to various liberation initiatives beyond traditional class struggle, which primarily characterised the global New Left.[2] Though briefly a part of that international upsurge of '1968', the British New Left originated from the crises of 1956 and followed an unparalleled course until the mid- to late 1970s. As a very loosely organised movement, it was rather confined in its national context to individual and collective activities associated with certain key publishing and research enterprises which formed the bases or organs of the movement. As an intellectual tendency, it differed from the new leftism of the 'Sixty-Eighters' by being far more profoundly inspired by Marxist theories. One of the reasons for the absence of any systematic study of the trajectory of the British case, among a quite rich literature on the new left in other countries and as a global whole, lies in the neglect of its distinctiveness.

There were roughly three major trends constituting what was nevertheless an integral New Left in Britain:
(1) dissident communism based on working-class culture and politics and other nineteenth-century native radical traditions;
(2) independent socialism, stemming from a fusion of the radicalism of the Oxbridge professional middle class and the tradition of London populist protest;
(3) theoretical Marxism, inspired by classical internationalism and continental European Marxist currents.

Other components such as revolutionary Christian thought, socialist feminist thinking and 'green politics', and the aesthetics of sub-culture or counter-culture were also visible. These trends clashed with each other from time to time but were more often mutually inclusive. Basically, differences in political style and intellectual orientation did not divert those who carried out the project of the New Left from what they saw as the fundamental task of rejecting the politically and morally bankrupt and intellectually paralysed forms of the old left – Stalinism and social democracy. Somewhere between these forms, they sought to define the space in which renewed socialist ideas and agendas could develop. This is why the New Left can be reconstructed, despite internal incoherence and oppositions, as a common tendency. (Such a position, of course, has been reclaimed at other times and places by those who believed in the possibility of a 'third way'.)

The difficulties in tracing the history of the British New Left are caused, among other things, by the lack of a unifying organisational identity and the complexity of the profound divisions between its two generations and, within the first generation, between the two initial groups. Besides, its leading theorists were

outstanding scholars in their respective fields: since they owed their standing to
their scholarly accomplishments as well as to their politics, it becomes problematic to decide where the two realms are linked together and where they are not.
Moreover, it has to be conceded that individual participants often moved between
the new and the other lefts, from the Labour Party to the Trotskyist groupings.
As a result, the label 'new left' is not necessarily liked or even accepted by all the
figures whose work I straitjacketed in this study. (On the other hand, there must
be non-aligned Marxists and socialists without any party affiliation who consider
themselves to be on a broad 'new left' but are not included in my narrowly
defined New Left circles.) I see my controversial approach as a price paid for a
way in which both the totality of, and differences among, what is called the
British New Left movement and the larger environment can be effectively
grasped and understood. I discuss some of these difficulties and my justifications
of my own attempt at overcoming them in a special section of chapter I on the
question of definitions, and in section 4 of chapter IV as well.

   This history can be divided into three stages: the early New Left of 1957–62;
the continuation of the movement from 1963–9 that was contributed to, though
in quite diverging directions, by both New Left generations; and the theoretical
construction of 1970–7. The year 1977 seemed to me the most convenient in
which to end the story because, against the background of the second half of the
1970s – the great rightward drift in politics resulting from the regeneration of the
conservative and liberal 'new right', and the realignment of forces on the left in
response to that drift – the long-admitted exhaustion of the New Left as a
political movement was now in conjunction with the completion of a body of its
theoretical work. At the same time, clearly the rapid growth of the new social
movements belonged to another moment of history, when arguments for a new
kind of politics were no longer identifiable as distinctively 'new left'. I explain
this displacement in concrete terms in the Epilogue. The book is simply
organised as follows: the first chapter examines the origins and formation of the
British New Left, and the rest deal with each stage of the movement in turn.

   It is undeniable that the British New Left never grew beyond being an
intellectual opposition and indeed failed to become a major interventionist social
force of any significance in actual political struggles. The value of any historical
work here is precisely to investigate why this was so. Yet 'cultural permeation' of
even a small movement of ideas, having taken place so often in history, can be
much more profound and lasting than its transitory political appearance. The
New Left apparently had an impact on the post-new left developments in radical
thinking and politics. Its living spirit of constantly reappraising ongoing changes
in society ensured its continuing contemporary relevance. It is, however, still too
early to reach a reasonably comprehensive assessment of something that is not yet
distant enough from us. What I shall try to do in the remainder of this
introduction is to present some of my preliminary conclusions and unsolved
questions in outline form (detailed discussions of them can be found in the
corresponding parts of the text), in order to warn the readers of the incomplete

nature of this work. Further research is needed, and I believe the British New Left deserves much more attention from serious historians, not only within the 'left academy' and the capitalist 'first world'.

One of the immediately observable weaknesses of this New Left was its political incapacity. It not only missed all of what seemed to be the real opportunities to build itself a stronger position with a wider political platform and support for its ideas, and therefore in turn, shared some responsibility for the victory of the New Right, but also failed to formulate any long-term programme for the future regeneration of a socialist movement.[3] In stressing the cultural dimension of politics and a substantive social function of criticism (beyond its old role of rebelling against ruling-class culture from within the confines of that culture itself), the New Left had been confronted with but never worked out the following question: how do radical thinking and theoretical analyses directly affect politics? Or, to put it differently, can a lively but solely intellectual force play any decisive role in bringing about social change? This is partly a question of how to translate theories into concrete political discussions since radical theorists are absolutely marginal in the polity (and indeed the question is also how the theory that a socialist movement requires is produced), and partly how these two levels of 'cultural struggle' are to be communicated to the agencies or potential agencies of the actual movement. Are these gaps ultimately unbridgeable? Far from commanding the mechanisms of cultural control and far too remote from the centres of power, to what extent can socialist intellectualism successfully combat the dominant influence of capitalist ideologies, or, in other words, how possibly might 'cultural hegemony' be achieved before and for an economic and political transformation of the existing system? Given the complex relationships between ideas, ideological institutions and institutional power, by what means, in any case, could at least a major section of the population be not only won over culturally, but also mobilised politically?

In fact, it took a long time for the New Left critics to realise how distant their culture was from reality, the common-sense morality of Labour and popular will under the conditions of welfare social democracy: the old belief in a firm unity between socialism and its 'natural' and traditional constituencies was seriously challenged, and the assumption that socialism was inevitable had long been abandoned. Socialism had to be redefined along the lines not only of class struggle but also of other emancipatory politics, and a socialist project had to begin with a struggle against some root values, concepts and images of the social consciousness of the day. This recognition was virtually a post-New Left achievement, but has now for more than a decade been most forcefully argued by the former participants of the New Left. This New Left while existing, however, never gave up what C. Wright Mills called the 'labour metaphysic',[4] even though it was not itself located in the organised Labour movement. This was a faith in the industrial working class, in Britain at least, as the central counter-force to capitalist domination; a faith that distinguished the British New Left and continuously characterised some of its leading thinkers.

The isolation of the New Left may explain something about, though by no means serve as an excuse for, its intellectual elitism, especially in the form of the super-theoreticism of the second New Left and the dislocation of Marxism from the current issues of national political economy. Being much criticised for its abstract approach that made no direct appeal in everyday language to an audience beyond a specialised intelligentsia, the highly successful 'theoretical practice' of the Marxist New Left nonetheless provided rigorous leadership to the drastic radicalisation of British intellectual life, a cultural gain that is seen by many as an authentic enlightenment. Related to this elitist strain there was also a sadly infective sectarianism that gave the New Left no escape from the 'rule' that the left is always ready to split. Both were at once causes and outcomes of the political defeat of the New Left.[5] The narrowness and inapplicability of New Left politics as a whole was above all manifest in its preoccupation with opposing the old left and later with opposing each other among its own competing trends, as though the enemy – the Conservatives, the right, the capitalist power – did not need to be really fought.[6]

Struggling with a 'new' identity, the New Left's ever-recurrent dilemma was its departure from and continuity with the great tradition of labour. By definition, of course, the rupture of the left between the old and the new cannot be thorough.[7] However, among the British New Left, both in its younger critics' total challenge to the national culture and the essence of Anglo-Saxon social thought and in the critiques of 'labourism' (and 'corporatism', 'parliamentarism', etc.) by its founding members, the positive and vital elements in the legacy of traditional English socialism were often seriously neglected or underrated. Whilst sympathetic to their creative stance, one cannot help wondering whether the values of the valuable had been fully weighed up. Have many of the imaginative ideas of utopian socialism (for example, the Owenian commitment to feminism and the architecture of a future co-operative community) or the work of an earlier generation of truly progressive socialists such as R. H. Tawney and G. D. H. Cole (Cole's objection to statist management of nationalised industry is surely highly relevant today) been carefully reconsidered? As another example, have the depth and strengths of English literary criticism – not only its romanticist motive of anti-capitalism (which offers a vantage point for the arguments of the present ecological movement) but also its remarkably anti-positivist inclination – been properly appreciated? And there are yet more examples: the moral and democratic traditions of the working class; the undogmatic Marxism of the old Independent Labour Party, the work of the Social Democratic Federation (whose slogan, 'Educate, Agitate, Organise', remains sound), and the unofficial currents of the Communist Party; the exemplary interaction between theory and practice in Workers' Adult Education programmes; the voluntary socialist principle introduced by the co-operative movement; the revolutionary self-liberating commitment of guild socialism.

In comparison with the old left, a major failing of the New Left was its lack of any organisational strength. Unlike pioneer British socialists (say, the Fabians) who were actively engaged with the daily work, either propaganda or educational campaigns, of strong political organisations and were therefore of significant influence on immediate policy debates and actual struggle over the decision making process, New Left people, with only one or two outstanding exceptions, at no point showed any intention of creating an alternative organisation to the stagnant left-wing bodies.[8] Without an independent party of their own, those of the New Left who did try were also unable to be more functional in the established parties. Both the attempts to revitalise the Labour Party from within and to develop the New Left into a force parallel to that party fell through. But had the New Left ever been in a position to organise a substantial new party even if it had so wished? Was it true that the existence of the Labour Party, the only historically formed expression of mass opposition, left too little room for the construction of an organisationally based New Left politics? In the broader milieu of the shattered hope of social democratic parties (and lately of most Communist Parties too) in western Europe as vehicles of socialist transformation, how might this crisis of political organisation, of the decay of the old forms and the absence and reluctance of the new, be surpassed?

On the one hand, the experience of the New Left seems to suggest that the conception of avoiding party bureaucracies defies the classical science of politics; on the other hand, it must be said that it was an important gain of the socialist movement to breach the limitation of the traditional framework of 'party' as the only channel of forging the conditions for effective political education and mobilisation.[9] This is a predicament that has trapped the New Left ever since it came into being after 1956 and recruited during 1968, one which had its root in the ambiguous collapse of vanguardism with all its not altogether good consequences.

What was, after all, accomplished in the twenty years of the British New Left movement? What impacts has it made on British society and socio-political thought, and beyond? I have mentioned some of my own answers, such as its leadership role in advancing a Marxist scholarship and radicalising the national culture. The benefits of this, from the viewpoint of regenerating socialism, could be very considerable. I shall examine fruitful New Left ideas in the following chapters, including those concerned with participatory democracy, workers' control and human self-emancipation; with community, communication, culture and cultural politics; with the alliance between mental and manual labour and between socialist and other emancipatory social movements; and with complexity, openness and pluralism in the nature of socialism and a socialist society. These ideas constitute a serious contribution to progressive social thought and represent long-term challenges to the existing order of capitalism. I emphasise, as the New Left critics themselves do, the 'libertarian' (not in its American sense of laissez-faire) core of new leftism. To discuss the legacy of the British New Left is to discover what far-reaching changes it brought about, if not institutionally then in terms of lifestyle, moral attitude, intellectual thinking and political culture, and is also to listen to the creative thinkers that the New Left movement was able to produce, who became main voices of late twentieth-century British socialism.

I hope my sympathetic criticism will do justice to the British New Left. In the light of the current worldwide crisis in socialist self-confidence, reviewing the lessons of the New Left may help us with the difficult task of recasting socialism in the years to come.

NOTES

1. A group of independent British socialists who were to become among the first New Leftists in Britain met Claude Bourdet, founder and editor of *France Observateur*, in Paris in 1956 for the conference called to consider setting up an International Socialist Society across the divisions between western and eastern Europe. The term was then borrowed from Bourdet (cf. Stuart Hall's recollection in 1989, pp. 14–15).

2. For the basic characteristics which are more or less commonly suggested to identify a general 'new left', cf. Birnbaum, 1969b, pp. 148–9; Cranston, ed. 1970, Foreword; Oglesby, ed. 1969, pp. 17–19; Teodori, ed. 1970, pp. 36–7; Katsiaficas, 1987, pp. 23–7.

3. Neither Raymond Williams's cultural 'long revolution' strategy (see, esp. essays in 1983a) nor the rather fragmentary New Left *May Day Manifesto* (1967–8, see III.3) can serve as such a programme. It was not until much later that Michael Rustin wrote *For a Pluralist Socialism* (1985) within a Labour/New Left tradition, arguing for 'social ownership', equality, democracy and pluralism, which is an important contribution in the direction toward a socialist programme.

4. See Mills, 'Such a labour metaphysic, I think, is a legacy from Victorian Marxism that is now quite unrealistic' (1960, p. 22).

5. See Bernard Crick's critique of the tendency of 'political anti-politics' among socialists including some of the first New Left people (1962, pp. 125–34). This critique is also applicable to the second New Left whose detachment from real politics, to be sure, took a different form.

6. This is not to suggest that there was no serious work engaged in combating Toryism. I discuss important writings of this kind in the text. My point is simply that much more attention could have been paid to the 'frontal enemy'.

7. The formative influence of the older CP Marxist generation and earlier socialist thinkers on people of the first New Left (typically William Morris on Edward Thompson, Harold Laski on Ralph Miliband and John Saville, G. D. H. Cole on Stuart Hall) was immense. By contrast, the second New Left was more under the impact of recent continental currents.

8. Miliband was almost alone in arguing that giving up the old left parties ought to have posed the whole question as 'in what other existing or to-be-created organisation it would be possible for Marxists to further the socialist cause'. But there was no adequate perception that such a new organisation was needed, and where there was some kind of perception of it, 'there was no clear view as to what it should specifically stand for, in programmatic and organisational as well as theoretical terms' (1979, pp. 25–7).

9. For the more recent arguments around the question of organisation in the light of the New Left experience, cf. Rustin, 1985, chapter 2, for an active Labour engagement; Hall, 1988, esp. pp. 180–1, on the need of a 'party' in Gramsci's sense. Marcuse's earlier formulation – in opposition to traditional centralised parties – of 'organised spontaneity or spontaneous organisation' (1968) still needs to find a form in actual political practice.

CHAPTER I

The Making of the New Left

1. PRELUDE: 1956

A s the birthplace of the first New Left movement, Britain's particular social, economic, political and cultural context of the 1950s was striking. Despite a boom after the Second World War, it was evident that Britain lagged behind almost all of her industrial competitors.[1] The consequences of this were significant; the retreat of the oldest and greatest capitalist empire from being a leading power in the world indicated the end of a historical era.

Neither the Conservatives nor Labour supporters quite grasped the decline of Britain at that time, and indeed the Left was even slower in breaking from a false national self-image.[2] But what was more difficult for the Left was to acknowledge the rapid changes in the class and social structures of post-war advanced capitalist society. The achievement of material affluence and the remarkable rise of working people's living standards (though with the rise of a new form of an 'underclass' as well that combined the unemployed and the discriminated ethnic groups), for example, involved some basic theoretical and ideological problems which challenged conventional Marxist beliefs. Political analyses now needed to be based on the changed and changing social conditions and relations of contemporary capitalism; all kinds of living sources of opposition within capitalist society, old and new, needed to be identified. It was this requirement of a renewed intellectual and political perspective that fundamentally divided the Left. Meanwhile, the 1950s were also marked throughout the west by massive Cold War mobilisation. The circumstances from which the New Left emerged were then, roughly speaking, consumer capitalism and the Cold War.

But the origins of the New Left in Britain were also highly specific. It came into being in 1956–7 under the double shock of the Hungarian uprising and the Suez Crisis, which had shaken the political configuration of the British left.[3]

The twentieth Congress of the Communist Party of the Soviet Union (CPSU), to which Khrushchev gave his secret speech concerning the truth about Stalin, was the watershed. Although criticisms of Stalin and some disputes within certain Communist Parties about Soviet polity and policy became more open and acute immediately after Stalin's death in 1953, Khrushchev's fierce denunciation of the purges and 'the cult of the individual', followed by a series of large scale rehabilitations, set off a chain reaction and profound crisis in the communist world. Among those bitter consequential events, the Hungarian revolt made a powerful impact on the western left. Whether the events there were regarded as an authentic revolution (by many independent socialists) or as a real political tragedy in terms of its western incited counter-revolutionary elements (for some honest communists), it was a decisive factor in reaching a common awareness of the brutally repressive nature of the Soviet regime in general and of Soviet hegemony over the communist movement in particular.[4]

The coincidental Suez Crisis produced an even more extensive and traumatic shock. The Left had taken some action against the attack on Egypt, including huge street demonstrations not seen since the 1930s. But what they found was that when Anglo-French troops launched their offensive, the position of the government was widely shared. Moreover, many Labour critics attacked the invasion not because of their anti-imperialist commitment, but only because the Tory venture endangered the American alliance and divided the country.[5] The 'imperial nostalgia' was not the special preserve of the Conservative ruling class: the imperialist legacy had been carried by people at all levels;[6] reflections on Suez as a 'loss of empire' were psychologically rooted nationwide. The reluctant recognition (with the ambivalence towards Europe) of the genuine decline of Britain as a major bourgeois state and world power expressed itself among the Left and the peace movement in a popular slogan, 'Let Britain Lead Again'.[7] At all events, it was Suez that helped people to wake up to the survival of imperialism and aroused a whole new radical protest in Britain.

The essential lesson received from Hungary and Suez was a final rejection of both Stalinism and western imperialism. The two events defined for the emerging New Left, in Stuart Hall's [8] words, 'the boundaries and limits of the tolerable in politics' (1987b: p. 13). In the British context, they also prepared moral as well as political ground for a significant mass peace movement.

2. DECLINE OF THE OLD LEFT IN BRITAIN

The organised labour movement was prominently strong in Britain in comparison to most of its counterparts in the industrialised countries before the mid-twentieth century. It had however experienced major setbacks since then due to the crisis of demoralised communism with its Stalinist shadow and the equally demoralised Fabianism in its Cold War context. In addition, the pre-war generation of Marxist and socialist thinkers (Christopher Caudwell, Ralph Fox, R. H. Tawney, G. D. H. Cole, Harold Laski, to name but a few, and the distinguished communist/socialist scientists) was by and large gone. While some of them (e.g., Maurice Dobb, Isaac Deutscher and of course, Cole) were still active and intellectually influential (not to mention those who shifted more or less to the right such as John Strachey or George Orwell), they no longer had formative influence on the post-war generations. (Deutscher might be an exception in a small circle of academic Marxists.) It was from the space created by the retreat of traditional left aspirations and organisations that the first New Left was to emerge to bridge these gaps and discontinuities, making what Ralph Miliband[9] called 'the transition to the transition', namely, the growth in renewed socialist ideas and politics in ways that would effectively revitalise the Labour movement (discussed in Saville, 1960, p. 8).

The 'Lost World' of the Communist Party

The Communist Party of Great Britain (CPGB) has never been a powerful, mass party like the French or Italian Communist Parties. However, it did have a solid base in the working-class movement of the 1920s and the 1930s, and then continued to have strong influence in the industrial struggles of the post-war decade. It was also strikingly a party of 'high intellectuals', especially in the pre-war period, with bases at leading academic institutions like Cambridge, Oxford and the London School of Economics, and even, to a lesser extent, the Royal Society. It pioneered discussions of political as well as cultural and scientific issues, British as well as international, in the journals *The Left Review* and later (1938) *Modern Quarterly*, and through the Workers' Educational Association (WEA), the Left Book Club and other publications or organisational efforts. The anti-fascist Popular Front won the party broad support throughout the country.[10] On the whole,

> the function of the Communist Party in British Labour politics has been as a cadre party, especially as a school for working-class trade union cadres, and as a center for the elaboration of policy and theory for the mass movement. Thanks to Marxism it has been able to act as a sort of 'brains trust' for labour at certain periods. (Eric Hobsbawm in a letter to the author, 13 July 1987)[11]

The election in 1945 of the first Labour government should have brought the CPGB the chance to play a greater role in national politics when the widespread demand for radical social reforms was emotionally strong. Although the party gained some local successes in the few years immediately after the war,[12] under the rather tight control of the CPSU and with rigid ideological limitations it proved to be unable to take the chance – the party had little intellectual and organisational strength in seeking the economic or political answer to the problems of socialism in Britain.

But it was not until the final blow of 1956 that the CPGB began to lose its last and most sustaining ground in the trade unions and among intellectual leftists. Recalling those days in 1976, Margot Heinemann, a veteran communist, wrote that 'it is hard to convey now the degree of shock and horror with which the CPSU critique [of Stalin] was received among British Communists' (1976, p. 45). The damage Stalinism did to the world communist movement was to be permanent; for the traditional Marxist left this meant a severe loss for the future. During and after a short period of the leadership's sway and limited debates on the issues of Stalin, the withdrawal of Soviet troops from Hungary, inner-party democracy and the independence of each individual party,[13] the CPGB lost altogether some one-third of its members, intellectuals as well as workers, many of whom had been active in and loyal to the party for decades, and come through the worst period of the Cold War.[14] In *The Golden Notebook* (1962), her beautifully-written account of the experiences of 'free women' and 'red' intellectuals, Doris Lessing[15] told the story of the 'ideological feel' of those years, of the bitterness and disillusion and the great wrench of separation between people who were leaving the party and those who were staying. For a majority in both groups, communism had been a political belief as well as 'a moral vocation'.[16]

The consequences of this shake-up were significant. Not only that commitment to Marxism no longer led naturally to a communist affiliation,[17] and that a historical change in the party itself had become inevitable,[18] but also, from the moment when the whole left was deeply fragmented and divided, new political forces were to emerge and realign, which would open up a wider field for socialist politics. The core of the first New Left was partly composed of those committed ex-communists who, after failing to shift the party line, determined to leave and continue to fight for socialism outside the party.

Labour Revisionism

It was supposed that there had been a 'peaceful revolution', beginning with Labour's victory in 1945, which developed during the period of the first decade after the war. With the Attlee government and even the subsequent Conservative administrations, inspired by the wartime hope and belief in post-war reform and reconstruction, a whole system of social security was introduced with the benefit of a growing economic affluence, and all that went to make up the welfare state. The Labour movement that fundamentally sustained this reform process should have been enjoying ever more favourable conditions to develop its potential of not only transforming British society, but also playing a role in building a new welfare democratic Europe.

However, such a prospect proved not to be the case. The rise of Labour 'revisionism' helped stifle the movement's imagination and opportunities. From the mid-1950s, with Labour's second defeat at the general election of 1955, the social-democratic consensus attained by the Labour Party in the previous decade faced a serious challenge. The conflict between the militant Bevanite Left and the timid party leaders was replaced by the reconciliation of Aneurin Bevan with Hugh Gaitskell and consequently the victory of the Labour New Right at the 1957 Brighton Conference.[19] The rise of this Labour conservatism was brought forth and accompanied by an intellectual offensive against Labour's traditional socialist commitment, in the forms of Keynesian theory and various new Fabian claims. Many of the views expressed in the later debates on the future of the Labour Party and socialism in Britain can be found in clues in the texts attached to this 'revisionism'.

Anthony Crosland's *The Future of Socialism* (1956) was a principal item of that literature. Developing a thesis first argued in his 'The transition from capitalism' (1952, in Crossman, 1970), the book advocates a mixed economy necessarily containing a large private sector and an industrial management that will need state regulation but deny workplace democracy. Within the 'post-capitalist' framework, his version of socialism can be achieved steadily without labour/ capital conflict which, he asserts, had ceased to be the primary focus of class struggle (1956, Preface; 1952, p. 38; cf. 1960). The importance of Crosland's work lies in its radical abandonment of the long-standing Fabian tradition of concern with central control and efficiency in government. Unlike the Gaitskellian programme, Crosland defines socialism not in terms of nationalisa-tion or state planning, but of social welfare and social equality. It is striking that this emphasis on the connection between socialism and the quality of life was also emphasised by the New Left who nevertheless lacked an anti-'revisionist' alternative programme.

Another major step made in the similar direction was by John Strachey in *Contemporary Capitalism* (1956) and *The End of Empire* (1959).[20] A leading Communist economist of the 1930s, he was now a convinced Keynesian and attempted (like Joan Robinson and others) to reconcile Marxism and Keynesianism. His influential books give an empirical account of the so-called 'new stage' of capitalism and the effect of Keynesian techniques in modifying the nature of capitalism, presenting a reformist neo-Fabian position midway between the New Right and the left. 'Labour revisionism'[21] to a great extent successfully united the New Right and the old Fabian centrists (such as R. H. S. Crossman[22] and the *New Statesman* group) who were by then only able to maintain traditional Fabian state-socialist ideas verbally.[23]

The revised commitment and policy of the Labour Party with its bureaucratic organisational structure profoundly disappointed more radical elements of its traditional constituency. The party increasingly failed to win the loyalty or active participation of its own rank-and-file, especially of young people who were hostile to the leadership's constant fear of losing votes and the party's consequent colourless presence and predicament. Terrified to attack capitalist power, even its official ideology had formally changed, with the publication of the new party programme, *Industry and Society* (1957), from striving for a new kind of society to bargaining for 'fair shares' within the existing system. Such an outlook is surely what had long been dominant in the undynamic American and most European labour movements.

But the Left (intellectually represented by the *Tribune* group and the Fabian socialists) was not innocent in the reorientation of the Labour Party. Its own disorientation weakened the normative socialist arguments for common owner-ship and industrial democracy which were nevertheless persisted against 'revi-sionism'.[24] The problem the Labour leftists had been confronted with was that they did not understand the changing social relations and conditions of post-war Britain. Their prevailing formulations of capitalism were still those of the 1930s which concentrated on inevitable crisis and dire poverty. Thus their rejection of capitalism was ineffectively pursued either in outdated terms or with prejudices. Moreover, the Labour left was no longer capable of desiring an independent platform based on socialist theory. Many 'idle claims' for the social revolution only made Labour supporters confused by the large gap between these claims and their own experience. Its impotence in encountering intelligent revisionism was also a failure in offering a concrete, feasible vision of the future.[25] Besides, there was a general problem for the British left as a whole. On the one hand, it seemed hardly anything could be achieved for socialism by and within the Labour Party under its current leadership; on the other hand, left-wing politics in any serious sense was just impossible without reference to the Labour Party because that party had been the only mass party based on the organised working class in Britain. Thus the Left was always struggling with the issue of whether to work within or outside the party. This central dilemma of British socialism had never been resolved.[26]

3. THE FERMENT OF 'MIDDLE-CLASS RADICALISM'

'Middle-class radicalism' was a phrase quite commonly used in the late 1950s to refer to the non-traditional popular protests, intellectual as well as political. The typical cases that then characterised British society were the movements identified as 'angry' literature/drama/arts and, on a larger scale, anti-bomb. The earlier background of these excitements was nonetheless the tremendous sense of boredom, disillusion, and defeat of the Left during Churchill and Eden's post-1951 governments. The concept of the 'establishment', the British social establishment of the church and the crown since the mid-eighteenth century, the institutional and cultural power, was revived in the discourse of the new radical movements which attracted public concerns and transformed general atmosphere. The newborn New Left was at once part of and a force to be distinguished from them. While sharing the anger with the young cultural rebels and actively engaged in the peace protest, it sought to move beyond middle class radicalism by channelling it into a broader and conscious political movement for socialism.

'Angry Young Men' and Non-aligned Intellectuals

John Osborne's play *Look Back in Anger* (1956) was a historical event that brought the phrase 'angry young man' into vogue as a description of all those 'sharing a certain indignation against the apathy, the complacency, the idealistic bankruptcy of their environment' (Maschler, 1957, p. 7).[27] The hero Jimmy Porter is angered at his wife and friends for having no genuine beliefs and enthusiasm. But he himself is a spokesman for the post-war generation that looks round at the whole wrong world and feels frustrated by finding no cause to fight for: 'I suppose people of our generation aren't able to die for good causes any longer. ...There aren't any good, brave causes left'. Unlike the heroic age of the 1930s and 1940s, the sense of life in the 1950s is so confused, aimless, empty and miserable, 'like the old bear, following his own breath in the dark forest'. This mixed feeling of being 'lost' and dissent made the question of political commitment 'historically the central issue' (K. J. Worth, quoted in J. R. Taylor, 1968, p. 114).

The play created a furore as it 'burst on London' for its 'authentic new tone of the 1950s', the tone being protest (cf. Worsley, A. E. Dyson and Tynan, quoted in Taylor, 1968, pp. 50–1).[28] When a commentator questioned 'are young men angry?', in a BBC programme, even more anger was provoked at established values and orders.[29] *Look Back in Anger* expressed a specific political mood of 'rebelling without a cause': vigorous but cynical, idealistic but negative, refusing the status quo but seeing no alternative. It was the interlinked movements of the New Left and CND (see the next section) that finally provided a cause for those of the 'New Drama' school and their young audience, especially those of lower class origins.[30] Angry Young Men were part of a generation who, in Edward Thompson's[31] summary, knew about the Soviet Union from the Great Purges and the Hungarian smoke, who learned about western Christian conduct from the examples of Kenya and Cyprus, Suez and Algeria. Thereafter they judged with critical eyes and did not 'give their enthusiasm cheaply away to any routine machine' (1959a).[32]

The publication of collective essays entitled *Declaration* (1957) and *Conviction* (1958) represented intellectual disenchantment and protest with an explicit socialist aspiration.[33] The more seriously political volume, *Conviction*, was regarded as a 'new left' or 'new socialist' manifesto.[34] In Raphael Samuel's[35] words, it 'suggests the emergence of a distinctively new pattern of socialist ideas; a "New Left" which is renewing the socialist tradition, reaffirming the humanist, utopian and revolutionary elements of the tradition' (1958, p. 67). The discussions in these two volumes ranged from the welfare state to changing class structure, from Britain's decline to the colonial crisis, from economics to philosophy, from popular culture to personal experience. The spiritual sources of the contributors varied widely: from Marx and William Morris to D. H. Lawrence and F. R. Leavis; from the Webbs and Shaw to George Orwell. Some of them had previously been considered Fabians, but now their critique of contemporary capitalist society is 'informed by values which are radically different from those of Fabianism – new or old' (Samuel, 1958, p. 68), such as existentialist Marxism and Morris-like communism. The label of Angry Young Man did not suit those who thought themselves to be of another generation – the war produced a real gap (Lessing, 1957, p. 21; Mackenzie, 1958, pp. 7–8). What brought these people together was their common attitude in rejecting 'the Establishment'. The British establishment of power, orthodoxy and institutions was seen to parallel the American power elite on the one hand and the Soviet bureaucracy on the other,[36] an 'economic and social framework' that was, as Lindsay Anderson[37] put it, 'corrupt and killing' (1957b, p. 5). Rather different from the angry young man tone, the *Conviction* people positively believed that 'the stalemate state' (Mackenzie, 1958, pp. 7, 17) could be broken. Iris Murdoch went further to attack English philosophical traditions of empiricism and scepticism, demanding 'theory'.[38] This would find an echo later in young New Left theorists in the 1960s. As a genuine expression of the search for a moral and political stand, the two books marked a transitional period of post-war British history in which many 'non–aligned' intellectuals, either formerly affiliated to a political party (Communist or Labour) or not, sought the renewal of socialist ideas and politics.

Ernest Gellner's *Words and Things* (1959) was an intellectual rebellion of different kind. The book was a fierce criticism of orthodox (Oxford) linguistic philosophy and its allegedly absurd approach, mysticism and irrationalism, as well as its eclectic or conservative political implications. Radical as it was, the book was not written in a socialist spirit.[39] This was also an indication of the lack of theory on the socialist left, for so far, pointed out John Saville,[40] 'the only sustained critique of Oxford philosophy has been by a liberal' (1973a, p. 225).

The Campaign for Nuclear Disarmament

The Campaign for Nuclear Disarmament (CND) was formed early in 1958 with eminent progressive intellectuals and politicians as its founding members, people such as Bertrand Russell and Julian Huxley, as well as Kingsley Martin (editor of the *New Statesman*) and Michael Foot (spokesman of the Labour left). By then the New Left, through its publications and discussion clubs (see the next section), had already taken shape. It developed simultaneously with the first wave of CND until the latter declined in the early 1960s.[41]

At one point, disarmament became a basis of New Left politics, for CND presented the essential possibility of freeing the stagnant Labour movement and revitalising political activism away from conventional left routines. The two movements were so closely connected that neither can properly be studied without the other. As the editors of the *Universities and Left Review (ULR)* stated, 'if any event has transformed the course, tempo and tone of politics since the crucial dates of Suez and Hungary, it is the formation of CND'. The young New Leftists were 'proud' to contribute to the disarmament movement and 'to develop some of its socialist implications' *(ULR 7, editorial)*. On the other hand, many in CND who were not necessarily socialists considered the New Left to be a coherent and desirable alternative to the old left. Peggy Duff, one of the founders and the first secretary of CND, was convinced that it was the New Left who 'provided a political leadership and a hard background of political analysis to what was basically a moral crusade' (1971, p. 128).[42]

At first glance, it might have appeared that the two movements were by nature distinct from each other. It seems difficult to understand how the policies of CND (and of the Direct Action Committee or the Committee of 100)[43] could be the New Left's 'main political expression' (Williams, 1970a); or, how the New Left socialists could identify themselves with a middle-class-based movement for pacifism. The aftershock of the storm over Hungary-Suez was the background for an answer which was twofold. Ideologically, pacifism could be justified within socialist thinking. Moreover, support for CND meant more than merely an opposition to nuclear weapons. Organisationally, socialist potential seemed to be there in a popular protest movement.

Although the New Left was politically ambitious, it regarded the moral ground of CND as by no means conflicting with its own inherited radical traditions. The experience of 1956 also brought about an increasing demand for the rediscovery of moral or political conscience in socialist politics. Thompson appealed to a 'rational, humane public opinion' for strengthening the peace movement, which, he concluded, was 'the authentic expression of a tradition, deeply rooted, not only in an intelligentsia, but in the trade unions and constituency parties' (1958a, p. 51). The Labour left, in particular, were seen to have a long tradition of morally based pacifist internationalism (Coates and Johnson, 1983, p. 215). This evaluation, however, proved not to be the case when the majority vote went to Labour's conventional nuclear and Anglo-American alliance-based defence policy at the 1961 party conference, after a short period in which the trade unions did back unilateralism and CND. The peace movement had never been successful in attracting massive support among workers.

It was the time when many came to believe that there was no contradiction between struggling for peace and for socialism. Williams,[44] witnessing an extraordinary development of militarism in west and east, recalled that he reflected on the Cold War that 'in that epoch of wholly technological war, I was very near ... to reconsidering the whole pacifist response as being the correct position' (1979, p. 89). Saville and Thompson's slogan was 'Beyond the Bomb'. The idea of 'positive neutralism' was put forward by the group of ex-communists. While neutralism was not directly linked to socialism, it could create a place where people would be able to find their path towards it. As there would be no way for socialist advance unless bloc politics was broken, they called for a unity of 'moral fervour with political realism' in CND *(NR* 4, editorial). It was simply clear, in Mervyn Jones's[45] words, 'To be a socialist today one must be a pacifist, ... And to be an effective pacifist one must be a socialist' (1958, p. 201).

CND had formally adopted the New Left position of Britain's withdrawal from NATO and 'positive neutralism', which appeared to be a political rather than moral issue, even though it was taken largely at a moral level in terms of neutralism and disarmament (cf. Rustin, 1961, pp. 51–3). However, despite much practical effort – the publication of the NLR bulletin *This Week (This Week, a NLR Daily*, October 1960), Thompson's byelection proposal (Hinton, 1989, pp. 192–3); John Rex's New Left pamphlet, *Britain without Bomb* (1960), Jones's CND pamphlet, *Freed from Fear* (1961), and Hall's CND manifesto, *Steps Towards Peace* (1963)[46] – the New Left failed to convert the campaign into a socialist movement and its influence was very much limited by the basically apolitical approach of many CND members. Moreover, apart from recalling classical Marxist internationalism in a very weak sense and classical socialist thesis of 'self-determination' in relation to the non-aligned movement, arguments given at the time to bridge the position of socialism and pacifism were not persuasively based on consistent theoretical considerations.[47]

Objectively, the radical and dynamic potential of the disarmament movement lies in the fact that at the moment when the major traditional left-wing bodies were discredited and weakened, CND opened a new 'rallying point' for its participants opposing to the political power and certain aspects of the prevailing political culture which might be independent of the Bomb issue, but which the latter served to symbolise. Much of the campaign's attraction derived from its uncompromising style in its response to the Cold War network which gave a large number of its supporters a sense of moral standing. CND had proved an example of the most radical type of 'single issue campaign' which questioned the whole politics of the system, in the light of its chosen issue (Williams *et al.*, 1968, pp. 163–4; Parkin, 1968, pp.3–5, 58). This helps to explain the New Left's true commitment to disarmament, in contrast to other left groupings such as the Trotskyists who were also engaged in CND for tactical reasons (Parkin, 1968, pp. 77–92).

Inseparably, the organisational need for those who had just lost or given up their membership cards, as well as those who had been wandering between the existing parties yet found no proper place to stay, made CND a 'natural' focus of political belonging and a favourable recruiting ground for reframing the structure of British politics. In this regard, it is worth noting that ex-communists were often seen in those early Aldermaston marches and running local CND groups (Williams 1979, p. 361), contrasting sharply with the CPGB's official opposition to unilateralism. Equally notable, they were also different from resigned communists of previous generations who would usually resign from political struggles altogether.

4. THE JOURNEY TO THE *NEW LEFT REVIEW*

The actual process of the formation of the New Left began with the creation of two important journals, the *Universities and Left Review* (*ULR*) and *The New Reasoner* (*NR*) (originally entitled *The Reasoner*). The former represented independent socialists, the latter dissident communists. The merger of the two into the *New Left Review* (*NLR*) indicated the unification of two New Left generations who had different political experiences and styles.

The Reasoners

The New Reasoner, a quarterly subtitled 'A journal of socialist humanism', was edited by John Saville and Edward Thompson from the summer of 1957 until 1959.[48] The journal was launched to provide a vehicle for continued dissenting activities outside the Communist Party, when the editors were suspended and then resigned from party membership for producing the mimeographed *Reasoner*.[49]

The first issue of *The Reasoner*, published independently of the party press in July 1956, intended to discuss 'questions of fundamental principle, aim and strategy' (1, editorial). The context of this publication and the reason for continuing it were summarised by the two editors as
(1)   the major and growing crisis in the party;
(2)   abundant evidence that no serious debate was ever going to be permitted in the official party press in response to the revelations of the 20th Congress of the CPSU;[50]

(3) the need for the fullest and frankest discussion;

(4) the fact that *The Reasoner* was not engaged in factional activity (see Saville's statement to the Party Yorkshire District meeting on 10 August 1956; the District Committee resolution of 26 August, published later in *World News*, 22 September; Thompson's letter to the party chairman of 5 September, quoted in Saville, 1976, pp. 9–11).

In the first editorial, they wrote that being emotionally, politically and morally shocked at what Stalinism really meant, they felt obliged to analyse seriously the causes of the crimes which in the past the British Communists had defended or apologised for. In their view the shock and turmoil engendered by the revelations were 'the result of our general failure to apply a Marxist analysis to socialist countries and to the Soviet Union in particular'. They also believed that for the future of the whole Labour movement the democratisation of the party was urgent and necessary. To take a proper part in this movement would in turn require a thorough analysis and honest acknowledgement of past dogmatism and sectarianism, including the history of the CPGB and Communist-Labour relations.

The second issue of *The Reasoner* was published just a day before the executive committee meeting of the Communist Party (13 September 1956) which instructed the two editors to cease the journal. This meant that any further publication would be followed by party disciplinary action. How difficult they found the dilemma to be was shown in their bitter decision to cease publication in 'the best interests of the party' (Saville, 1976, pp. 11–12). It was not until the Hungarian events that Saville and Thompson gave up hope of shifting the party line. The third issue, which was thus also the final one, was printed at the very moment of Soviet intervention.[51] Thompson wrote 'through the smoke of Budapest' that no chapter would be more tragic in international socialist history than if the Hungarian people were driven into the arms of the capitalist powers by the crimes of a communist government. He appealed to 'the Communist Party, my party', to support Hungarian working people: 'Shame on our leaders for their silence!' With these words, *The Reasoner* was itself silenced.

Both Saville and Thompson were highly committed communists[52] and members of the earlier Communist Historians' Group which was well known after the war.[53] Saville, a member of twenty-two years' standing and Thompson, on the Yorkshire District Committee, were both very active in their respective party branches which were deeply connected with the grassroots and developed a strong socialist movement especially in West Yorkshire. This practice was the ground on which *The New Reasoner* and its predecessor were run and maintained a clear identity:

> We have no desire to break impetuously with the Marxist and Communist tradition in Britain. On the contrary, we believe that this tradition, which stems from such men as William Morris and Tom Mann, ... is in need of rediscovery and reaffirmation. (editorial, *NR* 1, p. 2)

Even at the time of ending *The Reasoner*, the editors would rather have reformed the party than abandoned it. By the time of closing NR later in 1959, they still defined it as 'a journal of the democratic Communist opposition' (3, p. 7). It was precisely according to the communist principle which they believed to be free and open criticism that they started their journals and honourably named them 'reasoner'.[54] Quoting from Marx at the masthead, they declared, 'To leave error unrefuted is to encourage intellectual immorality'.

In a broader sense, the reasoners consisted of the most well-known CP historians, scientists and artists. However, there was a strong feeling among many other party members, especially union activists, against any dissident publications and therefore against the *Reasoner* 'splitters', because for them unity was an especially important value (Heinemann, letter to the author, 13 July 1987). As a result, inner-party discussion was diverted from the original questions relating to Stalinism to those of discipline and organisation;[55] and this further closed the possibility of open debates inside the party over difficult and painful issues. It was not until October 1957 that a new journal *Marxism Today* was founded, in which views not conforming to party policy could in principle be expressed.

Between the two *Reasoners*, in April 1957, the Wortley Conference of Socialist Forums was held near Sheffield. It was a national meeting of ex-communists and other socialists, who resolved to form 'an organised movement of the Marxist anti-Stalinist Left' (Widgery, 1976, p. 451; Palmer, 1981, p. 55). Criticising Stalinism and regenerating Marxism were set the keynotes of *The New Reasoner*, whose editors and most contributors identified themselves as 'democratic communists' and/or 'socialist humanists': 'We take our stand with those workers and intellectuals in the Soviet Union and eastern Europe who are fighting for that return to Communist principle and that extension of liberties which has been dubbed "de-Stalinisation" '; and in Britain with socialists fighting 'for a similar rebirth of principle' within the Labour movement (NR 1, p. 2). Here 'socialist humanism' was what the 'principle' referred to. Beginning with Thompson's long article on the theme which appeared in the first number, a focused discussion was developed by others. Socialist humanism was rediscovered as a common objective for a new left in the west and the Left opposition in the east. Thompson, in particular, put stress on the eastern dissidents' potential in light of the international outlook of active neutrality and future revolution (1959a, pp. 8, 10). No wonder the New Left was attacked for its 'revisionism' not only by the CPGB authority (for example, Kettle, 1960, p. 191) but also by official Soviet publications (see for example, Lvasheva, 'Revisionism of Marxism in Britain', *October*, 8, 1958, Moscow; translated in NR 7, pp. 143–8).

With a more balanced concern with problems directly related to the British Labour movement, from the second issue analyses ranged widely from the actual situation to theoretical questions of politics, economics, history and literature.[56] Although NR only sold about 2,500–3,000 copies, its readers were scattered around the world. In the last issue published in late autumn 1959, before its amalgamation with the *Universities and Left Review*, the editors reaffirmed their

commitment to 'the rational, humane and libertarian strand within the communist tradition' and took 'a communist leave' of their 'old comrades' *(NR* 10), for a
younger socialist generation was in the making and the two groups would appear
as one to form a new movement.

Universities and Left Review

The editors and supporters of the *Universities and Left Review*,[57] differing from
'disillusioned radicals', would fight for 'brave causes' (Hall's comment made in
1959 on *Look Back in Anger*, quoted in Taylor, 1968, p. 193), and many were
moved to take up political action, some for the first time. The founding of *ULR* in
spring 1957 was a real initiative, indicating the first significant break of the
university left with the orthodox political language and conventional framework
of politics. *ULR* was a well-designed name: 'universities' referred to the common
platform for the independent intellectual left; 'Left Review' signified the
connection of the new journal with an earlier tradition of the Marxist *Left Review*
of the 1930s which was unorthodox and greatly concerned with cultural questions
(Branson, 1971, pp. 273–4). *ULR* soon represented 'an authentic voice from the
critical post-war generation' (Thompson, 1959a, p. 11).

All of the first four editors, whose average age was twenty-four, had Oxford
connections and, symbolically expressing anti-imperialist sentiment among the
young, were of non-English origin. Stuart Hall, from the West Indies and a
graduate in English, was to become a leading figure of the New Left movement.
Gabriel Pearson was a graduate student in English at Balliol, a college known
especially for its communist students under the influence of Christopher Hill.
Charles Taylor,[58] an elected Fellow of All Souls College, was a Canadian
Christian socialist and active in a group of independents who were intellectually
without any party affiliation. The youngest at twenty-two, Ralph Samuel[59] was a
historian at Oxford and then a research student at the London School of
Economics. He was from a Jewish communist family and himself a passionate
party member until 1956. With two (Samuel and Pearson) from a communist
background and two (Hall and Taylor) from the independent left, the editors
intended to furnish broader based but clearly defined socialist ideas and politics.
Working closely with the whole circle of the *ULR* collective,[60] they pushed further
their earlier discussions either in the 'Cole Group' (formed by the members of
Cole's Oxford seminar in politics) or in the pages of *Clarion* (the Oxford Labour
Club magazine) of post-war capitalism, colonial questions, Soviet socialism and
many cultural issues.

The *ULR* group represented, in a sense, a new intelligentsia which, compared
with the older generation, came up by way of scholarship rather than privilege,
and lacked some of the social graces or class snobberies of its predecessors.[61] A
sociological analysis of this intelligentsia stated that it preferred films to the
theatre, American to French literature, popular to classical music (Arnold, 1962,
pp. 302–3). It favoured the avant-garde and abstract art. Accordingly, *ULR* was
distinguished by its lively but somewhat lightweight appearance, with such new

focuses as youth culture and lifestyle. Defending their own understanding of politics, the editors wrote: 'We want to break with the view that cultural or family life is an entertaining sideshow, a secondary expression of human creativity or fulfilment' *(ULR* 4, editorial).[62] Devoting itself to the burning problems of the day, the journal quickly sold 8,000 copies in all parts of the country; its clubs (and the Partisan Coffee Bar in London) were well attended and successful in opening up new areas of discussion. Peter Sedgwick recollected how young people were anxious to meet in the *ULR* London Club which

> used to attract hundreds to weekly lectures and discussions in the large basements of central London and further regular meetings were held by such autonomous sections as the Education, History of Socialism, Left Scientists, Social Priorities and Literature groups, the International Forum, and the London Schools Left Club, a self-governing unit for youngsters still at school. (1976, p. 132)[63]

Yet ULR was seriously political, attempting to link criticism of capitalism to that of modern culture. The old British capitalist system was attacked in terms of an ancien régime with its class prejudice, privileges and oppressions from the viewpoint of popular 'modernisation'. Allied with the Movement for Colonial Freedom and the Labour Victory for Socialism group, the journal represented in the more strict sense the Aldermaston generation, a generation that had revolted against the existing state of affairs. Most ULR contributors used Marxist concepts and many were said to be inspired by the 'young Marx' and his concept of 'alienation', or 'neo-Marxism' (existentialist Marxism, humanist Marxism, etc.). 'This journal', announced the first editorial, 'seeks to provide a forum where the different fruitful traditions of socialist discussion are free to meet in open controversy'. It also intended to reach beyond any narrow sectional appeal in the search for new ideas.

The first issue, already demonstrating a translation from the boundary of the student left, had contributions from people of different generations or traditions: Deutscher, Cole, Thompson, Hobsbawm, Joan Robinson and Lindsay Anderson, among others. Thompson's 'Socialism and the intellectuals' evoked an interesting discussion (issues 1 and 2). The important debate over 'Classlessness' (1, 5, 6, 7) was informed by the new conditions of post-war capitalism (see II.3 in the present volume). Nationalisation and Labour's economic policy (3, 4, 6, 7) were carefully examined, notably in Barratt Brown's [64] long study of the managerial organisation of industry and banking entitled 'The Controllers' (5, 6, 7). After a couple of issues dealing with extensive concerns, the editors tried to locate a centre which was to be fourfold: analysis of contemporary capitalism as a social and economic system, reportage and critique of the culture of 'post-welfare' Britain, study of the nature of a future socialist society, and re-examination of the values of socialist humanism (no. 4, p. ii). The fourth editorial was a move towards *The New Reasoner*, shown in its emphasis on *NR*'s 'socialist humanism', which was claimed to be at home here too as 'a real redefinition of the aim'. The *ULR* would pursue 'a deep, radical critique ... informed by humanism' of the quality of contemporary life and to take revolutionary perspectives on a socialist and humanist transformation of British society.

One of the heroes of the *ULR* group was Raymond Williams. Belonging by age and personal inclination to the *NR* circle, but being closer in interests to *ULR*, he would rather see 'energy devoted to exploring current changes in cultural experience' than going through the pain of re-working the past (the Cold War epoch, the traditional Marxist arguments, etc.).[65] A powerful cultural critic committed to the working class, he could in many ways be seen as an intermediary between the two traditions.

New Left Review

The *Universities and Left Review* and *The New Reasoner* were merged into the *New Left Review* in January 1960. One cannot overlook those original differences between the communist tradition of the anti-fascist movement joined with working-class politics based on the northern industrial areas (mainly Yorkshire) and that of Oxbridge middle-class radicalism combined with the metropolitan culture of London which to a certain extent characterised the *ULR* group. If the former can be said to be 'classical', the latter was 'modernist'. Or, in Miliband's judgement, the *NR* group were intellectuals *of* the labour movement, the *ULR* group *for* it (1979, p. 26). The *ULR* was attacked by some *NR* contributors for its blind hostility towards the Soviet Union and a sort of western European parochialism. The *NR* was in turn criticised by some *ULR* members for its rigid tone and for being less close to current transformations of the British scene. However, the resemblance became strong enough to outweigh the difference when both had attempted to overcome their own narrowness and undertaken several joint projects.[66] Labour's defeat in the 1959 General Election helped to bring the two groups together.

The Yorkshire editors showed great initiative in the fusion.[67] Some of them had already been sitting on the editorial board of *ULR*, which was now seen as 'the other journal of socialist humanism' (*ULR* 7, p. 1). Obviously, a renewed Left movement required an influential journal with wider readership and greater appeal. It was necessary for the achievment of such a journal to collaborate with young critical thinkers who were assumed to have the potential to revitalise socialist tradition in Britain. The new journal could then offer 'a unique combination of real contacts with the older and younger socialist generations' (Thompson, 1959a, p. 11). Once an open, unsectarian politics of the New Left is built up, wrote Thompson, 'the bureaucracy will hold the machine; but the New Left will hold the passes between it and the younger generation' (*ibid.*, p. 17). Being even more ambitious, he spoke at the founding meeting of *NLR* about the perspective of a popular movement based on the new *Review* and its clubs that would transform the mentality, if not the organisation, of the Labour Party. Others, however, were less optimistic. Although the merged group was scarcely identifiable in terms of organisation, the joint movement displayed an expansive dynamism and the participants were excited by the prospects of its future development.

As there was from the very beginning a sense of lacking a truly coherent unity, the *NLR*'s editorial team had to be so large that it embraced all the active members of the two old boards.[68] The editorship was entrusted, by mutual consent, to Stuart Hall. Attempting to clarify the purpose of the journal and the now widely called 'New Left movement', the editors considered the New Left to be 'a movement of ideas', because the poverty of theory had long undermined British socialism. Accordingly, the movement would commit itself to socialist education, analysis and propaganda *(ULR* 7, p. 2), from which the concept of leadership or hegemony was to be articulated. Bringing to life 'a genuine dialogue between intellectuals and workers' *(NLR* 1, editorial), or a dynamic connection between theoretical and practical works, was a designed task of *NLR*. In clubs, informal groups and local centres of socialist activities, in schools, colleges and trade union branches, the job of the New Left was, as William Morris put it long ago, 'making socialists'.[69] The opening editorial of *NLR* reads:

> The Labour movement is not in its insurrectionary phase. We are in our missionary phase. ... The New Left ... must pioneer a way forward by working for socialism as the old missionaries worked as if consumed by fire that is capable of lighting the darker places in our society.

Although the creation of the British New Left was not marked by the *NLR* but by its two forerunners, its foundation symbolised a decisive development of the movement. The journal became the voice of this growing movement and an alternative centre of socialist ideas in which Marxism could develop outside the Communist Party and other formal Marxist organisations. Despite internal turbulence, splits and even major changes in the Review's direction in the following years (see III.1), *NLR* continued to be a great organ of the New Left, carrying part of its intellectual weight and political authority. For all its mistakes and defects, the Review nevertheless initiated a renaissance of Marxism in Britain and established itself as one of the leading left fora in the west, and a distinguished international publication of socialist theoretical reconstruction.

5. WHAT WAS NEW ABOUT THE NEW LEFT: SOME NOTES ON DEFINITIONS

1. In a very broad sense, the whole traditional Left (in Britain, Communists, Trotskyists, trade union militants, the Fabians and radical intellectuals, with or without party affiliations) had gradually been changing during the post-war process of social transformation. But the only movement that was 'new' enough to occupy a special place in the history of socialism was the New Left, uniquely created outside the old system of politics.

Historians who touch the subject find, as one acknowledges, that 'it is hard to define the common features of all groups and sects which claim to belong to the New Left or are considered by others to form part of it' (Kolakowski, 1981, p. 487). In the case of the British New Left, the situation is even worse due to the existence, as will be shown, of two or more New Left generations or traditions. One cannot expect that all the people whose works are discussed in the following chapters would like the label of 'New Left'. Those who do admit it might prefer to lay emphasis on its diverse components and constant tensions. As Williams remarked, there was no single line and certainly no kind of intellectual submission: the New Left ranged

> from dissident communism ... through new kinds of Marxist encounters with other systems of thought such as Existentialism and psychoanalysis, to kinds of revolutionary socialism drawing on different radical and syndicalist traditions. Anybody closely involved in it ...will know how much controversy there was inside what was nevertheless a movement. (1970, p. 785)[70]

On the other hand, however, the New Left in Britain can be in a way rather easily identified. For as an intellectual movement it by and large involved people around certain publishing and research enterprises.

When former communists no longer believed that a reform of the party was possible,[71] while many socialists looked for new politics rather than being paralysed within the Labour Party; when an extraordinary potentiality was evolved by the '1956–60 vintage' (Palmer, 1981, p. 56) so that thousands of either (ex-)membership card holders or 'non-aligned' people converged on CND and other forms of protest; when space was made for a new and independent socialist movement as the main received political traditions of the left had irretrievably broken down; then a New Left came into being. Speaking of the rejection of both 'Stalinist communist' and 'social-democratic' orthodoxies, the New Left never clearly defined this 'third space' for socialist politics in positive terms. Nevertheless, such a position is where the British New Left can be roughly located.

2. The problem of this location becomes obvious if we consider the Trotskyist tradition which can be similarly identified. The uniqueness of the New Left must lie somewhere else, such as its preoccupation with 'culture' and its primary attention to current social changes (see the next chapter). Its moral concern and populist inclination with roots in native English radicalism also distanced it from Trotskyism. The more the New Left should lose these distinctions, the closer would it move to Trotskyism. In general, not to confuse the two, we need simply point out that the latter belongs to the traditional ideologies of the 'old left', although it revived and indeed to some extent mixed with a new left position especially during the student revolt and workers' control movement (see III.4).[72] (Editors of *International Socialism*, for example, were enthusiastic and 'very welcome' participants of New Left club activities; the journal was viewed by Thompson as 'the most constructive journal with a Trotskyist tendency in this country' (1960c, p. 22).[73] In any case, new leftism was not a substitute for old Trotskyism in terms of intellectual inspiration, strategic perspective and political practice (cf. Rowbotham, 1979a, pp. 23–6; Rustin, 1961, pp. 51–3). Situated at a historical juncture, the New Left claimed an authentic rupture with the old left.

3. It was clear that the New Left grew up outside the existing framework of political organisations. However, in his New Left 'manifesto' (1959a), Thompson maintained that the 'majority of those actively associated with the New Left will, as a matter of course, be active members of the Labour Party and trade union movement'. The New Left did not propose itself as an alternative organisation to

those already in the field; rather, it would pursue the experience of the pre-war Left Book Club movement: publications, journals, clubs, educational and conference programmes. The first *NLR* editorial stated that 'we shall ... be parallel to, rather than competing with, existing organisations of the Labour Movement' (Saville, 1960, p. 9; Barratt Brown, 1961a). Or, in a sharper statement (Thompson, 1960c, p. 19), 'We are embarking on a struggle, not to "win" the Labour Movement, but to transform it'. From the very beginning many New Left people did intervene actively in Labour debates and activities and called for retaining this involvement all along.

Much less wishfully, Saville believed that the Labour Party could not be any kind of vehicle for socialism (interview with the author, 19 October 1987). Similarly, Williams confessed that he 'could never establish real collaborative work with the Labour Left' who understood little of any new initiatives (1979, p. 368). Many New Leftists eventually moved into the Labour Party 'for the very good reason that socialism requires a mass organisation of working people in order to become anything more than an abstraction' (Coates, 1971a, pp. 241–2). But many others remained independent for equally good reasons. The paradoxical New Left attitude and relation (rather than strategy) to the Labour Party was described by Hall as 'one foot in, one foot out' (Oxford Conference, November 1987).

Despite this heavy 'traffic' between new and old – with the Labour Party remaining too overwhelming a formation to be bypassed – as a political intervention in conventional British life the New Left was certainly disturbing enough to have made itself outstandingly noticeable. Unlike, say, the United States where the old left was already largely gone when the new left emerged, the British New Left had been marginal in a traditional Labour dominated politics. Yet this by no means implies that new left in Britain must be less 'new' than it was in the US.[74] Still less plausible is it to dismiss the 'newness' of the New Left for its intellectual links with the old socialist traditions.[75] The two words, 'new' and 'left' are of equal importance in historical perspectives.

It is vitally relevant to mention that a few in the original *NR* group, notably Ralph Miliband (as a well-known Marxist theorist, he was the only one in that group who had not been in the Communist Party), dimly (at the time) perceived the need to re-group the New Left into an independent organisation. But the strong feeling generated from the lessons of 1956, especially among the *ULR* generation, of anti-'democratic-centralist' vanguards and anti-bureaucracy or authoritarianism led to a sort of anarchist position that would nullify any organisational proposals. The mass movement of CND with its self-organising and participatory manner of political mobilisation also disputed the need for or validity of a different organisation that particularly stood for the 'New Left'.

The single attempt endorsed by the New Left at forming an alternative 'genuine socialist organisation' was Lawrence Daly's[76] Fife Socialist League. In its few years' existence (1957–64), the League seriously challenged the Labour/ Communist electoral dominance in the local elections in West Fife (Daly, 1960;

Saville, 1959). While strongly supporting the Fife initiative, the NR editors had no expectation of an organised national new left. Whether they had missed the opportunity (if there was any) of creating an organisation of their own, or were unwilling or unable to take it, the New left carried on with political strength and intellectual vigour. The movement for a time being seemed to be pregnant with many possibilities.

NOTES

1. Among many works on the causes and consequences of Britain's economic decline, M. J. Wiener's *English Culture and the Decline of the Industrial Spirit* (1981) is particularly interesting and controversial. Beyond 'the limits of economic explanation', the book identifies 'a century of psychological and intellectual de-industrialisation', an attitude that was shared by the elite of every class and affected economic behaviour.
2. The activists of the Campaign for Nuclear Disarmament, for instance, still largely believed in Britain's capacity to 'lead the world'.
3. For a brief account of the two events and their impact on British politics, cf. Mervyn Jones, 1976, pp. 67–88.
4. For Raymond Williams, one of the key figures of the British New Left, the decisive event was the East German uprising of June 1953. He was then badly shocked by the intervention of Russian troops and ceased believing that there was in any sense a just international communist cause for socialism. See Williams, 1979, pp. 88, 93.
5. For some Labour politicians' own imperialist opinion on public matters, cf. Peter Worsley, 1960, pp. 110–11. The Labour leader Gaitskell, for example, before changing his attitute, denounced Nasser as another Hitler. See Anthony Nutting, 1967, p. 47.
6. See Andrew Gamble, 1981, p. xvii; John Strachey, 1959, p. 204; Tom Nairn, 1965; R. Skidelsky, 1970. The British workers' movement, in Williams's remark, 'can be frequently limited or even corrupted by nationalism as it was so grossly corrupted by imperialism (1965, p. 22).
7. See James Hinton, 1989, pp. 158–9, 180–1.
8. Stuart McPhail Hall, born in 1932, educated at Jamaica College, Kingston and then Oxford. Secondary school teacher (1957–9), university lecturer (London University 1961–4), Assistant Director and later Director of the Centre for Contemporary Cultural Studies (Birmingham University 1964–80). One of the editors of *Universities and Left Review* (1957–9) and the first editor of *New Left Review* (1960–1), he was active in both the New Left and early Campaign for Nuclear Disarmament (CND).
9. Ralph Miliband was of Belgian origin and exiled to England at the age of fourteen. He lectured on political science at the LSE where he was deeply influenced by Harold Laski. Professor of Politics at the University of Leeds from 1972 till 1978, Visiting Professor of Brandeis and several other American universities. He was on the editorial boards of all the three early New Left journals. Later, with John Saville, and more recently Leo Panitch, he edited *Socialist Register* from 1964.
10. For the pre-war British communism, cf. James Hinton and Richard Hyman, 1975; Noreen Branson, 1985; Branson and Margot Heinemann, 1971; S. Samuels, 1969; Gary Werskey, 1978, part II; John Callaghan, 1987, chapter 2; Eric Hobsbawm, 1989, pp. 103–17.
11. He continues, 'It would have been better if the CP had itself been or become a mass party like the French and Italian CPs. But it didn't. You ask what justification for independent existence it therefore has. I answer, its best policy (recommended by Lenin) would have been to operate *within* the Labour Party as an affiliated organisation. It failed to affiliate for reasons which cannot be summarised in a sentence. Its chances of affiliating as an organisation today are negligible. It could be argued that today it has no strong justification for separate existence left'. This is of course surprisingly straightforward and 'liquidationist' in view of Hobsbawm's

own eminent status in the party. But the irredeemable decline of the CPGB, what was described by Raphael Samuel as a 'lost world' (1985b, 1986a), has been so evident since the late 1950s. It should be an important but separate enterprise to investigate why the communist world is lost in Britain and what the nature of the party really is today. About the tension between the CP and LP, see David Priscott, 1974.

12. The party membership had reached a peak of about 64,000 in 1942, stood at 55,000 in 1943 and 1944, and had fallen to 45,000 in 1945. But in 1945 two communists were elected to parliament and in November 1946 the CP won 256 councillors in local elections. See John Callaghan, 1987, pp. 48–50.

13. One crucial issue was about the party democracy on the established basis of 'democratic centralism'. The most massive expression of dissidence was a letter which the party refused to publish, and which subsequently appeared in *Tribune* and the *New Statesman* (1 December 1956) disagreeing with the party line on the Hungarian event. The signatories include the *Reasoner* group (see 1.4 below) and others like Maurice Dobb and Eric Hobsbawm. Christopher Hill, among others, was involved in producing the 'Minority report on party democracy' at the 25th (special) Congress of the CPGB in April 1957. The issue concerning 'the Jewish question' was also highly critical. At the respected mathematician Hyman Levy's insistence, who was one of the top academics in the CP, delegates were sent to the Soviet Union in the autumn of 1956 to investigate anti-semitism there and came back with a report on the persecution of Jews in the years 1948–52. Levy signed the report which then, only in a summary version, appeared in the CP's weekly *World News* (January 1957) and spoke at the party's special congress, attacking the leadership for having so misled party members about the real situation in the Soviet Union. These dissenting voices were taken as 'revisionist views' by the party majority who denounced 'wavering intellectuals'.

    About the inner-party struggles of CPGB, cf. Malcolm MacEwen, 1976; Heinemann, 1976; L. Gardner, 1976; *Workers International Review*, vol. 2, no. 2, 1957; Neal Wood, 1959, chapter 7; G.Werskey, 1978, pp. 309–13.

14. The membership reported at the 25th Congress was 33,960, some 7,000 members left in 1956, more followed in 1957. See *SR* 1976, pp. 16, 50, 57.

15. Doris Lessing was born in 1919 in Persia to British parents and lived in Southern Rhodesia from 1924 until she moved to England in 1949. She became a member of the CPGB in 1950 and left the party around 1953, because of the Stalinist shadow which then heavily affected party life. A well-known novelist and a representative of 'non-aligned intellectuals' she was an editorial member of the *New Reasoner* and early *New Left Review (NLR)*. See IV.5 for her pioneering contribution to the women's movement.

16. Lessing, 1973. 'Somewhere at the back of my mind when I joined the party was a need for wholeness, for an end to the split, divided, unsatisfactory way we all live. Yet joining the party intensified the split ...' (p. 161).

17. See Raymond Williams, 'From 1957 onwards, there was a rapid proliferation of other organisations and groups which claimed, if in different ways, the significance of inheritance of revolutionary socialist practice and Marxist theory' (1976b, p. 82).

18. The CPGB eventually changed in terms of a democratic reform during the last three decades before it abandoned its name altogether in November 1991. According to Hobsbawm, who had remained in the party, this change 'has been achieved partly by the changed international situation since 1956, but certainly also to some extent by those who, while critical of the 1956–7 time, stayed in the party'. But the CP never recovered from its loss during the crisis of 1956–7: 'I believe that then it missed the chance of renovation – though at the time it might have been impossible to convince the USSR of the need to change (the USSR was still seen as the "leading force" in our movement)' (letter to the author, 13 July 1987). Margot Heinemann, who decided to stay in the party and work to change it, spoke in defence of the party line: 'I don't think there was at the time much widespread feeling that the British party was itself very undemocratic in its normal functioning (i.e. as disliked from the critics of 1956 onwards). The Comintern once described it as too much a "party

of good friends" – it had indeed had much fewer schisms and divisions than most. We in 1956–7 understood that the EC [CPGB Executive Committee] shared many of our doubts and fears, and that they believed that the Soviet comrades, having exposed the crimes and abuses, were well on the way to putting them right. We thought, too, that the fight for a cleaner analysis of what had gone wrong and a more critical line could have been won through the democratic processes of the party if the critics had stayed rather than resigned ...'. 'In the event, of course, the fall of Khrushchev and the coming of the Brezhnev era indicated that our EC's earlier analysis has been too optimistic. But, it was nevertheless serious as far as it went...' (letter to the author, 23 Nov. 1987). I have quoted her at some length here in consideration of the need for a useful background reference from a different standpoint.

19. For a fine account of the Labour Party in this period, see V.Bogdanor, 1970, esp. pp. 85–103.
20. These were said to be a series of studies 'on the principles of democratic socialism'. Strachey afforded a critical discussion of Leninist theory of imperialism in 1959, pp. 98–108. See R. L. Meek's critique, 1959, pp. 41–57 and Michael Barratt Brown's 1963a; 1963b, pp. 92–6.
21. Other typical texts include Hugh Gaitskell, 1956; Roy Jenkins, 1959. See Stephen Haseler, 1969.
22. See his 1960 and *New Fabian Essays* under his editorship.
23. For a record of Fabianism and G. D. H. Cole's post-war effort in revitalising the Fabian Society, see Margaret Cole, 1961, chapters 18, 19 and the epilogue.
24. For the battle over Clause 4 of the Labour Party Constitution of 1918, see III.3.
25. See John Saville, 1960, p. 9; 1964, p. 192.
26. See Ralph Miliband, 1966, p. 24. This means that even the New Left would eventually fail as an independent political movement.
27. However, Osborne himself and John Wain, whose *Hurry on Down*, together with *Look Back in Anger*, jointly started the 'angry young man movement', denied such a label. About the movement, see D. E. Cooper, 1970; G. Martin, 1959, pp. 37–40; J. R. Taylor, 1968; K. J. Worth, 1963; D. Potter, 1960; M. Kaye, 1960, pp. 64–6.
28. See John Barber: the play 'is intense, angry, feverish, undisciplined. It is even crazy. But it is young, young, young' *(Daily Express, 9 May 1956)*.
29. The BBC commentator says that history may 'judge us as a whole to be the most unangry, most reconciled younger generation of modern times'. See Potter, 1960, p. 20. This remark, however, turned out to be not altogether inaccurate.
30. In a letter to *The Times* entitled 'Damn You England!', Osborne spoke for the young dramatists and artists who became supporters of CND and the Committee of 100. Paradoxically, Bogdanor and Sidelsky point out (1970, p. 14), the very fact of worldly success marked the end of the angry young men's 'outsider' status and their absorption into the literary establishment. J. Klugmann (1969, p. 166) comments that many of the angry young men later on had become 'show-pieces in the British Museum of Social History as examples of British imperialism's capacity to absorb'. See Frank Parkin, 1968, pp. 99–101.
31. Edward Palmer Thompson was born in 1924 and educated at Cambridge, joined the CP in 1942 and left in 1956. He grew up in a liberal family that was closely associated with the Indian liberation movement. His father was a continuous critic of British imperialism and a friend of Nehru's. His brother Frank was a communist and died heroically during the anti-fascist resistance in Bulgaria; his life had significant influence on Edward's political and moral commitment (see T. J. and E. P. Thompson, 1947). After his war service in Italy 1942–5, he returned to Cambridge to finish his degree in history. In 1947, he worked on railway construction in Yugoslavia as a volunteer. Afterwards he became a tutor in adult education in WEA and Leeds University, and then taught at Warwick University. He was one of the founders and leading figures of the British New Left.
32. For a representative communist attitude towards 'angry young men', see Arnold Kettle, 1958.

33. *Declaration*, edited by Tom Maschler, with Lindsay Anderson, Kenneth Tynan, Stuart Holroyd, John Osborne, Doris Lessing, Colin Wilson, Bill Hopkins, John Wain as contributors. *Conviction* was edited by Norman MacKenzie, of *New Statesman*. Peter Shore, B. Abel-Smith, Raymond Williams, Peter Townsend, Richard Hoggart, Nigel Calder, Hugh Thomas, Peter Marris, Mervyn Jones, Paul Johnson, Iris Murdoch made contributions. Most of these writers also wrote for the New Left journals.

34. See Samuel, 1958a, p. 67; Dennis Potter, 1960, pp. 7–8. For a critical review, see K. Alexander, 1959.

35. Raphael Samuel, born in 1935, an Oxford graduate and social historian, taught at Ruskin College at Oxford (for adult students from the Labour movement) and initiated the History Workshop movement. He was a founding member of *Universities and Left Review* and then *NLR*. Twelve members of his family, including his mother and stepfather, were organisational communists. Chimen Abramsky, his uncle and mentor, was an outstanding figure of the Communist Jewish community. Samuel himself joined the Young Communist League at the age of seven and politically developed from that point. He left the party in 1956 and remained a highly committed socialist.

36. See Thompson, 1959a; Mackenzie, 1958, 'Foreword'. See MacIntyre's critique of the vague meaning of the term in *New Statesman*, 3 October 1959.

37. Lindsay Anderson, the leading figure of the Free Cinema movement and a contributor to the New Left journals. His films include *If*, *O Lucky Man* and *Britannia Hospital*. See Anderson's statement in 1957a, pp. 51–2; A. Lovell, 1961a, pp. 52–3 and 1961b, pp. 54–5.

38. She identifies British political thought under the three heads of 'Tory scepticism, scientific scepticism, and liberal humanist scepticism' (1958, pp. 220, 227).

39. In Perry Anderson's comment, the book has 'never aggregated into a cumulative attack on contemporary British culture', and hence has not had its proper impact. Still, 'all critics of English philosophy owe a great debt to Gellner's classic' (1968, pp. 227, 280; cf. Gellner, 1958, pp.67–73).

40. John Saville, born in 1916, of Greek origin, educated at the London School of Economics; economic and social historian at the University of Hull. He joined the CP in 1934, worked as a volunteer for the Union of Democratic Control and the China Campaign Committee in 1937, and served in the army between 1940 and 1946. He was appointed the only teacher in economic history at Hull in 1947. He was seen as the 'father figure' of the British New Left in terms not only of his founder status but also his personality (This remark was made by Stuart Hall on 9 June 1987, interview with the author). See Miliband, 1979 and Saville, 1991.

41. CND's first Chairman was Canon Collins, with Peggy Duff as his organising secretary. See Paul Byrne's (1988) and James Hinton's (1989, the last four chapters) historical accounts of the two waves of the Campaign. See also, R. Taylor and K. Ward, 1983. For early CND's decline, see Taylor, 1970, pp. 247–9; J. Minnion and P. Bolsover, 1983, pp. 56–63; detailed analyses provided in Taylor and Pritchard, 1980.

42. According to Peggy Duff, the New Left was important in the Campaign because people like Stuart Hall, Peter Worsley, Edward Thompson, and young New Leftists from the universities, like Alan Shuttleworth and John Slater, John Gittings and Richard Gott, 'brought politics to it, independent of the Labour Party, together with an understanding of the urgency of this new movement'. They organised, from that well-known New Left address, 7 Carlisle Street, the distribution of millions of leaflets before each Easter march. However, Duff also observed that 'in one way, CND did them [the New Left] no good. It swallowed them up as a political force' (1971, p. 128).

43. For the differences between CND and the two other organisations, see Duff, 1971, pp. 165–83; Byrne, 1988, pp. 45–7. After being the President of CND from 1958 to 1960, Russell became President of the Committee of 100 from 1960 to January 1963.

44. Raymond Williams, born in 1921 in a small village in Wales, the son of a railway

signalman. He was educated at Trinity College, Cambridge. During the war he served as an anti-tank captain, became an adult education tutor in literature at Oxford after the war, returned to Cambridge in 1961 and became Professor of Modern Drama. He briefly joined the CP and was periodically an LP member. He was one of the founders of the New Left and later the Socialist Society, died in January 1988. 'British intellectual life', remarked Stuart Hall, 'has lost its most distinctive and original mind, and the left its most outstanding socialist intellectual' (1988, p. 20). In Robin Blackburn's words, Williams was 'the most authoritative, consistent and original socialist thinker in the English-speaking world' (Introduction to Robin Gable, 1989, p. ix).

45. Mervyn Jones, born in 1922. Assistant Editor of *Tribune*, 1955–9; of *New Statesman*, 1966–8. He left the CP in 1953, was active in both early New Left and CND. Editorial member of the *New Reasoner* and a contributor to *NLR*.

46. See R. Gott, who talks about 'the genius of Stuart Hall, in my view CND's most original strategic thinker as well as its most brilliant platform orator' (1983, p. 60).

47. See section '"Positive Neutralism" and the Third World' in II.4 and Epilogue below.

48. The editorial committee listed Ken Alexander, Doris Lessing, Ronald Meek, Randall Swingler and later, Derek Kartun, Malcolm MacEwen, Ralph Miliband, Michael Barratt Brown, Peter Worsley, Alfred Dressler, D. G. Arnott and Mervyn Jones. See personal recollections offered by Saville (1976) and MacEwen (1976). The journal had general sympathy from the CP historians, Christopher Hill, Victor Kiernan, Rodney Hilton and Eric Hobsbawm. Lindsay Anderson (film artist), Hyman Levy (scientist) and Gabriel Friel (cartoonist), among others, were also close to the *NR* group.

49. Saville and Thompson were co-editors of *The Reasoner*; with them there were Alexander and Dressler. For an inside story of the journal, see Saville, 1976, pp. 7–21.

50. Saville's long letter to *World News* (19 May 1956) was the first letter appeared in the official party press which set out in some detail the issues that required serious arguments. Thompson's 'Winter wheat in Omsk', a discussion of morality and democracy, was published in *World News* (30 June). But their further letters were rejected and many criticisms from other party members were refused publication.

51. Saville recalled that Constance, his wife, who morally and politically sustained him throughout, threatened to leave him if he and Thompson would not publish this issue (1976).

52. See Saville, 1976, p. 7 and Thompson, 'Although I have resigned from the Communist Party – I remain a communist' (1957b, p. 31).

53. Communist historians such as Dona Torr, Maurice Dobb, Christopher Hill, Victor Kiernan, Rodney Hilton, Eric Hobsbawm, John Saville, Dorothy and Edward Thompson met regularly between 1946 and 1956. Torr's influence on the group was highly appreciated. Some of them (e.g., Dobb and Hobsbawm) remained in the party after 1956. About the history of the group, see Hobsbawm, 1978; H. J. Kaye, 1984, pp. 10–14; B. Schwarz, 1982.

54. Tracing the origin of this name, there were John Bone and his *Reasoner* rekindling English radical Jacobinism. See Thompson, 1963a, pp. 497ff.

55. See Heinemann, 1976, p.49 and her letter to the author (23 Nov. 1987). It seems though she was not very fair to lay the blame on the Thompson and Saville group for such a shift of the focus. Moreover, the question of party organisation was itself 'central' and unavoidable in any serious discussion of the degeneration of the Russian revolution and Stalinism.

56. See, especially, Miliband, 1958a, 1958b; John Hughes, 1957 and discussions around it in the following numbers; debate on a socialist wages plan in both *NR* and *ULR*.

57. Edited by Stuart Hall, Gabriel Pearson, Ralph Samuel and Charles Taylor. From no. 6 (1959) M. Barratt Brown (who also sat on the editorial board of *NR*), Norman Birnbaum, Alan Hall, Michael Kullmann, Alan Lovell and Alasdair MacIntyre also became members of the board.

58. Charles Taylor, born in 1931, educated at Oxford in History and PPE, was a

French-Canadian Rhodes Scholar and became a well-known student of Hegel writing about epistemology, psychology and language, humanism and liberation theology at McGill University, Montreal.

59. His original name was Raphael, and he became a noted social historian known as Raphael Samuel again.

60. In his recollection of thirty years later, Hall named the following: Dodd Alleyne, Sadiqal Mahdi, Clovis Maksou, Alan Lovell, Alan Hall, Stanley Mitchell, Robert Cassen, Anna Davin, Luke Hodgkin, Rod Prince, David Marquand, David and Michael Armstrong, and Perry Anderson, several of whom were not English. Alan Hall, a Scots classicist, went to Balliol College from Aberdeen. According to Stuart Hall, he 'played a key role in the early New Left' (1989, pp. 19-20, 114).

61. For 'the scholarship boy generation', cf. Richard Hoggart, 1957, pp. 238-49; A. Lovell, 1957, p. 34.

62. Hall: 'We raised issues of personal life, the way people live, culture, which weren't considered the topics of politics on the left. We wanted to talk about the contradictions of this new kind of capitalist society in which people didn't have a language to express their private troubles, didn't realize that these troubles reflected political and social questions which could be generalised' (quoted in R. Fraser, 1988, p. 30).

63. The first club lecture series were given by Deutscher, Cole, Hobsbawm, Lindsay Anderson, Thompson and others. About the activities of the local clubs, see for example P. Rose, 1960 and G. Clark, 1960.

64. Michael Barratt Brown, born in 1918, joined the CP after the war and left it in 1956; member of the editorial teams of *NR*, *ULR* and *NLR*. He had been working for adult education since the 1950s (note the family tradition – his father was the principal of a Labour college) at technical colleges, WEA, the Extramural Department of Sheffield University and Northern College, Barnsley, of which he was the first principal. He was one of the leading economists of the Labour left and a persistent New Left advocate for 'workers' control'.

65. He said in 1977 that 'but I now think, with the advantage of hindsight, that the pain of reworking that past was necessary' (1979, p. 362).

66. These projects include the first joint *ULR/NR* publication of the Hughes-Alexander pamphlet on wages policy, an industrial conference held in Yorkshire, the sponsorship of several new local Left clubs and contributions to each other from each group.

67. Miliband was almost alone in opposing it. Saville was also sceptical but at last agreed to act as chairman of the *NLR* board, which he later regarded as a mistake. See III.1.

68. The *NLR* editorial committee listed Alexander, Arnott, Barratt Brown, Birnbaum, Hall, Jones, Kullmann, Lessing, Lovell, MacEwen, MacIntyre, Miliband, Meek, Pearson, Rex, Samuel, Saville, Taylor, the Thompsons, Williams and Worsley.

69. By the end of 1961, there were about forty New Left Clubs around the country. They were intended 'both as open local forums of socialist theory, and as local points of socialist initiatives' (Thompson, 1973, p. 231). In fact, these clubs were once strong enough to exert pressure upon *NLR* and its editors had to state that 'our board ... is *not* the executive of a political body' (no. 12, 'Notes for readers').

70. Hall: 'the New Left was far from politically monolithic and certainly never became culturally or politically homogeneous. ... It would therefore be quite wrong to attempt to reconstruct, retrospectively, some essential "New Left", and to impose on it a political unity it never possessed' (1989, p. 23).

71. The New Left with a communist background was one of the peculiarities of the British situation. Different from the previous generation of ex-communists who moved either into political quietism or to the right, most of those who left the party in 1956/7 remained active in politics on the left. (But many Jewish former CP members became very anti-communist after the revelation of repression of the Jews in the USSR.) It has been unclear, however, why there had not been a single person ever to return to the CP regardless of all its changes actually achieved in the years subsequent to the crisis of 1956.

72. Trotskyism never had a chance to flourish in Britain. By 1956, it was further fatigued as 'an aging, beleaguered and faction-ridden force' (Coates, 1976, p. 112). After

1956, however, there were people who had left the CP and did not quite know what to do, and this 'provided the first basis intellectually speaking for a certain revival of Trotskyism' (Hobsbawm, 1986). A number of trade union activists, highly experienced and influential in factory agitation, went over to the Trotskyist groups (Callaghan, 1987).

73. Both Thompson and Saville, however, unlike their younger successors (see IV.2), did not find Trotskyist interpretation of Soviet problems attractive. Cf. Thompson, 1957c, p. 139.

74. Cf. Nigel Young's unconvincing argument that because Labour could not be bypassed the formation of a 'new' Left was problematic (1977, pp. 144–5).

75. Cf. Samuel's weak challenge to the earlier New Left confidence in its rupture with the old left: 'From the viewpoint of socialism, the New Left marked an end rather than a beginning' (1989, p. 57).

76. Lawrence Daly, born in 1924, joined the CP at the age of fourteen and left the party in 1955 (his father was one of the founders of the CPGB). A miner himself, he was member of the Scottish and later the National Executive of NUM. Representing a new left position in direct union politics, he was, in Saville's assessment, 'an extraordinarily outstanding working-class politician and spokesman' (interview with the author, 19 October 1987).

CHAPTER II

Traditions and Culture, 1957–1962

I. 'THE CULTURAL IS POLITICAL'

This was not a phrase that any New Left writer ever used. But it is no distortion to formulate the 'culturalist' position of the early New Left as such. The phrase makes a unique synthesis of culture and politics, in which cultural questions are of political significance in the process of social changes and transformation. Culture was thus conceived as a way in which a great deal more than political power was involved in politics; in which political identity took form. Consequently, the old distinction between what was political and what was not was rejected: politics could no longer be defined as and confined to parliamentary debates, party and union bureaucratic routine or periodical elections. A definition of it must be based on an understanding of the real forces and deep movements of society. Any political project for socialism had to connect with immediate experience or lived 'culture' of ordinary people whose action ought to count in politics. This conviction was made long before the feminist slogan 'the personal is political' prevailed. As the first *ULR* editorial put it, 'when socialist values lose their relevance for the total scale of man's activities, they lose their "political" point as well'.

Restating this expanded conception of politics, Stuart Hall recalled the New Left case thirty years later:

> the discourse of culture seemed to us fundamentally necessary to any language in which socialism could be redescribed. The New Left therefore took the first faltering steps of putting questions of cultural analysis and cultural politics at the center of its politics. (Hall, 1987b, pp. 25–6)

For the New Left, culture was neither a mere reflection of social relations nor a subordinate aspect of political power. But this was certainly not a New Left discovery. Lenin's conception of 'cultural revolution' or Trotsky's polemics against the idea that culture will change automatically when society changes, were already challenges to Marxist orthodoxy. The Gramscian concept of cultural hegemony had further made a genuine advance in Marxist political theory. The novelty of New Left thinking can be seen in its 'culturalist totality' which framed new political perspectives. In what was later on known as cultural studies, for the first time a discourse of culture became central in political discussions, and culture was used to 'designate a central process and area of social and political struggle' (Williams, 1980a, p. 255). This militant, interventionist cultural engagement was where the New Left contribution to socialist theory and practice can be first identified.

Four background factors might be suggested to explain the rise of this tremendously extensive concern with culture. First, post-war capitalist prosperity and profound changes in class structure, standards of living and lifestyle, combined with the new power of the rapidly growing mass media, highlighted issues concerning the quality of life and working-class attitudes. Socialists could not answer political questions without referring to what was expressed as a cultural crisis of capitalism that went far beyond the point of production or economic exploitation.[1] Second, a major extension of education and communication had a powerful impact on society and social thinking which needed to be studied and addressed, and this could not be properly done without a much broader critique of capitalism in terms of culture and ideology. It was greatly to the New Left's credit that they first recognised the immense power of the communications system (newspapers, broadcasting, television and press) as a major political institution.[2] Third, the new art forms of political protest initiated in the movements of New Drama ('Socialist Theatre'), 'Free Cinema' and similar creative activities[3] constituted a vital dimension of the New Left movement itself. This dimension also reflected and related to the emerging rebellious youth culture of which folk music and pop art developed as outward signs. Finally, for those confronting the Marxist tradition, the exposure of the grave limitations of Stalinism and subsequent criticism of economic reductionism made it clear that cultural problems concerning morality, community and the question of the aspects of 'alienation' other than wage labour, etc., had for a long time been ignored or misrepresented by many Marxists. This required that the absence be filled and the errors of theory revised.

The New Left's preoccupation with 'culture' also reflected its leading participants' earlier professional or intellectual interests. Those who were 'trained' in the CP Historians' Group under the guidance of Dona Torr had been engaged in a kind of cultural reading of history and inspired by the 'social history' approach that opened up to investigations in the cultural processes of historical transformations. Those who were students of English literature were immensely influenced by Leavisite criticism for its 'moral seriousness' and opposition to the mechanical/reductionist versions of Marxism, but were also looking for a way out of the impasse of the elitist *Scrutiny* tradition. In more general terms, they inherited the protest tradition of English literary criticism against industrial capitalism. This tradition, according to Perry Anderson,[4] constituted a profound critique of capitalism, but that critique never became encapsulated in any major social force. 'The New Left represented, in effect, the first time that this tradition found an anchorage in society, and became the inspiration of an actual political movement' (1965a, p. 15). It was a 'detour', however, Anderson wrote later in

1968, that the New Left thinkers had to make because literary criticism was a refuge or base-camp from which systematic socialist thought could develop in an empiricist national culture (1968a, pp. 55–6).

Moreover, most of the New Left people believed in the virtues of and need for adult education and were tutors themselves, for longer or shorter periods, at WEA and university extra-mural departments or Labour colleges. It is especially worth noticing this connection between the New Left and the workers' education movement which, after its height between the wars and immediately after the Second World War, gradually declined and lost its political significance in the late 1950s. As a radical tradition of political education associated with the communists, the Plebs League and such Labour figures as Tawney and Cole,[5] it stood for common-sense values of public and equal education, and a non-elite culture (in contrast to the elitist programmes of political training by the Fabians on the one hand and of the *Scrutiny* 'grammar school' on the other); and it sought to build a new social consciousness and a new civilisation that involved the participation of the working class. These ideas attracted the New Left not only because of their moral commitment but also because of their political conviction that a socialist transformation could be achieved only by long-term struggle 'from below' rather than simply the seizure of power by an elite revolutionary party. From such a perspective, the very dignity and strength of this tradition lay in its dynamic links between what Gramsci called 'organic' intellectuals and shop stewards and other working people, where the two groups educated each other in the way that theories were taught to be understandable by ordinary people in their own language and practicable in real movements. It meant to help the great cause of working-class self-emancipation by way of overcoming the dilemma of education as a mechanism of imposing ruling-class culture and as a means of countering that culture. At a more personal level, the reason for a choice by the leading figures of the British New Left to work in adult education, as Williams recalled, was that

> this was the social and cultural form in which they saw the possiblity of
> reuniting what had been in their personal histories disrupting: the value of
> higher education and the persistent educational deprivation of the majority
> of their originary or affiliated class. (1986, p. 25)

The departure of tutors like Thompson and Williams in the early 1960s contributed to the further weakening of this tradition which, for all its consequences, ought to be regretted.[6]

It would be a mistake to regard the early New Left as a cultural unity, although the confluence of different intellectual stances in the movement was seen by most participants as a source of strength.[7] However, what was common to these different stances was their roots in the national cultural tradition that generated the very mode of thinking and intellectual outlook, what was later fiercely attacked by the second generation of the New Left (see chapter III). The tendency of a new left 'culturalism' was an attempt at reformulating socialist theory from within the moral tradition of English social criticism.

This attempt turned out to be only partially successful because the confrontation of Marxist arguments with the native cultural tradition did not achieve any theoretical depth. The result was twofold: in criticising 'economism', there was a confusion of economic concern with reductionism and an analytic inability to attain a materialist cultural philosophy. The nature and implications of cultural changes were thus expounded from time to time as if spontaneous and isolated from actual historical movement. On the other hand, in promoting cultural analysis, the very limits of it were much neglected. An all-embracing theory of culture was pursued, in some cases not only to be indistinguishable from theories of particular arts but also to replace general sociological or historical studies. While the cultural can be political through articulation, it was still a question as to where the interconnection between culture and politics ought to be articulated, beyond moral criticism and the issue of consciousness. It was also, as a matter of practice, important to elaborate why and when political situations needed to be analysed in cultural terms and how such analysis could (and how far it may) be translated into effective political intervention, thus avoiding abstract or idealist perspective in the realm of cultural politics.

2. TO RECALL A NATIVE TRADITION

William Morris

Edward Thompson's *William Morris: Romantic to Revolutionary* was published in 1955 before the creation of the New Left. As a book that rediscovered and reinterpreted an old romantic tradition in light of socialist humanism, it was an important contribution to the very first 'internal' revolt against Stalinism. This is why the book should be included in any intellectual history of the British New Left.

In disagreement with Mackail's standard biography, *Life of William Morris* (1899), which treated Morris's political activities and writings inadequately, Thompson made his own work a political biography in which Morris was studied, with immense zeal, as one of the greatest Englishmen and a pioneering revolutionary socialist. The academic response to this new biography at the time was virtual silence. However, it was better received than most products of Lawrence and Wishart (the communist publishing house), attracting a few reviews with 'anti-Marxian bias' (Thompson, 1976c, pp. 812–13, 817), a typical case in the climate of the Cold War period.

William Morris, poet, artist, and political thinker, was a founder and leader of the Socialist League in the 1880s. His criticism of 'modern civilisation' – industrial capitalism, in Thompson's interpretation – was a moral rebellion, stemming from the long romantic tradition nourished by Carlyle and Ruskin. This finally led him, by way of an acute personal and intellectual crisis, to the burgeoning socialist movement. Thompson's major argument is that Morris's moral criticism marked the transformation of the romantic tradition in English cultural history. What makes this argument unique is not the personal sentiments it contains, but its focus on the juncture of Marxism and Morris, hence the relationship between historical materialism on the one hand, and romanticism, moralism and utopianism on the other, and its favourable emphasis on the strengths of the latter elements.

The romantic tradition is easily and usually criticised as being regressive and escapist because it is grounded in an appeal to pre-capitalist values. Morris too was driven by a 'hatred of modern civilisation' during his youthful revolt (see especially his 'The Society of the Future' and 'How I Became a Socialist'); and later he carried through into his socialist notion of a 'true society' some of the terms of the romantic critique of utilitarianism and capitalism. Here 'romanticism' is nevertheless of positive significance in Thompson's view, as it was transformed by Morris whose derivation of Marxism was 'out of the logic of the romantic tradition' and resulted in a 'great enrichment of the ethical content of communism' (1976c, p. 802; 1961, pp. 6, 17).[8] Morris therefore demonstrated that it was possible to envisage the romantic tradition 'entering into a common communist tradition to which it could contribute its particular emphases, vocabulary and concerns' (1976c, p. 785), namely, that of 'moral', 'human' and 'utopian'.[9]

To relate Morris's moral standpoint to the Marxist tradition, Thompson's Morris was first and foremost a conscious revolutionary within a society which lacked any revolutionary context, and one of the most determined fighters against the reformism of the (later) Fabian tradition.[10] At the same time, however, he was a 'profoundly cultured and humane' person, a moralist. Standing within the romantic tradition, he rejected those 'one-sided socialists' who saw a moral critique of society as irrelevant to scientific socialism. With the aid of Engels's passage on 'class morality' (*Anti-Duehring*), Thompson defends Morris's 'moral realism' as different from traditional romantic criticism. Morris's realistic moral criticism represented the morality of the working class and flowed directly from 'his scientific understanding of social development, his Marxism' (1976c, pp. 782–3; 1955, pp. 839–40, 832–4, 828; 1961, p. 7).

This implies an appeal to moral consciousness as a vital agency of social change, opposing mechanical materialism that gives society over into the hands of necessity. The chapter entitled 'Necessity and Desire' is specially devoted to Morris's contribution to Marxism. It is an independent discovery of Morris's that, whilst human desires are ultimately determined and limited by their material environment, 'desire must and could assert its own priorities'. Then the task of socialists would be to help people find out their interests and choose their own future (1976c, pp. 803–6; 1955, p. 837; see 1955, pp. 758–841).

Thompson stresses that this is not utopian in any ordinary sense, because the possibility of human desire is placed within a historical and political argument that does not lose sight of the economic and social foundations of change. Meanwhile, however, he also insists that Morris's thought was also exemplary of utopianism. Here utopianism becomes a matter of definition: it can be 'scientific' and 'communist', and so without contradiction 'Morris was a Marxist and a

Utopian'.[11] The term 'utopian' is thus rehabilitated as a challenge to the inability to project any images of a future society and the lack of initiative within mainstream Marxism (1976c, pp. 801–3, 815, 791–2; 1955, pp. 790–1, 797).

The political climate intensified after the turning point of 1956. Having experienced all those battles inside and outside the Communist Party, Thompson reached the conclusion that Morris's moral position was one equal in importance to that of Marx's economic and historical theories. In a lecture given in 1959, he revised his former suggestion that moral argument was in some ways secondary and the analysis of power and production relations primary. Now, 'I see the two as inextricably bound together in the same context of social life' and in fact they 'reinforce each other'. Thus the construction of a communist community would require a moral revolution as profound as the revolution in economic and social power (1959d, pp. 17–19). This idea was further elaborated in the second edition of *Morris* (1976c, pp. 803–4). Marking a crucial point in Thompson's intellectual development, he moved from defending Marxism as a theory that originally contains moral concern to attacking a 'certain silence' of that concern in Marx himself (1976b; 1976c, p. 818).

In 1955, Morris's moralism was rather carefully argued as 'entirely compatible with dialectical materialism' and 'paralleled' the criticisms developed in Marx's and Engels' writings. Those critics of Marxism who constantly averred that there could be no meaningful morality within a materialist interpretation of society confused the Marxist position with mechanical materialism (1955, pp. 828; 831–2; 839). In 1959, Thompson made his target 'the later Marxist tradition': without a historical understanding of 'the evolution of man's moral nature' to which Marx 'scarcely returned' after the 1844 manuscripts, Marx's 'essential concept' of the whole man became lost (1959d, p. 6; p. 18). As common to 'humanist Marxism' which called for Marx's early writings to legitimate moral and humanistic values, Thompson saw a distinction between Marx whose earlier ethical revolt led to an ability of responding to the moral issues and 'positivistic' Engels who failed to sense Morris the moralist communist (1959d, p. 6l; 1976c, pp. 785–6, 803).

The 1976 Postscript reintroduced Morris directly into contemporary socialist debate and questioned the possibility of 'a reordering of Marxism'. Thompson went further to say that, based on the fact of the lack of moral self-consciousness (and even vocabulary) which turned the major Marxist tradition into something worse than confusion, Morris ought to be understood as a (transformed) romantic more than a (conforming) Marxist; and Morris's importance within the Marxist tradition must be seen less in his adhesion to it than in the failure of Marxism to meet that adhesion halfway. Thus Morris could be assimilated to Marxism only in the course of a self-criticism of Marxism itself. Speaking very unfavourably to Marxism, Thompson claimed that what it might do, 'for a change, is sit on its own head a little in the interests of Socialism's heart' (1976c, pp. 802, 806–7). But he actually had little confidence in reforming mainstream Marxism:

> it should now be clear that there is a sense in which Morris, as a Utopian
> and moralist, can never be assimilated to Marxism, not because of any

contradiction of purposes but because one may not assimilate desire to knowledge, and because the attempt to do so is to confuse two different operative principles of culture. So that I've phrased the problem wrongly, and Marxism requires less a re-ordering of its parts than a sense of humility before those parts of culture which it can never order. (1976c, p. 807)

Obviously, by tracing out the evolution of romanticism and its trajectory in Morris's life, Thompson asserted his own commitment and ideas. The book was written during the height of McCarthyism and a 'muffled' resistance to Stalinism, and also in a period when Thompson was teaching worker-students and participating in the independent discussions within the CP Historians' Group. This very experience of producing *Morris* helped him eventually move towards becoming a historian, and more importantly, a Morrisian socialist who would go on arguing from the plenitude of Morris's spirit to seek to rehabilitate 'lost categories and a lost vocabulary in the Marxist tradition' (1976c, p. 810; 1976b, p. 13).

The weaknesses of *Morris* are obvious: it leaves untouched the reactionary characteristics of the romantic tradition, such as anti-industrial sentiment or Morris's medievalism and a simplism or naïveté of utopian passion derived from his nostalgic sentiment; it is uncritical of the moral critique of capitalist society for its being limited by the very terms of that society itself; it lays greater stress on moral protest and neglects the whole problem of class power (especially in the revised edition where the original militant polemic against reformism is mitigated); and it dismisses the fundamental moral credibility of a Marxism which, after all, stands for the interests of the oppressed and the working class. In his *Arguments within English Marxism* (1980), a systematic criticism of Thompson's work, Anderson points out that there is insufficient analysis in *Morris* about the historical conditions of Morris's utopianism and why Marxism long failed to take up Morris's legacy. Although Thompson's study contains materials for a portrait of Morris as an original socialist strategist, 'the whole strategic dimension of his thought is given virtually no weight' (1980, pp. 160-3, 176).

The excuse for such a partiality is that Thompson had every reason to feel in 1955 that 'never before in history have the moral issues facing mankind been more challenging' (1955, p. 843). The following remarks by Anderson are a valid assessment:

> in criticising it, with whatever justice, I committed the serious mistake of failing to see the real force and originality of Thompson's engagement with the issue of communist morality proper in his major work ... we come full circle, to the need for a revival of the faculties of moral and political imagination – what was traditionally called utopian thought – on the Left today. No one has done more to bring this need home to us all than Edward Thompson. (1980, p. 205)

Socialist Humanism

'Socialist humanism' as the basic intellectual position of the early New Left was a response, rather crudely expressed, to the moral discredit surrounding the old left. Passionately inspired by such a position – in Alasdair MacIntyre's words: 'All other forms of society have been suffered by men, socialism is to be lived by them' (1958/9) – the New Left critics nevertheless did not develop a systematic philosophical basis for it. In revolting against Stalinism with all its hard background of political hegemony and ideological authority, socialist humanism at first served as an immediately available weapon for the dissident communists in the east as well as the west. This 'new rebellious humanism', in Thompson's opinion, was crucially relevant to the entire socialist movement and 'must be of the profoundest importance to British socialists' (1957c, p. 107; 1957a, p. 36). It was also fundamentally a New Left outlook, because the old Left, according to him, could only speak in the language of power but never of socialist humanity (1960a, p. 188). This was certainly not the case of either the humanist tradition within the communist literature (which Thompson himself deeply appreciated earlier in the *New Reasoner*) or the moral concerns presented by the Fabians. His anger was directed at the inhuman nature of Stalinist theory and practice which to a great extent poisoned the notion of 'scientific socialism' and credibility of the old Left.

Even as early as *Morris*, Thompson appealed to 'courage' – and the conscience of Marxists was urgently required at a time when people were turning to a re-examination of their socialist principles and challenging what was orthodox (1955, p. 843). In his *Reasoner* article on the Hungarian events of 1956, the primary critique of Stalinism focused on its 'mechanical idealism' and loss of 'the ingredient of humanity': its doctrines of the party, class struggle and the proletarian dictatorship; its fear of independent thought and identification of all disagreement with counter-revolutionary conspiracy, which he saw as 'anti-intellectual'; its elimination of moral criteria from political judgement; and a mechanical understanding of human consciousness – 'Stalinism is Leninism turned into stone' (1956a, pp. 1–7; 1957b, p. 22). Thompson acknowledged the need to dig deep to reveal the roots of the Stalinist phenomenon, which could not be sufficiently explained by the accident of an individual personality.

'Socialist humanism', published in the initial issue of NR, was the first articulated anti-Stalinist statement by a British communist. As Thompson saw it, to criticise Stalinism was:

> a revolt against the ideology, the false consciousness of the elite-into-bureaucracy, ... as such it is expressed in the revolt against dogmatism and the anti-intellectualism which feeds it. Second, it is a revolt against inhumanity – the equivalent of dogmatism in human relationships and moral conduct ... so the positive content of this revolt may be described as 'socialist humanism'. (1957c, p. 109)

Three distinctive characteristics of the Stalinist ideology were summed up as anti-intellectualism, moral nihilism and denial of the creative agency of humanity. Their common political expression is 'veiled hostility to democratic initiatives in every form'. In this analysis, 'economism' that sustained a historical determinist view of men as passive objects is taken as 'the original sin of Marxism'. It is not laid at Stalin's door alone but can be traced to ambiguities in the thought of Marx and 'mechanistic fallacies' in Lenin (1957c, pp. 112, 132–4; 1959a, pp. 9, 13). This critique carried out by Thompson and many others contributed to the long-standing polemic against economistic determinism which had become clearly disclosed in the arguments around the communist movement from 1956 onwards. Meanwhile, Thompson insisted that Stalinism had never been the same thing as the Russian revolution or communism. He reaffirmed his faith in 'the fundamental humanist content' of the indigenous socialist tradition represented by Morris and Mann, Fox and Caudwell (1957c, p. 137; 1959a, pp. 6–7; 1957b, pp. 35–6, 22).

On the part of the younger *ULR* circle, the excitement evoked by the rediscovery of Marx's 1844 manuscripts (in French) which were brought to Oxford from Paris by Charles Taylor in 1958 coincided with the New Left indignation at the impact of Stalinism. Convinced that the politics of the Left could not function without moral ideas, they found a humanist Marx to counter a determinist one. They were especially attracted by the young Marx's themes of 'alienation'; 'realms of necessity and freedom' or self-fulfilment in work as artistic-like activities of a liberated human life (which was part of the inspiration to the politicising of culture); and 'needs' (debated in terms of a distinction between true needs and the false or manipulated needs of consumerism).

By enlarging the key notion of 'alienation' from its early confinement to the conditions of 'wage slavery', the *ULR* critics took it also as a concept applicable to the 'outsiders' in British society, outsiders whether falling into class, racial/ethnic or cultural categories. In terms of political advocacy, Samuel recalled that at the time 'alienation' was a unifying concept that 'rapidly came to occupy the imaginative space accorded to "exploitation" in earlier schools of socialist thought, and "hegemony" in more recent ones' (1989, p. 43). Perry Anderson, who was to become the fiercest critic of the early New Left's 'moralism', wrote in the *New University* that 'if there is one word which the Labour Party lacks, it is alienation' (quoted in Samuel, *ibid.*).

These young Marxists, in their discussions of socialist humanism, came to doubt later Marxism. In a response to Thompson, Taylor forcefully argued that at the theoretical level Stalinist ideology was not mere economic automatism, but a kind of 'historical solipsism' or 'subjectivism' which refused human limitations or negative sides of human beings on the part of the judges of history. He was careful in questioning the relationship between Stalinism and Marxism: is the assimilation of communism to Stalinism false? Can we repudiate Stalinism without also repudiating something of Marxism? The answer, for him, could not be simply an unqualified 'yes' or an unqualified 'no'. He saw the dilemma which Marxism itself had been facing since 1917 – the communist movement had chosen inhuman means to pursue what was in principle a human end. He concluded that 'Marxist communism is at best an incomplete humanism', and 'a really consequent critique of Stalinism cannot be a simple return to the original tradition [of Marxism]' (1957, pp. 92, 95, 98).[12]

In his reply to Taylor (whose conclusion he accepted) and others, but mainly to Harry Hanson who denied any possibility of uniting socialist humanism and scientific socialism (Hanson, 1957), Thompson placed great stress, again, on human agency and choice, in opposition to any form of determinism, whether that of 'economic necessity' or 'historical laws' (1958b, pp. 89–106). Without referring to the work of Lukács or Sartre or any other humanist currents of continental Marxism but surely in accord with them, humanism here is taken not merely as a moral appeal but as a conception of history (see IV.2). In political terms, Thompson claimed that humanist socialism was a practicable and desirable goal which must commence with the needs of people (1957c, p. 106; 1959a, p. 10). He did not go further to elaborate the meaning of the highly ambiguous word 'needs', nor did he define a form in which such a socialist and humanist desire to meet needs could be achieved.

In a philosophical commentary, Alasdair MacIntyre criticised Hanson, but perhaps also implicitly Thompson, for the fallacy in their otherwise opposite arguments of a 'moral liberalism'. This moral liberalism takes the 'ought' of principle as completely external to the 'is' of history, as against the Stalinist 'is' that swallowed the 'ought' altogether. Such an arbitrary, groundless morality is characterised by its empiricism, which is in fact what it has in common with Stalinism: history occurred, whether theory can grasp it or not, independently of human agency. He sought for a third position which would reject both the naked utilitarianism of Stalinist method and the romantic liberal belief in the autonomy of ethics, and bridge the gulf between morality and history (1958–9). Beyond a somewhat idealist moral criticism (e.g. Thompson's), he looked for solid theory. MacIntyre's and Thompson's discussions, tentative as they were, highlighted NR's major effort in seeking an adequate approach to criticising Stalinism and proposing an alternative.

Thompson's 'Outside the Whale', published in the New Left collection Out of Apathy in 1960, was another influential statement of socialist humanism. His new theme was the making of 'socialist human nature': 'The aim is not to create a socialist State, towering above man and upon which his socialist nature depends, but to create a "human society or socialised humanity" ' (NLB, 1960, pp. 183–5, 199). By not confronting the immensely important issue of political power, this sounds 'utopian' indeed, in a negative sense. The other part of the article concerns 'Natopolitan culture', addressing socialist humanism in different terms of nuclear disarmament and 'positive neutralism' (see II.4). Thompson's lifetime position of what might be called 'socialist pacifism' was then already in shape.

3. CULTURAL TRADITIONS AND THE WORKING CLASS

The Uses of Literacy

The Uses of Literacy, written by Richard Hoggart and published in 1957,[13] was the 'solemn, earnest, heavy voice' of an educated working-class generation (Williams, 1957a, p. 29). A major contribution to the cultural studies of the lived experience of social change, of the current trends and feelings and their impact on the pattern of working-class life, the book was tremendously inspiring at a time when the New Left began to look at culture in terms of its political dimensions and implications. On the one hand, Hoggart sought to show the remaining strength of class attitudes in spite of the great changes since the post-First World War period, while on the other hand, he saw them as so profound that they in some ways led to a culturally classless situation. In approaching these the author relied more on personal experience (mainly in Leeds) than specialist analysis, which drew serious criticism from his fellow New Left critics (for example, Williams, 1957a; Thompson, 1959c).

One of the focuses of *The Uses of Literacy* is the effect of modern popular culture on the working classes.[14] The former, with its worst aspect of commercial advertising, was regarded as a corruption of and threat to the traditional culture of the latter. Hoggart warned that once popular publications were successful in holding their readers at a level of passive acceptance and the newer mass art became a 'money-making game at bottom' for working men, the old 'urban culture of the people' would be destroyed (1957, pp. 196–7, 260–1, 271–3).[15] In fact, he wrote, the popular press stood as one of the greatest conservative forces in public life today, and most popular entertainments were in the end what D. H. Lawrence described as 'anti-life'. These, together with the 'extraordinarily low level' organs of the mass communication system, effected a real gap between the material improvement and the 'cultural loss' of working people, hence a worsening rather than a progression in the quality of their lives (pp. 196, 277, 11). Cultural changes were therefore tending to cause the working classes to lose much that was valuable, while failing to achieve the new life to which they aspired.

> No doubt many of the old barriers of class should be broken down. But at the present the older, the more narrow but also more genuine class culture is being eroded in favour of mass opinion, … The old forms of class culture are in danger of being replaced by a poorer kind of classless… culture, and this is to be regretted. (p. 260)

This regret for a cultural degeneration inherited Scrutiny's governing theme yet differed from that of the Leavises in emphasis. Hoggart's was not a defence of high culture, nor a nostalgia for the golden age of an organic community, but an elegy for a genuine working-class culture.[16] However, being hostile to the standardisation and commercialisation of cultural activities, like F. R. Leavis who tended to romanticise seventeenth-century folk art, Hoggart idealised certain non-political aspects of old working-class life, such as the world of club singing, music halls and brass bands; as well as the solidarity of the neighbourhood community. This in turn strengthened his view that people of the working classes were less affected by the newer approaches to them than might be assumed. While their earlier cultural tradition was no doubt weakening in the process of urbanisation that made life more public and uniform, they possessed some inner resistance and largely preserved a decent, local, personal and communal way of life (pp. 16, 27, 31–2, 164, 265).

The theme of 'classlessness', which preoccupied *ULR* for quite a while, was first raised in *The Uses of Literacy*. According to Hoggart, newer products appealed to more than a single class. They could not reach an audience of the size needed for commercial purposes except by cutting across class boundaries, and so class divisions became less clear as circulations increased. In at least one sense, he said, 'we are indeed becoming classless – that is, the great majority of us are being merged into one class'. This emerging culturally classless class was likely to be a compound of working-class and lower-middle to middle-class elements who consumed the same mass products. Yet in another sense, even if the label 'working classes' ceased to be used, there would still exist a huge body of people who would have to take the less interesting and more mechanical jobs – a 'kind of new caste system' would be as firm as the old (pp. 201, 276, 279–80).

Hoggart's cultivated rejection of 'mass culture'[17] was an appeal to those who were loyal both to a non-polluted culture and to self-consciously working-class people, and indeed democracy: democracy in the sense of anti-elitism, what Williams would put in a simple phrase as 'culture is ordinary' (1958a). It was also a gesture of returning to the class- and community-based cultural life and politics which Hoggart outlined in terms of 'Us' and 'Them'. However, his under-estimation of the political quality of the working-class tradition and partial acceptance (from the viewpoint of consumption) of, in Williams's words, 'the extremely damaging and quite untrue identification' of mass culture with working-class culture (1957b, p. 30),[18] reduced the weight of these messages. At this point, Williams offered a much sharper observation: mass culture was 'instituted, financed and operated by the commercial bourgeoisie' and remained 'typically capitalist in its methods of production and distribution' (*ibid.*).

Unlike Williams, who did have serious criticisms but in general greatly admired *The Uses of Literacy* for its successful engagement with issues of 'exceptional contemporary interest', Thompson viewed the book as a failure in several aspects: its conservative assessment of resistance to 'commercialism' that actually views the working classes as merely passive recipients; its near dismissal of the vital political tradition of the working class (Williams had the same criticism); and its 'anti-historical framework' (1959c, p. 53). He himself emphasised tensions between the actual (class?) nature of the audience and the false consciousness of the media. Extending his objections, Thompson found a tendency particularly strong in *ULR* of asserting 'the absolute autonomy of cultural phenomena' without reference to the context of political power and class struggle (pp. 51, 53–4). This last point is an important one, but it applies as well to some of Thompson's own writings. As to the nature of the book, an empiricist and sociological narrative is not necessarily anti- or less 'historical', although the limitations of Hoggart's approach, such as the danger of broad generalisation, must be acknowledged.[19] Obviously, the problems of the book have something to do with its strong romantic inclination to idealise traditional working-class culture in opposition to the social and cultural consequences of industrial and technological development under capitalism. It is far from sufficient as a socialist analysis, which ought to examine political power and control over both cultural institutions and the means of communication. Nevertheless, *The Uses of Literacy* revealed some profound truths about the great process of change, especially the decline of class consciousness, which seemed to have been ignored by many Marxist critics.

Culture and Society

Culture and Society (1958) was written in effective political isolation during a personal crisis of retreat from immediate politics. Although Raymond Williams was still cast as a communist by many people until 1956, since leaving the party a decade earlier he had been seeking an intellectual position in the difficult Cold War context. Being 'negatively marked by elements of a disgusted withdrawal', the book was nevertheless a seminal enterprise that set the author's 'first-stage radicalism' between a left-Leavisite and a steadfast socialist (1979, pp. 106–10). Williams recalled, about twenty years later, that *Culture and Society* was an 'oppositional' work written from within the tradition of English literary criticism to refuse what he termed 'cultural conservatism', namely the increasingly reactionary use of the concept of culture *against* democracy, socialism, and working-class or popular education (1979, pp. 98, 112, 121). This political motivation of writing something 'non-political' reflected the new distinction made between routine politics and politics as conscious struggle in relation to deeper movements and changes in society (the chapter on Burke is most closely along this line).

In different ways, *The Uses of Literacy* is of the same character. That Williams and Hoggart worked coincidentally on cultural history with many similar interests and ideas, and published their books almost simultaneously without knowing of each other's project, only indicated a new common trend in political thinking in which culture became the focus.

Williams started looking at the concept of culture in an adult education class between 1949 and 1951. During the subsequent process of writing, of 'almost constant redefinition and reformulation' (1979, p. 132), the notion eventually extended into a historical complexity of ideas, values and reference. Confronting the 'crisis' of social consciousness and human relationships, *Culture and Society* was intended to be 'an account and an interpretation of our responses in thought and feeling to changes in English society' since the late eighteenth century (1961a, pp. 11, 17). As an original attempt to bring literary criticism to a wider field across 'cultural studies' and social history, this ground-breaking work established the 'culture and society tradition'.[20] This was at once profoundly novel in its depth and scope of inquiry and methodologically conventional in terms of its inherited practical criticism in a particularising and empirico-moral mode of discourse,[21] a discourse to which he himself would later adopt a critical stance.

Williams divided the English history of culture into three main periods: from about 1790 to 1870, the major analysis was undertaken and the major opinions emerged; then a kind of interregnum between 1870 and 1914 (this is, however, contradicted by his account of William Morris); and finally after 1914, there was a growing concern with new problems arising from the development of the mass media and large scale organisations. The focus of his analysis is the historical formation of culture as a very concept, of its structure of meanings. The emergence of this concept merged two general responses: the recognition of the practical separation of certain moral and intellectual activities from the driven impetus of a new industrialising society, and the emphasis of these activities, as a court of human appeal, to offer an alternative (1961a, p. 17). The strongest stream of 'thought and feeling' presented in *Culture and Society* might be said to be a romantic/humanistic tradition of anti-utilitarianism, involving both radical and Tory writers: from William Blake and William Wordsworth to Shelley, Keats, the industrial novelists and D. H. Lawrence; and more widely, from William Cobbett, Robert Owen, Thomas Carlyle, John Ruskin, William Morris, R. H. Tawney, George Orwell to F. R. Leavis.[22] There is an important remark in the chapter on Orwell explaining how the particular characters of this tradition, generated within a paradoxical situation, logically created contradictory and tragic figures:

> England took the first shock of industrialism and its consequences, and
> from this it followed, on the one hand, that the humane response was early,
> fine and deep – the making of a real tradition; on the other hand, that the
> material constitution of what was criticised was built widely into all our
> lives – a powerful and committed reality. (p. 276)

Later in 1965, Williams made the much more controversial point that 'the moral critique of industrial capitalism, which has mainly informed the British working-class movement, has been paralleled, throughout, by a literary tradition of comparable importance' (1965 p. 23). Morris was viewed as a significant figure who linked the two.[23]

Williams's reading of such a unilinear, generalised tradition of culture was seen by some of the same 'culturalist' New Left critics as inadequate, divorced from the effective historical context of class contradictions and the altered conditions of British society (e.g., Kiernan, 1959, pp. 75–8, 82; Thompson, 1961a). The French revolution and Jacobinism, for example, seemed to have no influence on the thinking of English intellectuals. Thompson thus challenged the notion of the tradition itself, arguing that there were actually not one but two major traditions under review in *Culture and Society*, with sub-traditions within both: a socialist or revolutionary tradition and a tradition of bourgeois self-criticism. Williams's loss of 'the sense of the whole way of conflict in which the two traditions are involved' resulted in his own partial disengagement from the former tradition (1961a, pp. 24–5; 1961b, pp. 34–5; cf. L. Johnson, 1979, pp. 200–7). Later, Terry Eagleton, a young Marxist critic and a pupil of Williams, attacked *Culture and Society* for its handling merely 'the Romantic radical-conservative lineage' from which the radical elements were extracted and of which the reactionary characters were systematically neglected (1976a, p. 10).

What is interesting here is that from a shared Marxist point of view, Thompson's and Kiernan's original criticism of the blindness to antagonism between classes and hence traditions in *Culture and Society* had been entirely taken over and developed by younger writers like Eagleton. But when Eagleton sniffed at the 'humanist standpoint' and viewed romanticism as 'the nineteenth-century bourgeois exploitation' of 'an ideological crutch', he irritated Thompson. The latter would eventually come to a strong defence of Williams's position which was identified with his own much accused infection of 'romantic populism' or 'moralism' (Eagleton, 1976a, pp. 10–11; Thompson, 1976a, pp. 110–11). This is a case of what was later known as 'a serious continuing quarrel of principles' (Thompson, 1976a, p. 110) between some of the first New Left and their Marxist critics of the second New Left generation.

For Williams's part, while he did not distinguish in his tradition, which indeed was full of the interaction of different ideas and values, between two or more lines on a class or political basis, where his political sympathies lay is evident in the contrasts made between Burke and Cobbett, or Southey and Owen, and also in the Conclusion where he sought a common culture and reasserted the concept of socialist democracy. But more importantly, he wanted to examine the established patterns of English culture rather than deal with a selected set of radical heritage. To the charge that *Culture and Society* had 'an inadvertently conservative bias', he replied, long after making his 'final break' with the 'reformist' outlook (Labour reformism in particular) in 1966 (Williams, 1976b, p. 249), that he had discovered themes profoundly related to the current social crisis and the socialist way out of it, 'not in the approved list of progressive thinkers, but in these paradoxical figures'; and that the only correct way of discussion should be to argue critically each case individually (1979, pp. 103–6). Since the original strategy of the book was to recover a specifically English tradition of social thinking about culture, it is quite convincing that we are offered a single tradition composed of writers of different political tendencies.

As to Williams's own stand at the time, he believed that 'the argument between Morris and Webb, between communism and social democracy, still rages; neither has yet been proved finally right' (p. 185). This statement refers to the question of strategy rather than principle – his political gradualism was a major factor in making *Culture and Society* less enthusiastically welcomed by his fellow leftists than by a liberal reading public.

Looking at the changes in language since the last decades of the eighteenth century, Williams suggested five concepts as the key points: industry, democracy, class, art, and culture. Among them culture was the most striking one. The development of this word is a record of important and continuing human reactions to the changes in social, economic, and political life; by means of it the nature of these changes can be explored (pp. 13, 16). He thus examined the very concept of culture[24] through tradition, the various ideas formulated, in particular, by Coleridge and Carlyle (the nature of and relations between culture and civilisation), Arnold (culture as the entire way or process of human development), Ruskin (the perfection of man and wholeness of being), Tawney (equality and culture and common culture), T. S. Eliot (the conceptualisation of culture as a whole way of life) and Leavis (organic society, tradition and community).[25] Williams, as he himself acknowledged, was profoundly in debt to this 'great tradition'. Attempting to make sense of culture and to find the internal network of relations behind the nature of the concept, he tended to defend the traditional framework of its values and meanings that had been written about since the nineteenth century, and was most marked in twentieth-century anthropology and sociology: 'culture is not only a body of intellectual and imaginative work; it is also and essentially a whole way of life'. What was a personal assertion of value is now a general intellectual method (1961a, pp. 18, 229, 311).

But Williams had made his own significant contribution which highlights the idea of a 'common culture' – 'an educated and participating democracy' (1961a, pp. 306–23; 1968a, p. 32). The historical heritage of the tradition and the revelation of interrelation between true communication and community[26] offered, in his view, an opportunity of establishing a common ground for ways of life. The body of intellectual and imaginative work which each generation receives as its traditional culture is something more than the product of a single class. It is thus misleading to describe a 'bourgeois culture' and to manufacture an artificial 'working-class culture' in opposition to it. The working class has not produced a culture in the narrow class sense. The culture which it has achieved is a great creative accomplishment: 'the collective democratic institution, whether in the trade unions, the co-operative movement, or a political party' (1961a, pp. 307–8, 313). That is to say, the very distinction between different class cultures is no longer useful; instead, a common culture could be built (though not in any final sense) with a common process of industrial development and democratic extension (*ibid.*, pp. 320–3).

From a Marxist point of view, Kiernan and Thompson both emphasised the actual historical context of power/class structures and ideological conflicts, which seemed not really to matter in Williams's conceptualisation. Williams did realise, however, that attention would have to be concentrated on 'the nature of the controlling social relations' (p. 300). What he did not realise was that it was mistaken to leave the problem of class behind at the economic level and trust cultural possibility alone to effect great change, thereby failing to gain a coherent theory of culture (self-criticism in 1979, p. 364). His Marxist critics, on the other hand, more or less underrated the increasing power of the new means of communication and the profound social implications of this major technological advance, and neglected the enormous importance of cultural institutions and organisations, of which Williams pioneered an analysis.

Confronting himself with Marxism in pursuing a definition of culture, Williams was of the opinion that 'Marx himself outlined, but never fully developed, a cultural theory'; and Marxist writings in England from the 1920s to the 1950s continually failed to formulate a Marxist theory of culture. However, he had no intention of working out such a theory other than to expose the confusions within a vulgar Marxism and the 'self-contradictions' of English Marxist critics (1961a, pp. 258, 262–71).

In opposition to 'a rigid methodology' of economic reductionism, Williams argues that to understand different cultures of, say, English society and French society which are both in certain stages of capitalism, 'we are committed to what is manifest: the way of life as a whole' (pp. 119, 272). Since economic change never in practice appears in isolation and the basic economic organisation cannot be separated and excluded from its moral and intellectual concerns, the question whether the 'economic element' is determining is ultimately unanswerable. This understanding of economic-cultural totality enables him to evaluate a cultural revolution to be as fundamental as a social revolution (pp. 271–2; Introduction to 1961b). In his opinion, a general inadequacy among Marxists in the use of culture is that the term is taken to indicate something belonging to the 'ideological superstructure'. This could be even worse if the superstructure is believed to be simply and directly determined by the economic base, because from such a conception naturally arise theoretical difficulties and errors (1961a, pp. 268–9, 272).[27]

To interpret culture as an ambiguous 'whole' way of life is surely incompatible with the classical Marxist framework. Even those Marxists who tend to abandon the standard 'mechanical metaphor' of base and superstructure, yet persist in the position of historical materialism, can hardly accept such a concept. For it collapses the central categories – mode of production, socio-economic formation, production relations, the political system, the state apparatus, ethics and ideology – without any sense of priority, into an all-embracing concept of culture. Moreover, such a categorically neutral and ideologically innocent 'culture' is at odds with the Marxist tenet of class and class struggle (Eagleton, 1976b, p. 26). This is why Thompson not only counterposed a formula, 'way of conflict', but was also forced narrowly to define culture as 'intellectual products' and to attach it to the pole of social consciousness.[28] The notion of socialist culture is thus understood and justified as something that must have its basis in the co-operative production relations, which means that a revolution to change the mode of production is required (1961b, pp. 38–9). A sharp comparison can be made here between Thompson the critic of Williams and Thompson the Morris-like moralist.[29] The conceptual clash between a culturalist and a Marxist or materialist solution cannot be simply resolved by a flexible interpretation of dialectical interactions.

A related issue that Williams emphasised for discussion is the tendency towards a theoretical simplism as a consequence of mechanical determinism. He points out that the isolation of economics as the key to change has led, in its turn, to dangerous simplification and abstraction. Even in an argument which does not break away from the formula of base and superstructure, the latter is necessarily very complex because it is always diverse and historical. 'This recognition of complexity is the first control in any valid attempt at a Marxist theory of culture' (pp. 259–60). Criticising Morris's utopianism for attaching the notion of social simplicity to communism, Williams sees no incompatibility between social complexity and a genuinely common culture (pp. 308, 318). As he would later put it, essentially 'the break towards socialism can only be towards an unimaginably greater complexity' (1979, pp. 128–9).[30] This was indeed a fundamental observation, an observation that anticipated the more recent debate over the question of pluralism and socialist arrangement of a future society.[31]

Looking at the English attempt at a Marxist theory of culture, all that Williams can see is an interaction between romanticism and Marx, between the ideas of culture which constituted the tradition and Marx's revaluation of it. It is hard for Williams, however, to distinguish much of the Marxist writings on cultural themes of the last few decades from the literature of old romantic protest. Their concepts are very near to Arnoldian and their terms inherited from the tradition proceeding from the romantics through Morris (1961a, pp. 258, 263, 271). If a self-proclaimed Marxist like Thompson could take 'the ideological role of art' as an 'active agency in changing human beings and society as a whole' (1955, p. 770), it is sufficiently reasonable for Williams to ask for a distinction between the idealist and materialist position and to view ideas like Thompson's as romantic because only a romantic attitude bestows such great power on the arts. Then 'it certainly seems relevant to ask English Marxists who have interested themselves in the arts whether this is not romanticism absorbing Marx, rather than Marx transforming romanticism' (1961a, p. 265).

The problem is, partly, a matter of assessing romanticism itself. As a major literary tradition, it attracted several generations of moral critics of capitalism, but never transcended its own critical basis as a part of that very society against which it protested. Reconfiguring the history of English literary thoughts, Williams seemed then to be not quite aware of his own romantic inheritance.[32] Thompson, who was proud of being a 'Morrisian Marxist', with an increasing emphasis on the former term rather than the latter in the years after the publication of *Morris*, wrote in 1976 that:

> It was a distinctive contribution of *Culture and Society* to show how tough this long Romantic critique of industrial capitalism had been; and I would add that Williams's own writing, over two decades, has exemplified how tough a mutation of that tradition can still be, and how congruent to the thought of Marx. (1976c, p. 785)

But Marx's famous remark in the *Grundrisse* suggests something rather sceptical about this 'congruence': 'The bourgeois viewpoint has never advanced beyond the antithesis between itself and the romantic viewpoint, and the latter will accompany it as its legitimate antithesis up to its blessed end' (1973, p. 162). The romantic perspective must be transcended in an outlook that foresees capitalism's 'blessed end'. Or, in other words, Thompson's 'mutation' of the romantic tradition must go beyond that tradition.

The massive success of *Culture and Society* lies in the fact that it confronted contemporary cultural issues by way of examining and evaluating changes of society and social consciousness. In seeking a new analysis adequate to those changes which had their deep root and striking expression in culture, the book initiated a significant step toward a new sort of socialist debate: a whole range of 'cultural studies' subsequently developed, in richness and diversity, from that very starting point. Having acquired a centrality within an entire new intellectual generation, the book, as the NLR editors put it, 'has played an extremely important and liberating role for socialist thought in this country' (Williams, 1979, p. 106).

Class, Classlessness and Working-class Attitudes

The debate over the issues concerning working class culture following the publication of *The Uses of Literacy* and *Culture and Society* was a major event in the early history of the New Left. The problem at first appeared as 'the myth of classlessness' that reflected complex social changes in post-war Britain: the novel conditions and new forms of capitalism, the altering forces in social and class structures, the effects of these developments on political relations and consciousness. Stuart Hall opened the debate with his 'A Sense of Classlessness' printed in *ULR* in the spring of 1958, speaking of a breaking up of the old sense of class in terms of discontinuity between economic class position and class politics – the objective factors which shaped and were in turn shaped by an industrial working class, the subjective ways in which these factors grew into consciousness, and the degree to which these factors changed and were still changing (1958, pp. 27, 29).

Three major processes that contributed to the idea of an emerging classlessness and required a reconsideration of class formulations are the spread of mass communication, public education and consumerism. Hoggart and Williams first observed a cultural classlessness in the light of commercially sponsored mass culture – publishing, cinema, broadcasting, television and advertising – which tended to be 'classless' since it penetrated all classes. The extension of education (including adult education)[33] together with a growth in belief in educational equality constituted what was called by an NLR editorial a 'learning revolution' (*NLR* 11, pp. 38–9). In a real 'inter-class movement' through educational opportunity, according to Hoggart, numbers of people from the working classes transferred into membership of other classes by the scholarship system (1957, pp. 238–49, 275; 1958, p. 137).[34] The development of this new education for public servants, in Williams's opinion, helped to create 'a new and expanding class' (1961b, pp. 148–9). In any case, the proportion of technical and professional people in the labour force had expanded, and the social intake widened, which must have consequences (*NLR* 11, editorial).

To an even greater degree, the New Left saw an 'undifferentiated consumerism' which was remaking class relations. A mass of consumers formed within the context of a growing equality in consumer patterns, to which a merging of the working class with the middle class was related in terms of a consumption-directed character and general lifestyle (Hall, 1958, pp. 26, 30–1). For Hall, consumption had become the most significant relationship, one which represented a new form of exploitative relations between capital and labour, and commodities had accumulated a social value and thus became 'insignias of class and status' (1958, pp. 28–9; 1959, p. 51). As Williams put it, politically, under the domination of the concepts of organised market and consumer, 'hardly any principled opposition remains' (1961b, p. 305).

Nonetheless, such a 'classlessness' was taken by these viewers only in a limited and definite sense. It is not that classes had disappeared, but rather a recognition was occurring of class confusion in a more 'open' society, in which class, class formation and class relations were being profoundly transformed. In this sense, 'classlessness' was something developed as 'false consciousness' (Hall, 1958, p. 30). While the so-called 'deproletarianisation' was taking place, it became very complicated; on the one hand many people who felt themselves middle-class were selling their labour and on the other hand the working class itself was internally divided. Both 'working-class' and 'middle-class' needed radical new definitions.[35] In the end, in Hall's summary, the nature of 'classlessness' was that a working class had 'freed itself only for new and more subtle forms of enslavement' (1958, p. 31; 1960, p. 93).

It is worth noting that the New Left also held in common that material improvement played no decisive role in changing class attitudes. This was among several other points that notably distinguished the New Left position from that of Labour revisionism. 'The working class does not become bourgeois by owning the new products', as Hall quoted Williams (1958, p. 26). Working-class struggle, Thompson asserted, 'has never been a blind, spontaneous reflex to objective economic conditions' (1959c, p. 52). Samuel wrote that it was nothing else but the failure of socialists to offer a meaningful picture of a new society that weakened socialism among workers (1958b, pp. 49–50).

Taking a surprisingly Old Left position which would stress every unchanged aspect of capitalism, Samuel, basing his argument on some social surveys, maintained that the trend was 'towards not classlessness but a strengthening of the English class system'. The Left should therefore fight for 'reconstructing socialist ideas' rather than accepting the notion of the 'manipulated mass' (1959, pp. 45, 48–50). In another article he reaffirmed that Britain was one of the most class-bound countries in the world with the reality of 'two nations' (1960, p. 55). For him the message of *The Uses of Literacy* was not classlessness, but rather a return to class perspective and politics. Thompson did not deny the actual changes in class consciousness, especially that of younger workers who accepted the new classless ideology, yet insisted on a 'way of struggle' in a society 'grounded on antagonism' (1959c, p. 52; 1960a, p. 291). His fairly traditional approach was best shown in a proposed speech rejected by the BBC, a militant statement of class struggle (1961c).

The idea of 'classlessness' is apparently related to the idea of 'common culture'. Hoggart wrote that:

> for the first time in our history, cultural intellectual matters need no longer be associated almost entirely with selected social groups. Here is a particular and fairly precise point at which one good kind of classlessness might begin to emerge, a classlessness neither that of outsiders nor that of massed consumers. (1958, pp. 136–7)

This 'good kind of classlessness' has an echo in *Culture and Society*, in the discussions of true communication, community and common culture. Reversing the Leavisite thesis of extension of the minority culture, Williams restated his idea in *ULR*, proclaiming a culture that is not merely commonly shared, but commonly made by the participation of all. In the process of this democratic participation, the defensive element of workers' solidarity would be converted into wider and more positive meaning, and the development of a genuine broadening of the values of the working class would bring about 'a common way of life' (1957b, pp. 31-2; 1961a, pp. 318-23).

A related debate over the nature of these cultural values or the tradition of class consciousness and its present crisis was waged between Hoggart and others. Using the term political in its conventional sense, Hoggart argues against the assumption that the working-class outlook is primarily social and political. For him, grass-roots working people's lives are rather personal, concrete and local, focusing on family and neighbourhood. This general character is in contrast to, but not affected by, a politically active 'earnest minority'. Traditional working-class attitudes are at most and typically cynical (1957; 1958, pp. 132-3). Here, a conscious minority seems to be isolated from or even opposed by the majority workers. Although such a view, as Williams pointed out, can hardly be differentiated from a hostile bourgeois conception (1957b, pp. 29, 32), Hoggart's critics were not able to provide a sufficient counter-argument.[36]

This minority/majority problem is to a great extent also a question of the role of intellectuals in the socialist movement; or more specifically, what the New Left could do with the 'crisis' in class consciousness. Discussions in the pages of *ULR* and *NLR* focused on the two aspects of the question: one was old and more general, the other new and more personal. Thompson talked about breaking down the 'Left anti-intellectualism' which had deep roots within all working-class movements and had been particularly strengthened by Stalinism. But he also censured a 'withdrawal' of intellectuals themselves, their retreat from socialist humanism to varieties of liberalism, which helped sever ideas from effective social energies (1957c; 1957a). However, as he believed that there was no political organisation now acting to set on its feet a principled socialist movement, he actually inclined to the view of an inevitable isolation of intellectuals from the class majority. Rodney Hilton and Mervyn Jones, among others, insisted that it was wrong for socialist intellectuals to stand aloof from the Labour Party which was not simply a slick electoral machine but still the only mass party of British working people (*ULR* 2, pp. 15-20). On the other hand, Williams and Hoggart were concerned with the relationship between community life and class consciousness, and the particular tensions lived by those intellectuals who had a working class background but took opportunities within a bourgeois framework. The most interesting part of their discussion was about the relationships with society of intellectual individuals as 'the rebel', 'the exile' and 'the vagrant' (Williams, 1957b, p. 32; 1961b, pp. 88-93), or as members of a lost 'classless intelligentsia' (Hoggart, 1957, p. 246; 1960, p. 30).[37]

The themes, with their differing viewpoints, rhetorics, and emphases, of the cultural degeneration of contemporary life that encourages working people to modify their old, narrow, but genuinely class-based culture to a false sense of 'freedom' (Hoggart, Williams); of a 'democratic control' of the mass media (Williams,[38] Thompson); of a common culture to which the working class would make a decisive contribution by creating democratic institutions (Williams); of 'reshaping' class consciousness through careful examination of 'working-class psychology' and the reformation of socialist theory in the light of social adjustments (Hall: 'in that sense, the changes in working-class life and attitudes are gains, not losses', 1960, p. 95); of a transcendence of the interests of the working class to 'the common good', or 'self-renewal' of the great traditions of labour (Thompson, 1960c, pp. 29–30; 1959a, pp. 11–12): these are all of the special New Left character in contrast to the old Left's virtual blindness to rapidly transforming realities. Looking back thirty years later, while admitting many of the criticisms of the early New Left, Hall made no apologies for the debate on 'classlessness':

> On the question of the complexities of class, of how class relates to the current conjuncture, of the problems of class formation in Britain and why it is so difficult to organise a class and popular socialist movement, the New Left's instincts were absolutely correct. (1989, p. 133)

Some of these 'instincts', of course, can be traced back to the inspirations of an earlier critical literature.[39] But what is significant is that later socialist discussions have had to return to them again and again. Historical investigations and political criticism of 'Labourism' in the mid-1960s (see III.3), and the debate evoked by Eric Hobsbawm's 'The Forward March of Labour Halted?' in the late 1970s, are two striking examples. The more recent development of this new left line of argument has been the feminist theory concerning how class identities are cross-cut by varieties of other identities. The initial New Left discussion was without a solution as in the end it was obscure what would replace the old channels by which political consciousness formed and expressed itself. It was only the beginning of a long process in which the profound transformation of classes and class relations, and especially of the serious political division of the industrial working class itself was being recognised: economic position and political attitudes, or class interests and ideological formation, do not necessarily coincide.[40] The only sense that did prevail during and after the debate was the crucial importance of cultural argument – the whole New Left began with the project of grounding socialism in a new analysis of changed and changing society. 'To understand this society', said Williams, 'we have to look at its culture, even for political answers' (1960b, p. 29).

4. LOOKING FOR A REVOLUTIONARY CHANGE

Out of Apathy

The widely felt 'moral decline of socialism' contributed much to the political apathy of the late 1950s: while Fabian social democracy reached an impasse, the

Soviet model was rejected without a workable alternative. But such a particular
climate had deeper roots in British culture, as pointed out by the New Left
critics, a culture in which even indifference and cynicism were often an active,
ironic negation (Williams, 1961b, p. xii; Thompson, 1960c, p. 29); at that time it
was a negation of celebrated successes, either those of the old empire, or of newly
achieved 'affluence'. The failure of the traditional Labour movement to adjust to
social changes and to fight in new ways only reinforced the apathetic attitude.
Thus how to approach contemporary capitalism became central in the strategic
thinking of the New Leftists who sought to build up strength out of apathy and
towards a socialist resolution.

Out of Apathy, a collection of papers based on local club discussions, was
published in 1960 as the first volume of the New Left Books series. With three
pieces contributed by Thompson, the book highlights his theme of revolution.
Joined by others on the nature of British society, Thompson's famous judgement
was that 'Britain is over-ripe for socialism'. By 'over-ripe' he meant decay after
the point of maturity. The ideology of apathy was exactly the form which this
decay took in public life (1960d, p. 10). The book's analyses of the existing
system, whether a decayed nation-state and bastard capitalism (Samuel, 1960,
pp. 23–5), or new imperialism (Worsley,[41] 1960, pp. 106, 110–11), contain two
crucial points: first, capitalism had changed and second, it retained its fundamental character. In view of both, the practicability of a socialist revolution was
under consideration, to which orthodox Labour had for years paid no serious
attention.

But further questions that have to be asked are what socialism means and how a
socialist transition is to take place. The common position of the New Left laid great
stress on 'humanised' social arrangements: 'quality of life' and 'democratic self-
activity' in opposition to the over-centralised bureaucracy and state monopoly. For
them the essence of socialism, something which is more fundamental than the forms
of ownership and distribution, is individual participation in decision-making and
collective control over the economy and social environment. The point is that there
is no automatic relationship between common ownership and socialist institutions
and socialist attitudes. Socialism is not possible without a 'moral revolution'
(Thompson, 1960a, p. 289; Alexander, 1960, pp. 264–6; Taylor, 1960b, p. 4).

As to the question of whether socialism can be achieved without material
abundance, Thompson's answer, as appeared in his introductory chapter to *Out
of Apathy*, was surprisingly idealist:

> A socialist society might be underdeveloped or overdeveloped, poor or
> affluent. The distinction between socialist and capitalist society is to be
> found, not in the level of productivity, but in the characteristic relation of
> production, in the ordering of social priorities, and in its whole way of life.
> (1960d, pp. 3–4)

The elimination of poverty is surely not a sufficient end for socialism; but the
twentieth-century experience of largely failed struggles of 'poor socialism' for
survival alone is painful enough to require a radical revision of the 'revisionist'

assumption that socialism can succeed without overcoming material scarcity.

Although an evolutionary model, based on some discussion of the limits of reform, was denounced, 'the iron dictatorship of the proletariat' or 'a cataclysmic revolution' were not acceptable for the New Left. Thompson proposed a 'democratic revolutionary strategy' in between, aiming at a reorientation of the labour movement towards the attainment of a total but peaceful socialist transformation. Specifically, it would involve the breaking up of certain institutions (for example the House of Lords), the reformation or modification of others including the House of Commons and the nationalised boards, and the transfer or regulation of some functions at the level of town councils and the rest (1960a, pp. 10, 13; 1960b, pp. 301–5). A practical opportunity for such a revolution could arise from both local/domestic and international causes; a British withdrawal from NATO and imperial retreat, for example, would have positive consequences. Once people break through the conventions, wrote Thompson optimistically, they will find that they have moved from the edge to a real revolutionary situation and Britain might be the best place of all western countries to effect it. Otherwise, 'we might easily miss "our" revolution just as we missed it in 1945' (1960a, pp. 10, 13; 1960b, pp. 301–5, 307–8).

For many readers Thompson's concept of revolution suggested a very remote contingency. Those who did appreciate the topic only did so because they wanted to get away from the stalemate of debates within the Labour Party (Taylor, 1960, p. 5). A more serious response printed in NLR focused on the question of the agency and class consciousness (cf. Saville, 1960, p. 8). Thompson replied with 'Revolution again!', devoting himself to a concrete analysis of the transformation of consciousness.

In an open letter to the British New Left, C. Wright Mills suggested that 'the cultural apparatus, the intellectuals', instead of the working class, were 'a possible, immediate, radical agency of change' in the advanced capitalist world. In the face of historical evidence, he wrote, one could not assume anything more 'unrealistic' than a revolutionary working class consciousness within an affluent society (1960, p. 22). Unlike some other Marxists such as Miliband, who thought Mills was 'mistaken' to lose his confidence in organised labour and to only speak to 'conscious' intellectuals (1962; 1964b), Thompson was quite willing to take a fresh look at the problem. But, from a different angle, he found an echo of 'economic reductionism' in Mills, namely, some significant values beyond economic and status conditions, wherein such components of 'the common good' as peace and democracy, were denied the category of class interests. He therefore asked to 'conceive of new forms of class consciousness' which arose 'both more consonant with changed reality and more revolutionary in implication' (1960c, pp. 23–4, 27–8). He challenged a static concept originating, in his view, from Engels who regarded the working class as an unchanging entity with a fixed characteristic consciousness which emerged and grew as a social force based on the factory system. He read the history differently and was to develop his argument soon in The Making of the English Working Class (see III.2).

For Thompson it was dangerous to divide workers into an old industrial working class which held traditional class appeal and a new working population which was uninterested in or hostile to the current labour movement and scarcely conscious of its own class identity. The consciousness or 'false consciousness' of the latter seemed not to bother Thompson much. He talked about the possibility of binding together old and new into a majority movement with a new class consciousness which was 'broader and more generous than that which was dominant in the 1930s; less "class-bound" in the old sense, speaking more in the name of the whole people' (1960c, pp. 27–8). And, reclaiming the Leninist thesis of anti-spontaneity, it was the constant business of socialists to 'fix' this consciousness.[42] Here he would agree with Mills in emphasising the crucial role that socialist intellectuals must play.

Discussions of class consciousness grounded the new idea advanced in 'Revolution' of drawing the line 'between the monopolists and the people', an idea that reflected the New Left's deep commitment that socialism would be 'impossible without the participation of the whole people at every level' (Thompson, 1960b, p. 305; 1960c, p. 29). Or as the slogan put forward by the first *ULR* went: 'Socialism at its widest stretch'. To define 'class alignment' like this, intending the broadest possible socialist alliance, became one of the foundations of what later was known as 'the Euro-Communist strategy'. Accordingly, revolution was understood as a movement that must arise from below by popular activity and not merely a 'structural change' or 'seizing power' by a small vanguard, which implied a socialism as something for or to but not done by the ordinary people. Thompson's concept of revolution is therefore not of a moment of transition, nor need it be one of cataclysmic crisis and violence: 'It is a concept of historical process', whereby democratic pressures can no longer be contained within the capitalist system; this leads on to a chain of interrelated crises which result in profound changes in class and social relationships and in institutions. The breaking point can be found only in practice, where socialist potentiality is liberated, the public sector assumes the dominant role, and the priorities of need overrule those of profit in social life. Thus, only in the widest 'epochal sense' can this transformation be seen as a transfer of class power (1960b, p. 303; 1960c, p. 30).

One can hardly find in Thompson's scheme the actual role of either the state apparatus or class struggle. He did not even mention the major centres of power (finance, the army, police, etc.). In the same article he admitted that 'I and other New Left writers have failed to discuss sufficiently the "theory of the State"' (1960c, p. 30).[43] The problem for him was not about beginning to 'smash' the old state machinery, but about how far pressures for a democratic change were compatible with the preservation of the bourgeois state. He had the confidence that:

> it is possible to look forward to a peaceful revolution in Britain, ... not because it will be a semi-revolution, nor because capitalism is 'evolving' into socialism; but because the advances of 1942–48 were real, because the

socialist potential has been enlarged, and socialist forms, however imperfect, have grown up 'within' capitalism. (1960c, p. 302)

The Leninist conception that socialism cannot settle within capitalism, and thus
a socialist transformation only begins with the seizure of political power, no
longer possessed any authority over the New Left thinking which in many ways
obscured the traditional demarcation between revolution and reformism.

Returning several times to the theme of revolution, Thompson distanced
himself more and more from the classical Marxist proposition except in his
critique of Williams's *The Long Revolution* (see the next section).

'Revolution' in the early New Left's discussion was confined to the specific
British conditions and was basically a cultural category without implications of
political cataclysm, even though the belief in a qualitative 'breakthrough' was
retained. Rediscovering that culture came to carry political weight, what it
actually could not carry was nevertheless much neglected. As a result, the
revolution discourse was somehow one-sided or empty of content and had little
impact on immediate politics.

The 'Long Revolution'

The 'long revolution' originally (in *Culture and Society*) meant continuing
changes in British society as well as the world which were brought about by the
forces of industry and democracy. Moving from discussing the English cultural
tradition to reinterpreting and extending certain ideas and values of that tradition
based on pioneering historical studies of an 'expanding culture', Williams took
the phrase as the title of the second part of his project, which was published in
1961. *The Long Revolution* received intense attack from the right, as an alert
recognition of its power and quality as a serious socialist work. Williams's central
theme was the hidden significance of a long term struggle against all forms of
alienation or denial of human needs, and the general effect of this process on
social thinking and feeling. A 'long revolution' unaccompanied by any claim for
political power and necessary means to defeat resistance is obviously gradualist
with a quite utopian perspective, and this is why it was, again, fiercely criticised
by the Marxist critics of the New Left. However, the book provided a fresh
analysis which made an original and important contribution to twentieth-century
socialist thought and debate.

In Williams's definition, the 'long revolution' indicates that democratic,
industrial and cultural revolutions constitute an integral historical process. This
process involves real and substantial changes in the four interrelated systems:
'decision', 'communication and learning', 'maintenance' (production), 'generation
and nurture' (family) (1961b, pp. 36, 347, 354). It is a pity that his discussion
actually ignored this last system, as the 'absolute centrality' of it (1979, p. 147)
was then not yet acknowledged. Concerning the nature of this process, great
emphasis was laid on the common experience of cultural expansion, which
transformed, in the direction of democracy, social change itself. As a general
assessment, Williams saw the progress of the long revolution in Britain as 'at a

relatively advanced stage' yet also 'a very critical phase'; but in a global perspective, it was, in all the three aspects, 'at a very early stage'. 'It is a genuine revolution', wrote Williams, 'transforming men and institutions; continually extended and deepened by the actions of millions, continually and variously opposed by explicit reaction and by the pressure of habitual forms and ideas' (pp. x–xiii, 120–2, 354ff).

Criticism of the book from the Left concentrated on two aspects: cultural theory and political strategy. Williams provided a great deal of factual revision of received cultural history together with detailed discussions of the current situation. He also developed his theory of culture by distinguishing three categories or levels in a general definition: lived culture, recorded culture, and socially defined culture as the selective tradition. Links among the three exist where culture as creative activity and as a whole way of life can be reconciled (pp. 41–53). These variations of meaning and reference were seen by him as a genuine complexity, corresponding to real elements in 'experience' and 'structure of feeling'.

'Structure of feeling' is an essential concept for Williams with which to explore the mode of relations between literature and society, or the comparison between articulated and lived culture, and the whole pattern, the true presence of impulses, restraints, tones and styles that is deeply and widely possessed, of a given society (pp. 43, 46–9, 64–8, 293). The best part of *The Long Revolution*, Williams felt when he reread it years later, was the theoretical analysis of the structure of feeling of the time which grasped the particular 'dissent' as a largely negative reaction without much promise of reconstruction (1979, p. 163). This concept had been consistently emphasised in Williams's later work, from *The Country and the City* (1971) to *Marxism and Literature* (1977).[44]

In his critical review which appeared in NLR just two months after the publication of *The Long Revolution*, Thompson rejects Williams's definition of culture simply because it is by and large identical with society. 'Any theory of culture must include the concept of the dialectical interaction between culture and something that is not culture' (1961a, pp. 32–3). For Williams, 'culture' implies a total human order and does so more conveniently than the notion of 'society'. To define working class culture as the institutions of the labour movement rather than a few proletarian novels, for instance, is a gain in talking about culture as a whole way of life (1979, pp. 154–5). If this is more a matter of personal preference, the main argument was over the phrase 'way of life'. Thompson insists on what he believes to be a formula in line with Marx: a 'way of struggle' (1961a, p. 33; 1961b, p. 34). Although Williams's phrase does not necessarily exclude struggle – in fact he writes on 'the changes and conflicts of the whole way of life' (1961b, p. 122) – where the divergent emphases of the two writers lie can certainly be pinpointed.

The crucial point here is whether a further long episode of expansion or growth is possible: without revolutionary foresight, in Thompson's opinion, Williams had not yet achieved an adequate general theory of culture (1961a, p. 28). To identify the whole historical process with struggle, however, contains the danger of falling into, say, social Darwinism or political adventurism and, as

Williams argued, prevents one from a comprehensive understanding of social relationships and cultural process. It is necessary to distinguish certain periods and situations in which struggle is intense and 'determinant' from other periods and situations, in which there is not only relatively smooth progress (or regress) or a stability without serious conflicts, but also 'incorporation'. The unheroic 1950s is an example in which many institutions in Britain had been neutralised and incorporated (Williams, 1968a, pp. 298-9; 1979, pp. 135-6).

As to the question of political strategy, there were two approaches, neither held decisively, within the early New Left: Williams's work on the one hand, and consciously Marxist writings on the other. Thompson wished the New Left to make a synthesis of the two, hence a political and intellectual coherence through a dialogue 'about power, communication, class, and ideology' (1961b, pp. 37-9). It was a time when many of these people, by different paths, came to the point of realising the outdated mechanical and rhetorical opposition between reform and revolution, and sought to bypass it by reformulating a strategic thinking for socialism. The idea of a long revolution, seemingly contradictory in terms, might serve such a purpose.

Williams himself, who later admitted his reformism and indeed made a break from it, considered in *The Long Revolution* that the goal of the revolution could only be achieved gradually, and this 'slow reach for control' was a long process under the capitalist system. Since active radical politics in Britain had never been revolutionary, he believed in the effect of steady reforms rather than revolution-ary rupture. Particularly, the case of the historical expansion and integration of culture was more convincing for him than that of a socialist culture which would be established immediately after economic and political change. The cultural revolution was therefore in fact seen as the dominant front of the long revolution, proceeding by breaking through the pressures and restrictions of the old society, and by discovering, defending and developing new common institutions. The growth of 'a common general education', for example, was itself revolutionary, since it had increasingly 'placed the quality of the whole national culture in the hands of the people as a whole' (1961b, pp. 347, 150).

At a deeper level, Williams elaborated his thesis later in his conversations with NLR interviewers, making the cultural revolution explicitly a fundamental one: what capitalism produces in commodity form excludes certain crucial kinds of production which are permanent human needs, such as health, habitation, family, education and leisure. These exclusions and the accompanying social processes of repression and discrimination have involved profound contradictions - more difficult for capitalism to solve than those which are generated within the market.

> This is not to diminish its economic contradictions in the traditional sense, which I think it will never resolve. But the cultural revolution finds its source in the perennial resistance to the suppression of so many basic and necessary forms of production by capitalism. The cultural revolution is then against the whole version of culture and society which the capitalist mode of production has imposed. (1979, pp. 150-1)

This is a very powerful proposition. However, the problem remains of how to achieve it. There is surely an overestimate of the possibilities of cultural change – given the reality that the left lacks the basic means of cultural struggle within the concrete power structure of a capitalist society. Thompson fairly questioned (as if he too was questioning an earlier self): can this 'revolution' go on – and for how long – 'without either giving way to counter-revolution or coming to a point of crisis between the human system of socialism and capitalist state power?' If old forms and institutions would be broken and remade, can revolution and growth remain compatible terms? The revival of the key importance of state power in Thompson found an expression in his assertion that 'the tactics of reform must be developed within a revolutionary strategy' (1961b, p. 39; 1961a, p. 13).

Observing Labour's impasse of the 1960s, Williams finally departed from his gradualist position in *The Long Revolution*. It was a remarkable personal achievement especially because most of his left wing contemporaries were moving precisely in the opposite direction. In his self-criticism, two points were made: one, it was wrong to 'assume that a cultural and educational programme alone could revitalise the left or alter areas of popular opinion sufficiently to change the traditional institutions of the labour movement' (1979, p. 364); two, it was 'stupid and in the end vicious' to talk about the inevitability of gradualism for, he now realised, social transformation had an active enemy. Not that he ever envisaged a revolution without opposition and struggle, but that there was in his analysis a 'radical underestimate of the political power of the capitalist state' (*ibid.*; 1975, pp. 69–71).

On the other hand, however, Williams's splendid discussions of the crisis in social consciousness, of the relations between society and the individual, of the true nature of democracy as not merely a political system (in a participating democracy; see 1961b, pp. 305–16), of the myth of the class foundation of political parties (pp. 311–35; 1960a, p. 28), of varied thoughts and social forces resisting the revolution, are all the more stimulating and concrete in revealing deeper or hidden aspects of a revolutionary process rather than a simplified or abstract class analysis. Thompson admitted that Williams had 'a more constructive insight into the possibilities of socialism in this country than anyone living' (1961b, p. 34). Williams identifies, besides the opposition of vested interests, a version of ordinary people, whom the version misrepresents and insults, that is nevertheless accepted by a large number of those very people who unconsciously reproduce the existing order by accepting offers of any inferior job and thinking and feeling in old ways. This is the end of any hope for change (1961b, pp. 348–52). As a matter of consciousness, Williams's revolution is a huge process of transforming both society and people as individuals as well as social beings, and therefore must be a long and very profound process. Despite the fact, as Marxist critics commonly noted, that *The Long Revolution* failed to be a strategic intervention because its arguments were unclear about the enemy, its author certainly took 'revolution' seriously, meaning not just to 'modernise' an ancient society, but to transform capitalism.

In the end, the thesis of a broad cultural revolution held firm and became a general New Left conviction in the decades following the publication of Williams's book. Absorbing the Gramscian notion of hegemony, he was to restate his innovation and commitment in a more balanced manner:

I know that there is a profoundly necessary job to do in relation to the processes of the cultural hegemony itself. I believe that the system of meanings and values which a capitalist society has generated has to be defeated in general and in detail by the most sustained kinds of intellectual and educational work. This is a cultural process which I called 'the long revolution' and in calling it 'the long revolution' I meant that it was a genuine struggle which was part of the necessary battles of democracy and of economic victory for the organised working class. (1975, p. 76)

'Positive Neutralism' and the Third World

Not quite a component of the long revolution, which was conceived by and large within the national context, at the global level the immediate political focus of the New Left was nuclear disarmament and then on the non-aligned movement. Inspired by the national liberation movements in the Third World, the New Left advocated a foreign policy of 'positive neutralism' in opposition to Labour's 'Atlanticist world-view' and pro-USA/NATO convention that had contributed a great deal to the post-war military and political establishment. Actively engaged in CND, the only mass protest movement with a compatible base, and through this engagement pressuring the Labour Party, the New Left filled the 'ideological vacuum' of the Campaign (Anderson, 1965a, p. 16) and successfully won the vote for unilateralism at the Labour Scarborough Conference in 1960.

'Positive neutralism' was initially formulated by the Reasoners in relation to their moral position of 'socialist humanism' and 'socialist pacifism'. For them, the future of the socialist movement still depended on the Cold War. Under the shadow of bloc confrontation and superpower hegemony, the first task for any New Left must be to propagate and support active neutrality (Thompson, 1958a, pp. 49–50; 1959a). Peter Worsley, among the first of the New Left to pursue a systematic analysis of the 'third world' (see IV.3), saw the emergent peoples as vital new forces challenging imperialism and the international deadlock. In this context, he believed that Britain could generate immense pressure, in alliance with countries like India, Ghana and Yugoslavia, and backed by the uncommitted nations, for world peace and prosperity. In building non-exploitative relations between the developed and underdeveloped countries, most uncommitted nations 'could, under such stimulus, move towards socialism' (1960, p. 136; 1961, pp. 18–25). Similarly, Thompson expected a possible British initiative in creating something like a 'Bandung' group in Europe, of which the implications could be far more explosive: they might lead to a socialist revolution (1958a, pp. 50–1; 1959a, p. 8; 1960a).

Concerning the economic content of the concept of positive neutralism, Barratt Brown emphasised the link between disarmament and development:

without economic co-operation through planned and equal international trade, there would be no solution to the arms race (1958, pp. 54–5; 1963b, pp. 465–8). The New Left proposed, addressing both the Labour leadership and the United Nations, to introduce planned trade with newly independent countries through a 'fundamentally neutralist bloc' of free trade associations.

The central commitment sustaining all these over-optimistic views and proposals was the principle of self-determination: positive neutralism would entail real chances for national self-rule in the former colonies and for a common effort by non-aligned peoples in dismantling the old world order which continuously produced bombs on the one hand and poverty on the other.

Talking about the 'third way' of positive neutralism and democratic and humanist socialism, the New Left radically underestimated the grave obstacles to their alternative way. They had been unable to convert either CND or non-aligned groups into socialist movements. After the 1961 Blackpool Conference, at which Gaitskell defeated the unilateralist policy, the first wave of CND declined, due to internal difficulties as well as external pressures. The unexpected events including the Sino-Indian border conflict (1962), the Cuban missile crisis (1962), a succession of reverses for the radical 'neutralist' forces and the collapse of the populist and nationalist regimes in the Third World: all these undermined the viability of positive neutralism and proved that the hope of the New Left for a socialist outcome was unfounded.[45]

NOTES

1. According to Williams, post-war developed capitalism showed that it could for a long time avoid depression by a series of adaptions, even if those adaptions in turn produced other kinds of crises (1979, p. 150). In a more general Gramscian perspective (Gramsci was not yet available to English readers), the cultural front is extremely important in advanced capitalist societies where the ruling class rules less by force than by 'consensus'.

2. Raymond Williams's small but important book, *Communications* (1962), will be discussed in IV.4.

3. The Free Cinema movement was led by Lindsay Anderson at the National Film Theatre and the New Drama by Arnold Wesker. There were also new developments in music, documentary photography, design and typography. See Bicat, 1970, pp. 321–38, for the characteristic changes of folk music and popular songs. Jazz in Britain was partly pioneered by the communists. See *NLR* 10, pp. 41–50; *The New University*, nos.2 and 5; and Francis Newton (i.e., Eric Hobsbawm), 1959; Coe, 1982.

4. Perry Anderson, born in 1940, educated at Eton and then Oxford. He helped Hall in the editorial work of *NLR* and eventually replaced him as the editor. He retained the post for 20 years until Robin Blackburn succeeded him in 1983. Anderson left Oxford in 1962, since then he had never 'found it necessary to compromise with the institutions of capitalist England' (in Scruton's words) by finding a job in them. A commonly acknowledged brilliant theorist, he was a leading representative of the 'second New Left' (see section III.1).

5. This movement was able to provide a predominantly socialist and Marxist education to working people. For example, the Plebs League preferred a Marxist alternative to conventional economics, philosophy and history in its educational programme offered to a generation of working-class LP activists. For the origins and development of workers' education, see Harrison, 1961, pp. 261–99; Kelly, 1970, chapters 15, 20 and 21; Rowbotham, 1981; Ree, 1984, pp. 15–22, chapter 2, 3, 4;

Williams, 1979, pp. 78–82; McLennan, Schwarz and Sutton, 1982, pp. 39–40. For the distinction between the old 'Labour' tradition of the movement and its new development and new concepts, see Samuel and Stedman Jones, 1982, pp. 328ff.

6. Some others, like Royden Harrison (Sheffield), Barratt Brown (Northern College), John Hughes and Raphael Samuel (Ruskin College) and later Stuart Hall (Open University), remained faithful to their engagement in (workers') adult education.

7. See Thompson: 'the dialogue of the early New Left was a fruitful one, from which both traditions gained' (in Samuel, 1981a, pp. 398–9).

8. Thompson held that romanticism was 'capable of undergoing this transformation independently of the precipitate of Marx and Engels's writing' (1976c, p. 779). For a convincing criticism of this point from Perry Anderson, see 1980, pp. 168–9.

9. Later in 1956, he came back to this central theme, saying that moral characters of the protest tradition had been always seen by Marxists as a source of weakness. 'Rightly so. ... But if we do not also see it as a source of strength, then we are damming up sources of energy of ourselves, we are cutting ourselves off from our people' (1956b).

10. This character most remarkably expressed in Morris's writings on the labour theory of value, class struggle, and the state; and, in Thompson's own manner of presentation, the 'dictatorship of the proletariat'. Morris is also revealed to be the first creative artist of major stature in world history to take his stand with the working class and participate in the day-to-day struggle for the socialist movement. He is seen as an outstanding member of the first generation of European communist intellectuals, and his contribution to the Marxist tradition, as significant as those of Plekhanov or Labriola (1955, pp. 841, 794; 1976c, p. 818).

11. By 'communism', Thompson means especially those values which Morris attributed to a future society.

12. To the classical dilemma – does the end justify the means? The best solution might be to reject the dichotomy itself between the two. As Taylor put it, the means are in a real sense part of the end (1957, p. 95). Thompson also believed that a moral end could only be obtained by moral means (1957c, pp. 125–6; cf. 1956b). Taylor's attitude toward Marxism had come to a very hostile one in his later writings. See IV.2 below.

13. Richard Hoggart, born in 1918, was a cultural critic and educationist. He wrote for *ULR* and was greatly influential in the area of cultural studies. He founded the Centre for Contemporary Cultural Studies at Birmingham in 1964 when he was Professor of Modern English Literature. He acted as its director until 1968 and was succeeded by Stuart Hall. Later, he was Assistant Director-General at UNESCO.

14. By a plural 'working classes', Hoggart meant to emphasise 'the great number of differences, the subtle shades, the class distinctions, within the working classes themselves'(1957, p. 21).

15. 'Popular art' was employed by Hoggart differently from 'popular culture' as a Morrisian positive term. 'Good art, whether highbrow or popular, embodies its moral sense in specific details'(1958, p. 129).

16. To be sure, Q. D. Leavis also saw the cinema as a 'disruptive' force that threatened to extinguish traditional working-class culture.

17. As pop art rose in the 1960s, 'mass culture' became a term of praise among some left-wing critics. The term was long available in the modern revolutionary traditions from Russia to China, where it was defined as being opposed not to 'high culture' or class culture, but to elitist/aristocratic culture; and derived from an entirely different, and positive, concept of 'the mass'. In its western usage, the moment of the formation of a 'mass culture' has been a subject of debate. See, for example, Hoggart (1957; most cultural changes came just after the First World War), Williams (1961b; popular press began with the Sunday papers of the early nineteenth century), and Thompson (1963a; important changes took place well before 1780).

18. Williams regarded mass culture with its destructive elements as a disinheritance from the 'great tradition' and believed in the need of establishing the sense of 'community' as an aim of the working-class movement, which had some images in past societies (cf. III.4).

19. See Gwyn Lewis's critique of the 'geographical limits' of *The Uses of Literacy* based on his own Welsh experience (1957, pp. 34, 39–40).

20. See Williams: this important tradition was the one in which writers like Cobbett, Ruskin, Morris and D. H. Lawrence asserted their ideas and feelings of humanist protest against industrial capitalism. (1965, p. 23).

21. See Hall's criticism of *Culture and Society*: 'since Williams's method underpinned the idiom it was analysing, the book itself offered no rallying point outside this empirico-moral discourse from which its limitations (as well as its strengths) might have been identified' (1989b, p. 59).

22. A passage in Williams's later piece (1965) on the British left can be seen as a fine annotation on this tradition: '...there has been an important tradition of ideas and feelings which is not Puritan, and which in my view lies just as deeply in the moral consciousness. ...what is asserted in this tradition is the claim to life, against the distortion of humanity by the priorities and disciplines of industrial capital-ism'(1965, p. 23).

23. It is interesting to compare Williams's more critical treatment of Morris (1958, pp. 153–4, 161) with Thompson's. See, for example, disagreement between them over 'News from Nowhere' and 'The Dream of John Ball' (Williams, 1958, p. 159; Thompson, 1976c, p. 794). However, they both highly appreciate Morris's 'transformation' (Thompson) or 'extension' (Williams) of the romantic tradition.

24. For his redefinition of this concept, see 1976a, pp. 76–82.

25. For Williams, until the Industrial Revolution, the word 'culture' served to indicate a process of training. At the beginning of the nineteenth century, this idea of a process was extended to, and became dominated by, the idea of culture as a product: an achieved state or habit. By the second half of the century, 'culture' came to mean 'a whole way of life'. These major senses have all survived into our own period (1957b, p. 29).

26. Williams sees the process of communication as in fact the process of community, and therefore any real theory of communication is a theory of community (1961a, pp. 301–6). For the problem of definition of community in *Culture and Society*, see his reconsideration in 1979, pp. 118–9.

27. Williams's examples are Christopher Caudwell's description of modern poetry as 'capitalist poetry', and in the same way the judgement of twentieth-century western literature as 'decadent' because its social base is judged so. For a rethinking of Caudwell, see 1979, pp. 127–8.

28. Later in 1963, he actually situated culture in the dialectic between being and consciousness in his study of the English working class (see III.2).

29. One can find in *Morris* even a critical remark on Morris's fault of seeing 'man's economic and social development always as the master-process' upon which the arts are passively dependent (1955, pp. 763, 770). Surely 'passively' is wrong. But isn't this 'master-process' Marx's own assertion?

30. See R. Wollheim's challenge to the concept of 'common culture' for its vagueness (What is the meaning of 'common'?) and danger (How to avoid introducing a common culture forcefully?). He himself preferred a concept of 'pluralist culture' (1961).

31. Concluding his conversations with the *NLR* interviewers in 1978, Williams said that 'I have been pulled all my life ... between simplicity and complexity, and I can still feel the pull both ways. But every argument of experience and of history now makes my decision ... clear. It is only in very complex ways, and by moving confidently towards very complex societies, that we can defeat imperialism and capitalism and begin that construction of many socialisms which will liberate and draw upon our real and now threatened energies' (1979, p. 437).

32. He wrote in 1965 to admit that 'The New Left is a group of writers and political thinkers, essentially based on the tradition of the moral critique of industrial capitalism which has been so important in the British working-class movement' (1965, p. 26).

33. There were about 150,000 adults taking part in study organised by voluntary bodies and university extra-mural departments; WEA had about 90,000 students at the

time when *The Uses of Literacy* was being written. For workers' education, see Barratt Brown, 1969.

34. A. Lovell offered a personal example in *ULR* based on his grammar school and Oxford experience: 'My education has made it very difficult for me to go back to the class from which I come ... because many of the things that interest me and some of my values find no place in working-class life'. This is, he considers, not a matter of economic privilege, but attitude (1957, p. 34).

35. See a joint analysis by Hoggart and Williams in 1960 when they first met in *NLR* (*NLR* 1, pp. 26–30); Hall, 1958, p. 31; Birnbaum, 1960, p. x.

36. See Taylor's discussion in *ULR* 2, pp. 18–19. Later, Hoggart changed much of his opinion; see 1960, p. 28.

37. See Lesley Johnson's comment that through the notion of common culture Williams seeks to resolve the tension between his two fundamental commitments based on his personal background of both Welsh country and Trinity College: a commitment to the working class and its tradition; and a commitment to high culture and the value of education (1979, p. 160). Later, in 1967, when a group of the early New Leftists gathered to produce the *May Day Manifesto* (see III.3) at Jesus College, Cambridge, Williams 'was the only person who did not find it any way odd' (Hall, 1988, p. 21).

38. For Williams, it is especially important to develop a 'really adequate educational system, which will make people more free to use these media critically' and to work for 'clearing the channels' (1957b, p. 30; cf. 1961b, pp. 125ff).

39. F. R. Leavis, for example, had argued much earlier about the results of machine-made goods: the 'standardisation of commodities' led to the 'standardisation of persons' (*Culture and Environment*); there were no longer class divisions of the kind that could produce class cultures ('Under which King, Bezonian?'). See F. Mulhern, 1979, pp. 48–9, 65.

40. Based on some voting statistics of the period between 1924 and 1955, Williams observed that 'there's no kind of automatic correspondence between being working-class, objectively, feeling working-class, and voting for a working-class party' (1960a, p. 28).

41. Peter Worsley was born in 1924, served in the war in East Africa and India, studied anthropology at Cambridge University, Manchester University and the Australian National University, lectured sociology at Hull since 1957, Professor of Sociology at Manchester since 1964, President of the British Sociological Association between 1971 and 1974. He joined the CPGB in 1943, and left it in 1956. He has been a member of the *NR* and *NLR* editorial committee, and a long-standing activist of CND.

42. 'Since – if we do not do it – the capitalist media will "fix" it for us' (1961c, p. 28).

43. Miliband was to develop an important body of work in the 1970s on the theory of the state. See IV.3.

44. Williams, 1971; 1979, pp. 156–74.

45. Barratt Brown admitted this in the second edition of his *After Imperialism* (1969, p. xviii).

CHAPTER III

Society and Politics, 1963–69

I. DISCONTINUITY AND CONTINUITY OF THE NEW LEFT

The 'red decade' of the 1960s was marked by the international Vietnam Solidarity Campaign, the continuing third world liberation movements, Czechoslovakian protests against Russian tanks, the Chinese cultural revolution, and massive campus/factory occupations in the west. When Isaac Deutscher, who died in 1967 just before the high tide of the global New Left movement, used 'red' to term that decade, what he referred to in particular were the possible political changes in the USSR and the Soviet Bloc. He believed that the bureaucratic system there could be reformed 'from above' by a new generation of communist leaders. Neither he, nor any others, however, had foreseen the revolutionary sentiments and rebellions which not only shook certain parts of the east (Warsaw, Prague, Belgrade, the whole country of People's China), but also swept across the entire advanced capitalist world.

Against this background, the New Left movement in Britain transformed itself from a small but populist tendency into a wider political intervention with more vigorous theoretical engagement. This transformation, however, was by no means identical with the transition from what came to be known as the 'first' to the 'second' New Left. While the transition was made in the editorial policies of NLR, it was not the case that the earlier participants had abandoned the cause of the New Left, nor was it true that the newcomers distorted, if not destroyed, that original cause. Rather, the two generations joined forces in the later stages of the movement, despite their differences and bitter arguments over some theoretical as well as practical issues. The result of these arguments turned out to be generally constructive from the viewpoint of the larger enterprise of British socialism.

If the initial New Left was intellectually notable for its outstanding cultural analyses basically within the native radical traditions, the succeeding New Left concern, more informed about European political thought, extended to a thorough examination of each dimension of contemporary British capitalism, their particular origins in history, and a socialist strategy to confront them. This is not to suggest that culture became less important in the New Left arguments, certainly not for the old New Leftists. Even the second generation who, with their distinct characteristics, came from the same tradition of Oxbridge radicalism which produced *ULR*, were also preoccupied with cultural questions and the politics of intellectual practice. However, what should be emphasised here are

(1) despite a common focus on culture, their emphasis on priorities had been quite different;

(2) by the time of the reorganisation of *NLR*, it was already clear that the first New Left had failed as a political movement;

(3) there afterwards developed a remarkable body of theoretical analyses to which both generations contributed, and therefore the second stage of the New Left movement involved not only the 'second' but also the 'first' New Left.

The *NLR* crisis of 1961–2 marked this transition. From the very beginning the *Review* had suffered a considerable uncertainty of purpose and direction, generating endless arguments within the editorial committee over whether it was running a political movement or a journal. Increase of tensions between the senior and junior groups was a sign of coherence lacking in *NLR* which tried to balance different tendencies within itself. Pressures on the overworked Stuart Hall were enormous, including criticism of his *ULR* style.[1] A 'reconstruction' of *NLR* was under way by the end of 1961, when personal exhaustion mounted among the editors and some of them had already prepared their departure. The state of the *Review* at the time was best indicated by a question raised by its readers and supporters: 'What is wrong with the New Left?' (*NLR* 12) In December 1961, *NLR* announced the loss of Hall, Taylor and Don Arnott, and the formation of a new editorial team.[2] This transitional team was soon dissolved and twenty-two-year-old Perry Anderson took over the editorship in May 1962. He quickly built up a board of young colleagues who were in touch with New Left politics through Left clubs and the *New University* edited from Oxford,[3] setting up a restyled and reoriented *NLR*.[4]

Previous issues produced under the old board had mainly discussed Labour politics, with special interest in cultural and industrial questions, as well as imperialism and colonialism with particular reference to Anglo-European relations and nuclear disarmament. Renouncing the partiality of emphases and the former New Left's 'almost complete failure to offer any structural analysis of British society' (Anderson, 1965a, p. 17), the new *Review*'s ambition was to reform and regenerate the intellectual landscape and political culture of Britain.

It was said that *NLR* passed out of the hands of the libertarian and humanist editors into the control of a group who were committed to theoretical elitism and vanguard politics; and consequently, it developed a left-sectarianism in a mandarin journal of abstract or super-Marxism which had little influence outside an academic circle (Rustin, 1981, pp. 67–9; Widgery, 1976, pp. 512–13; Palmer, 1981, pp. 131, 59–63). The gradually widening division between the two New Lefts became even sharper in the Thompson–Anderson/Nairn[5] polemical exchange (see the next section). Later in 1973, Thompson summarised his criticism of the new New Left: its exclusion of the *NLR* founders without examining their thought, and denial of the existence of a Marxist tradition before 1963; its ignorance of communist revisionism and dissent which characterised the NR tradition; its 'narrowing of intellectual referents' and reassertion of Marxism as dogma, and hence its inability to eliminate Stalinism; and its preference for a 'heuristic and structural organisation of concepts' over 'substantive analysis' (1973, p. 315).[6]

From the viewpoint of the other side, however, the old New Left, as critics of their society, never moved beyond attacking that society on its own terms and thus marked no more than a renaissance of traditional social criticism (Anderson, 1965a, p. 17). This renaissance, in Anderson's opinion, was in itself a major achievement, but lacked any programmatic edge: 'its concepts cannot be cashed in the arena of practical politics'. Thompson's writings of 1958–61, for example, constituted the weakest part of his work, which was 'a reflection of un-negotiated strains and difficulties in the New Left of the time' (1980, pp. 157–8). The difference between the two New Lefts was more than a matter of political style. It was also intellectual. Besides the contrasted emphasis on morality or culture on the one hand and strategy or power on the other,[7] their theoretical approaches were also radically different. With the passage of time, these gaps became clearer as they came to subsume the remaining differences between the two original traditions of ULR on the one hand and NR on the other.

Critics of the post-1962 NLR highlight its fatal weakness of separation between theory and practice, or between theoretical practice and practical politics. Its abandonment of the Review's movement policy and devotion to pure theorising can hardly be excused as a necessary reaction to the traditional British working-class contempt for theory, or as a natural response to a deeply conservative strain of class consciousness. The new NLR's lack of serious contact with the life experience of ordinary people and thin relationship with the actual labour movement cast doubt upon the quality of its work, and contrasted unfavourably with its predecessors who sought to make their ideas available to and effective in the popular protest movements.[8]

In return, culturalism, in relation to the gradualist, empiricist and populist labour traditions, was made the object of the new New Left attack on the older generation. The term was used (though not by such key critics as Anderson) to identify a specific idealist tendency in analysing cultural problems inherited from the tradition of English literary and social criticism. To a great extent this attack, despite its many overemphases, was justified and actually accepted later in one way or another by some who were then under fire (the reaction of Williams or of Hall). Williams and Thompson, for all their differences, were representatives of that 'culturalist tendency'. Both owed a great deal to the native traditions of critical thought. Their humanistic perspective was no doubt rooted in the political situation of the time, but intellectually speaking, inspired more by Wordsworth or Morris than by Marx. Their line of argument for socialism was often pursued without confronting the real antagonisms between the ruling power and its material foundations on the one hand, and funding the working-class movement culturally on the other. A successful Labour policy was believed to be able to keep and extend the channels of popular education and publicly controlled communication. They both, moreover, were quite confined to an empiricist approach which can be seen, in a way, in the almost deliberate avoidance of constructive theorisation in their earlier works. Not that the term 'experience' was given an extraordinary conceptual importance which it certainly deserves, but that in seeing it as an 'objective form' (in reversing the subjectivist Leavisite usage) and source of 'structure of feeling' (Williams, 1961b), or a necessary middle term between social being and social consciousness (Thompson, 1963a), they seemed to be not fully aware, then, of the epistemic limits of primary experience, and thus of the power of ideology.[9]

Much attention had been paid to a common ground of the early New Left (the *ULR* group in particular) and the traditionalist *Scrutiny*, a journal founded in 1932 and representing the major radical tradition of social criticism in England.[10] There was in the New Left discussion of cultural changes, mass media and classlessness a clear echo of *Scrutiny*'s central themes – the destructive effects of industrialism and commerce, and Leavisite critique of vulgar Marxism. Williams acknowledged that he was greatly indebted to F. R. Leavis in respect of the humane values that Leavis emphasised, the cultural insights that he communicated and the critical approach that he employed (1958b, pp. 245, 247).[11] But at least on one basic point the first New Left stood remarkably opposed to *Scrutiny*: they compared the concept of common culture with *Scrutiny*'s minority culture, and looked at the contrary idea of 'cultural expansion' as an enlargement of working-class culture and as a rescue of the degraded mass by the enlightened elites.[12] It is precisely here the second New Left turned out to be not very different from the *Scrutiny* group whose ideology Eagleton consigned to the side of the petty bourgeoisie. Thompson was right to point out the danger of intellectual elitism (represented by some 'new revolutionary' *NLR* critics) that severed theorisation from larger non-intellectual audiences and from living experience and values of working people (1976a, p. 111).

From these sometimes extremely bitter exchanges, a whole range of socialist cultural analyses, being for the first time thoroughly informed by continental intellectual trends and consistently tested in view of its own militant social function, had developed in Britain after the mid-1960s. What ought to be emphasised here is that a substantial Marxist cultural theory in the Anglo-Saxon world, where an empiricist and idealist dualism in methodology of liberal philosophy had never been seriously challenged before, was an achievement that owed its development not only to the younger theorists, but also to the older 'culturalists' who continuously searched for new ideas and played an active role in the cultural debates. One can easily cite a list of names of outstanding contributors; but above all, of course, Williams 'almost single-handedly' transformed the landscape of cultural studies in Britain (Eagleton was to appreciate this in 1989, p. 9).

Discussing the transition from the initial to the second stage of the New Left, in any event, is to admit that the original New Left as a political movement was defeated. Most of those who created the movement did not realise or were unable to overcome the contradiction between their commitment to political involvement and their lack of both a coherent programme and an organised mass base of its own. As a result they failed to arm the workers and other popular struggles with an appropriate strategic theory that would help a renewed labour movement to emerge; they also missed the opportunity of developing CND into a sympathetic movement for socialism. Decline of the first wave of the Campaign in the early 1960s was naturally followed by the ebb of the first tide of the New Left. This double defeat was also due to the specific political situation of the time. International circumstances began to change with the early signs of detente in the Cold War that had underlined the political life of the whole previous decade. At home the influence of the old Labour left revived after Gaitskell's death and the succession of Harold Wilson in 1963. Many independent socialists went back to the Labour Party with an illusion of a real reform of the party, which was eventually shattered during the period of the Wilson government.[13]

Thompson wrote at that particular moment of transition, venting his personal anger at the new NLR editors, that 'the movement which once claimed to be "the New Left" ... has now, in this country, dispersed itself both organisationally and (to some extent) intellectually'.[14] It was not surprising that he, among others, was so pessimistic that he considered the ground of a new left to have been already completely lost. But he was wrong. The 'ground' or 'space' for a culture and politics of the New Left in subsequent years proved to be substantial and remained to be historically demanded, even though the next wave of the movement might have to be viewed in quite different terms.

A Note on the Main Participants

After the succession of Anderson to the editorship of NLR, members of the old board left, of whom some regrouped in 1967 to produce the May Day Manifesto (see III.3). Stuart Hall joined with Richard Hoggart in establishing the Centre for Contemporary Cultural Studies (CCCS) at the University of Birmingham in 1964. Raphael Samuel started the History Workshop at Ruskin College, Oxford, in 1966. These two remarkably successful projects carried forward the original ideas of the New Left. John Saville and Ralph Miliband founded in 1964 the annual Socialist Register (SR) which, in Thompson's opinion, was 'the last survivor in the direct line of continuity from the old New Left'.[15] Its contributors were often from the old NR circle but also of other socialist groups and other countries that granted SR an impressive international dimension. NLR created its own publishing house and began to produce New Left Books in 1970. Together with NLR,[16] we shall follow the tracks of SR, History Workshop and CCCS as four parallel institutional New Left tendencies, which made up the general development of the movement. Thompson also launched the Centre for the Study of Social History at Warwick University in 1965. After that he fell into 'political silence' for eight years (1978a, p. 313), avoiding involvement in debates of the Left.

2. AN ANATOMY OF BRITAIN

The Making of the English Working Class *(1963)*

Thompson's *The Making of the English Working Class* was written during the period of CND and New Left activities, and came out in 1963 at the moment of CND's collapse and the reshaping of NLR. This context accounts for its polemical style, and, to some extent an absence of conceptual analysis. An excuse for the latter point is that the book was not addressed to the academic public, but rather to concerned working people when Thompson was teaching in WEA evening classes. This powerful and tremendously influential account of early working class experience was not, however, without theoretical significance. It revised, in a way, some orthodox Marxist assumptions about class formation and class consciousness, and more generally, relations between economics, politics, and culture. Representing an effort to return history to its roots, it also considerably transformed the study of the first Industrial Revolution within the tradition of social history. The book met with 'a generous but critical reception' at the time of its publication. More serious and sophisticated criticisms, however, came later not from the conservatives, but from younger left-wing theorists (Thompson, 1968 Postscript, p. 917; 1976b, p. 7).[17] In any case, *The Making of the English Working Class* not only made itself a classic in contemporary Marxist literature, but also became 'a source of political inspiration well outside the ranks of professional historians' (Samuel and Stedman Jones, 1982a, p. 378).

According to the author, the book arose from a two-sided polemic against the Fabian tradition of empiricist economic history;[18] and against an abbreviated economistic notion of Marxism, around which questions and some answers had been theoretically proposed since the moment from 1956 onwards of the creation of the New Left. What was lost in the mood of these prevailing orthodoxies was a sense of the process – the whole political and social context of the period in which change and conflict, class and class struggle, actually occurred (1963a, pp. 12, 195–6; 1976b, pp. 6–7, 20).

Focusing on the themes of exploitation and standards and experiences, Thompson argues against the way of seeing class formation as externally determined: 'steam power plus cotton-mill = new working class'. Such an over-simplified idea, according to him, did affect the 'bourgeois' schools, but especially penetrated into Marxist historiography, including Engels's *The Condition of the Working Class in England* (1844). In Thompson's view, the creation of the working class between 1790 and 1832 was not an automatic generation of the factory system, nor a product solely of the Industrial Revolution. Based on his richly detailed narrative, he believes that 'the making of the working class is a fact of political and cultural, as much as of economic, history. ... The working class made itself as much as it was made' (1963a, pp. 191, 194). The points he emphasises here are that

(1) class is not a thing, a static structure or a sociological category, but a process, a historical happening, unifying events in both primary experience and

consciousness – class can only be defined in terms of historical relationships by people who live their own history (pp. 9–12);

(2) there is a continuity of political and cultural traditions in the formation of working-class communities, such as eighteenth-century religious dissent, popular rebellion, constitutional conviction and the 'liberty tree' movement of the English Jacobins; but no automatic correspondence between the dynamic of economic growth and of social or cultural life (pp. 192–3 and part 1);

(3) class consciousness is the way in which class experiences are handled in cultural terms (seen in the plebeian consciousness refracted by new experiences in social being giving rise to a transformed consciousness of the working class);[19] and

(4) workers themselves contributed, by conscious efforts, to the making of history: it is here the title of *The Making of the English Working Class* meets its purpose – 'a study in an active process, which owes as much to agency as to conditioning'(pp. 9, 12).

The core of these arguments is the dialectical interaction of social being and social consciousness, related to the Marxist tradition but without recourse to the 'simple' received formula. In the classical Marxist approach, a class is basically defined by its objective position, namely, by its relationship to the means of production. (Marx's negative conception of defining a class in *The Eighteenth Brumaire* and his positive conception in *The Poverty of Philosophy* and *German Ideology* are both very brief but clear, 1961, pp. 188–9; 187–9, 64–5.) Thompson's own definition reads:

> class happens when some men, as a result of common experiences (inherited or shared), feel and articulate the identity of their interests as between themselves, and as against other men whose interests are different from (and usually opposed to) theirs. … if the experience appears as determined [by the productive relations], class-consciousness does not. (1963a, pp. 9–10)

In his essay on what for him were mistakenly conceived peculiarities of English society, published in *SR* in 1965 and his 1968 Postscript to the revised edition of *The Making of the English Working Class*, Thompson reasserts the principle of regarding class as a social and cultural formation which cannot be defined abstractly or in isolation (1968 edn. p. 939):

> class is not this or that part of the machine, but the way the machine works once it is set in motion... [Class is] a very loosely defined body of people who share the same congeries of interests, social experiences, traditions and value-system, who have a disposition to behave as a class, to define themselves in their actions and in their consciousness in relation to other groups of people in class ways. (1965, pp. 357–8)

The earlier impulse behind Morris of 'rehabilitating' the 'lost' vocabulary of moral concerns in Marx is once again given a voice here,[20] supported by concrete studies of how the different groups of labourers came to struggle, think and value in a class way, while out of their experiences came a new stance and new solidarities. It is only after 'people commence to struggle in a class way that then one can begin to talk about class formation'. In other words, class formation is the result and consequence of class struggle (1963a, p. 212, ch. 16 and part 3; 1968 edn. p. 938; 1978b, p. 21). This is not quite what Anderson generalises as 'the conversion of a collective experience into a social consciousness which thereby defined and created the class itself' (1980, pp. 30, 42), but rather, class consciousness is indispensable to composing the class. Thompson did not ever deny the 'objective reasons within production relations' for people to identify their common interests and share attitudes in class way (1978b), and actually examined the historical development of capitalist economic relations.[21] Here since consciousness is brought to the process of class formation, the distinction between class-in-itself and class-for-itself in Marxist terms (taken from Hegel) is dismissed. As Thompson accepted the Kautskyist–Leninist thesis of fixing class consciousness 'from the outside',[22] he contradicts himself unless his concept of class formation implies that class consciousness is not brought to the working class by those who are not themselves belonging to the same class, but from inside that class by those who become conscious first and are in part constitutive of it. They could be either Gramsci's organic intellectuals produced from within the ranks of workers, or individuals of whatever origin who attain working-class consciousness 'from the observation of the situation' of that class (Marx and Engels, 1845, p. 65).

It is not surprising that criticisms of *The Making of the English Working Class* directed later by the younger Marxist generation were largely from a structuralist point of view.[23] This also helped manifest the book's remarkable long-term influence on contemporary socialist debates. Anderson insists on the 'objective' position of a class which is regardless of will or attitude.[24] He holds that as by 1832 industrial transformation had been far from completed, Thompson's class formation is quite independent of the new mode of production. Such an absence of any material framework laying down the whole pattern of capital accumulation provides little possibility of assessing the role of subjective experience. The underestimation of the importance of the factory system led Thompson, in Anderson's view, to a loose study of the history of the 'highly atypical' class history of artisans, outworkers, agricultural labourers, domestic workers and the casual poor, without necessary reference to 'the overall occupational composition' of the working class (1980, pp. 32–40). Moreover, in emphasising Marx's thesis that men make history but not freely, Nairn points out that one of *The Making of the English Working Class*'s limitations is its blind-spot to the tragic evolution of working-class consciousness under the specific conditions of British capitalism (1964b, pp. 52–4). In other words, Thompson has missed the fatal weaknesses, the defensive character, of the English working class which are of vital importance in understanding the problems of the contemporary labour movement (see the next section). This is a major point on which the two New Left generations radically divided.

A common critique of Thompson focuses on his understanding of consciousness which is somehow confused with experience from time to time in his analysis, and taken as feelings and immediate self-reflections of the subject. Experience is so crucial a category for him that it serves as both the origin and the bearer of the process of class formation and class consciousness. The central concept of exploitation, for example, is perceived by workers from their experience of poverty and solidarity, rather than from the way that Marx revealed, in which the historically specific production relations guarantee a capitalist ownership and control. The critique of the empiricist approach of *The Making of the English Working Class* found an echo more recently in feminist historians who effectively challenged an essentialist and 'universalised' definition of class. Joan Scott demonstrates how Thompson's singular and homogeneous conceptualisation of experience entails a class identity that is constructed in gendered terms and overrides all differences (1988, pp. 68–90; 1990, esp. pp. 26–8). Barbara Taylor, among others, argues against the unitary notion of a working class which cannot locate the sources of different political attitudes arising in that same class (1983).[25] But this point applies well to both Thompson's subjective 'common experiences' of workers and his critics' 'objective' structural conditions.

Two other questions that made the argument of *The Making of the English Working Class* problematic are concerned with the conjunction of class and class consciousness.[26] First, if class is only formed with class conciousness, what about certain periods prior to nineteenth-century industrial capitalism when classes were not conscious of themselves as classes? (This is of course less acute wherever Thompson tends to reduce consciousness to experience.) Thompson's 'class struggle without class' in eighteenth-century English society (between gentry and common people; patricians and plebeians), that is, people behave in class ways before the actual formation of the class, is obviously not a satisfactory solution. Thus, he is in fact forced to go back to the dichotomy of class-for-itself and class-in-itself (1978c). He tries to overcome the difficulty by distinguishing two senses of class:

(1) with reference to real, empirically observable historical content;
(2) as an analytic category without much direct correspondence with factual evidence.

The concept may be employed in both ways (1978c, p. 148) on the presupposition that class struggle does not happen because of the existence of classes, but rather, people 'discover' themselves to be in a struggle in a class-specific way.

The second problem is that if the working class was made in the 1830s when, as Thompson suggests, class consciousness matured, coupled with the great growth of working class political and industrial organisations, then how to explain the 'discontinuity' of the period 1850–80? Surely he knows well that the failure of Chartism marked a very significant turning point, a rupture that separated the period, and which ended with the falling apart of working-class agitation and an entirely new phase of class politics and institutions decades later (1963a, pp. 194, 712; 1968 edn. p. 937; 1965, pp. 342–6). But, Anderson questions, if the same class could be made by the 1830s, unmade after the 1840s, and remade during the

1880s, how ultimately satisfactory is the whole vocabulary of 'making' itself (1980, pp. 45–7).[27] Gareth Stedman Jones's[28] study of the 'remaking' of a working class was a decisive contribution to the debate (1974),[29] yet the questions concerning the meaning of 'making', the sociological demarcation between artisans and proletariat or the definition of the proletarian class, remained open.

The dispute exemplifies, in a way, the division between a humanist and a culturalist perspective, so as to place it on subjective/internal elements on the one side, and objective/external determinants on the other. The concept of labour aristocracy, which combined both ideological and economic considerations, was then reintroduced to explain the retreat of class politics in the mid-nineteenth-century. It generally helped to further discredit Thompson's argument. Among the best known attempts to work out the trajectory of the British labour movement in this direction are those of Royden Harrison[30] (1965), Hobsbawm (1954) and James Hinton (1965).

The 'Peculiarities of the English'

In Anderson's opinion, by 1964 when people on the left confronted the evident national crisis of British capitalism[31] and urgently needed to comprehend the current situation, they could benefit little from the early New Left. In more general terms, he observed that 'we must be unique among advanced industrial nations in having not one single structural study of our society today', and logically this absence followed the complete lack of any scholarly tenable global history of twentieth-century Britain (1964a, p. 12). To remedy these failings, NLR set itself the programme of providing a systematic examination of modern British society since the emergence of capitalism, especially the configuration of class relations and conflicts, in order to achieve an effective historical perspective on the current struggle. 'Any worthwhile socialist intervention today must be based on a serious, coherent view of our total society and the conflicting forces within it'(NLR 27, 'To our readers'). In so doing, Anderson and Nairn radically revised the established historiography by illuminating Britain's unique development among major capitalist nations at every political and cultural conjuncture. Thompson, based on what he believed to be 'grand facts', fiercely attacked such 'English exceptionalism'. Anderson struck back violently, to which Thompson never replied. However sharp the tone of both sides, neither of them regretted it much.[32] The Thompson/Anderson-Nairn debate[33] represented the first vigorous theoretical engagement by the British New Left. The original arguments advanced from this polemic are of great significance, for they stem from the creative ideas and new modes of thinking which eventually changed the character of British Marxism.

The nature of the seventeenth-century English revolution came to be the starting point of the debate. The traditional picture that presents a struggle simply between the rising bourgeoisie and the declining aristocracy was no longer conceivable. Rather, in Anderson's and Nairn's view, it was primarily between factions within the landed class and not between classes of opposed economic positions and interests. Conflicts between urban capitalism and the old rural order appeared only as secondary episodes in the larger span of English social history. As a result, although the outcome was a typically bourgeois rationalisation of the state and economy, and in this sense, the revolution was supremely successful ('by proxy'), 'it left almost the entire social structure intact', and its ideological legacy 'was almost nil' (Anderson, 1964a, pp. 13–17; Nairn, 1964c, p. 22; 1964b, pp. 44–5).[34] Thompson, though he stresses 'certain changes in the institutional superstructure' brought about by the 1640 revolution (as cultural achievements), actually shares with his two opponents the imperfect and unfulfilled character of it, from which legacy Britain's social and political problems constantly arose. 'The revolution which did *not* happen in England is as important for understanding England as the French Revolution is for understanding France' (Thompson, quoted from Nairn, 1964c, p. 19).

The controversy centres on the nature of contending class forces. Thompson follows the classical Marxist tradition in seeing the landowners and tenant-farmers as already composing a 'powerful and authentic capitalist nexus' during the seventeenth-century revolution. But, he reproaches, neither Anderson nor Nairn appear to be able to accept the notion of an agrarian class as a true bourgeoisie (1965, pp. 315–7, 319). For the two *NLR* editors it was only after 1640 that a landed aristocracy, underpinned by a strong mercantile group, became a basically capitalist class. The revolution had only 'made possible' such a transformation (Anderson, 1964a, pp. 17, 29; 1966, p. 6). Whether the subordination of industrial capital to commercial activity was the case remains crucially controversial;[35] it nevertheless seems an agreed idea that agrarian capitalism preceded industrial capitalism, that the latter developed upon the social and political framework created by the former.[36] The independent thesis that Anderson proposes against the implication of Thompson's 'epochal' bourgeois revolution (from the fifteenth to eighteenth centuries) is that:

> Capitalism does not automatically or everywhere require a victorious industrial bourgeoisie to launch it – any more than socialism necessarily requires a victorious industrial proletariat to impose it; although in time capitalism inevitably creates an industrial bourgeoisie, just as socialism in our century has always created an urban proletariat. ... There is no simple, technical fatality which allocates mandatory roles univocally to social groups. (1966, p. 9)

He does not explain, in this connection, the complexity of industrialisation itself which produces both a bourgeoisie and a proletariat, if not necessarily a capitalism and a socialism.

The very essence of the English Revolution, according to Anderson and Nairn, must be seen in the same origin of the nobility/landed gentry class and the industrial bourgeoisie. Moreover, the bourgeoisie always rallied to, polarised towards and compromised with its senior partner or 'master'. This resulted, in the subsequent two centuries, in the eventual formation of a hegemonic or dominant social bloc in the form of the archaic contemporary British upper class.

The most important single key to modern English history is the fact that the ·
aristocracy was 'the vanguard of the bourgeoisie' (Anderson, 1964a, pp. 18–20,
29; 1966, pp. 14, 16; Nairn, 1964c, p. 21; 1963, pp. 116ff).[37] In addition, the
whole process was reinforced by the building of the empire and imperialism.
'The English capitalist class', writes Nairn, 'because of the peculiar circumstances
attending its birth, was conservative from the outset', and 'did not revolutionise
society as a whole' (1964c, pp. 20, 21; 1964b, p. 44). The failure of this class to
attain hegemony is substantially and directly relevant to the present crisis, in
terms of Britain's belated 'modernisation'.[38]

Following Marx, who saw England as the 'most bourgeois of nations',
Thompson would not lay stress on the aristocratic privileges and influence which
were largely displaced or, at least, began to lose control before the Reform Bill of
1832. So as not to confuse the persistence of the old styles or ethos with 'the real
movement and equilibrium of social forces', he concludes that the 'capitalist
gentry' had never performed as a ruling class since the settlement of 1688,
whereas the industrial middle class exercised political ascendancy from the mid-
nineteenth century onwards. He thus leaves the whole period in between without
categorising clearly its power identity.[39] Having acknowledged important differences between the English and, say, the French way of capitalist formation,
neither for him, however, can be claimed typical.

What is at issue is the bourgeois ideological legacy. In the Anderson/Nairn
assessment, the English bourgeoisie achieved almost nothing but 'the insular
destiny of its civilisation'. Radical Puritanism that founded no significant
tradition and left no major after-effects was a politically 'useless passion';
empiricism, as a transcript of the fragmented, incomplete character of the
historical experience of this very class, fused traditionalism into a 'comprehensive
coagulated conservatism'; utilitarianism was the only 'authentic, articulated
ideology' of industrial capitalism and a 'timid and dreary species' of economic and
social rationalism, but too crude and one-dimensional to triumph over society at
large; liberalism, as both a refinement and enfeeblement of the original utilitarian
doctrines, was a more contradictory and intrinsically limited phenomenon
(Anderson, 1964a, pp. 16–17, 31–33; 1966, p. 17; Nairn, 1964b, pp. 44–45; 1964a,
p. 44; 1962, p. 31). As for political economy, which Thompson regards as a
'systematic, highly structured ideology' that Marx had to devote his life's work to
overthrowing (1965, pp. 318–19, 335–6), it is seen by Nairn as only a part of the
parochial, shallow English Enlightenment and by Anderson as a 'hypnotic,
monocular account' of economy. Anderson does not even bother to mention it in
his survey of those at least 'comprehensive' social thoughts (Nairn, 1964b, pp. 45,
56; Anderson, 1966, pp. 22, 40). Instead of building a 'unified bourgeois culture'
that is said to have been established in continental Europe, the new ruling bloc in
England was incapable of attaining a 'creative total view of the world', and lived
only with 'English separateness and provincialism; English backwardness and
traditionalism; English religiosity and moralistic vapouring; paltry English "empiricism", or instinctive distrust of reason' (Nairn, 1964c, p. 22; 1964b, p. 48). Both the

darkness of its time when the material conditions for an adequate consciousness were absent and the peculiarities of its post-seventeenth-century development set the English bourgeoisie a record of nullity in terms of political philosophy (Anderson, 1964a, pp. 28, 30; 1966, pp. 17, 41, 22; Nairn, 1964a, pp. 60–1).

What the two young authors fail to see is, in Thompson's criticism, the enormous importance of (1) the Protestant inheritance which composed much of the best of the 'tradition of dissent'; (2) the bourgeois democratic culture that 'contributed vastly more to the intellectual universe of the English working class' than utilitarianism; (3) political economy represented in Adam Smith's theory and (4) achievements of natural science (Bacon, Newton, Huxley and above all, Darwinian evolutionism) and the positive relations between the bourgeoisie and the scientific revolutions. More might be added, Thompson goes on – for instance, the realist novels and romanticism. In short, 'they have never imagined the great arch of bourgeois culture' (1965, pp. 318–19, 330–5). In his reply, Anderson simply excludes Protestantism (which was not bourgeois in any narrow sense) and Darwinism (which cannot be attributed so speedily to a specific social class or even a nation) from the bourgeois ideology, and treats political economy as a specialist discipline that should be passed over. Bourgeois culture and political theory are separate categories, says Anderson, and the original thesis he and Nairn formulated is no more and no less than that the English bourgeoisie 'produced no major political philosophy that became hegemonic in the society' (1966, pp. 17–19, 40).[40]

It is noteworthy that neither side was prepared to examine seriously the heritage of liberalism. Anderson and Nairn tend to dismiss any 'bourgeois' achievement on this aristocratic territory at least in terms of systematic theory. Thompson seems to have collected all the evidence against a nihilism, although even he does not mention Locke, for example, the great thinker of the English Revolution. All three Marxist polemicists ignore this figure, who was viewed by Marx as the father of the modern liberal thought of the bourgeoisie.[41]

By a logical extension, Anderson and Nairn apply their thesis to the working class, the 'victim' of the peculiar evolution of the bourgeoisie. The latter did not provide the popular masses and workers with a political and general education, and handed on to them no impulse for liberation, no revolutionary values, no common language. 'Given the time and circumstances of its birth', Nairn remarks, the working class was 'fated to repeat, in certain respects, the historical experience of the English bourgeoisie itself' (1964b, pp. 44, 46–7). In Anderson's short formula, 'a supine bourgeoisie produced a subordinate proletariat' (1964a, p. 39). Just like the bourgeoisie who missed the Enlightenment philosophy, the working class missed socialist theory. The unfortunate destiny of the first proletariat was not its immaturity, but that it was premature in a crucial sense: in contrast to the countries that industrialised afterwards, Marxism came too late to England (the *Communist Manifesto* was written two months before the collapse of Chartism) and penetrated the consciousness of workers far less than anywhere else (Anderson, 1964a, pp. 17, 21, 25–6; Nairn, 1964b, p. 56). The two *NLR* editors seem to have no problem here with Thompson's notion of the working class making itself in the pre-Victorian period, which Anderson would reject later without reapproaching his theme of prematurity. Nairn draws the conclusion that 'the formation of the English working class was a major tragedy', perhaps the greatest single phase of the modern tragedy: that the European working class failed to overthrow capital and fashion the new society for which the material basis was long ago made possible. Fascism, Stalinism, the problems of 'underdevelopment' and the Cold War, in Nairn's eyes, are all products of this disastrous failure that was ultimately caused by the fact that the working class of Great Britain did not lead the way (as Marx used to expect) toward socialism (1964b, pp. 52–3). Once again we see that even the most revolutionary mind is somehow haunted by British chauvinism. Surely if the working class of one major industrial nation had succeeded, the course of human history would have been different. But advanced capitalist societies do not have a privileged position or necessarily play a decisive role in many of the great changes of the modern world.

Now, the question is what the English working class actually developed instead of a Marxist outlook? The Anderson-Nairn evaluation focuses on reformism, trade unionism, and 'immovable corporatism' as genuine class consciousness. It was 'wedded to the narrowest and greyest of bourgeois ideology' and has remained so (Anderson, 1964a, pp. 29, 33–4; Nairn, 1964b, pp. 44, 54–5; 1964a, pp. 39–43). The three striking manifestations of this bourgeois root are Fabianism, 'British socialist empiricism' (as an ideology of anti-ideology), and imperialism. The first was derived from and has been immediately subordinate to utilitarianism. The second has led the entire history of the Labour Party to a repetition of the road along which the bourgeoisie transformed society blindly and empirically without ever accomplishing its mission. The third nurtured the dream and reality of the empire and penetrated deeply into the effective political culture of the socialist movement (Nairn, 1964a, NLR 27, pp. 38, 44, 52, 56; NLR 28, pp. 40, 43; Anderson, 1964a, pp. 24, 36–7). Speaking of the established 'English ideology' as a whole, Anderson's famous thesis (cf. III.4) is that the 'overwhelming fact of British intellectual history in the last 50 years has been the simultaneous failure to produce either a Marxism or a classical sociology of any serious kind. This double absence is what fundamentally defines our cultural situation today' (1966, p. 22). Correspondingly, a true intelligentsia is yet to emerge in this country.[42]

Here, the debate touched the most sensitive issues and soon became rather emotional. Thompson traced the unique historical context of the formation of the English working class originally in The Making of the English Working Class, emphasising (a) the first entrance of England into the Industrial Revolution and (b) the coincidence of the zenith of this process and the French Revolution. Confronting from the outset the truly catastrophic nature of capitalist development and the counter-revolution of the ruling classes against French Jacobinism and hence a potential 'English revolution', the working class formed its consciousness in opposition to both economic exploitation and political oppression (1963a, pp. 177–8, 185, 197–9). It is interesting that from the same observation of the co-existence of the emerging proletariat and an international counter-revolutionary tide, Thompson and Anderson reach opposite conclusions. As against the Anderson/Nairn pessimistic and negative viewpoint, Thompson argued that developed class consciousness cannot be reduced to unchanged sociological composition, nor to a hermetically sealed corporate culture (1965, p. 358).[43] This brings him to a major disagreement with them on the questions of the part that Communism played in the labour movement and the impact of Marxism on British political culture.

The only criticism Anderson has ever accepted during these exchanges is that he and Nairn indeed neglected the role of the Communist Party (1966, p. 24).[44] But he insists that the Labour left and the communists shared a common pragmatism in their occasional inter-dependence, and the categories of Nairn's analysis of the Labour Party are applicable to much of the CP's record. Even to see British communism as the opposite pole to orthodox right-wing labourism (Thompson, 1965, pp. 338–9, 347–9) is a 'fantasy', and so is the view that the CPGB has made important political and intellectual contribution to the socialist movement. He can only see a 'modest and marginal presence' of the party and therefore, for him, Thompson wildly exaggerated its influence (1966, pp. 24–5, 40). But Thompson was not alone – the gulf here was not so much between the two sides of the debate as between the two generations of British Marxists.[45] It was a remarkable adjustment that three years later, under Anderson's editorship, NLR started printing some studies of the CP's history, based on an acknowledgement that 'one of the great gaps in labour historiography in Britain has been the lack of any adequate account of the development of the British Communist Party' (NLR 41, 'Themes').[46]

Thompson's exaggeration, Anderson explains, is linked to his belief in a major Marxist permeation in Britain: a systematic grass-roots Marxist education and a traffic of Marxism and anti-Marxism. Anderson asks that as Britain has not produced a single Marxist thinker, let alone a consensus Marxist culture, can we speak without hesitation of a British Marxism (1966, pp. 25–6)?[47] Nairn talks about a 'very weak and limited indigenous Marxist tradition' which was quite unable to resist the pressures of Stalinism – did this not mark the first effort of the New Left? (1964a, p. 61) The reason for the failure of Marxism in Britain in their view is twofold: the very intensity of the corporate class-consciousness left little room for an alternative; and Marxism itself, more so in the elementary form earlier embraced and propagated by the Social-Democratic Federation, did not really echo the conditions of life in England, especially in the area of 'superstructures' (Anderson, 1964a, p. 34; Nairn, 1964a, pp. 43–4).[48] They have thus dismissed the achievements of British Marxists, all the way from that of pioneer socialists, the whole generation of Marxist intellectuals of the 1930s and the 1940s, the Communist Historians' Group, and the old New Left. There was allegedly virtually no Marxist tradition in Britain prior to the second NLR. Such an 'injurious judgement' was obviously the immediate ground for Thompson's indignation.[49]

The relationship between Marxism and the British working-class movement and socialist groups was of course not a new topic to debate. But Anderson and

Nairn had reworked it in an extraordinarily critical way, and their denial of any significant Marxist past in Britain became a tenet of the post-1956 Marxist generation. The publication in 1965 of a balanced study, *Karl Marx and the British Labour Movement*, by Collins and Abramsky,[50] did not end the controversy but brought it new excitement. The authors offered original analyses of the First International and its London-based General Council in relation to the industrial and political struggles of the working class in mid-Victorian England and Scotland, and the 'anti-colonial' campaign over the Irish question as well. What remained true, however, was the smaller influence of Marx's theory on the British Isles than on the continent. In any case, as Anderson pointed out, to say that British Labour lacked Marxist ideology was not his and Nairn's original contribution. Saville (1965, p. 149) and Miliband (1964a, 1966), for example, long held that the dominant Fabian political tradition had never been effectively challenged by Marxism in England.

In regard to the power structure of British society, Thompson finds himself in a 'exceptionalist' position similar to that of his two critics. Anderson and Nairn emphasise that out of a particular historical and geographical situation Britain had a very specific configuration of hegemonic system, characterised by the relative insignificance of bureaucratic and military forms, immediate strike-capacity of economic forms, and crucial importance of ideological and cultural forms. The combination of all these is a supremacy of civil society over the state. 'In England, democracy was the ransom of hegemony' (Anderson, 1964a, pp. 42–6). While having no substantial objection to this observation, Thompson does not like the way it is addressed. It took several years for him to admit his own 'inadequate' understanding of the Gramscian notion of hegemony and Anderson's 'authority' on this particular point (1965, pp. 347, 356; 1978a, p. 404).[51]

A brief comparison might be made of the methodological difference between the two sides. First, as Anderson and Nairn pursue a 'totalising' understanding (not Thompson's sort of fragmentary history) and 'schemata of a unified theory of the past' (Anderson, 1966, p. 33), their approach is somewhat over-schematic and lacks control of historical evidence. This can be seen in the first place in a rigid double claim of British exceptionality (explicitly) and continental uniformity (implicitly). They even consciously reject the need for any empirical testing of theory (Nairn's statement in 1964b, p. 47). Thompson, on the other hand, refuses what he calls fatal blindness in criticising empiricism and believes that an empiricism based on the dialectic between conceptual hypotheses and 'grand facts' is in line with the Marxist analytical tradition (1965, pp. 333, 337).[52]

Secondly, Thompson seems to be mistaken in seeing the Anderson/Nairn method as economic reductionist (1965, pp. 351–4). It is rather, as conceded by the two younger theorists themselves, idealist in emphasis, in view of their assertion of the primacy of political and ideological factors (Anderson, 1966, pp. 30, 40).[53] In his recent return to the debate, Anderson offered a self-criticism that in their earlier essays the 'Gramscian polarity was given too cultural a turn', and the crisis they analysed was 'deduced too narrowly from the character of the hegemonic order alone,' although, he added, their essential intuitions were not wrong (1987, p. 57). An idealism also manifests itself in a teleological ring to their style: the two authors frequently criticise in accordance with ideal types of events or somehow fixed path of movements. Thirdly, the theoretical lineage of the Anderson/Nairn argument, they declared, comes from the major tradition of Western European Marxism, a tradition with new idealist currents (Anderson, 1966, pp. 31, 41; see IV.2). While Thompson stayed within an old framework combining English intellectual occupation and a Marxist revisionism, as pronounced by himself (1976b, p. 18; 1973, pp. 313, 319), his younger challengers employed a set of different concepts, raised new questions, and urged, following the European pattern, the creation of an Anglo-Marxism (Anderson, 1966, pp. 32, 41).

Fourthly, Anderson and Nairn engaged themselves in investigating the past in order to comprehend the present. Their writings were indeed directly related to the nature of the current crisis of the labour movement and the essential features of Britain's political economy. They charged Thompson, not altogether unfairly, with being incompetent as a keen political analyst. Thompson's discussion in 'The Peculiarities of the English' of reformist tactics within a revolutionary strategy (1965, pp. 344–5) for a socialist transition, for example, suffers by comparison with Anderson's critique of Wilsonism (1964b) in terms of both political concreteness and theoretical vigour.[54] Finally, Anderson attacked Thompson's populism, for its replacement of any structural examination of specific classes or social groups with a characteristic terminology, 'the people'. He saw this populist idiom as a curious form of 'messianic nationalism', and the tendency behind it was a moralisation of all social and political phenomena (1965a, p. 17; 1966, pp. 34–8). NLR's commitment, on the contrary, was that 'socialist strategy must be founded on a unified sociological analysis of our society, and not only on moral protest' (NLR 32, 'Themes'). What Anderson failed to recognise, however, a failure so fatally serious, was the vital importance for socialism of the genuine humanist essence and strong moral appeal of English radical traditions which people like Williams and Thompson always defended.

Radically breaking with the English cultural inheritance, the new NLR group attempted to overcome what was called 'the general crisis of socialist thought' (Nairn, 1964a, NLR 28, p. 61). The judgement that 'the nullity of native intellectual traditions proved to be the most serious of obstacles to socialism' (NLR 27, p. 44), iconoclastic and uncompromising as it is, does contain some real truth. Even Thompson would agree with Nairn that the British working class, immunised against theory like no other class, needs theory like no other (1965, p. 337). Yet the question is what kind of theory? Referring to the Anderson/Nairn conceptualisation and speaking for those who backed Thompson from the old New Left in the 1960s, Barratt Brown made it clear again recently that the focus of socialist discussion must shift away from the peculiarities of English development to the global crisis of which Britain was not an atypical part (1988). But the problem was unsettled. Nairn and Anderson still had good reasons for insisting on their original thesis (IV.3).

3. TOWARDS SOCIALISM

Critique of New Capitalism and Old Labourism

In contrast to the traditional left who overlooked the changes of capitalism, the New Left confronted the realities and set itself the task of revealing the true content and nature of these changes. A great many writings were devoted to this task, in the debate over 'class and classlessness', the critique of 'Labour revisionism', and in the pages of NLR, SR and other New Left publications, most notably *Out of Apathy* (1960), *Towards Socialism* (1965) and *The May Day Manifesto* (1967–8). Employing the phrase 'new capitalism', the emphasis was placed on the second rather than the first word as a reaction to the theory that capitalism had gone and Britain belonged to something called 'post-capitalist' society (Williams, 1968b, pp. 15–6).

It was largely agreed that the long boom of post-war capitalism had been accompanied by far-reaching institutional changes: increase of rationalisation, macro-planning, and state intervention by means of introducing a public sector, welfare service, taxation and so on. Advanced capitalism, at least for a period, had exhibited a great flexibility in assimilating the pressures upon it. It integrated some originally socialist proposals. In the case of Britain, Hobsbawm saw what had been happening since the early 1950s as in some ways 'much more revolutionary than what happened in the early stages of industrialisation' (1978b, p. 43). Pressed by a powerful labour movement, capitalist society showed the ability to meet certain basic human needs – a marked reduction in primary poverty, a considerable stability of employment and an extensive welfare network (Anderson, 1965a, p. 15; Miliband, 1964a, p. 101; Rowthorn, 1966, p. 15; Thompson, 1965, p. 356). The questions the New Left tried to answer were thus how did these happen? What did they actually mean to capitalism itself as well as to the socialist theory and practice? Was it true that capitalism had been overtaken by a managerial revolution and government regulation? Had all these, as the massive liberal and revisionist literature suggested, fundamentally altered private ownership and class division?[55]

The New Left critics firmly rejected these 'disastrous' revisionist views. What had changed, in Barratt Brown's analysis, was not the nature of the controllers from being owners to managers of capital, but the scale of the capital they controlled (the concentration of giant corporations) and so the economic power they possessed. The search for maximum profit, the anarchy of the market and the tendency to over-production all remained the case (1963b, pp. 293–307, 320–4, 452–3; 1958/9; 1963a, pp. 23–4; 1968b). Similarly, Williams pointed out that the economy, while not controlled by ordinary shareholders, was not controlled by managers and technicians either, but by 'powerful interlocking private institutions' (1961b, final part). In an essay contributed to *Towards Socialism*, Robin Blackburn[56] examined the relationships between managers and owners, the logic of the market and the decomposition of management (new technology, such as computer automation, tended to undermine top managerial functions), concluding that there was a change in the forms of property income, but that a managerial revolution had never occurred (1965, pp. 115–26). He and Nairn both considered Keynesian techniques adapted at the level of national policy to be in no way a solution to capitalist contradictions, only that capitalism had taken a radically new form, a state-supported monopoly (Blackburn, 1965, pp. 131–44; Nairn, 1964c, p. 25). Miliband and many others argued in the same spirit (Miliband, 1968, pp. 215–29; Williams, *et al*, 1967/8, sections 11, 12, 30, 33, 34).[57]

On the related question of the welfare state, arguments were advanced to distinguish socialism from the 'contemporary myth' of welfarism.[58] Certain achievements in social welfare were part of the change of capitalist society and a result of the long struggle, historically connected with the nineteenth-century utopian socialist tradition, to remove poverty and attain humane services. The popular base of welfare social democracy formed the real ground on which socialism had to be built. However, the welfare state had not actually solved problems of poverty and inequality (most significantly manifested in the distribution of wealth and power), and nothing in its policies could be seen as specifically socialist. As Dorothy Wedderburn remarked, the effect of, or the values embodied in, welfare legislation represented no more than an 'unstable compromise' between the market and laissez-faire on the one hand, and planned egalitarianism on the other (1965, p. 143). But such compromises did bring real benefits for a while.

Parallel to the critique of new capitalism, there was an increasing concern with the issues of imperialism and underdevelopment, which were strikingly given little weight in major works that appeared during the first wave of the New Left. *Culture and Society*, for example, included neither 'nationalism' nor 'imperialism' in its list of some forty new key words.[59] The first *NLR* printed very little between 1960 and 1962 on international relations and the third world.[60] In spite of the shock of Suez and the growing inspiration of the national liberation movements in the tottering colonies, the entire question of imperialism as both a world system and a national legacy of British society was not yet centred in political debates at a theoretical level. Instead of pursuing new analyses of twentieth-century imperialism, Marxist critics had left the subject more or less as Lenin outlined it in 1916 (Saville, 1957, p. 73). It was not until 1963 that *NLR* announced its commitment to internationalism and began to remove 'the fixed habit' of conceiving capitalism as a single, undifferentiated phenomenon (editorial statement, *NLR* 18 and *NLR* 20). Barratt Brown published *After Imperialism* in 1963 and Peter Worsley *The Third World* in 1964. Both authors, with origins in the Communist Party and *NR*, wrote in the Marxist tradition of political economy and a New Left spirit of cultural analysis (see II.3). Later, protests against the Vietnam War and distaste for the neo-imperialist foreign policy of the Labour government extended discussions in this area.

The New Left exposure of the new capitalism would not be effective in any concrete sense unless it was accompanied by a ruthless criticism of 'labourism', a term that had become prevalent since the early 1960s. Labourism was not a homogeneous entity but a historical product of the theory and practice of class collaboration. It was, wrote Saville, a tradition which 'emphasised the unity of Capital and Labour, and the importance of conciliation and arbitration in industrial disputes' (1973a, pp. 215–16). In Anderson's analysis, the history of the British Labour movement developed within a set of structural limits that placed strict bounds on its identity. The modern form of that binding is labourism (1987, p. 58). Apart from a series of essays, Miliband offered *Parliamentary Socialism* (1961), a book widely recognised as one of the most important contemporary accounts of the labour predicament. He documented the process from 1900 onwards by which the Labour Party had institutionalised to the extent that it was incapable of curing 'the sickness of Labourism' (cf. 1961b, p. 66).

One of the 'permanent weaknesses' of the Labour leadership, according to Miliband, is that it always seeks to escape from the implications of the party's class character and proclaimed goal of socialism, hence from any kind of political action which falls outside the framework and conventions of the parliamentary system. Even the Labour left is in general 'parliamentary' as well. Indeed the fundamental question is about the very nature of the party – whether it could really adapt itself to the task of creating a new society or whether it would merely make capitalism more efficient and humane. Unfortunately, socialism never seems seriously to underlie its ideology and politics, and it is simply unrealistic to expect this organisation to change into an adequate agency for radical social transformation (1961a, ch. 3, 9, 10; see esp. pp. 14–15, 344; 1966, pp. 15, 21–2 and 1973 edn., Postscript, pp. 372–3, 376). Speaking of the Labour Party as a coalition, Williams pointed out that this single fact led to an evident poverty in theory, for any attempt to go beyond general definitions at once evokes strains on the complicated alliance. Moreover, the left was locked into this coalition, dominated by undemocratic voting rules in a 'moral paternalist' fashion (1965).

Miliband argues against the assumption that the origins of the present crisis of the Labour Party were in the new circumstances of the affluent society. In 'Socialism and the Myth of the Golden Past' (1964a), he reaffirms his rejection of the notion of a socialist decline from a supposed militant and committed stage. For him, neither poverty nor affluence can serve as a fundamental explanation of social behaviour and political conviction, though a general improvement in the conditions of the working class might be actually one of the preconditions for developing socialist consciousness. There is nothing in the development of contemporary capitalism which had made the socialist road harder than before – 'rather the reverse' (pp. 92–3). Similarly, Anderson claims that there is little need for fear of a seemingly working-class 'affluence'. The 'great, permanent landmark of real abundance will not be the end of ideology, but the end of necessity' (1965b, pp. 289–90). Blackburn even believes that under welfare capitalism, 'a more far-reaching class consciousness than any we have witnessed hitherto' would be fostered by the struggles over the share of labour in the national income (1965, p. 144). Optimistic as these views are, they share the same negative conclusion concerning the past and shed no light on the question of why the future could be different. The Anderson-Nairn thesis of the fatal tragedy of the British labour movement (see III.2), can indeed be traced to Miliband who was the first to suggest that 'the present difficulties can only be properly understood by seeing them in the perspective of what has gone before' (1961a, p. 16), and he recorded that history as a total failure.

Nairn's historical study of the Labour Party (above all in 'The Nature of the Labour Party', 1964a) was a unique contribution to the attempt at a theoretical explanation of why the British Labour movement had never been predominantly socialist. It is mainly concerned with

(1) the empirical and indigenous origins of the party which came into being with 'organisational deficiencies' such as bureaucratic control;

(2) the permanent hegemony of trade unionism, Fabianism, evolutionism, parliamentarism and, in a single term, labourism, over socialism as the ideological identity of the Party, including its left wing;

(3) the overpowering conservatism of British society that was deeply embedded in the working class itself [61] and aggravated by long lived British imperialism; and

(4) the great failure of intellectuals to furnish the working-class movement with a 'more revolutionary ideology'.

The most important feature of the British ideology – consonant with the whole British way of life – was that it always reflected the past. Likewise, the Labour Party always lived in the shadow of the spirit and situation of workers and the intelligentsia within the triumphant social machinery of Victorian imperialism (1970, pp. 4, 24, 29–35; 1964a, NLR 27, pp. 47–8, 55; NLR 28, pp. 34, 60–1). Nairn's central theme is that because the source of the weaknesses of the left is the absence of a coherent intellectual position, the tragic evolution of the Labour Party and the whole labour movement can never be turned unless socialists work first to fill this absence in order to transform the very consciousness called labourism.[62]

During the term of the Wilson government which began in 1964, a Labour government that disregarded socialism and was wholeheartedly dedicated to NATO and the American alliance, 'Labour imperialism' became a focus of New Left critique.[63] Shifting from the old theme that the working class of the metropolitan states benefited materially from colonial exploitation, Anderson saw the primary impact of imperialism on this class as rather at the level of consciousness. This was the 'real-negative-achievement of social-imperialism' which created in Britain a powerful national framework for social contradictions (1964a, p. 24). There were strong disagreements with the Anderson-Nairn approach of seeking a direct continuity in the political and ideological spheres from the formative period (the third quarter of the nineteenth century) of 'corporativism' to Wilsonism (see for example Hinton, 1965, pp. 72–7); yet it was a commonplace that the British working class had been seriously poisoned or corrupted by the imperialist heritage and outlook. What was most enraging was

Labour's support for the American involvement in Vietnam. But Vietnam only symbolised the position of the capitalist British state in the capitalist international nexus, which quite prescribed both Britain's foreign and domestic policies. Witnessing a Labour government acting as an imperialist military power, Williams wrote in *Modern Tragedy* (1966):

> it is impossible to believe that as a society we have yet dedicated ourselves to human liberation, or even to that simple recognition of the basic humanity of all other men which is the impulse of any genuine revolution. To say that in our own affairs we have made this recognition would also be too much, in a society powered by great economic inequality and by organised manipulation. (1966, p. 79)

In the end, the question that had to be answered was how to break down this politically and ideologically bankrupt labourism. The whole socialist strategy, for Anderson, 'depends on one immense precondition: a socialist ideology'(1965b, p. 282). Great emphasis was laid on 'a broad and sustained effort of socialist education' which was seen as not an alternative to an immediate involvement in concrete struggle, but an essential element of it (Miliband, *SR* 1966, p. 25); the Centre for Socialist Education (CSE) was formed in 1965, aiming at 'the spread of socialist consciousness' (see *NLR* 35, pp. 105–6).[64] More directly, appeals were made to the union Left to organise a socialist opposition to challenge the Labour leadership. [65] The lack of strategic perspectives on the left was, after all, due to the specific historical limitations. As Anderson put it, an authentic socialist strategy can only be born within the internal dialectic of a mass political mobilisation or movement – it would have no meaning or possibility outside such a movement. Since the Labour Party is non-socialist yet the sole mass organisation of the British working people, 'any attempt to consider some of the problems involved in a successful march towards socialism must necessarily be abstract and inorganic'. His own strategic suggestions are therefore basically 'utopian' (1965b, pp. 222–3).

In spite of this fatal utopian character, Anderson's analysis of the strategic problems is of considerable help to a clearer self-examination by socialists. Discussing ideological struggle, he distinguishes between three main currents of a broad left: working-class consciousness which sustains the Labour left; classical English liberalism which remains vigorous in a significant section of the middle class and CND; moral and aesthetic criticism from the Romantics to *Culture and Society*, which constitutes the major creative tradition of British critical social thought since industrialisation. A fusion of these currents in a new Labour ideology is not necessarily an illusion (1965b, pp. 283–4; 1965a). This essay can be read even today as a forceful reminder of how all the problems remain unsolved more than two decades later.

'Labourism' as a category was questioned later on by two History Workshop editors, Ralph Samuel and Stedman Jones. They argued that to enumerate indigenous empiricism, Protestant moralism, philistine utilitarianism, reverential parliamentarism and intellectual poverty as the symptoms of labourism is no more than a 'polemically brilliant phenomenology' of the disease. It does not help with the complex location of labour history in specific political contexts and at particular moments of time (1982, pp. 325–6). Because the Labour Party was a broad church that represented a coalition of separate interests (essentially a coalition of middle-class progressivism and working-class corporatism) rather than a coherent unity, their claim for a new approach refers to a change of focus for research: one should look at what happened outside the Party, seeing the history of Labour politics not as that of a self-sufficient organisational or ideological identity, but rather as a shifting fulcrum between contending extra-party pressures from left and right (p. 328). The New Left's criticism of 'labourism' was a theoretical step forward, but perhaps they sometimes under-estimated the welfare institutions that Labour had created.

The Question of Ownership and Workers' Control

The battle, a symbolic rather than substantial one, around 'Clause 4' within the Labour Party became white-hot after Labour's defeat in the general election of 1959, for which it was condemned as being responsible. Clause 4 of the Party Constitution, written by Sidney Webb in 1918, declared its commitment to 'the common ownership of the means of production'.[66] Nonetheless, the Labour revisionists had argued quite successfully that nationalisation was largely irrel-evant to economic efficiency, full employment and income redistribution.[67] From the socialist point of view, the public sector of industry within the capitalist framework continued to fail to prove any interconnection between nationalisation and socialism. Confronting all this, the New Left, while sharply critical of the existing statist form of common ownership, was unable to offer a serious alternative theory to revisionism and was in fact driven into a weak defence of Clause 4.[68] In the course of the events, it was an alliance of right-wing trade unionists, the old Fabian state socialists and the New Left which won a verbal victory, subsequently written into the new Labour programme, *Signposts for the Sixties* (1961). In his analysis of this paradoxical result, Anderson pointed out that Clause 4 never came near to being an operative goal in the history of the Labour Party, and did not spell out any fundamental will to transform capitalism. 'It was saved, in a sense, by its very innocuousness' (1965a, p. 7).

As a careful New Left examination of the British experience suggested, nationalised industries were subordinated to the interests of capital and the private sector, and without any strength of competing with, let alone combating, capitalism. Barratt Brown's 'controllers' who had power in the big private financial centres were also controllers of the public enterprises. Moreover, the old industrial relations and position of workers remained virtually untouched inside these enterprises.[69] John Hughes,[70] one of the leading economists of the first New Left and a constant contributor to the New Left effort to formulate an alternative economic strategy for Labour, focused criticism still more on the exploitative nature of nationalised industries in light of the relationship between the public and private sectors, especially in terms of price policy. The whole poorly mixed system was a degeneration of the price mechanism and profit-making, a capitalist reorganisation of production under a single management of capital, equipment and technology (1960a, 1960b; 1963). Precisely because of this underlying factor, Anderson disagreed with those who saw the problem as the imbalance between social and private goods, which was not, for Anderson, an insoluble contradiction of the capitalist system. 'The real significance of public ownership is situated at a much more fundamental level, in the recovery of an alienated economy and society' (1961; 1965a, pp. 7–8).

So, widespread doubt arose as to whether nationalisation in the form that it took was a move in the direction of socialism. However, as the doctrine of the first priority of property rights and relations was not then seriously challenged, New Left writers were generally in agreement on the necessity of public ownership as the single major prerequisite for a socialist transformation. The crux of the matter was to find alternative forms or paths to achieve such ownership. Criticisms of traditional nationalisation should not affect the socialist commitment to 'eliminating private ownership' (Anderson, 1964b, p. 13; Taylor, 1960a). People like Miliband still believed in the principle of nationalisation, seeing its vast extension as a necessary condition for the transcendence of capitalism (1973 Postscript to 1961a, p. 350; 1977b, pp. 44–5). Barratt Brown, too, expected that further nationalisation might become an effective instrument of both planned economic growth and radical social changes (1964, pp. 242, 246). But most others were more sceptical. Even though nationalised industries could be reorganised and become dynamic, they cannot be the sole possible way to shift power over the means of production. Anderson's study of the Swedish model (1961) and Hughes's proposal for regulating economy by means of price control and a wages plan (see below) suggest some clues to an alternative programme.

Two crucial and combined questions raised from the debate were first, about the nature of the nation-state (is it an unproblematic entity in relation to ownership? Why has not nationalisation automatically achieved genuine public, common or social character?) and second, the unity of democratic decision making and rational central planning (can the two be reconciled? How would a decentralised local management work within a planned economy?).[71] Both are still open questions today.

If nationalisation was a formula which appeared unable to confront the problems of bureaucracy and monopolistic power, the idea of workers' control, as distinct from worker participation, offered the most significant remedy or even an alternative. It was within this context that the great concern for industrial democracy re-emerged on the basis of the conviction that political democracy could not proceed in a meaningful way in an arbitrarily and oligarchically operated economy.[72] The revival of the movement for workers' control in the mid-1960s drew its inspiration from European socialist traditions, above all British guild socialism, but also from contemporary Yugoslav and Algerian experiments of workers' self-management and perhaps west German experience of co-determination as well.[73]

It was *ULR* and then *NLR* that first reintroduced serious discussions of militant union activism at shop-stewards' level and workers' representation, and argued that industrial struggle had become the current main-front for the Left. Notable earlier contributions included the *ULR* pamphlet, 'The Insiders' (1958), and an *NLR* collection, *The Incompatibles* (eds. Blackburn and Cockburn, 1967).[74] Trotskyist groupings also helped spread the slogan of 'workers' control' throughout the trade union movement. The first *NR* sponsored Industrial Conference held in April 1959 gathered more than thirty union delegates. *Searchlight, A New Left Industrial Bulletin* was launched in January 1960 in West Riding, aiming to translate some socialist beliefs into 'practical, down to earth language' and tackle immediate problems of workshop organisation (cf. Saville's piece in *Searchlight*, no. 1). Although these early efforts toward agitating a lively working-class movement failed to attract sufficient support from the shop floor,[75] they were the only direct connection between ordinary union militants and the New Left. The issue of workers' control was also one actual point at which an intellectual and political unity of the old and the new New Left could be fruitfully manifested.

The Institute for Workers' Control (IWC) was formed in spring 1968. It was a loose organisation for conferences, publications and liaison, with the backing of the Russell Peace Foundation, the Labour Party Left (notably Stuart Holland), the Voice of the Unions (Ernie Roberts and others), and individual activists.[76] A group of New Left/Labour economists and policy analysts, Barratt Brown, John Hughes, Ken Coates[77] and Tony Topham, became leading spokesmen of the movement.

A key point of Coates's argument is that capitalist property relations sustained by the state power is what must be challenged in the process from workers' control to self-management, which is essentially a process of democratic planning:

> it seems sensible for us to speak of 'workers' control' to indicate the aggressive encroachment of Trade Unions on management powers in a capitalist framework, and of 'workers' self-management' to indicate attempts to administer a socialised economy democratically. ... Between the two, however it may be accomplished, lies the political transformation of the social structure. (1965, p. 291)

An intensified campaign for workers' control could be a most valuable school for practically preparing self-management, a leap towards the ultimate overcoming of the division of labour and human alienation. It is self-management rather than empty 'equality' that should be the goal of socialism (1965, pp. 232–3, 291–3, 313–15; 1968a, p. 15). For him, the meaning of workers' control is thus well beyond that of industrial democracy which is not necessarily connected with politically revolutionary method. In this direction, Coates and Topham, and Anderson too, expected the shop-stewards' mobilisation logically to move beyond a struggle within the capitalist framework and to achieve a total challenge to it (Coates, 1971b, pp. 60–1; Topham, 1964, p. 13; Anderson, 1964b, p. 25). The question thus highlighted by Barratt Brown is the relationship between workers' control and central control – a distinction regarded by Royden Harrison as essentially a contradiction in socialist thought (Harrison, 1960; Barratt Brown, 1964, pp. 251–5). In his IWC pamphlets, Barratt Brown not only confronted theoretical problems, but also proposed concrete procedures (beginning with 'opening the books') for actual workers' control and effective democratisation of the trade unions.

Workers' control was viewed, not by all but by a few forceful New Left commentators, as above all measured by wage control (not traditionally defended free collective bargaining), because income distribution was always the most critical field of economic power in light of the confrontation between wages and profits. Ernest Mandel was to assert later (1971) that the centre of gravity of class struggle in the west was shifting 'from questions of dividing the national income between wages and profits to the question of who determines what is produced, how it should be produced, and how labour should be organised to produce it' (p. 40). For the New Leftists who advocated wage control, however, the two were not separate questions. As early as in 1959, Ken Alexander and John Hughes proposed *A Socialist Wages Plan*, promoting consensus between the future Labour government and organised labour for a balanced long-term growth of both the economy and real incomes. It failed to be put into practice during the Wilson years when the debate about socialist attitudes towards Labour's incomes policy was grounded on a total distrust of a discredited Labour Government.[78] Yet many still believed in principle in a 'correct' incomes policy and regarded it as a political issue. Barratt Brown and Harrison even talked about revolutionary possibilities behind it (*Tribune*, 8 January 1965). In more accurate terms, Topham stressed workers' control of wages as a major challenge to the trade union and socialist movement in western Europe (1965, p. 163). Putting it rather differently, Anderson saw workers' control as 'the only negotiable exchange for an incomes policy: it alone offers a genuine counterpart – powers and not pence' (1964b, pp. 24–5). Bob Rowthorn,[79] a Marxist economist attached to the younger New Left generation, offered his distinct opinion drawn from an analysis of the internal logic of the capitalist economic system, insisting that the whole strategy of 'socialism-through-an-incomes-policy' or, in other words, 'probing the limits of capitalism from within', was 'wrongly conceived in the first place' (1965, pp. 4, 10; 1967, pp. 215–26; 1966, p. 21).[80] From the older generation, Miliband wrote that 'an incomes policy would do nothing to cure the chronic ills of British capitalism' (1966, p. 17).

The underdeveloped movement for workers' control completely disappeared from the scene in the mid-1970s, without any achievement of a permanent kind in terms of class consciousness and institutional change. Factory occupations inspired by the idea of workers' control only lasted for a couple of years in 1970–2 in a 'revolutionary' atmosphere extended from the late 1960s. It was another marked failure of the New Left as a political movement, after it had failed to transform the early CND. This, however, is more than mere impotence of the New Left, for the vast majority of workers themselves were concerned more with wages than 'control'.[81]

The May Day Manifesto

The question of workers' control was taken up, among a whole range of current political issues, by the New Left *May Day Manifesto*:

> The need to gain control over the productive process and over real wealth is the same need as that for the extended care of people, in work, education and housing, or in old age, sickness and disability. It is the assertion of different priorities, against the internal and limited priorities of capitalism. Only when there is democratic control, over the whole process of production and investment, can a human distribution be steadily achieved. (Williams, *et al.*, 1968, p. 133)

This is a very general assertion. Although the *Manifesto* was not an abstract statement, it failed to investigate the way to get there, especially in terms of removing the obstacles. The same can be said about several other questions though by no means all of what it so ambitiously included in its wide range of discussions.

The May Day Manifesto Committee was formed, on the initiative of Williams, in August 1966, by those who had more or less lost touch with one another after the breakdown of the original New Left. The well-attended meetings of these people were 'like a regrouping again of the early New Left board' (Williams, 1979, p. 373). The first version of the *Manifesto* was almost written by Williams alone and printed in 1967.[82] The double-length second version, published as a Penguin paperback in 1968, was jointly edited by Williams, Thompson and Hall, with a large group of contributors, including a few younger New Leftists such as Michael Rustin,[83] Bob Rowthorn, Terry Eagleton and George Clark, whose various analyses presented a common perspective.

The *Manifesto* was designed to be itself an influential challenge and to evoke an effective resistance to the further rightward shift of the Labour Government. Its editors believed that it was 'the first connected and closely argued statement of socialist views' on the specific and changing conditions of Britain and the world of the 1960s (p. 10). However, the collaboratively written text reads as rather fragmented, uneven in quality, and occasionally incoherent in argument. A striking example is the unstated yet grave difference between Williams and Thompson, and people around each of them, over the importance of parliament for radical social change. While Thompson still anticipates a Labour-dominated House of Commons as the ultimate focus of the democratic process, Williams renounced that possibility on the factual ground that the Labour machine could not work on behalf of socialism (*Manifesto*, pp. 148–9; Williams, 1979, pp. 413–20). The nevertheless unitary programmme the *Manifesto* offered was therefore a compromise between more or less divided political analyses and strategic thinking within a generally New Left framework. As a direct intervention in the current trend of the Wilson administration, a large part of the document was devoted to the discussion of concrete social forces, organised or not, and the authors put first the necessity of unifying of theory and practice in a mass socialist movement.

The second *Manifesto* was launched in May 1968, the very moment of the May events in France. Although, as Williams recalled, he and others felt that 'this was a different manifestation of the same kind of movement' (1979, p. 375), it had little influence on the student demonstrations and other popular protests. Indeed it was simply overtaken by the latter which, in a very different way, hit the entire western world.

The effort in producing the *Manifesto* can be seen as a brief revival of the early New Left, in terms not so much of the background of its main participants as their intellectual emphasis ('We define socialism again as humanism'), political concern (the intention was 'to have not only theoretical but practical consequences') and actual politics (a National Convention, for example, was called to hold together divergent socialist organisations and to set up new local left groups for the broadest possible discussions and alliance) (*Manifesto*, pp. 11, 16). Williams, on behalf of the Manifesto Committee, declared that:

> What we are attempting is not a revival of 'the New Left', considered as some specific organisation which it has never really been, but a development of what we are content to call the New Left emphasis, which has continued throughout, in specific work, but which in the present crisis leads necessarily to a different kind of political manifestation. (p. 11)

Beyond the image of this manifestation, a 'revolution' erupted.

4. REVOLUTION IN PRACTICE

Pursuing a Cultural Revolution

The events of May 1968 and the subsequent revolutionary movements in advanced capitalist societies were on the whole unforeseen. In terms of actual history they combined student revolt with the civil rights struggle in the United States; with strikes and factory occupations in France, Germany and Italy; with protests against the Vietnam War everywhere. In Britain where the new political generation of the 1960s had failed to build a major movement of a scale and impact comparable to what had developed in North America or continental Europe, it was a very confused time for the veteran leftists, old and new alike. For the attempt to feed new currents of ideas, styles and politics into the labour movement was not merely ignored but actually repulsed (Williams, 1988, p. 177). At the same moment, inspired by the unexpected events, quite separate from the *May Day Manifesto* initiative, a group of young NLR editors ventured on a uniquely heroic undertaking, namely, to disestablish the whole architecture of 'English bourgeois culture'.

Radical students in Britain, like passionate rebels elsewhere, worshipped third world revolutionary models and heroes such as Che Guevara and Ho Chi Minh. Ideologically, they were influenced by the so-called 'new Left Thinkers' – Herbert Marcuse in the first instance, but also, to name but a few, C. Wright Mills, Jean-Paul Sartre, Louis Althusser, Mao Tse-Tung, Frantz Fanon and Regis Debray.[84] The only native guru was Dr R. D. Laing, a Scottish psychiatrist.

His work, in a way similar to that of Marcuse, was an inquiry into and critique of the spiritual exploration of alienation and sexuality, an area of far-reaching significance opened up by the New Left (see IV.2 and IV.5).[85]

The earlier thesis of the 'nihilism' of English culture twinned with impoverished intellectuals seemed now to be proved correct by new evidence: British society was the only major industrialised society which did not generate a competitive militant student movement, nor a vigorous and coherent theory for such a movement. The *NLR* editors' repeatedly stated task was to achieve the total critical foundation for a socialist ideology that was missing in their country, and to destroy the reformist nature of English social thought that helped maintain the ruling class hegemony. They attempted to do so primarily in two ways: introducing revolutionary theoretical trends developed elsewhere to the British audience; meanwhile going further to attack the general pattern of national culture. 'In intellectual approach', Stedman Jones recalled years later,

> *NLR* set its face against most indigenous traditions and styles of thought from linguistic philosophy to labour history and deliberately opened itself to heterodox theoretical currents in France, Italy and Germany, which it considered to have been submerged beneath the complacent assumptions of Anglo-Saxon empiricism and positively anathematised by the conservative imperatives of the Cold War. (Preface to the 1984 edn. of 1971b, p. xiii)

These new positions had found their first expression in Anderson's 'The Origins of the Present Crisis' (1964a), followed by a series of *NLR* articles. The British Left, they claimed, had never truly internationalised its outlook and thereby never questioned its indigenous inheritance before. Anderson's famous 1968 essay, 'Components of the National Culture', was a remarkable step forward in the latter direction.

The culture of British bourgeois society, Anderson reaffirms, is organised about an 'absent centre' – the absence of a total theory and an intellectual universe of itself, neither a classical sociology nor a native Marxism; neither a Weber, a Durkheim, a Pareto nor a Lenin, a Lukács, a Gramsci. While the 1950s and 1960s saw the proliferation of important Marxist schools on the continent – Althusser in France, Adorno in Germany and Della Volpe in Italy, England remained unaffected. Such is the essential characteristic of English culture, unique among the major western countries (1968a, pp. 218–25, 276). The trajectory of English social structure – the non-emergence of a powerful revolutionary movement of the working class in the first place – is an explanation or the 'secret' of this absence. Not only that society was never challenged as a whole from within, but also its culture as it exists is still a 'profound obstacle' and 'deeply damaging force' to any revolutionary politics. This point is contained within Anderson's and Nairn's original theme of bourgeois failure: the class which first accomplished the technological explosion of the Industrial Revolution never achieved a political or social revolution (1968a, 214–16, 225–8, 276–7).

Anderson claims a 'structural analysis' of the 'totalising' culture of which each discipline is a part. The English culture, he argues in an exaggerated manner, has actually been pushed along by the 'white emigration': philosophy by Wittgenstein (from Austria), political and social theory by Berlin (Latvia) and Popper (Austria), history by Namier (Poland), psychology by Eysenck (Germany), aesthetics by Gombrich (Austria) and anthropology by Malinowski (Poland). The established national culture naturally welcomed these essentially 'counter-revolutionary' allies, whereas the 'red' emigration found difficulty in settling here because of 'basic cultural and political incompatibility'. Isaac Deutscher, seen by Anderson and his NLR colleagues as 'the greatest Marxist historian in the world', was reviled and ignored by hostile British academia throughout his life (1968a, pp. 229–34, 276; 1966, pp. 22–3).

The only two areas that Anderson excludes from that foreign system of thought resident in Britain are economics and literary criticism. Keynes's international reputation lent British economics a peculiar status among its fellow disciplines, but for Anderson he had no successors and the discipline stagnated after him. Even here, Anderson points out that many of Keynes's ideas were first posed by Kalecki, a Pole; and the most influential economists were now Nicolas Kaldor, a Hungarian and Piero Sraffa who was from Italy (pp. 230, 250–1).[86] Literary criticism is thus actually the only natively generated sector and the only discipline in which the notion of totality finds a home. Williams, Anderson does not fail to appreciate, was able to develop a remarkably systematic socialist thought from within the literary critical tradition; and that tradition has insights which parallel some of the philosophical bases of Marxism. Yet that tradition as a coherent and far-reaching critique of capitalism, as a hotbed of magnificent trends of truly radical social thinking with their bearers, is not fully recognised. As it is so often 'irremediably divorced from the realities of economic structure and political conflict', for Anderson literary criticism in general rarely encountered the question of class struggle and social revolution, and hence remained politically naive or could even be reactionary (1964a, p. 36). Leavis's unwillingness to develop a theoretical framework for his extraordinarily fine local criticisms mirrors the very ethos of English thinking. His paradox is his empiricism which rests on a metaphysic that he could neither expound nor defend. Here Anderson's idea of unique 'refuge' in a culture which in his view everywhere represses the ideas of totality and critical reason (1964a, pp. 11, 36; 1966, p. 23; 1968a, pp. 268–76) needs some qualification again.

The national culture that sustains empiricism and conservatism 'instinctively', Anderson concludes, is simply composed of empirical, piecemeal, incoherent intellectual disciplines:

> Philosophy was restricted to a technical inventory of language. Political theory was thereby cut off from history. History was divorced from the exploration of political ideas. Psychology was counterposed to them. Economics was dissociated from both political theory and history. Aesthetics was reduced to psychology. The congruence of each sector with its

neighbour is circular: together they form something like a closed system. (1968a, pp. 233, 276)
This sounds like a dead end.

Anderson also explains this terrible situation in terms of, tautologically, intellectual default, based on an idealised image of the intellectuals. His constant thesis is that modern English society has never given birth to an intelligentsia of the kind that has marked other European countries. He writes elsewhere that the majority of the three types of British intelligentsia – a traditional literary one, a newer technical one and an even newer social science one – all 'have a fundamentally conservative outlook' (1965b, pp. 269–71).[87] Marxist and socialist intellectuals (at least he praises, for example, Christopher Hill's 'serious, scientific intellectual achievement' and Williams's 'systematic critique of "all forms of utilitarianism and Fabianism – the political avatars of empiricism in the Labour movement" '; see 1968a, pp. 278, 275–6) seem to be too weak or marginal to alter anything that is characteristic about this peculiar intelligentsia and peculiar national culture.

Anderson's all-round dismissal together with an arrogant tone was irritating to many people for good or not so good reasons. Typically, Roger Scruton, a New Rightist (of the Oxbridge Salisbury Group formed later in 1977), argues that if a healthy culture can be guaranteed only by a 'total theory of itself', the owl of Minerva has begun flapping in the dawn (and, 'why should our "totalising theory" be Marxism?'). He questions what the 'white emigration' has in common and accuses Anderson, fairly, of his 'careless identification of the enemy' (1985, pp. 134–5). He is quite right here to attack left sectarianism. To give an example at hand, Isaiah Berlin, a 'white' émigré whom Anderson made a sloppy target in his general attack, in fact held not only exactly the same ideas about the parochialism of English culture as Anderson did, but also an almost identical view as his on stagnant English society:

> The issues which shook the Continent took many years to cross the English Channel, and when they did, did so in some new and peculiar shape, transformed and anglicised in the process of transition. ... the immense stability which the capitalist regime appeared to possess in England, the complete absence of any symptom of revolution at times tended to induce a sense of hopeless stagnation.... (1963, pp. 180–1)

Needless to note that these words, among similar remarks made by a number of others, were written earlier than Anderson's project, though the latter developed the idea much further in an indisputably novel direction.

Engaging in the same *NLR* enterprise, Blackburn attempts to identify the prevailing ideology in the social sciences as taught in British universities and colleges. Post-classical bourgeois social theory, for him, has fallen into confusion and sterility: it consistently defends the existing capitalist arrangements, and mystifies social consciousness by either imbuing it with fatalism or blunting any critical impulse. He recalls 'the revolutionary kernel' of Hegel's dialectic, the vocation to change the world, which is so much lacking in the established cultural formation, reformation and transmission in Britain. However, he suggests that one should not fail to see, no matter how ingrained the bourgeois ideology is, the advance of modern classics of Marxism – for him the works of Lenin, Lukács and Gramsci, as well as Mao and Che, Althusser and Balibar – that have emerged from the most diverse surroundings (1969, pp. 163–4, 211–13).

Before Anderson's and Blackburn's assault, Stedman Jones published his critique in *NLR* of a single discipline, English historiography. The most striking thing he had to say was that British historians had largely remained impervious to the solutions put forward by Marxism, psychoanalysis and classical sociology, and never thoroughly questioned their inherited positivist research method. This positivism was reinforced by an uncritical acceptance of the basic tenets of 19th-century English liberalism, the optimistic assumptions implicit in the idea of progress but also the dilemma of moralism without progress. Between the 1890s and the 1920s, Europe experienced an intellectual revolution in the human sciences (Freud, Weber, Durkheim, Pareto, Croce, Simmel, Dilthey and Sorel are significant figures for the study of history) which indicated a decisive rejection of the simplistic assumptions of positivist methodology, but England was virtually unaffected by it. In Stedman Jones's explanation, the main reason for this contrast lies in the fact that Marxism, a complete antithesis of the liberal positivist framework, had a momentous impact upon the entire intellectual generation in Europe but not in England. While utilitarianism and positivism were there challenged differently by Marxism as well as by European irrational-ism and romantic conservatism (from such a 'philosophical maelstrom' modern sociology emerged), the liberal-individualist tradition was sustained by reformist British intellectuals. Tawney, who represented the romantic anti-capitalist tradi-tion, and Namier – the reactionary anti-liberal tradition – were the first to be seriously influenced by the European intellectual revolution, yet both lacked a theoretical framework or conceptual system that armed typical continental thinkers (1967, pp. 29, 32–5, 40–2).

What happened in the discipline of history as portrayed by Stedman Jones is just what happened to the national culture as a whole as portrayed by Anderson. It is a history without centre: to political history is added each branch of history; no attempt has been made to fuse this aggregate of specialist routines into a meaningful totality. Even Marxist and left-wing scholars are unable to demolish fragmentation and empiricism in their own work. British historians, with very few exceptions, 'have never aimed to construct historical totalities' and never 'reached the promised land of theory' (*ibid.*, pp. 36–41).[88] In a brief review of E. H. Carr's *What is History?*,[89] Stedman Jones, obviously inspired by Althusser and the French *Annales* historians (who were associated with the journal *Annales* and its editor Fernand Braudel (1957–68); cf. Stuart Clark, 1985), asserts that

> it was only theory that could constitute them [facts] as facts in the first place. Similarly ... events are only meaningful in terms of a structure which will establish them as such. In effect history is theory, and cannot logically be otherwise. It is the formulation of theoretical concepts with which to

> construct history that determines the greatness of the historian. ... In a
> minimal sense at least, all great history is structural history. In England,
> this has never been acknowledged. (1967, pp. 42–3)

A revolution in historiography, for Stedman Jones, cannot be achieved unless
socialist historians in Britain engage themselves in theorising and totalising, with
support from their own institutions, journals, and debates (p. 43).

Another discipline, anthropology, occupied together with history a prominent
place in the culture of British imperialism. David Goddard attacked British
anthropologists who for the most part, according to his unduly negative
assessment, avoided questioning the foundations and ideology of imperialism.
They chose to see the peoples who became victims during the process of
colonisation in a 'primitive' setting, and failed to articulate a total and structural
conception of the colonial situation. But anthropology only exemplifies British
social thought at large which, he maintains, has never placed itself in relation to
its society 'as a total historical phenomenon requiring critical structural explanation' (1969, pp. 79–80).[90]

Anderson and his NLR colleagues were the vanguard of British intellectuals in
breaking from their national boundary. They were not only well informed about
the international development of contemporary social sciences, but also consciously advocated a cultural revolution in Britain. The admirable uncompromising critical mentality of these cultural revolutionaries worked side by side with an
ahistorical or prejudged bias, which marked their weakness as well as brilliance.
Writing more soberly some twenty years after that youthful offence, Anderson
admitted, probably not only reflecting his own reconsideration, that the earlier
attempt had many failings.

> Written at a time of rebellion, in a spirit of *outrance*, it mounted a
> peremptory broadside on its chosen target. The price of this general
> excoriation was paid in a variety of local simplifications or misjudgements.
> Overstatement in critique was also accompanied by over-confidence of cure
> – a theoretical triumphalism that was no service to the radical alternatives
> advocated. (1990, NLR 180, p. 41)

Besides, he also saw a broad methodological problem there. First, how could such
a wide diversity of subjects be brought into a single focus? Second, why was it a
set of academic specialisms, rather than 'major popular manifestations of the
national culture', that was made the unfortunate dominant pattern of social
thought (*ibid.*, pp. 41–2)?[91] In any case, a new culture cannot be built from a sheer
denial of any positive elements for grounding the depth and strength of a national
tradition. The NLR intellectual revolution was therefore, to use Marcuse's words
in referring to the anti-aesthetic and anti-classicist arts, 'without soil and basis in
society', and appeared indeed 'as the abstract negation rather than the historical
heir of bourgeois culture' (1972a, p. 93).

Defined in a very different direction, 'cultural revolution' was also a central
concern of some former ULR editors, including Williams, Hall and Taylor, who
gathered at the Slant Symposium (the journal *Slant* was produced by the Catholic

Left) in 1967 to develop ideas of a common culture, Christian socialism, and the culture/politics synthesis. The proceedings of the symposium, edited by Terry. Eagleton and Brian Wicker, were published in a volume entitled *From Culture to Revolution* (1968). Eagleton, a student of and later a prominent Marxist critic of Williams, expressed the general perspective of these ideas as a 'socialist cultural revolution', for the socialist revolutionary is now confronted with a total system, so pervasive and deep-rooted in our culture. His toughness of criticism and readiness for rebellion must therefore combine with 'a richly flexible and resourceful humanism' in order to challenge at root the old social formation (1968, p. 2). This must be therefore a cultural revolution with a definable socialist content: it relates a radical analysis of the existing society to a practical drive to transform that society's institution into the means of human liberation.

The key point here, stressed by Williams, is to achieve democratic control over the process of 'the creation of meanings and values' as a necessary condition for the human community's self-realisation. Since one would not be fully qualified to participate in this process unless the education which provides its immediate tools were made commonly available, 'a common culture is an educated and participating democracy' (1968a, p. 308; 1968c, pp. 34–7). He did not develop a discussion, however, of the connection between community and communications, of the dilemma of education itself that at once provides the means of access to and critique of a culture, and imposes the established rules and values. But it is already significant to highlight the struggle over the creation of public meanings as the detailed practice of revolution and counter-revolution. It was in this sense that Williams and Hall claimed that the problem of a common culture was itself the problem of revolutionary politics (Williams, 1968a; Hall, 1968b). Taylor's critical interpretation of the common culture thesis concerned a dialogue between Christians and non-Christians on the left (1968; see IV.2).

All of these discussions, of course, require a politically conscious readership. The object a cultural revolution confronts itself with is the systematic political-ideological power and such a revolution is therefore very difficult to achieve; especially when it is divorced from the economic struggle of the organised working class, and from other kinds of emancipatory struggle.

Student Power

The student movement, as an international phenomenon, arose in Berkeley, rapidly spread to the rest of California, to New York, Boston, Madison; to Berlin, Strasbourg, London, Paris, Turin, Rome, Brussels, Tokyo, Mexico City and many other places, pounding at the world system of capitalism.

In Britain,[92] student direct actions (sit-ins, occupations, strikes) took place most notably at the London School of Economics and at Essex, Hornsey, Hull and Birmingham. There was no linked development of these actions and workers' control. 'Student power' was simply separated from the workers' movements of the time (the seamen's, motor workers' and dockers' strikes and protest campaigns) and from larger Left activities in opposition to the Wilson government.

94 THE BRITISH NEW LEFT

Another major factor was that militant students were also organised and influenced by the far-left groupings whose 'Leninist' tradition was rather old left in character. The Trotskyite revival in British politics in the late 1960s was an outstanding phenomenon. It owed a great deal to the Vietnam Solidarity Campaign (VSC), around which scattered Trotskyites emerged from their isolation and began to work in a united front. However, it is important to acknowledge that the International Socialists (IS) and the International Marxist Group (IMG), the two principal organisations representing this revival, were on the stage as a consequence of an ideological break with orthodox Trotskyism.[93] This neo-Trotskyism had much in common with the NLR position though it would be a mistake not to distinguish between the two with regard to both historical background and intellectual emphasis.[94]

Moreover, the rather peculiar development of the British New Left movement was above all shown in the following divergent aspects: many activists of the 1968 generation did not know much about the already existing indigenous New Left and were not previously involved in it. On the other hand, a number of the leading original New Leftists did not actively participate in the events of 1968–70. In other words, in Britain, the New Left and student radicalism must be to a great extent analysed in separate terms. People like Thompson kept a respectable distance from the movement which, for him, did not belong to a serious and deeply rooted, rational revolutionary tradition.[95] Others like Worsley, who were by now university professors or senior lecturers and thus themselves part of the privileged in that educational hierarchy, were in a somewhat difficult position. Such an ambiguous attitude toward the students, paradoxical in relation to their own general standpoint in supporting anti-imperialist movements and struggles for the democratisation of cultural institutions, made these veteran and 'rational' socialists embarrassed or passive. These factors, however, should by no means overshadow the other side of the story: there were older New Left people such as Saville, Miliband and Hall who did stand firmly for a pro-student politics.[96]

It is clear that there was no economic crisis to provoke a revolution. On the contrary, the post-war boom lasted through the 1950s and 1960s.[97] The student revolt can only be interpreted by structural analysis of its sociological, political, cultural and psychological contexts. Two overriding direct causes that gave birth to the series of events were the war in Vietnam and the conditions in higher education at home. The Vietnam Solidarity Campaign was the most important political mobilisation of the left in the 1960s in Britain, which inherited much from, but also represented an advance over, the tradition of CND. For it called, as Anderson put it, 'not for peace but for victory, not for neutralism but for socialism in Vietnam' (1980, p. 152; he referred to Vietnam, but Vietnam was only a symbol). Admiration for the Vietnamese (and the Cubans, the Algerians, the Yemenis, etc.) and sympathy for the third world led to broad criticisms of global social relations which were exploitative and repressive. Likewise, revolt against the existing educational system became, by logical extension, revolt against the social system and its ideology which continually produced the poor, the neglected and the oppressed. It was here that the 'New Left', as a general term accepted internationally, makes sense – a loose amalgam of student rebels, war protesters, civil rights activists (especially 'Black Power' and 'Free Speech' in the USA), new industrial militants, and intellectual dissenters.

The New Left analysis of the student movement had to examine what had happened in higher education since the post-war settlement:

(1) a rapid increase in the number of students because developed capitalism required not only a traditional elite but also a large, well-trained intellectual labour force through mass expansion of universities;[98]

(2) a worsening of the immediate conditions in academic institutions – contents of curriculum and methods of teaching, inequality between students and staff, authoritarian control over the learning process and bureaucratic administration;[99]

(3) continued discrimination against working-class children and women;[100]

(4) a radicalisation of students, due to the rise of the third world and the changing structure of international conflicts, from the political passivity related to the Cold War experience.[101]

Beyond higher education, the larger area of communications is closely relevant. Control of both the educational system and the means of communication is, according to the New Left critics, crucial for capitalist power under which all revolutionary and new ideas are stifled.[102] As students protested against their intellectual manipulation and demanded a democratisation of cultural institutions, they were ultimately to demand a fundamental social change. Moreover, it is no accident that after a long period of what Marcuse called repressive tolerance, they were tempted to revolutionary methods.[103]

The strategic ideas provided by and debated among the second generation of the British New Left for the student revolt are about the meaning of student power itself and the 'Red Base' theory.[104] The movement for student power, in its best sense, was a natural descendant of the tradition of workers' councils which embodied the basic principle of democracy. Democracy 'will only be concrete and authentic when it is extended to all the institutions of society – economic, political and cultural' (Stedman Jones, 1969b, p. 52). Inspired by Regis Debray and the successful examples of guerrilla warfare, Blackburn and Cockburn[105] advocated 'Red Bases' on campuses. They were possible because education is a comparatively weak link in the capitalist chain and necessary because they could serve revolutionary agitation and preparation. From such bases, they believed, student revolutionaries (joining force with workers and others) would undermine other key institutions of the existing social order.[106] The background promise of the 'Red Base' strategy was that traditionally the left had the idea of becoming a government through winning an election (or a civil war) and then changing everything at once. For the New Left, however, before the advent of a socialist government, socialists would have to find a place (in educational institutions or in regional governments) where an anti-capitalist struggle could be waged and socialist relations can be prefigured.[107] Neither Blackburn nor Cockburn rejected the classical notion of the proletariat as the major and leading agency of change, but the implication of their 'Red Base' theory seems to contain something of the opposite.

The question concerning the role of the students who were actually revolting against the system without a powerful working class involvement requires a definition of the social identity of students and, by the same token, of the larger circle of intellectuals as a whole. Not themselves constituting a class, students were nevertheless believed to have remapped the relations of capitalist production. Mandel's idea of the 'proletarianisation of intellectual labour' (1969, pp. 47–53; 1971, pp. 37–8) was then influential, so were the ideas of Mao about intellectual vanguards and Gramsci on the 'organic intellectuals'.[108] According to Stedman Jones, there had emerged a permanent contradiction within the universities between the capitalist need for a mass of intellectual workers and the inevitable growth of the critical potential of this mass. Thus, students can play a vanguard role at certain specific historical moments when the most explosive contradiction of capitalism resides in the university and the proletariat is temporarily passive. But he insists that while the industrial proletariat has no monopoly of socialist potential, it remains 'the revolutionary class' alone, capable of freeing itself and all others from the old world (1969b, pp. 26–30, 32, 35, 52–3).

In a similar spirit, Fred Halliday[109] maintained that the militant student movement would only succeed in revolutionary objectives where it allied itself with the major exploited classes of society (1969, pp. 323–4). Even Nairn, who in a timely study of the French May spoke of the validity of the self-definition of students as workers, would not renounce the crucial importance of the traditional working class in a meaningful revolution (1968, p. 123). NLR carefully placed students only in a 'general revolutionary alliance' in which they could play 'a key role' (NLR 50, 'Themes').[110]

A remarkable comparison can be made here between the young British New Leftists (not to mention the older faithful working-class defenders like Williams or Miliband) and the internationally most prominent New Left thinkers. Mills, for example, denied any revolutionary potential of the western working class because he saw it as having been integrated into the structure of the bourgeois state. He identified the young intelligentsia as a 'new historical agency of change' (1960, pp. 18–23; cf. 1963, p. 232). Fanon's 'the wretched' were composed of the 'key classes' supporting the revolution: the impoverished peasantry and the sub-proletariat.[111] Marcuse wrote that when the working class was absorbed by the system and politically passive, revolutionary forces would be:

(1) 'the substratum of the outcasts and outsiders, the exploited and persecuted of other races and other colours, the unemployed and the unemployable';

(2) students ('these alleged infantile radicals are... the weak and confused but true historical heirs of the great socialist tradition');

(3) peoples of the economically and technologically backward countries (1964, pp. 256–7; 1970a, 1970b, p. 473).

Such a mixed new proletariat, in the mainstream (non-British) New Left thinking, could perform the historical mission of the socialist revolution which the industrial working class in the west seemed to have abandoned. Not without doubt or reservations, most of the NLR group, however, preserved the classical Marxist confidence in the workers' role given in a long-term perspective.

Hall did raise the question as to who might be 'the carriers of a potential revolutionary consciousness', referring to the forces resisting the system from without, that is, those whom that system systematically excluded and dispossessed. The gap between reformist formal left organisations and the fluid form of revolutionary consciousness struck him; but he did not confront himself directly with the question of the political assessment of the working class (1968b, pp. 217–18). The most impressive revisionism in this regard that had been ever made within the British left was by Kiernan, and his is still less 'radical' than the typical New Left line of either Mills or Marcuse. Kiernan distinguished himself from many others of his own Marxist generation by his insightful solidarity with the 'Sixty-Eighters'. Considering whether the intelligentsia could be thought of as an alternative force to workers to bring about revolutionary change in advanced capitalist societies, he argued that surely intellectuals were always divided[112] and class struggles necessary, but in the light of the new historical experience,

> no single class or social force can be expected to drag us out of the rut, though one or other may take the lead for the time being. There is no chosen class, any more than a chosen people. ... the working class remains indispensable to any thorough-going social change, though it can no longer be expected to make one by itself. Something similar can be said of the intelligentsia. (1969, pp. 68, 76–7, 83)

It was therefore a reasonable expectation for him that the world student movement might lead the way toward 'the reborn humanist socialism'.

Another focus of the discussion was the social-political category of the young, since the New Left had to a great extent become a youth movement.[113] Obviously the identity of a student combines the more extensively defined terms of 'youth' and 'intellectual'. Serious attention was naturally also paid to the analysis of 'young people as a class' or 'classless youth',[114] in the context of the growing gap between generations highlighted by the student revolt, and by a moral and aesthetic upheaval which was transforming the lifestyle of the young and which profoundly underlay their political movement and commitment. The appeal to 'counter-culture' or 'anti-culture' – a form of political protest which brought young people into conflict with the dominant ideologies and agencies of power – radically renewed the New Left tradition of cultural debate.[115] Hall's study of the youth minorities and youth sub-cultures and their genesis within the class structure and social consciousness in England (and American hippies as well) made a notable contribution to the debate, in which he pursued the political meaning of cultural rebellion (1968a; 1969; Hall and Whannel, 1964). Williams was to write in 1975 that the 1960s 'can now be seen as the decade of pop culture' that gave birth to a new generation, a new culture and a new consciousness, a change that was one of the major gains of the student movement (see 'Retrospect and Prospect', 1975 edn. of 1962, pp. 183–6). The conclusion, for Kiernan, has to be that a working class is only likely to attempt a revolution in its developmental phase. It may be equally true that a bourgeoisie can only make a revolution when it is young and romantic. 'When history is making a daring leap it does not find its agents among the solid men in the ruck of any class, but among skirmishers on the flanks' – young people, adventurers, idealists, women, intellectuals (1968, pp. 198, 200; 1969, pp. 77, 81–2).[116]

The 'agency problematic' in general and the question of limits and possibilities of student struggle in particular were posed to the New Left in very sharp terms, both theoretically and practically: discussions around these points were also a self-reflecting and self-examining process of the New Left. Their urgent need for such a process hardly requires explanation.

It was soon realised that however profound a crisis in the democratic values of western societies it revealed and provoked, '1968' was unworthy of comparison with any real revolutions, those which transformed a social-economic system or a cultural establishment. But quite opposite judgements among the left ranged at the time from warnings against 'left fascism' to celebrating a revolution of a 'classical type'. Once everything had become quiet again, the past storm was virtually neglected. Former student militants easily turned around and criticised themselves for their blind activism, utopianism, anarchism, ultra-leftism, infanti-lism, 'super' revolutionary style, and so on. Yet beside all these defeats and defects, 1968 was a historical landmark of the first mass resistance to post-industrial capitalism. For those participants who retained their conviction thereafter, it was a beginning and not an end.[117] The next revolution, in Lukács's or Marcuse's perspective, 'will be the concern of generations', because 'we are now at the very beginning of a crisis in capitalist society' and this final crisis may take a century (Marcuse, 1972a, p. 134; Lukács, 1970, pp. 44–5).

So, how to sum up that unprecedented 'red decade', foreseen by nobody, in modern history? What has survived from or been solidly accomplished by it? What were the major opportunities at the time and why were they taken or lost? What lessons can be learned from the history of the student movement, in terms of the particular features of the British state (the confrontation with the state and the revolt were fierce but without major violence), the political potential of young intellectuals (being at the lowest level of the hierarchy of the higher educational system, students nevertheless made up a small and privileged portion of the population), the structure of persistent conservative consensus (the existing order was less disturbed in Britain than in other major advanced capitalist countries), the complexity of possible future changes of society ('1968', exciting as it was, remains in many respects a historical myth), and so on? Research in this area has been poor and sparse.

The dynamic 1960s promoted a fresh force of emancipatory and democratic utopianism for the next decade. The 1970s saw the growth of a new socialist generation in both the labour movement and academic circles, the initiative of new social movements and the development of community politics,[118] a reluctant yet steady democratisation of the university system (student participation, curricular reforms, etc.),[119] a general radicalisation of British intellectual life, and a remarkable flourish of Marxist scholarship. [120]

NOTES

1. Miliband was of the opinion that the merging of *ULR* and *NR* was not a natural development and led to difficulties in the existence of *NLR* (1979, pp. 26–7). See Birnbaum's similar comment quoted in Young, 1977, p. 146 and Williams's recollection in 1979, p. 365. Hall recalled that many senior figures of the large editorial board who did not live in London worked little and criticised much. 'Looking back', he told this author, 'if you ask me my honest opinion, I would say I prefer *ULR* to *NLR*' (interview, 9 June 1987). People like Saville also admitted that it was a 'sort of mistake' to merge the two original journals.
2. The new team was made up of Samuel, Jones, Pearson, Butt and Anderson. The new Board Chairman was Thompson who took it over from Saville.
3. The *New University*, started in 1960, was 'a challenging and effective voice of what can roughly ... be called "New Left" student opinion in Oxford' (Hall, 1961a, p. 51). Its editorial group includes O. Williams (editor), Robin Blackburn (later, editor), Michael Rustin, Gareth Stedman Jones, Bob Rowthorn, Alan Shuttleworth and more than twenty others.
4. The new editorial committee consisted of Blackburn, Tom Nairn and Pearson. Later during 1962–3, Roger Murray, Rustin, Shuttleworth, Tom Wengraf and Juliet Mitchell joined in. By the end of 1965, there were more new members including Ronald Fraser, Quintin Hoare, Lucien Rey, Martin Rossdale, Stedman Jones and Orlando Patterson. According to Williams, there were for a brief moment grave conflicts between new and old editors. He chose a 'survival strategy', trying to quiet the arguments to save the journal (1979, pp. 365–6). But Hall said that there wasn't any disagreement (interview, *ibid.*). Thompson felt much more bitterness than most others (cf. 1978a, pp. 311–15). The typical attitudes of the old editorial members was 'Let them get on with it'. For more details, see Widgery, 1976, pp. 134–5, 144–5; Young, 1977, pp. 147, 436; Anderson, 1980, pp. 136–7.
5. Tom Nairn, born in 1938 in Freuchie, Scotland, educated at Edinburgh and Oxford, then taught social science and philosophy at the University of Birmingham and lectured in sociology at Hornsey College of Art until being expelled in 1968 for supporting the rebellious students; a member of *NLR* editorial board since 1962.
6. For Anderson, all these charges were untrue or wrong (1980, pp. 132, 135).
7. See the similar formulation of this contrast by Anderson, 1980, p. 206; Thompson, 1976b, pp. 16–17; Williams, 1965, p. 26.
8. Sheila Rowbotham: 'I could not understand how they could be socialists and not bother about being personally remote from working-class people. This made them very different from the initiators of the New Left' (1979a, p. 26).
9. They both returned to the concept of 'experience' with much more sophisticated reflections. See especially, Williams, 1979, pp. 163–73; Thompson, 1978a, pp. 170–1.
10. See Eagleton's critique, 1976b, pp. 12–16; Anderson's analysis, 1968a, pp. 268–76; and Mulhern's balanced study, 1979. About the confrontation of Leavis with the Marxism of the 1930s, see Baldick, 1983, chapter 7; Mulhern, 1979, pp. 63–72.
11. In Eagleton's sharp but exaggerated assessment, Williams's 'idealist epistemology', 'organicist aesthetics' and 'corporatist sociology' went logically together and the root of all three was a form of 'romantic populism'. Placing the matter within a wider intellectual context, Williams's 'mistaking of scientificity for positivism' linked him 'not only with some of the most myopic aspects of the *Scrutiny*, but also with the Romantic "anti-scientism" of Lukács and the Frankfurt school' (1976b, p. 27, 32).
12. It is worth noting that a cultural elitism can be also found in the Bloomsbury group,

another Cambridge rooted tradition of liberal humanism that was a dominant literary influence in the 1920s. But *Scrutiny* was in fact quite hostile to High Bloomsbury and very critical of the 'Etonian values' of the traditional privileged intelligentsia. See Branson and Heinemann, 1971, 265–6; Williams, 1980b.

13. Williams: 'the biggest mistake made was not the overestimate of the possibilities of an alternative movement from '58 to '61, but the resigned reacceptance of conventional politics which followed from '62 to '64' (1979, pp. 366–7).

14. 'We failed', he added, 'to implement our original purposes, or even to sustain what cultural apparatus we had' (*Peace News*, 29 Nov. 1963).

15. He was right to add that *SR* 'has not included all the tendencies which co-existed fruitfully in the older movement' (1973, p. 312). A warm review of the first volume of *SR* appeared in *NLR*, saying that it was 'an event in socialist publishing in Britain of great importance' (*NLR* 26, p. 90).

16. Saville acknowledged that *NLR* had become 'a very interesting and useful journal' since the 1970s, and was indeed more influential than *SR* edited by Miliband and himself (interview, 19 October 1987). Miliband had been closer to the new *NLR* circle than anyone else with a *NR* background, partly because of his friendship with Deutscher, the main contemporary hero of the young 'hard-line' Marxist New Leftists.

17. See F. K. Donnelly, 1976. It was debated whether *The Making of the English Working Class* represented a break with Dobb and the communist historians' tradition, see Richard Johnson, 1978, pp. 79–82; McClelland's comment in 1979, pp. 104–5; Kaye, 1984, pp. 20–2, 182–3, 220.

18. For the 'standard of living' debate, see Sutton's and McLennan's comments in Johnson *et al.*, 1982, pp. 41–2, 109. Thompson defended a 'classical' view and the contribution of the Hammonds to it that industrialisation was carried through with exceptional violence in Britain (1963a, pp. 194–9; 1968 edn. pp. 445–6).

19. For Thompson's view on the transformation of class consciousness since the eighteenth century, see also 1974; 1978c.

20. 'I hope with increasing theoretical consciousness – this remains a central preoccupation of my historical and political writing' (1976b, p. 21).

21. See 1963a, especially chapters 7, 8, 9. Thompson seems to deal inadequately with production relations and their connection with political and cultural activity – according to McClelland's critique, by treating those relations, at times, as 'over-objective' or 'passive' (1979b, pp. 111–12).

22. In fact 'working people' rather than 'working class' was used to avoid terminological confusion, since before this fixing, there would not exist a working class in the full sense. See 1960b and 1960c.

23. See, for example, Anderson, 1980, pp. 30–49; Richard Johnson, 1978. For discussions of these criticisms, see Donnelly, 1976 and E. M. Wood, 1982, pp. 45–75. See also Kaye's sympathetic review in 1984, pp. 168, 172–208; Palmer's defence of Thompson in 1981, pp. 12–14, 110–14, 165–82.

24. Here he shares G. A. Cohen's 'standard' Marxist concept of class. See Cohen, 1978, pp. 73–7.

25. Taylor's book on nineteenth-century socialism and feminism, *Eve and the New Jerusalem* (1983), can be seen as an important supplement to *The Making of the English Working Class*. See, especially, pp. 261–87.

26. It was not until the late 1970s that the conventional Marxist proposition of one-to-one correspondence between class position/interests and beliefs/ideology or between the economic situation and political attitudes of a class was theoretically challenged. See especially Jon Elster, 1982, pp. 123–48; Stedman Jones, Introduction to 1983; 1984b. See also Ellen Wood's systematic critique of the trend of 'retreat from class', 1986.

27. Anderson held that the English working class was not 'made' by the 1830s simply because, in the social logical sense, it was still far from being predominantly a labour-force operating genuinely industrial means of production (1980, p. 45).

28. Gareth Stedman Jones, born in London in 1942, educated at St Paul's School and then Lincoln College, Oxford. Currently a Fellow of King's College and Professor

in Modern History at Cambridge University. Member of *NLR* editorial committee between 1965 and 1983; with Raphael Samuel, among others, editing *History Workshop Journal* since 1976.

29. Thompson commented that it was 'a brilliant article ... [which] does very significantly modify some of the received wisdom that most of us offered as theory ten years or more ago' (1976b, p. 16). See Stedman Jones, 1983, in which the themes of the previous article were newly approached, pp. 7–12, 17–22.

30. Royden Harrison, a Marxist historian, was a member of the CP Historians' Group and later the *NR* circle; frequent contributor to *NLR* and *SR*, taught economic history at the Department of Extramural Studies, Sheffield University, Professor of Social History at Warwick University, the Editor of the *Bulletin* of the Society for the Study of Labour History, 1960–82.

31. This crisis was described elsewhere by Anderson as 'the great crisis of conservative Britain, which exploded in depth in 1961, supervened a few months after the left had collapsed, demobilised and exhausted' (1965a, p. 18). It was a 'prolonged crisis' which, he re-indicated years later, 'we have been living ever since' (1980, p. 148).

32. See Anderson, 1980, pp. 139–40; Thompson, 1978a, pp. 403–4.

33. It began with Anderson's large-scale historical analysis entitled 'The Origins of the Present Crisis' (1964a), which was followed by a series of *NLR* articles concerning 'fundamental recasting of our thought about British society and British socialism', including Nairn's 'The British Political Elite' (1964c), 'The English Working Class' (1964b), 'Anatomy of the Labour Party' (1964a), and Anderson's 'Critique of Wilsonism' (1964b). Thompson presented his comprehensive objections to Anderson and Nairn in 'The Peculiarities of the English' (1965), to which Anderson replied in 'Socialism and Pseudo-empiricism' (1966). The issue of *NLR* that printed Anderson's rejoinder carried bold headlines on its cover: 'Storm over the Left'.

34. See M. J. Wiener: in Britain, 'industrialisation was indigenous, and thus more easily accommodated to existing social structures, which did not need to change radically' (1981, p. 7).

35. See among relevant literature, Anderson's restatement of his and Nairn's proposition on this question, 1987; Barratt Brown's critical response to both Anderson's historical account and conceptual framework, 1988; Geoffery Ingham's rejoinder to Barratt Brown, 1988.

36. This idea followed from Dobb's position that capitalism must have developed through an internal dynamic of class society. See George Comninel, 1987, p. 183.

37. See Wiener's analysis in support of the Anderson/Nairn argument: Britain never had 'a straightforwardly bourgeois or industrial elite' (1981, pp. 8, 97, 127ff).

38. See Anderson's comment on A. J. Mayer, *The Persistence of the Old Regime* (1981), 1988; Alex Callinicos's critique, 1990, pp. 40–44.

39. See Thompson, 1965, pp. 319–28. See Hobsbawm on the actual use of 'mechanism of aristocracy' by the bourgeoisie in the age of the British empire, 1987, pp. 168, 176–7.

40. Anderson mentioned the 'disastrous effect' of Social Darwinism on Marxism in passing; see 1966, pp. 21, 40.

41. See Marx: 'free thought ... was brought to France from no other country than England. Locke was its father' (1850, p. 344). Anderson did mention 'liberalism' and its spokesman, Mill, once in 1964a, p. 33. The excuse he made for their radical dismissal of the bourgeois legacy was that he and Nairn confined themselves to discussing nineteenth-century political theories (cf. 1966, p. 40).

42. For Anderson's causal analysis of this failure, see 1964a, pp. 35–6. He developed the thesis in his seminal essay, 1968a. See Thompson's response in 1965, p. 342.

43. Compare this with his earlier critique of a 'hotch-potch' consciousness of the pragmatist British Labour movement which 'tends to accept, or half-accept, a framework of capitalist ideas but to fight hard for certain principles and interests within it' (1957c, p. 140).

44. Nairn's long account (25,000 words) of the Labour Party leaves no room for communism. This is almost the case with Anderson's essays.

45. See Hobsbawm: 'the CP never acquired a significant electorate, local or in national

politics, once its links with the LP were cut. On the other hand, the CP played an absolutely central role as the inheritor of the industrial (TU) left, and, in the 1930s and 1940s, as virtually the only school for young union activists and cadres. Consequently it was never a 'sect' in spite of its small size, but – unlike most other small parties – it played a role of major significance in the British [trade union] movement from the 1930s till the 1970s' (letter to the author dated 3 May 1987). On the other hand, there is a comparison between Thompson's new evaluation (1965) and his and Saville's earlier remarks on 'the weakness of Marxist tradition', 'the shallow growth of Marxist scholarship' and 'the failure of Marxism as a body of ideas' in England (*NR* 1, 1957).

46. Later Anderson himself got interested in the CP history in an international framework, (see 1981).

47. Ignoring British Marxists, Anderson asked: 'Who would deny that the only Marxist intellectual of world eminence in Britain today is Isaac Deutscher, who was born near Cracow' (1966, p. 23)? The fact of Thompson's 'lack of grasp of the subject of Marxism' (his ignorance of Gramsci, for example) itself demonstrates how weak a Marxism is presented even among distinguished Marxist historians (pp. 34–5, 39–40).

48. See Williams: Marxism failed because it was represented as a direct denial of the mainstream of the moral tradition of the British working-class movement (1965, p. 24).

49. See Anderson, 1980, pp. 138–9, 158. He made some minor revisions of his total dismissal after Thompson published his *The Poverty of Theory* in 1978.

50. See Stedman Jones's review, 1965, pp. 105–8.

51. Thompson later applied this notion willingly and powerfully to his analysis of eighteenth-century English radicalism, concluding that the ruling order was then located primarily in a cultural hegemony (1974).

52. See McLennan, 1982, pp. 103–4, 123.

53. See Hinton, 1965, pp. 76ff; R. Johnson, 1980, pp. 62–3. Poulantzas describes the Anderson/Nairn theoretical position as 'historicist and subjectivist', 1967, pp. 60–6.

54. See Poulantzas's review on the debate in favour of the Anderson/Nairn side whose essays are considered to be 'exemplary texts of Marxist political analysis'(1967, p. 57).

55. James Burnham's pioneering work *The Managerial Revolution* (1941) assumes that during the Second World War, there were rapid changes of social and cultural institutions, beliefs and power structure; a theory of managerial revolution can explain these changes. J. K. Galbraith's *The Affluent Society* (1958) argues that although private wealth is still increasing while the public service is degrading, the problem of production has been in large part solved in capitalist society where widespread poverty and class divisions have been decisively reduced. Without abandoning his influential 'convergence' (of capitalism and socialism) thesis, he nevertheless became much less optimistic later on.

56. Robin Blackburn, born in 1941, graduated from Oxford and LSE, with a degree in sociology; became Assistant Lecturer at LSE and lost the job in 1969 for his activities during the student revolt. He has been a visiting professor at several American universities and the University of Havana; joined *NLR* in 1962 as one of the two candidates (with Anderson) for the new editorship of the reshaped *Review* and has been the editor since 1983.

57. Mills's sociological critique of the thesis of managerial revolution in *The Power Elite* (1956) had an impact on the thinking of the British New Lefts.

58. See Barratt Brown, 1963b, pp. 452–3; Hobsbawm, 1961, p. 64; Wedderburn, 1962 and 1964; Coates and Silburn, 1970; Blackburn, 1967a and 1967b; Titmuss, 1964; Coates, 1971a, pp. 152–66; Westergaard, 1965 and 1964; Lipton, 1966; Anderson, 1965a, p. 7; Hughes, 1963, pp. 3–4; Williams *et al.*, 1967/8, sections 4, 5, 6, 7, 8. See also the exchange between Saville and Dorothy Thompson on the approach to the question of welfarism, *NLR* 3 and *NLR* 4.

59. See Kiernan's critique, 1959, p. 82. *The Long Revolution*, too, had hardly reminded its readers that Britain was an imperial power.

60. One can find only a single piece on imperialism yesterday and today by Barratt Brown (*NLR* 5), an introduction, which is of importance, to the Cuban Revolution by Hall and others (*NLR* 7 and *NLR* 9), and a review of the Third World revolution by Worsley (*NLR* 12).

61. On this point, see MacKenzie and Silver, 1962, which is a sociological study of Conservative working-class voters.

62. According to Saville, the absence of any sustained critique of bourgeois society by its traditional intellectuals helped the formation of labourism (1973a, pp. 222–3, 226).

63. For a general 'New Left analysis' of new imperialism and labour imperialism, see the *May Day Manifesto*, esp. sections 19, 23 and 24.

64. See a draft proposal for a workers' university jointly written by Coates and Topham, 1964; Coates, ed. 1968b which was produced by CSE; Mitchell, 1964.

65. See, for example, exchanges between Ken Coates and Frank Cousins, the General Secretary of the Transport & General Workers' Union (Coates, 1971a, pp. 131–2, 242–3). See Anderson's discussion of the limits and possibilities of trade union action (1967).

66. The whole passage reads: 'To secure for the workers by hand or by brain the full fruits of their industry and the most equitable distribution thereof that may be possible upon the basis of the common ownership of the means of production, distribution, and exchange, and the best obtainable system of popular administration and control of each industry or service.' 'That piece of formalism', Hall was to write later, 'contributed precious little to deepening the concept of social ownership' (1988b, p. 212).

67. See, especially, Gaitskell, 1956; Crosland, 1956, chap. 3, 4, 18, 19; 1962, chap. 3, 5, 14; cf. *Industry and Society*, the Labour programme adopted in 1957.

68. The most influential document of a joint defence made by the old Labour Left and the New Left was a *Tribune* pamphlet, *Socialism for the Sixties*, written by John Hughes and others. For a useful analysis of the battle, see Bogdanor and Skidelsky, 1970, pp. 94–109.

69. See *The Insiders*, supplement to *ULR* 3; Barratt Brown, 1958/9; Hughes, 1957, 1960a; Saville, 1965, pp. 155–6; Miliband, 1961a, pp. 288–90. See also Rogow and Shore, 1955, an influential study supporting the New Left argument. About the problems involved in the Wilson Government's renationalisation of steel and road transport and project of establishing 'competitive public enterprises' (*Signposts for the Sixties*), see Anderson, 1964b.

70. John Hughes was a former communist and a tutor in Economics and Industrial Relations at Ruskin College, Oxford, also an extra-mural lecturer at the University of Leeds, an active participant of the early New Left and a member of the first *NLR* editorial committee.

71. See Williams, 1983a, p. 27; Coates, (ed.) 1968a, p. 14; 1965, pp. 313–16; Barratt Brown, 1964, p. 251.

72. See Coates and Topham, 1968b and eds. 1968a, p. xiii.

73. See Cole's Foreword to Pribicevic, 1959; Coates, (ed.) 1968a, p. 11; Coates and Topham (eds) 1968a, pp. xvii–xxxii; 1969, pp. 24–8; Coates's introduction to Markovic and Cohen, 1975, promoting the Yugoslav experience. Industrial democracy had also been advocated by the Fabians without any resource from Marxism. I shall return to the theoretical discussions of workers' control in IV.2.

74. See important early analyses by Barratt Brown, 1958/9 and 1960; D. Butt, 1960 and 1961; Harrison, 1960; Hughes, 1960a. See *NLR* collection of personal experiences of workers, manual and mental, concerning the nature of work under capitalism (Ronald Fraser, ed. 1968; with a concluding essay by Williams). For later discussions, see, for example, Topham, 1964; Anderson, 1964b, section 5, 9, 15; Blackburn and Cockburn, eds. 1967.

75. See D. R. Holden's careful study of *Searchlight* in his doctoral dissertation, 1976, pp. 263–7.

76. See IWC pamphlets such as Barratt Brown's *Opening the Books* (1968a), *Declaration of the 6th National Conference on Workers' Control* (Nottingham, 31 March 1968),

and Coates and Williams (eds) 1969, a collection of papers submitted to and report
on the 1968 conference. See also Coates, 1968b, an argument for the 1967 teach-
in organised by the Centre for Socialist Education and the May Day Manifesto
Group.

77. Ken Coates, born in 1930, was a former CP member and a coal miner, chairman
of the Nottingham LP until his expulsion from the party in 1965 (he was restored
in 1969); taught in WEA for years, tutor in Industrial Relations at extra-mural
department of Nottingham University. He helped to found the International
Marxist Group (IMG), was an editorial member of the *International Socialist
Journal*; the editor of *Spokesman*, long-standing contributor to *NLR* and *SR*; a
director of the Russell Foundation and joint secretary of END since 1980.

78. For a general account, see Coates, 1967, pp. 56–92; 1971a, pp. 38–61.

79. Bob Rowthorn, born in 1943, Professor in Economics at Cambridge University,
since 1971 a leading member of the CP Economics Commission, since 1979 an
editorial member of *Marxism Today*. He was active in CND and the International
Socialist Group, *NLR* editorial member between 1967 and 1983.

80. For the debate between Rowthorn and Barratt Brown/Harrison, see *NLR* 37,
pp. 86–95.

81. In Saville's view, if its leading figures kept defending and developing the context
which had been already established, 'workers' control' would have remained an
important movement and probably succeeded in providing an alternative to current
Labour politics in terms of ideas and organisation (interview with Saville by the
author, 19 October 1987). Barratt Brown and Ken Coates, however, disagreed, for
it was wrong to give too much weight to the role of individual people (interview
with Barratt Brown by the author, 30 Oct. 1987; with Coates, 31 Oct. 1987).

82. See Oglesby, ed. 1969, pp. 111–43 for the most part of this version, including its
conclusion, 'The Politics of the Future'.

83. Michael Rustin was an editor of *New University* in Oxford and was the secretary
of the Oxford Labour Club in the early 1960s; joined the second *NLR* in 1962, was
a frequent contributor to the *Review* and a strategic thinker speaking to a New Left/
Labour tradition.

84. Marcuse's most influential writings at the time were *Eros and Civilisation* (1955),
One-Dimensional Man (1964), and papers, speeches and interviews concerning post-
industrial civilisation and revolution, printed in *Five Lectures* (1970), *Counter-
Revolution and Revolt* (1972), *NLR* and other publications. Mills's sociological
analysis in *The Power Elite* (1956), *The Causes of World War Three* (1958) and *Power,
Politics and People* (1963), for example, were very widely read. Sartre's existentialism
was especially attractive to youth in intellectual crisis. His view that violence was
necessary in political struggle was a popular moral recognition. Althusser's
structuralist Marxism quickly exerted a strong influence in Britain on left-wing
intellectuals rather than directly on the consciousness of students. Mao's thought
was introduced to western readers, together with very limited reports on the
progress of the Cultural Revolution, of which the image was immensely inspiring.
The title of Fanon's book, *The Wretched of the Earth* (1964), was taken as a moving
slogan of liberation, while those 'wretched' themselves became conceptual components of the mass base of the New Left. Debray's *Revolution in Revolution* (1967)
provided some ideas directly for the 'Red Base' strategy of the campus protest (see
the next section). For a general introductory reading, see Cranston, ed. 1970 and
Oglesby, ed. 1969.

85. For a brief introduction to Laing, see Martin, 1970 and Howarth-Williams, 1977.
For Laing's politics, see Mezan, 1972; Kirsner, 1976, pp. 143–54; Boyers and Orrill
(eds.) 1972.

86. For Anderson, Keynes 'was perhaps the last great social thinker produced by the
English bourgeoisie' (1968a, p. 250).

87. See Stedman Jones's brief analysis of English intellectuals in a similar negative manner.
The major intellectual approaches are summarised as reaffirmation of the values of a
liberal individualism, Fabian state socialism and 'the new liberalism'. Significantly, each
attaches to parliamentary politics (1967, pp. 34–5). In a different direction, Williams

wrote about 'a comprehensive development and reform of the professional and cultural life of bourgeois England between the 1910s and 1920s' (1980b).

88. He acknowledged, however, that Christopher Hill (and Trevor-Roper and Lawrence Stone) developed important implications of Tawney's work; Hobsbawm and Thompson established a history based upon Marxism and informed by psychology and sociology; Deutscher's, E. H. Carr's and Richard Cobb's creative work began to be appreciated. A 'genuine social history' is finally possible today (1967, pp. 37–40).

89. Stedman Jones views the book as a 'vigorous attack upon empiricism, pseudo-objectivism and the subordination of historical analysis to moral stricture'; it demolished the dichotomy between 'facts' and 'interpretations' which was the cornerstone of latter-day positivism. However, Carr's notion of time as a general relation in history is seen by him as inadequate (1967, pp. 41–3).

90. Anthropology (along with literary criticism and aesthetics), however, was seen twenty years later by Anderson as an area whose 'totalising impulses' had actually set it apart within traditionally empiricist and positivist English culture (1990, II, pp. 131, 135). The publication of Goddard's attack on British anthropology in NLR under Anderson's editorship was not mentioned.

91. Stedman Jones, too, admitted later that he was 'unduly dismissive' about British historiography (1984 edn. of 1971b, p. xiv).

92. Among an extensive literature, the following selected references (mainly on Britain, but also referring to international counterparts) may be helpful: Cockburn and Blackburn, (eds) 1969; Nagel, (ed.) 1969; Rowbotham, 1979a, pp. 21–50; Ali, 1972, pp. 152–74; 1978; ed. 1969; Teodori, (ed.) 1970, part two; Harman et al., (eds) 1968; Young, 1977, chapter 9–14; Widgery, (ed.) 1976, pp. 305–447, 469–76, 522–6; Hayter, 1971; SR 1969; NLR 48–53; Black Dwarf (June 1968–September 1970); International Socialism, no. 35 and 36, editorial. For recent publications in retrospect, see Caute, 1988; Katsiaficas, 1987; Fraser, 1988. The last book, written by an oral historian who was a long-standing NLR editorial member, and consisting of personal recollections by the participants of the events, is particularly important.

93. See Rowbotham, 1979a, pp. 26–7, 35–8; Shipley, 1976; Coates, 1976, pp. 111–27. The tensions between IS and IMG lie in the former's greater emphasis on the proletariat and so stronger 'New Left' orientation to the students and the Third World. About the IS (later the Socialist Workers Party) and IMG (later the Socialist League, official British branch of the Unified Secretariat Fourth International), see Widgery, 1976, pp. 437–47, 487. The organ of the IMG at the time was Black Dwarf set up in June 1968, focusing on the themes of anti-imperialism, student militancy, feminist questions and dissident culture. The International Socialist Journal, by contrast, held a more conventional 'Marxist-Leninist' line.

94. Blackburn was a member of IMG and eventually left it because of his disagreement with the majority line. NLR editors were active in VSC, in the Cuban and Czech Solidarity Committees which also involved Trotskyite groupings. They dominated the paper Black Dwarf (with Tariq Ali as the editor), and also once gained the leadership of the Revolutionary Socialist Students' Federation (RSSF), a typical 'Leninist' organisation that stated its commitment to 'the revolutionary overthrow of capitalism and imperialism and its replacement by workers' power' (see NLR 53, pp. 21–2).

95. See Thompson's critique of the 'irrationalist' 'revolting bourgeoisie' in 1976b, pp. 8–10 and 1973, p. 392. This distance can be partly explained by the old wound made over the regeneration of NLR. Compare Thompson to Hobsbawm who regarded the French events as 'classical revolution' in type: all serious observers of politics had long taken it for granted that such a revolution would no longer happen in the western countries, yet in Paris it did (1968a). He soon realised, of course, that 'it proved not that revolutions can succeed in western countries today, but only they can break out' (1969, p. 242).

96. Saville's professorship at Hull University was postponed for his backing of the students. Miliband supported radical students at LSE. Hall participated in the student actions at Birmingham University where he worked and his wife was a student militant.

97. Between 1952 and 1968, world capitalist output doubled, which was without historical parallel. See Glyn and Sutcliffe, 1980.

98. The figures are 122,000 (1954–5), 216,000 (1962–3), 300,000 (1965–6); 2.7 per cent of their age group before the Second World War, 11 per cent by 1967. See Stedman Jones, 1969b, pp. 30–5, 40–1. No doubt students then still composed an elite group, but their social destination has shifted (see *NLR* 43, p. 5). According to Kiernan, simple increase of student numbers must have had a transforming influence – students felt able to act on their own because they now had a mass basis (1969, p. 70).

99. See Newman, 1969, pp. 1–15; Atkinson, 1969, pp. 16–44; Hoare's earlier discussion with Williams of education reform programme (*NLR* 32, pp. 40–52). See also Cockburn: 'everywhere one finds education subordinated to exams, competition and grading: most fields of study are stunted by academic philistinism and hostility towards ideas ...' (1969, p. 11). Anderson talked about 'the reactionary and mystifying culture' that enveloped universities and colleges (1965b, p. 214) quite a while before the student movement.

100. According to Cockburn, class discrimination and sex discrimination combine, so that a working-class girl in Britain only has 1/600 chance of receiving higher education (1969, p. 17). See also Linda Tinkham, 1969, pp. 82–98.

101. According to Stedman Jones, the Cold War, or a 'competition between equals' in which neither side prevailed, was a decisive political experience for the radical students (1969b, pp. 36–8).

102. As Anderson sees it, cultural institutions are extremely important in the distinctive configuration of power in Britain (1964a, p. 44). In Nairn's words, capitalist control of these institutions in Britain has reached a degree of 'more intensive and stultifying monopoly' than anywhere else (1964a, *NLR* 28, p. 61). Williams devoted many of his writings to this subject, see esp. II.4.

103. See Marcuse, 1969c. According to Marcuse, Sartre and most other 'New Left' thinkers, violence could have a liberating purpose and is justified when the effect is liberation. A typical appeal to direct action appeared during the student movement in Britain was printed in *Black Dwarf*: 'Don't demand – occupy!'

104. Kiernan points out that 'student power' seems as vague a slogan as 'Black power' because students, like other social groups, are always divided (1969, p. 73). In Widgery's account, in general 'student power' was 'a description which most student militants disliked but couldn't avoid being labelled with' (1976, p. 525).

105. Alexander Cockburn, born in 1940, worked for *The Times Literary Supplement* and the *New Statesman* at the time of the student movement. A long-standing *NLR* editorial member since 1966, he moved to live and work in USA.

106. See Cockburn, 1969, p. 17. Blackburn announced in a leaflet against 'timidity' and 'opportunism' in the LSE Socialist Society that 'those who reject the strategy of the Red Base ... will be in serious danger of becoming the objective allies of social imperialism and social fascism' (quoted from Sedgwick, 1976, pp. 314–15). See RSSF Manifesto and *NLR* introduction to Debray in *NLR* 45.

107. Interview with Blackburn by the author, 26 November 1987.

108. See Cockburn's remarks on the role of intellectuals in the great revolutions in history (1969); a footnote on the New Left understanding of Gramsci in Stedman Jones, 1969b, p. 55. Stedman Jones, Anderson and Nairn all considered that it was not yet possible to make a political distinction between 'organic' and 'traditional' intellectuals in Britain.

109. Fred Halliday, born in 1948, was a student of politics at the School of Oriental and African Studies in London during the period 1968–9, and is a specialist in international relations of the post-1968 New Left.

110. See Barnett, 1969; debate between Brewster/Cockburn and Shaw, *NLR* 44, pp. 87–93.

111. See Worsley's review on Fanon, 1972.

112. It must be noted that intellectuals have played different roles in history. A striking negative example is, as Gramsci pointed out, that the cosmopolitan/nationalist intellectuals helped to make straight the path to Italian fascism.

113. The question was raised earlier in the context of the first CND, which involved a large number of young people. See Parkin, 1968, pp. 140–74.

114. See, for example, John and Margaret Rowntree, 1970; Dutschke, 1969; Nairn, 1968, pp. 170–3; Murdoch and McCron, 1975, pp. 192–207; Birnbaum, 1971, p. 387.

115. See Stedman Jones, 1969b, pp. 43–5; Rock and Cohen, 1970.

116. See Magri, 'It is not by chance that all the revolutions we know of have been made by young people and young parties' (1969, p. 53).

117. For discussions of the lessons of the student movement, see *NLR* 52, editorial, pp. 1–7; Mandel, 1968b; Gluksmann, 1969; Gellner, 1970.

118. See Michael Walzer, 1980, pp. 113–4; 175–85. Referring to the USA New Left, he called the new local concerns and activism in community organising a 'pastoral retreat'.

119. There has been also evidence that things changed very little in some universities (e.g. LSE): see Caute, 1988, p. 329. But on the whole, as Anderson remarked, a large change has been achieved over the last two decades: then, the academic institutions were the object of a left revolt from below, and now they are the target of the right-wing government from above (1990).

120. See Blackburn: 'The movement encouraged the growth of a radical, anti-capitalist current of thought, brought an interest in theory and ideas – look at the number of radical and Marxist sociological, economic and philosophical journals that have come into being since then – which went against the grain of the philistine anti-intellectualism of British society in general and the British Left and Labour movement in particular' (quoted in Fraser, 1988, pp. 325–6).

CHAPTER IV

History and Theory, 1970–77

1. THE AFTERMATH OF 1968

The storm of 1968 was an unusual historical conjuncture, more profound than it may seem, in the sense of the rebirth and stimulation of an expansive mood of radical resistance within capitalist societies, under conditions of peace, prosperity and political stability based on the bourgeois democracy.

In the subsequent few years, a new wave of working-class struggle and socialist politics surged forward in the heartlands of the capitalist world. Large-scale workers' strikes in Italy (and the continued electoral advance of the Italian Communist Party), industrial militancy in Britain, and the high point of the labour movement in Japan were a few striking examples. The Portuguese revolution (1974–5) reopened the question of the possibility of a socialist revolution in post-war western Europe. The Eurocommunist strategy of forming the 'broadest possible alliance' began to extend the traditional focus from confinement to the trade unions to a wider area of protests. The growth of the democratic opposition in eastern Europe after the Czech reform movement (1968), the peaceful socialist transition and its overthrow by the military coup in Chile, the victorious warfare against American imperialism in Vietnam and revolutionary movements in some other third world countries, were equally important events on the international stage that transcended the experience of 1968 in the first half of the 1970s.

In Britain, there was continuing student radicalism. The revolt over the Warwick files issue,[1] the Manchester and Oxford University sit-ins, the one-day action with 40,000 participants organised by the National Union of Students, students' demonstrations in support of the miners, and campus based youth groupings like Rock Against Racism all echoed the earlier movement. Many college militants had become activists in the Labour Left or the reinitiated feminist movement (see IV.5). The post-1968 period also saw the increasing dynamic of locally managed struggles over 'single issues', either housing or racial discrimination or environment or others. The violent civil rights rebellion in Northern Ireland, coincidentally, threw the unitary UK state into crisis.[2]

The Conservatives won the general election of 1970, which was followed by Britain's entry into the Common Market. Then Labour's turn came, in 1974. No matter who was in office, factory occupations and other forms of workers' struggle reached a scale that had not been seen in this country since the 1920s. After the dispute over the Industrial Relations Bill (which the Wilson government was forced to abandon in 1969), militant shop-stewards often went beyond the official trade union line.[3] In 1972, the miners went on strike and were supported by action in other industries, which paralysed the national economy and defeated the government.[4] The second miners' strike of 1974 brought about the electoral victory of the Labour Party. A more radical Labour programme was adopted and intellectually endorsed by the New Left/Labour socialists. Meanwhile, the Labour Left (led by Tony Benn) was reorganising itself and recruiting. These events did not, however, change the basic situation that, observed Williams, had been clear since about 1966: 'what I would call a post-social-democratic party is absolutely essential to the working of modern capitalism in Britain'. He meant to say that the historical role the Labour Party had come to play was 'a major neutralisation of the working class' in order to meet demands of the capitalist economy and society (1979, pp. 376–7). Yet, it was not until the latter half of the 1970s that the labour movement went into a total retreat, and a general rightward drift in politics began to take shape.

The events inspired by 1968 had been reflected in the pages of New Left publications. Socialist and feminist papers (such as *Black Dwarf*, the *Red Mole*, *Seven Days*) and new journals and forums engaged in Marxist analyses (notably the CSE Bulletin (1970); *Economy and Society* (1972); *Radical Philosophy* (1972); *Race and Class* (1974, previously *Race*) appeared in large numbers, and most directly involved New Left people.[5] *Seven Days*, for example, was edited by a group of NLR editorial members. Without a 'Leninist' vanguard flavour, it claimed, in language similar to that of the early New Left, to 'reach out beyond those already in organised left politics' and 'provide a focus for the Left that is rent by division' (editorial, 22 March 1972). In its six months' existence (1971–2), the paper gained for itself a fairly wide readership, amongst workers, shop stewards, radical women, art critics, students and others. All these developments had combined to transform the environment of the intellectual work of the left. By the end of the decade, Marxist traditions had been much strengthened in some fields in this notoriously parochial country, in sharp contrast to the collapse of Marxist strongholds on the continent at exactly the same time.[6]

It is not surprising that political crises and revolutionary ferment would release or generate critical energy with intensity. The disruption of liberal consensus in developed capitalist societies, the impact of the liberation movements in the third world, the 'geo-cultural break' catalysed by 1968 (see the next section) all contributed to a change in the British situation. Marxism was no longer isolated in a climate of hostility as in the past (Walton and Hall, Introduction to 1972). But why did such a divergence between Britain and continental Europe come about within similar political and social contexts? There seemed to be some question of leadership – it was to the New Left's credit that the revival of Marxism with its intrinsic openness in Britain was so vigorous. The *New Left Review* and New Left Books (Verso) had deliberately introduced a plurality of theoretical systems more or less within the Marxist tradition and encouraged heated discussions and debates around them in the English speaking world. The offspring of the early New Left, *SR*, CCCS and History Workshop (see III.1), also played important parts, among others, in building a new Marxist culture. Individual contributors associated with either generation of the New Left produced a great deal of the writing and thinking which characterised the final stage of the New Left movement.

2. ENCOUNTER WITH 'WESTERN MARXISM'

The Missing Traditions

One of *NLR*'s principal themes was the absence in English culture of any tradition of western Marxism, an absence registered in a negative light. Despite the fact that both *NR* and *ULR* in the late 1950s did publish some translations and discussions, of Sartre and Gramsci, for example, the whole range of continental Marxist traditions were virtually unknown to British Marxism until the 1960s.

In his overall survey of 'Western Marxism' (1976a), Anderson suggests the 'general co-ordinates' which define the term as a common intellectual identity. The structural unity of this identity, beyond its internal divergences and oppositions, is considered in the following context: the defeat of the proletarian revolutions in Europe and the isolation of Soviet Russia in the early 1920s, the dogmatisation of both the theoretical legacies of the Second International and the official Marxism of the Comintern, and the failure of communist ideology and practice in the Stalin era. Anderson's approach certainly contains merits which allow him properly to locate western Marxism in geo-political terms and to compare or assess individual schools and thinkers within a historical totality.[7] However, the inadequacy of his approach is also obvious. It is very difficult to encompass such a vast territory of conflicting intellectual trends within a unified phase and framework. It seems necessary at least to distinguish the scientific Marxisms of such figures as Della Volpe, Colletti, and Althusser from the Hegelian or humanistic mainstream. (Although both Korsch and Gramsci see Marxism as a scientific weapon of the working class, they are usually placed in the humanist stream due to the nature of their work.)[8] Marxism in Britain was a movement strongly influenced by the first tradition, especially by French structuralist Marxism which was an entirely imported system of thought that the English native soil could hardly produce. But this will be discussed separately (in IV.4).

The enthusiasm of the younger Marxist generation of the New Left for European Marxism was reflected above all in the pages of *NLR*. Between 1963 and 1977, the *Review* introduced, translated, published and discussed the work of Georg Lukács, Karl Korsch, Antonio Gramsci, Jean-Paul Sartre, Herbert Marcuse,

Theodor Adorno, Max Horkheimer, Walter Benjamin, Jürgen Habermas and Lucien Goldmann; as well as Galvano Della Volpe, Lucio Colletti, Louis Althusser, Etienne Balibar, André Glucksmann, Nicos Poulantzas, André Gorz, Maurice Godelier; and Claude Lévi-Strauss and Jacques Lacan.[9] A collection of research from this 'trans-English' standpoint under the powerful impact of structuralism, *Western Marxism: A Critical Reader*, was published by New Left Books in 1977, after the appearance of Anderson's *Considerations on Western Marxism* in 1976, an essay which was originally designed as an introduction to the former volume. This enterprise of NLR was in part an attempt to remedy what was seen by its leading theorists as a native deficiency exposed in their earlier criticism of the insular pattern of national culture. It was also, significantly, 'the product of an increasing awareness that the heritage that Britain had missed, to its detriment, was itself missing in certain of the classical traits of historical materialism' (Anderson, 1976a, p. viii). The young *Review* editors found, however, disapproval of their programme among the older generation (NLR Foreword to Williams, 1979, p. 9). Besides a few who disliked both Marcuse's and Althusser's Marxism (for example, Thompson, 1973, p. 352), quite typical attitudes of even those European-oriented Marxists long resident in Britain can be seen, for example, in Hobsbawm's comment on Korsch: 'What he says is often worth listening to .... But, in the end, there is no major reason today why we should have to read him' (1969, in 1973, p. 159).

Gramsci was exceptional, maybe because, for those who were still much under the shadow of a Communist Party background, he was the only major western Marxist thinker apart from either non-communists or condemned communists, who had escaped official criticism; and later himself became the source of Italian Communist orthodoxy. Gramsci's political theory was uniquely taken as directly relevant to the problems of socialism in the west today, to which classical Marxism offered no answers. The publication of a new edition of the *Prison Notebooks*, edited and translated by Quintin Hoare of NLR and Geoffrey Nowell-Smith in 1971[10] promoted new waves of studying Gramsci, to whom the intellectual left in Britain paid greater attention than in probably any other country besides Italy.[11] The outcome was overwhelmingly uncritical, partly due to the quality and richness of Gramsci's ideas themselves, partly maybe that these very ideas remained themselves beset by theoretical crises and with historical problems unsolved.

The only rebel against the current was Anderson, whose 'seriousness of real criticism' led to the finding of a series of theoretical errors and political mistakes not only in the 'premature' Gramsci of 1919–20,[12] but also in the *Prison Notebooks*. Focusing on the east/west problematic that the Italian thinker set out to reveal, Anderson's full-length essay (1976b) was the first critical evaluation of Gramsci's shifting concepts of theorising the nature of the state, civil society, and class rule. Their background was traced to the strategic polemics between Luxemburg and Kautsky, Lenin and the left adventurists. Not only did prison conditions make Gramsci's composition 'non-unitary', 'fragmentary' and 'incoherent' (p. 72),[13] but most important, according to this critique, there is in his analytical versions a 'structural asymmetry' (together with categorical confusions) in the distribution of the consensual and coercive functions of bourgeois power between civil society and the state.[14] These errors result in the absence in his work of an adequate examination of the power structure of capitalism. Moreover, as he at times suggests that consent primarily pertains to civil society, and civil society possesses primacy over the state, he allows the conclusion that bourgeois power is primarily consensual and basically takes the form of cultural hegemony. Here the idea of hegemony omits the role of the repressive machinery of the army and the police, whilst grounding the 'war of position', a long struggle against an immensely stronger enemy, with no visible clarity of outcome (pp. 45, 47, 52, 69–70). For Anderson, Gramsci no doubt embodied in his person alone a revolutionary unity of theory and practice in the tradition of western Marxism, yet his strategic formula failed to integrate the fundamental tenets of classical Marxism on the ultimate necessity of the violent destruction of the state, and therefore in the end sank into reformism (pp. 69–72; 1976, p. 45). Gramsci was unable to offer a political solution, Anderson asserts, to the future of the western working class.

Gramsci's perspective of a war of position is thus a deadlock, representing a kind of 'moral metaphor', a sense of 'stoical adjustment' to the loss of any immediate hope of victory, a latent political pessimism. This pessimism was shared by all the main departures or developments of substance within the Marxist tradition between 1920 and 1960 (1977, pp. 71–2; 1976, pp. 88–9). Anderson's observations are quite true in both cases, the scientific and the humanist traditions of Marxism. It is doubtful, however, if this was any less true after 1960: with or without exceptions, a darkness had enveloped the theories of the Left and their implications all along, including even the most cheering ideas produced during the revolutionary years marked by 1968.

Anderson's challenge did not appear to evoke noteworthy debates even though there was extensive disagreement. Not being sufficiently concerned with economics ('civil society' in Gramsci's usage often excludes economic relations), one of Gramsci's theses is that people experience social conflict not so much in direct competition for material interests as in the struggle of ideas or beliefs. In other words, interests are not given but must be politically and ideologically constructed (see especially his criticism of economism in 'The Modern Prince', 1971, pp. 158–68). At this particular point, Anderson claims almost the same: the ideology of bourgeois democracy is far more potent than any economic improvement or rise in the living standard of the masses won by welfarism in contributing to a consensus (1976b, pp. 28–9). This is of course a long-standing New Left tenet (II.3). Yet Kiernan argues the contrary: in advanced capitalist society today, class struggle is 'a squabbling over shillings or dollars quite free from illusion or ideal'; workers' demands are more on wage bargaining than any political issues. Gramsci's concept of the mission of a revolutionary party thus seems to Kiernan to have neglected an alternative, defensive function of protecting the working class instead of leading it to power (as in England, since the Chartists) (1972a, pp.

14, 19). In a similar spirit Miliband points out that the 'Modern Prince' lacks theoretical material for the resolution of tensions between the class and the party (1977a, pp. 148–9). In contrast to these local but serious criticisms, the whole question of the political party is omitted altogether in Anderson's global critique.

A more sensitive dispute focused on the question of whether the working class could win hegemony culturally before winning political power. Against most admirers of the Gramscian thesis of hegemony, Anderson's interpretation of him is that the hegemonic activity which can and must be exercised before the transition to power is related, in the text of the *Prison Notebooks*, only to the problem of the alliance of workers with other labouring classes, such as with the peasantry (as in the classical Marxist notion). In other words, a cultural ascendancy of the working class over the bourgeoisie is possible only after a socialist revolution; and even then, the culturally dominant class will remain the bourgeoisie in certain aspects and for a certain time (1976b, pp. 44–6). Hobsbawm, among others, holds that Gramsci was right to centre his attention on the struggle for hegemony rather than coercion as a crucial revolutionary strategy in the countries where the key to rule lay in the subordinate (and fragmentary) status of the masses. The question of hegemony is thus not how revolutionaries come to power, but how they come to be accepted as guides and leaders (1977a, pp. 210–1; cf. Thompson's similar remark in 1978b, p. 22).

Gramsci's powerful cultural emphasis (that the idea of hegemony requires) greatly strengthened the culturalist tradition within the British New Left.[15] As a substantial effort to reshape this tradition, at the risk of underestimating the political dimension of culture, Anderson criticises Gramsci for his constant tendency more towards the purely cultural institutions (churches, schools, newspapers and other means of communication, etc.) which secure the consent of the masses than towards the specifically political institutions (the state machinery, etc.) which assure the stability of capitalism (1976b, pp. 41–2). The unifying focus of culturalist Marxism is to forge the intellectual preconditions for winning the majority of the people over to the socialist side in the west. Here the danger of reducing the problem of socialist transformation to that of consciousness is reached. As Stedman Jones warns, 'the idea that revolution results from raised consciousness is a tautology'. What is at stake is to challenge the material structure that links the ruling classes and the ruled in capitalist societies (1972).

Despite (and indeed because of) other commentators arguing the significance of Gramsci's transfer of emphasis from the state to civil society in the light of radically different social conditions between east and west, Anderson insists on the determination (so long as classes exist) of the bourgeois–democratic state 'in the final instance' by coercion and the inevitable role of violence within any great historical transformation. At one point, he does accept the 'dominant role of culture in the contemporary bourgeois power system' as 'the most salient immediate difference between western parliamentarism and Russian absolutism'. He believes, however, that the development of any revolutionary crisis necessarily displaces dominance within the old power structure from ideology to force. The socialist transformation requires a maximum expansion of freedom and liberty, which must indeed start before the old regime is overthrown; and the enemy could be divided by winning over its major segments, yet the hard core of professional counter-revolutionary units can only be defeated by an armed conflict (1976b, pp. 42–4, 70, 76–7).[16] In place of Gramsci's cultural control systems within civil society, Anderson stresses the 'juridico-political component of consent' and the 'cultural-ideological role of the state' itself. In the end, he dismisses Gramsci's strategic perspective and offers his own: even with the achievement of the united front and dual power (rather than a cultural hegemony), the state with its military apparatus still has to be fought (pp. 28–9, 71, 78).[17]

Anderson, in opposition to the entire historical trend of reformist strategy (in his judgement) from that of Kautsky ('strategy of attrition') to Eurocommunism (the 'parliamentary road to socialism') mediated by Gramsci's 'hegemony',[18] recalls the politico-theoretical heritage of Trotskyism as 'one of the central elements for any renaissance of revolutionary Marxism on an international scale'. In comparison with Gramsci, according to Anderson, Trotsky provided a classical theorisation of the United Front and a scientific critique of the ideas of both 'war of manoeuvre' and 'war of position'.[19] Fighting against capitalism as well as official communism and existing socialism,[20] Anderson himself can be seen as a representative of such a revolutionary Marxist tradition among the younger generation of British Marxists – though not, to be sure, of a typical Trotskyist one. The fact that he and his NLR colleagues rejected catastrophist analysis of contemporary capitalism alone distinguishes their stand from the routine forms of Trotskyist doctrines.[21] Yet this revolutionary Marxism widened the gulf between the second New Left and its predecessors, many of the latter tending to combine originally New Left populist politics with newly penetrated Eurocommunism (for example in the pages of *Marxism Today*).

Apart from the work of Gramsci and, in another direction, structuralist Marxism, the western Marxist currents received little critical and creative examination among the British intellectual Left, in spite of the remarkable effort made by NLR and individual contributors over more than a decade. (*Screen*, preoccupied by literature and cinema, was also a devoted forum for Althusser, beside its special attention to Lacan and social psychology). By 1977, there had been only a few studies of Lukács, for instance, including the NLB edition of Michael Löwy's biography, *Lukács: From Romanticism to Bolshevism* (1976), two pieces on the Hungarian thinker selected in the NLB volume of *Western Marxism*, and an essay on Lukácsian false consciousness in the CCCS collection, *On Ideology* (1977).[22] Stedman Jones's Althusserian critique of Lukács's early writings traces the intellectual sources of their key categories in German philosophy and sociology against the nineteenth-century background of the dissolution of both Kantianism and Hegelianism, arguing that *History and Class Consciousness* (1923) represented 'the first major irruption of the romantic anti-scientific tradition of bourgeois thought into Marxist theory' (1971a, p. 33). The problem with western

Marxism, for Stedman Jones, is that this essay, rather than the one on Lenin (*Lenin: A Study on the Unity of His Thought*, 1924) which was a historical materialist adjustment of Lukács's own position, remained the central focus of interest (pp. 34–48, 50–4).[23] As another example, Korsch's main essays, including 'Marxism and Philosophy' (1923), were translated and introduced by Fred Halliday of NLR and published by NLB in 1970; yet Halliday has not offered any detailed study of him since then, nor has anyone else from the NLR circle.[24]

Compared to the situation of the two 'critical communists', Sartre's later work was better discussed, though hardly any contribution was made by British Marxists. R. D. Laing, generally seen as on the international New Left (rather than the peculiar British New Left; cf. III.4 and the next section), was an important interpreter and disciple of Sartre in Britain.[25] Inheriting a ULR taste, NLR published, among a few other pieces, Gorz's (French) review (1966) of *Critique of Dialectical Reason* (1960; NLB English edition, 1976) and Ronald Aronson's (American) sympathetic assessment of Sartrean individualist social theory (1977) which paid no attention to *Between Existentialism and Marxism* (NLB edition, 1972). As for critical theory, it too attracted little philosophical engagement from the Marxist British New Left.[26] Only two individual members of the Frankfurt School, namely Adorno and Marcuse (not counting Benjamin, of the outer circle of the School), have occupied a place in the New Left pantheon.[27] Even though there were, after all, some critiques from an Althusserian perspective, humanist Marxists in Britain altogether ignored a critical theory which not only inspired a whole radical student generation but also actually in several respects shared their own political and intellectual orientations. There was thus no active discussion of many of the profound issues raised by the Frankfurt thinkers concerning, for example, the methodological distinction or unity of natural sciences and social sciences (against positivism), critique of ideology in relation to the conditions of claims for truth and knowledge (against 'instrumental reason'), obstacles and possibilities of human self-emancipation (against the dominant 'technological apparatus'); and so on.

The New Left critics in Britain warmly responded, at last, to the aesthetics tradition in western Marxism.[28] This tradition, in Anderson's opinion, is far richer and more subtle than anything within the classical heritage of historical materialism, and 'may in the end prove to be the most permanent collective gain of western Marxism' (1976a, p. 78).[29] This is clearly a rather negative comment on both the alleged aesthetic poverty of classical Marxism as well as the general defaults of western Marxism. This Marxism was, as is now already clear, not only introduced to a British audience by the young NLR editors, but its defaults were also resisted by the same group.

A typical case is Anderson's *Considerations*. Four essential elements are suggested to characterise western Marxism (note that, in his usage, the term is all-inclusive):

(1) European idealism – Lukács's reassessment of Hegel had lasting influence, and methodologically it became common among western Marxist writers to

make use of pre-Marxist and bourgeois idealist systems of thought (pp. 56–62, 73). Here a careful examination of a key concept, praxis, which was not necessarily Hegelian and in most cases was intended to indicate materially grounded and conditioned practices, including theoretical elaborations (as 'the self-clarification of the struggles and wishes of the age' – Marx, 1843), might put the judgement of idealism in question.

(2) Political pessimism – the hidden hallmark of western Marxism is that it was a product of defeat (pp. 42–4, 88–92). But the proletarian defeat in the 1848 revolutions did not smash the political optimism of the two founders of historical materialism. The origins of this pessimism require more and deeper explanations.

(3) Silence in those areas most central to the classical Marxist traditions (with the exception of Gramsci's work) – western Marxism represented a shift of the focus of Marxist theory from economics and politics to philosophy or else removing them to the most abstract height of the hierarchy of superstructure (pp. 44–5, 75, 93; cf. pp. 49–51 for the external and internal background of this shift). This criticism is fair enough if what is positive or necessary in the new focuses be taken into account. However, the whole point can be arbitrary in the sense that it is made by the virtual exclusion of some Marxist political theories and all Marxist economics from western Marxism.[30]

(4) Divorce of theory and practice – Marxist theory had migrated into the universities after the Second World War, cutting itself off from the political struggle of the organised working class and speaking a language of obscurity and pedantry rather than of clarity and urgency. (Is this not also a self-critical reflection of the Marxist British New Left?) The divorce, as Anderson correctly points out, was subject to a wider historical filter: the gulf for nearly fifty years between socialist thought and the soil of popular revolution (pp. 96–101, 118–21).[31]

He concludes with an appeal to the Trotskyist tradition, ignoring what that old Left tradition had left behind. After all, why New Left at all?

But surely Anderson would not deny, given the nature of *NLR*'s own work, that an emancipatory discourse, a radical 'public sphere' (Habermas; or what Eagleton calls 'counter-public sphere'), a 'transvaluation of values' (Marcuse, 1969a, p. 32), or what had been so vigorously argued by some New Left critics (especially, Hall) as 'ideological struggle', can be itself part of the process of revolutionary ferment and change? Theoretical reflection is always grasped in the Marxist tradition as part of material practice. This defence of the asymmetrical development of theory is certainly not to argue that social transformation is essentially intellectual or a matter of winning the battle over ideas, and indeed any critical theory will lose its critical edge if it falls into such an illusory or idealist proposition. At all events, Anderson has led us to a point where it seems all the more strange why it should be regretted that British Marxism had missed western Marxism, idealist, pessimist, unduly superstructurally preoccupied and divorced from practice as it is portrayed.

The western Marxist schools, consisting of remarkably able political philosophers, never took root in British intellectual life. The reasons for the failure of
British Marxists to develop an established pattern of thought similar to that of
mainstream western Marxism are not difficult to indicate: the historically weak
position of Marxism in British political thinking, the strong native style of
empiricism and disinterest in metaphysical issues,[32] a cultural default that
England had not been the birthplace of either the Renaissance or the Enlightenment, and above all, in *NLR*'s analysis, the lasting stability of state and society in
this insulated part of Europe. Of course, each of these can be further questioned
with 'why?'. Lukács's remark is relevant if both classical and western Marxism be
seen as strongly Hegelian: 'It is a great weakness of English culture that there is
no acquaintance with Hegel in it' (1968, p. 58). (Charles Taylor traced the
background of the indigenous anti-Hegelianism that had been strengthened in the
twentieth century by Russell and Moore and later Oxford linguistics – the
Hegelian revival around the turn of the century was 'only an interlude in a long
tradition of philosophical empiricism', 1966, pp. 229–30.) This seems an exaggerated but true point, referring to the very essence of the English intellectual
climate which the younger New Left generation sought to alter, though actually
in a quite anti-Hegelian spirit, drawing support from French rather than German
sources.

The British Presentation

There were roughly four alternative currents within the New Left which had
developed in Britain independent of the various Marxist schools on the continent:
(1) socialist humanism;
(2) culturalism or (in a much more advanced form) cultural materialism;
(3) *NLR* Marxism; and
(4) advocacy of workers' control.

The work of R. D. Laing, however, does not fit any of these categories (see
III.4). Influenced by psychoanalysis and a Hegelian existentialism rather than
Marxism, Laing was distant from the intellectual orientation of the British New
Left, though his work was of considerable significance for the internationally
recognised New Left movement. He inspired not only the 1968 generation to a
radical criticism of the 'sane' society and family which repressed 'insane'
individuals, but also inspired some New Left critics in one way or another to his
politicising of psychotherapy ('anti-psychiatry'; the 'politics of experience') and
concern with counter-culture (youth non-conformity). Indeed in theoretical
terms Laing's writings linked to or prepared for the post-1968 feminist uprising
in reference to Lacanian linguistics as well as Foucault's clinical genealogy. It was
a pity that the Marxist New Left in Britain did not pay enough attention to his
contribution.

As discussed earlier, socialist humanism was reconstituted from political and
intellectual rebellion against the moral decline of socialism embodied especially in
the Stalinist era, and theoretical impoverishment exemplified in mechanical

determinism or economic reductionism which was supposed to be an ideology of Stalinism. In this respect, the 'socialist humanism' of the early New Left was close to the 'humanist-historicist' tradition of western Marxism, only it had not been given a systematically elaborated justification.

Continuing the line of argument first formulated in *Morris*, Thompson's book-long essay *The Poverty of Theory*, published in 1978 after the New Left movement subsided (and therefore beyond the period which this study intends to cover), was a notable attempt in English, and indeed in the tradition of English empiricism, at defending the position of socialist humanism in opposition to Althusserian theoretical anti-humanism. In an interview given in the same year, Thompson restated the need for Morrisian utopianism in a democratic struggle against an increasingly authoritarian state, and restated libertarian socialism within the socialist-humanist tradition that, he accused, had been long abandoned by the second New Left (1978b). Earlier in his open letter to Leszek Kolakowski, Thompson did no more than recall the radiating problems faced by the old New Left as historical determinism, on the one hand, and human agency, moral choice, and individual responsibility, on the other (1973, p. 303).[33] The significance of British socialist humanism, with its practical expression in a populist movement of the first New Left, should be expressed only in political terms, and is clearly without a sustained pursuit of its philosophical foundation.

Deeply rooted in the national culture, Thompson and others of the older generation of the New Left turned for inspiration to Morris and the tradition of English social-literary criticism rather than to either the young Marx as a philosopher of alienation or to figures of any humanist European Marxism. For Thompson, the adoption of non-native thoughts which are not fully worked through, interrogated, and translated into the terms of indigenous traditions would not produce any organic theories in relation to actual social conflicts in Britain and to the British people (1978a, p. iv). Even younger New Left writers who were really fascinated by the early Marx and by thinkers like Sartre, too, did little to develop a humanist theory. Without knowing much of the works of Herbert Marcuse or Erich Fromm or Ernst Bloch at the time, Thompson's 'utopian impulse' (1955) coincided with the emphasis which all these authors shared on untiring humanist struggle against existing human conditions and conformist social consciousness.

As a political banner, socialist humanism in Britain never had sufficient clarity, nor freed itself from romantic moralism, and was therefore subject to criticism from a non-sentimental historical materialist point of view. This characteristic weakness might explain something about the fate of the first New Left – essentially furnished in its ideas and politics with moralistic polemics, it was not able effectively to challenge the dominant ideology of the Labour movement.

There was yet another humanist current within the New Left, particularly influenced by Christian socialism (see III.4). Those who briefly gathered around *Slant* intended to reconcile Christianity and Marxism by way of a kind of syncretic humanism. They found that progressive Catholic and Protestant social thinkers also sought to humanise their ethics with the aid of Marx's theory of alienation; and they knew that the European left in general had been strengthened by the participation of socialists with religious commitments. Their discussions of human nature, of the social and natural conditions of human existence, of community and common culture, of a new political theology (whether liberation theology in Latin America or a new left theology in Europe) and of the socialist transformation of capitalism, can be found in two New Left *Slant* publications: besides *From Culture to Revolution* mentioned earlier in the last chapter, there was *The Body as Language* (Eagleton, 1970). Sartre and Merleau-Ponty were the two among western Marxists whose work was a source of inspiration for the non-Communist origin (in comparison with the NR tradition) of this different socialist humanism.

Being distant from ex-communists such as Thompson, Charles Taylor became more and more critical of the inadequate formulations of Marxist humanism and its lack of theory. This humanism, in his opinion, does not face issues of immediate personal relationships.[34] Its totally positive conception of human potentiality neglects the limitations and obstacles to human achievements. That Marxist error is precisely what was earlier attributed to Stalinist 'solipsism' (1957; see II.2 in this volume). Taylor, the Hegelian philosopher, would later develop his idea into a criticism of both Marxian unrealistic humanism and neo-Nietzschean anti-humanism, placing emphasis on what he saw as the emptiness and simplism of the Marxist self-determining notion of freedom (Taylor, 1983; 1985.) For him, humanism means 'the creation of a community' with which humanity can identify and maintain a recipient/donor relationship constitutive (in part) of their identity (1968). These are forceful arguments. The reactionary side to them, however, is the tendency to give in to a conventional religious preoccupation with perfecting the individuals long before the political struggle can be fought to a conclusion.[35]

Approaching from a different angle, Eagleton criticises the 'false sentimental belief' and 'populist' standpoint of the political thinking of the early New Left (1970, ch. 7, esp. pp. 81–2). He understands the elimination of alienation, or 'genuine communal liberation', as lying at the core of both Christian political commitment and Marxism, when the former is 'revolutionary in a Marxist sense' (*ibid*. pp. 69, 92). He even speaks of the church and the priest as 'the revolutionary vanguard of human history ... on the Leninist model' (pp. 75–6). Here (to leave aside the question of the reactionary aspect of the social function of the religious establishments, dissenting wings included) Eagleton's humanism, to be fulfilled politically by a vanguard movement, radically diverges from either Thompson's or Taylor's version, demonstrating an old rather than a New Left position.

The second current of New Left thought is not easy to define. On the one hand, there was earlier a common ground of Marxist humanism and culturalist discourse which was often out of tune with received Marxist formulations. On the other hand, cultural materialism (see IV.4), promoted by Williams and responded to by many radical critics, had developed into a systematic theory which, though it drew upon non-Marxist traditions as well, contributed a great deal to the revival of Marxism in Britain as a basis for political and literary critique.[36] Eagleton's criticism of Williams was fierce, yet at most crucial points he said the same things as Williams did and they shared a common focus on the western Marxist aesthetics. The publications of CCCS by and large belonged to this current in spite of the Centre's being seized for a short time by the structuralist perspective in what Hall would later recall as 'a hopelessly theoreticist way' (1989b, p. 63).

Typically British as it is, culturalist Marxism nevertheless cannot be cast exclusively within the national culture. Gramsci's influence was apparently powerful, for example; so were some ideas of the Frankfurt School. Indeed Williams's cultural theory, as Fredric Jameson persuasively illustrated (1990, pp. 139–44), was a significant advance from Adorno's thesis of the culture industry. Literary critics of the British New Left appeared to be informed about certain developments of Marxist thinking in their own field on the continent which 'had not previously come our way' – the work of Lukács, Brecht, the Frankfurt thinkers, and of Gramsci, Sartre and Althusser (Williams, 1977, pp. 2–4).

In his memorial lecture on Lucien Goldmann[37] given in 1971, Williams reindicates, in light of Goldmann's contribution to the sociology of literature, the problems and impasses set by Leavisite empiricism with which British cultural thought has always been confronted. The Cambridge *Scrutiny* won what Williams calls a 'local victory' in its clash with a dogmatic and reductionist form of Marxism in the 1930s. But this victory 'was bought at a price we have all since paid' and one must now go beyond that argument which contains 'a sense of certain absolute restrictions in English thought'. These restrictions made the search for alternative traditions and methods imperative. The active and developed Marxist theory of Lukács and Goldmann is seen by Williams, though not without difficulties, as having represented such an alternative. Particularly, he stresses the importance of the concepts of reification, structure and collective subject; the distinctions made between kinds of consciousness (actual and possible, etc.), and attention to the structure of the genesis of consciousness. Goldmann's understanding of relations between social and literary facts as mental structures is close to Williams's own idea of a 'structure of feeling'. The significance of Goldmann, according to Williams, is in the different methodology that he introduced: not something uncritically transferred from the physical sciences to literature and social studies, but a way in which not 'value-free observations', but a real totality, a human centre, might be found (1971, pp. 4, 6–7, 16–17).

At this point, Eagleton connects Williams with the 'romantic anti-scientism' of Lukács, Goldmann and the Frankfurt School. Francis Mulhern, standing at some distance from either Williams or Eagleton, doubts whether Goldmann's work could have any radical impact on an empiricist literary tradition, especially because, for him, Goldmann actually converged with the *Scrutiny* group in 'a unilateral insistence on evaluation, at the expense of the development of aesthetic theory proper' (1975b, pp. 34–8). The Goldmann controversy was one of those cases which mirrored the complexity of the interflow between British and European cultural thoughts.

Williams's resistance to empiricism was by no means effective in the eyes of his young Marxist critics. While they did appreciate him and others who made a 'cognate' transformation of the English themes into works of unparalleled richness and a substantial contribution to the subsequent development of Marxist scholarship, they insisted that the old situation of British Marxism had not ever really changed. As Eagleton put it:

> The Marxist writers and critics of the 1930s were on the whole Marxist *Englishmen*, whose historical materialism remained deeply entwined with the romantic, empiricist and liberal humanist motifs of the dominant culture. Much the same may be said of the only major British socialist critic to emerge in the following decades, Raymond Williams ... [and] of the magnificent work of the historian E. P. Thompson. ... these writers may be described in a rough sense as the English equivalent of Lukács; but there is no English Brecht. (1981, p. 96)

In contrast to Brecht's central concern with the problem of practical revolutionary art, in Eagleton's opinion, the academicism of western Marxism (with the outstanding exception of Benjamin) is also a feature in Williams's writings, even though he did so much to shift attention from literature in a restricted sense to the social relations of cultural practice (*ibid.*, p. 97). Concerning the typical charge of Williams's native intellectual limitation first made by the NLR 'cultural revolution' in the mid-1960s (see III.4; Nairn, 1972, pp. 106–8), Anthony Barnett, among others, retorted fairly in NLR that 'Eagleton and Nairn ... have tried to press Williams into the antiquated mould of the English traditions – but he does not quite fit' (1976, pp. 51–3).

From criticising the populist and culturalist tendencies, there had developed a theoretical trend primarily influenced by the Marxism of Althusser and followers. In an article published in NLR in 1969, Miriam Glucksmann attacked what she saw in Britain as a growing interest in the identification of Marxism with neo-Hegelianism: theory is denied any autonomy, and becomes an expression merely of class consciousness rather than a science capable of guiding political struggles. For her, 'to emphasise idealism and humanism is an effective way of defusing the revolutionary potential of Marxism' (1969, pp. 49, 62). This remark actually represented much of NLR's own position which will concern us later (in IV.4).

As discussed before (III.3), one of the key initiatives of the British New Left was the movement for workers' control. Drawing upon classical socialist ideas of self-government within a native tradition of guild socialism and revolutionary syndicalism, the movement was advanced through propaganda and agitation among shop stewards and trade unions, by the IWC. Their theorists constituted perhaps the only section of the New Left until the early 1970s that did maintain active contact with organised workers and had influence on union leaders. The marginal and short-lived movement exemplified one of the few meeting points between intellectuals and workers in this period and was one of the motive forces behind the later growth of the Labour Militant and far left.

In a dispute with Richard Hyman, a representative of what was called the revisionist Trotskyism of the IS group, Barratt Brown, Coates and Topham had an opportunity to give a clear-cut summary of their well-known strategic ideas about workers' control (SR 1975). These ideas are basically educational: as participants themselves, and not carrying out an intervention from outside, intellectuals educate workers and are educated among workers who develop their own theoretical apparatus from day-to-day experience as well as from learning theory.[38] This Gramsci-like argument, however, does not lead to Gramsci's 'Modern Prince'. The response of the IWC writers to the question of the need for a revolutionary party is rather simple: if the objective of socialism is to achieve a self-governing society with a self-managing industry, and not merely a transfer of power between elites or from market-dominance to bureaucratic arbitrariness, then a co-ordinating and information exchange centre, rather than a conventional party organisation, will be necessary. 'It could transitionally assume that part of the role classically assigned to a "revolutionary party" ... into an instrument for democratic revolutionary social transformation' (Coates, 1973; pp. 294–5). They see such a transformation not as a matter of overturning capitalist power, but as a disintegration of that power structure by gaining control from within: the extension of democracy, workers' control (from wages and conditions to employment and investment policies) and dual power. Here, educational becomes political:

> All concessions won by labour from capital ... can be seen as 'making capitalism work'; but, if they increase the knowledge and power of the workers and reduce the arbitrary power of capital, then increasingly capitalism is 'working' on the workers' terms. Such a situation of 'dual power' is, we believe, inherently unstable and after whatever length of time and fierceness of struggle would have to be resolved in the hegemony of the workers (Barratt Brown et al, 1975, pp. 303–4).[39]

Obviously there is in this passage an optimistic blindness to the possibility that such an 'inherently unstable' dual power could be resolved in favour of capitalism against workers. Whether the notion of 'conquest of power' can be replaced with that of a systematic dismantling of the old power relations remains an open question. In opposition to a 'state socialism' and preoccupied with the industrial battlefield, the IWC writers reclaim, in practical rather than theoretical terms, a selected set of ideas advanced and developed by Tom Mann (education and direct action), Lenin and Trotsky ('Soviet' and dual power), 'Council communists' such as Pannekoek, Lukács, Korsch and Gramsci, and perhaps also the Workers' Opposition in Russia (extending union democracy, and ascending from workers' power in factory councils to the future proletarian state). The chief contemporary inspiration was of course the Yugoslav experiment of self-governing socialism elaborated by the Praxis philosophers (see Coates's introduction to the Spokes-man edition of Markovic and Cohen, 1975).

One of a number of serious errors made by the young Gramsci, in Anderson's critique, is that he counterposed the workers' council to the party in 1919, holding that only the former was the true form of the revolutionary process. This was related to his belief, before his Turin experience, in the achievement of dominance in economic affairs by factory councils prior to the seizure of national political power (1968b, p. 26).[40] The IWC writers, however, seemed to be very close to the early Gramsci in stressing workers' political and managerial capacity for control while not confronting what became central in the Gramscian legacy: the thesis of the role of 'organic intellectuals' of the working class in the forging of a revolutionary party.[41]

The old problem of direct democracy had constantly re-emerged in different circumstances in the history of the roughly defined socialist movements, whether utopian socialism, anarcho-syndical socialism, guild socialism, workers' control, or more recently, student radicalism. In 1968, right after the French May, NLR editors wrote excitedly that the relevance of soviets or councils 'has never been greater than today' (NLR 51, 'Themes'). Similarly, Norman Birnbaum remarked that perhaps the most outstanding aspect of the events of 1968 was the seizure of bureaucratic institutions by their highly educated personnel. 'The battle for self-determination and participation in the workplace has been joined by part of the advanced labour force' (1969b, pp. 166–7). Far too optimistic in their perspective, these words touched the fundamental question of the form of socialist democracy: mediated by councils or other such institutions, can 'people's power' be actually realised? What is the relationship between workers' control and the function of the state – a capitalist state before the socialist revolution, and a temporarily maintained 'bourgeois state' after it? Miliband, among a few New Left theorists, is very sceptical about the entire project of direct or council democracy which (as Fernando Claudin points out) is essentially in conflict with representative or delegated democracy. The former is not viable in its literal meaning, least of all in a revolutionary period, because it 'represents a leap into a fairly distant future, and leaves the question of the exercise of socialist power unsolved' (1978, p. 165). From a different angle, Hyman argues that capitalism must be seen as a total power and system, against which the ideas of workers' control have not put enough emphasis (1974).

The IWC writers provided no theoretical answers to these questions but were more concerned with practical objectives. They were in fact joined, before the founding of IWC, by the younger New Left advocates for workers' control. Anderson also believed this control as 'not a utopian myth', but 'an eminently practicable political goal' (1964b, p. 25). What is fundamental in such a goal, in his view, is that it in effect implies more than merely immediate gains by industrial workers, namely, the restoration of meaning to work and the products of work. Much wider and deeper issues are thereby involved, concerning the entire and ultimate aim of human self-realisation (cf. 1965b, pp. 285–6). It was a pity that Anderson, as well as his colleagues in the second *NLR*, rarely returned to the theme of workers' control after the mid-1960s.

There are, of course, hardly any clear boundaries between the various political and intellectual tendencies of the British New Left sketched in this section. In general, compared with theoretically highly developed western Marxism, in Britain fruitful engagements in Marxist theory had been much fewer. In other words, as Saville put it, there was an 'absence of hard-line theoreticians capable of confronting bourgeois ideas at their strongest rather than their weakest points'. One of the strengths of *NLR*, he admitted, was that it had taken on some of the central problems of theory; but were it not for the 'unreadable jargon' that afflicted so much of its discussions, the *Review* would be more helpful (1970, pp. 210–11). This is to say, the common identity of British Marxism of the 1970s (at least and especially seen in *NLR*) and post-Gramsci western Marxism was simply their common academic nature. The demise of all the political movements inspired in one way or another by Marxist theory renewed the 'dialectic of defeat' that had haunted western Marxism from the outset, and continued to separate theories from history.

The International Dimension

However backward or, to be more precise, unbalanced, British Marxism appeared to be, one of the significant intellectual contributions of the New Left in Britain is that it had decisively broken the hitherto insulated national culture. Anderson is not exaggerating in saying that the ferment of 1968 represented not only a political break, it marked a 'geo-cultural' one as well. Much due to the technological and institutional developments of the communication systems, 'in this epoch, no cultures could remain national in the pristiner senses of the past' (1990, *NLR* 180, pp. 48).[42] He is only partially right though. On the one hand, in regard to the encounter with the theoretical systems of continental Marxism which was followed by a Marxist renaissance in Britain, it was indeed not until the mid-1960s that the second New Left initiated the project of overcoming an intellectual parochialism. It is also a fact that the impact of *NLR* and New Left Books (NLB/Verso) in other parts of the world, in USA, Europe and elsewhere (for example in Japan and China) had been far greater than before after the boundary changes that principally resulted from the emergence of a substantial Marxist culture in Britain. What he overlooked, on the other hand, is not only the international interactions between the old British New Left and its counterparts in the United States and continental Europe, but also the emerging tendency in the second half of the 1970s within his own generation to rethink the earlier total discard of the Anglo-Saxon tradition of critical thought; and to respond to the increasing recognition from outside Britain of the importance and merits of this tradition, after a disappointing tour of the landscape of western Marxism and a feverish engagement in French structuralism.

If the name of 'the Marxist *Englishmen*' fits people like Thompson,[43] Williams was nonetheless not only a Welshman (though the country and especially its working class had always been there in the background of his writings), just as Anderson was not only or even particularly Irish or Nairn only Scottish. While by and large the New Left was culturally preoccupied with the English intellectual inheritance, the 'little Englandism' that affected native liberals so much had never been a problem. Furthermore, the leading figures of the old British New Left had become internationally influential, far beyond the borders of their homelands. In a review of *The Country and the City*, Thompson wrote that:

> if his [Williams's] material is largely national, the moral inquiry which informs his book is not. It remains part of that stubborn, uncompromising clarification of socialist thought which historians will come to see as more important and more lasting in influence than better advertised products of the international New Left. ... The idiom is too English to fall easily into international discourse; but I believe that in time it will (1975b).

He was proven right about Williams, a distinguished representative of British socialist criticism, though what he belittled under the sweeping name of the 'international New Left' is unclear.

An intellectual isolation was of course felt long before *NLR*'s European programme. That is why C. Wright Mills, in those early days, was so highly appreciated. Formulating a 'new left' theory in America where there was not yet a new left movement, Mills's sociology of the power elite (1956), the middle classes (1951), world politics (1958, 1963) and intellectual radicalism (1959) was at least for a moment more effective on the other side of the Atlantic. A true defender of the Cuban revolution, a stern but open-minded critic (unlike those dogmatic anti-communists among old and new left alike) of the Soviet system, a passionate friend of the British New Left, Mills was, wrote Miliband in *NLR* to mourn his death, 'desperately needed by socialists everywhere' (1962, p. 20). Other US sources of support and inspiration include the two independent socialist magazines from New York: *Monthly Review* (*MR*), edited by the prominent Marxist economist Paul Sweezy and historian Leo Huberman (he died in 1968 and was replaced by Harry Magdoff), and *Dissent*, edited by long-standing democratic socialists such as Irving Howe, Meyer Schapiro and Michael Walzer (with Erich Fromm and others as contributing editors). The only advertising page of *NR* was solely reserved for *MR* which had contributions from New Left authors in Britain (such as Williams, 1960a). *Dissent*, later a key forum where the American New Left was criticised and also defended, was regarded as a 'sister publication' of *ULR* (Samuel, 1989, p. 44).

For the former communist elements of the New Left who belonged to 'an emaciated political tradition, encapsulated within hostile national culture' (that culture was, however, their 'reluctant host' in terms of intellectual familiarity and preference; see Thompson, 1973, p. 319), 'Marxist revisionism' initiated from eastern Europe was a natural focus. Contacts with these critics of orthodox institutional Marxism were made as close as possible, and these constituted the major alliance in the struggle against Stalinism. One of the best-known examples of critical exchange between the Marxist New Left and the disillusioned eastern dissidents was Thompson's open letter to Leszek Kolakowski (1973). Another example of general New Left attention to 'actually existing socialism' is Williams's discussion of a deserter, Alexander Solzhenitsyn (1972), and a reformer, Rudolph Bahro (1980, pp. 252–73).[44] These contacts were already part of Anderson's post-1968 geo-cultural emplacement, but have their origin in the early New Left preoccupation with the Soviet bloc. In promoting positive neutralism during the CND years, moreover, there was an active alignment with the national liberation movements in the third world pursued by *NR* and *ULR*. Worsley and Hall, for instance, went to Ghana for a conference; they both, as did Rex and Lessing, regularly appeared on anti-colonial platforms at home (Worsley, 1989, p. 90; not to mention Blackburn's and Tariq Ali's later Cuban adventure).

It is worth noting a special event of what might be called an international New Left gathering in London in July 1967. The Round House Conference on the Dialectics of Liberation was organised by the 'anti-psychiatrists': Laing, Cooper, Berke and Redler, and attracted, among others, Marcuse and Goldmann. The conference, in Blackburn's assessment, 'represented a definite shift to politics' compared to other typically New Left protests like the earlier counter-cultural poetry festival (quoted from Fraser, 1988, p. 143). The point is that the cultural is not spontaneously political but can be so only through deliberate articulation and conscious struggles. It is also worth mentioning the impact of the History Workshop movement (see IV.4) within the tradition of the British New Left, especially on radical US historians, as shown by their growing interest in oral history, and other scholarly as well as organisational activities inspired by the Ruskin Workshop (see, for example, Mary Blatt's report on the Massachusetts History Workshop, *RHR* 25, p. 184).

The 'failed dialogue' between British and continental philosophers (Meszaros, 1986, pp. 212–3) in general mirrored the similar failure between British and European Marxists. But there was also the failure of Marxism in Britain, at least by the late 1970s, to recognise and properly assimilate non-Marxist achievements on its own national scene. Writing around 1983, Alex Callinicos, a young analytic Marxist in Oxford, complains that:

> The past fifteen years have seen developments of the most fundamental importance in English-speaking (and especially American) philosophy. ... Collectively, they have drawn analytical philosophy away from the worst excesses of logical positivism and the ordinary-language approach – respectively, vulgar empiricism and complacent lexicography – towards epistemological and metaphysical issues of substance. Yet all this has passed English-speaking Marxist philosophers by (1983, pp. 4–5).[45]

He is blaming English-speaking philosophers because in other disciplines (history, economics, sociology, cultural studies), in his view, Marxism has been entrenched or made considerable impact; and because continental thinkers (such as Habermas) to whom many British Marxists once sought for salvation have turned to show respect for and interest in analytical philosophy (pp. 6–7).

The 1980s, however, was precisely the decade that saw the growing up of a vigorous school of Anglo-American analytical Marxism (G. A. Cohen, Jon Elster,

John Roemer, Erik Olin Wright and others) from the soil of an intellectual tradition that had long appeared to be so foreign to the mode of Marxist thought. Even more impressively, there had been indeed (contrary to Callinicos's somewhat exaggerated picture) resistance from some of those who were hitherto almost single-mindedly European oriented to the fashionable trends of the moment under the rubric of 'postmodernism' among the continental left.[46] Anderson's belated recognition of the achievements of a native scholarship, left and liberal alike, in sociology, anthropology, history, literary criticism, aesthetics, political philosophy, philosophy, economics and feminist studies (1990), is all the more remarkable, especially because NLR's 'cultural revolution' of the late 1960s was supposed to have been launched in an impoverished national desert. It might be more appropriate to say that all these came too late to be able to bypass the Marxist British New Left, and the latter's sectarianism, affecting both its generations, played a part.

As a general assessment, it is greatly to the New Left's credit that the British national tradition can no longer be isolated from the outside world and has more than ever promised fruitful intellectual yields in the political culture of Marxism and socialism.

3. BUILDING A NEW MARXIST CULTURE

Reassessing Historical Materialism

The New Left was a dynamic generator of creative ideas during the 1960s. However, theoretical reconstruction was undertaken mainly in the 1970s after the political movement of the New Left began to decline. The intellectual results of this reconstruction could be of political significance in the next period of radical change, but their real potential as a legacy must await the judgement of a future generation with deeper and fuller understanding of the two decades that brought the New Left into being and then took it away from the British scene.

In general, whatever the contrasts or oppositions among them, a common commitment of New Left writers was to see Marxism not as a dogmatic orthodoxy, but as a living tradition and a major scientific theory within the broader compass of socialist thought.[47] Classical Marxism, suggests Anderson, should be submitted to the same rigorous scrutiny and critical appraisal as the later Marxist traditions. 'The presence of errors is one of the marks of any science'. Historical materialism cannot be replaced so long as 'there is no superior candidate for comparable overall advance in knowledge', to be sure; it must nevertheless 'surpass' Marx's and Engels's own 'mistakes and omissions' on the basis of new scientific knowledge now available for theoretical development (1976a, pp. 113–14).[48] Although treating Marxism simply as a general philosophy for the interpretation of history was resisted, most sought a synthesis: above all, Marx's scientific critique of political economy transcended philosophy. The New Left theoretical project was by and large an undertaking to liberate Marxist thought from its various versions of positivism.

In Thompson's not very helpful classification, Marxism has been conceived as
(a) a self-sufficient body of doctrines;
(b) method;
(c) heritage (one of the items in the 'supermarket' of human culture); and
(d) tradition.
He identifies with Marxism in sense (d), which is against the scientism of sense
(a) and opportunism of (c), and entails some of the advantages but avoids certain
difficulties of (b) (1973, pp. 320–9). Since it is almost impossible categorically to
separate method and theory with reference to Marxism, and apparently 'tradition'
needs a qualification in order to be not identical to 'heritage', it is unclear where
Thompson stands in that complicated recasting process of Marxism by the New
Left.[49] By contrast, Anderson's overview of classical Marxism, referring only to
the works of Marx, Lenin and Trotsky, is more useful as he has suggested several
critical areas or unanswered questions for inquiry.[50] Engels is missing here despite
the fact that it was he who produced the first systematic expositions of Marxism
as a world view that inspired succeeding socialist generations and the lasting
tradition of the Second International.

     In rejecting the prevalent stereotype of Engels as the positivist vulgariser
and mechanical interpreter of dialectical Marxism, and the liberal attacks on
Marxism itself through Engels, Stedman Jones examines Engels's writings
against their background, showing how essential his contribution was to the
genesis and the worldwide diffusion of historical materialism, and why his
thought should be understood in the same light of German philosophy, next to
Marx himself (1973; 1977c). The roots for much subsequent controversy in
Engels's venture to systematise a general Marxist philosophy, however, is
found in Engels's mistaken attempt at borrowing Hegel's dialectical 'method'
while repudiating the Hegelian idealist 'system', for the two are not really
inconsistent (1973, pp. 35–6; 1977c).[51] It is surprising that no serious arguments
rose to challenge Stedman Jones's unusual treatment of Engels, in both its
positive and negative directions. Unlike fashionable Marxist discussions elsewhere, in Britain there has not been much debate on the intellectual relationship between Marx and Engels, and therefore the continuities and 'breaks' in
the trajectory of classical Marxism.

     Touching the very core of historical materialism, Hall explains the evolution
of the modes of production in a structuralist manner:

> What matters is not the mere appearance of a relation sequentially through
> time, but its position within the configuration of productive relations which
> makes each mode an ensemble. Modes of production form the discontinu-
> ous structural sets through which history articulates itself. History moves –
> but only as a delayed and displaced trajectory, through a series of breaks,
> engendered by the internal contradictions specific to each mode (1974,
> p. 154).

The problem of Hall's 'figurative language', remarks Eagleton, 'is a symptom of
the difficulty that any dialectical thought must confront in trying to think this

fraught issue': what is this unitary 'history' that moves through discontinuous structures? Is this 'history' at once always deconstructed yet always self-identical (1981, p. 65; 1989, pp. 166–7)? Hall's history seems to become independent and abstract from concrete social structures, but how is his different from Marx's own abstraction? More questions need to be raised and answered here for clarification.

The most telling and clear-cut amendment made to a basic tenet of historical materialism might have been best stated by Anderson, supported by the evidence reconstructed in his two-volume study of global social transformations:

> Contrary to widely received belief among Marxists, the characteristic 'figure' of a crisis in a mode of production is not one in which vigorous (economic) forces of production burst triumphantly to establish a higher productivity and society on their ruins. On the contrary, ... relations of production ... must themselves be radically changed and recorded before new forces of production can be created and combined for a globally new mode of production. In other words, the relations of production generally change prior to the forces of production in an epoch of transition, and not vice versa (1974a, p. 204).

He cannot claim much novelty here, of course, but this is still a bold generalisation.[52] It is always astonishing that, knowing well that the course of capitalist development had experienced its most fundamental leap forward after the bourgeois revolutions, why in the original Marxist formulations the dynamic or initiating capacity of productive relations was not given greater weight. No matter which changes first, the very idea that relations must correspond to forces of production remains legitimate. Once the former no longer corresponds to the latter, that can be (or indeed usually is) caused not by decisive advances in the forces of production but by decay, or collapse in the elements of productive relations themselves, then an epoch of transition begins. This is a matter of logical order rather than historical timing. Anderson's revision is therefore well in line with Marx's overall framework.

Much attention has been paid to the debate over base and superstructure. The complicated relation between the two realms is a lacuna in Marx, yet, as Ellen Wood puts it, the metaphor 'has been made to bear a theoretical weight far beyond its limited capacities' (1990, p. 126).[53] It is not surprising that most New Left writers would either simply abandon this metaphor altogether or be highly sceptical and attempt substantial refinements. The same underlying impulse behind such total or partial negative attitudes was a rejection of economism or reductionism which, it was said, became a common trend in the transition from Marx to Marxism, and was the focus of the very battle from which the New Left first emerged.

Thompson straightforwardly objects to 'the lamentable image' of the base/superstructure model because it offends the very profound 'sense of process' which has sustained his own work all along as a historian (1973, pp. 329–30; cf. 1959b; 1961, pp. 17–18; 1965, pp. 351–6). By 'process' he means the dialectical interrelations of social being and social consciousness in the concrete historical context, involving people and institutions in their daily activities. Earlier in *The Making of the English Working Class* and later in *Whigs and Hunters* (1975), it is not difficult for him to explore these relations without recourse to the base/ superstructure formula which he considers to characterise a 'schematic Marxism'. Concluding from his study of the origins of the Black Act of 1723 and the bourgeois legislation of eighteenth-century England, he asserts that law 'was deeply imbricated within the very basis of productive relations' (1975a, p. 261; pp. 258–69). This is a prestigious case against the base/superstructure distinction, yet it is far from sufficient.[54]

Like Thompson, Williams has 'great difficulty' in his own fields to see the processes of art and thought as superstructural in the sense of the formula as it is commonly employed (1980a, p. 36). But unlike Thompson, his more tactful manner leaves room for a sophisticated version: he prefers to reveal the methodological complexities and conceptual problems of the formula. He only opposes it when it constitutes, with a figurative element and the suggestion of a fixed and static spatial relationship, a reductionist form of the originally authentic proposition of social being determining social consciousness, an abstraction of the determining base and the determined superstructure as simple reflection, representation or ideological expression (1977, pp. 75–82; 1971, pp. 9–10; ;cf. 1979, pp. 136–50).[55] Moreover, he goes further from these usual grounds that sustain his and others' suspicion of a crude metaphor that is so often and so easily accommodated to mechanical simplifications, to establish 'cultural materialism', to include cultural practices or the forces of cultural production in the material base (see the next section). An important development from the problematic base/superstructure model seems to Williams to be an emphasis, primarily associated with Lukács, on social totality. For the concept 'totality' is in a way capable of overcoming the narrowness of the 'base' as being confined to economic sphere and is quite similar to his own solution – a theory of broad social process, 'of [the] relation between elements in a whole way of life' (1971, p. 10). The metaphor of 'base' is still more acceptable if it embraces the notion of human 'intention', especially the intention of the ruling class in terms of hegemony. However, Williams is aware of the inadequacy of totality if that is composed of different social practices but without any working of determination (1980a, p. 37).[56]

Others like Worsley, Saville and Miliband, are all seriously critical of the metaphor, but would not think it is legitimate to remove it.[57] In Miliband's view, the neglect of political theory in Marxist writings has something to do with the concept of base/superstructure and its implications. Certain parts of Marx's texts have been readily interpreted so as to give politics a mostly derivative, subsidiary, and epiphenomenal character. He suggests that as there remains in Marxism an insistence on the primacy of the economic base, it would be much more meaningful and apposite to treat this base as a starting-point, as 'a matter of the *first instance*', rather than as determining 'in the last instance' (1977a, p. 8).

The New Left theorists found helpful arguments in both Gramsci and

Althusser, for their respective strengths. Gramsci's contribution is seen by Hall as a concern with a Marxist theory of politics as the proper posing of the relation between base and superstructure (especially the specificity of the state), mediated by critical concepts such as hegemony and historical bloc. The controversial phrase of 'ideological state apparatus' in the post-Althusserian analysis is actually a direct reworking of Gramsci's passages on apparatuses of consent and coercion (1977b, pp. 64–8).[58] Miliband emphasises the Gramscian approach: the different elements, base and superstructure alike, which make up a 'historical bloc' would vary in their relative weight and importance according to concrete historical circumstances and human intervention (1977a, p. 8). Williams, on the other hand, acknowledges that Althusser's distinction between determinacy and domination and hence his creative idea of 'overdetermination', in opposition to an 'abstract determinism', is more useful than any other concept as a way of understanding historically lived situations and complexities of the contradictory process of interactions (1977, pp. 83–94; cf. 1976a, pp. 87–97). This distinction enables Anderson to analyse the structure of political power of bourgeois democratic states in fairly convincing terms, as in effect it is simultaneously and indivisibly dominated by culture and determined by coercion (1977, p. 42).

The distinction between determination and dominance, originally made by Marx himself in the 1857 *Grundrisse* and later, for instance, in a discussion in *Capital* of why politics in ancient Rome and Catholicism in the Middle Ages played the 'chief part' (1867, p. 82),[59] is a key to the 'genetic problem' of causal explanation. The primacy of economic base is asserted only in the sense that it is the source of superstructure. The latter must be both autonomous and related to, needed by and profoundly influencing or reinforcing what is generally called material production.[60] Althusser's contribution (in *For Marx*, and further in *Reading Capital*), according to Hall, is not only that he reinterpreted determinism in the form of a structured whole rather than a sequential causality, but also that he proposed to go beyond the purely descriptive limitations of the classical metaphor and reconceptualised the problem on the basis of social reproduction (1977b pp. 68–71).

But Hall also considers, disputing Althusser, that it is misleading to see the central premise of historical materialism as 'ultimate determination' always by the economic. Neither 'relative autonomy' nor 'overdetermination', though fruitful, are a theoretically final solution. He is thus attracted to the 'second template' in Marx (and Engels; for example, in *The German Ideology*), namely the tendency to attribute determination not to economics but to history itself – to praxis, an undifferentiated praxis which rolls throughout the whole social formation as its essential ground (1980, pp. 29, 33, 44, 52).[61] This is again too abstract a history or too general a praxis to be grasped. A dialectical distinction between historical object and human subject seems still necessary. Hall's explicit denial of the privileged economic determinants and overwhelming concern with superstructures was widely noted and evoked debate.

Political Economy and Socialism

Anderson concludes his considerations on western Marxism with a set of problematics, concentrating on the nature and structure of bourgeois democracy as a normal mode of capitalist power, the possible institutional forms of an authentic socialist democracy, the true configuration of imperialism as an international system of economic and political domination, the position and function of the nation-state, the complex mechanisms and meanings of national-ism, the laws of the motion of contemporary capitalism and the new forms of crisis specific to them, the basic characteristics and dynamics of the bureaucratic state that has emerged from the socialist revolutions, and the path to its abolition (1976, pp. 103–4, 121). The questions asked and discussed around these concerns have remained largely unsolved theoretically as well as historically. Another vital question that Anderson does not fully confront is why capitalism has been able, despite all its difficulties and contradictions, to achieve striking economic and political advances, some of which were originally proposed by socialists. This has to be followed by a series of sensitive and open questions with the reference to the nature of a socialist revolution and the revisionist legacies since the Second International.[62]

The State

Nicos Poulantzas, among others, pointed out that the theory of the state and political power had, with rare exceptions, been neglected by Marxist thought (1969, pp. 238–9).[63] It was also a commonplace that Marxist political theory in general was far from comparable to the coherent and developed Marxian economic theory of capitalism. Hall once admitted that the concentration on ideological problems, to which the New Left devoted so much of its energies, had obscured the 'absolutely critical question of the nature of the capitalist state'. Under his directorship, the Birmingham Centre made considerable efforts later on to remedy this neglect. One of the results was *Policing the Crisis* (1978), a collective analysis of British law and order, that anticipated the rise of Thatcherism. On the more theoretical level, the most distinguished work of the New Left at this aspect was done by Miliband, concerning the capitalist state in general and the British state in particular. The re-entry of the focus on the state within the Marxist tradition was an attempt at coming to terms with new political situations, especially after the student movement, the Czech events of 1968, and the revolution in Portugal, all revealed that many difficult questions around the 'myth' of the capitalist state were still to be confronted.

The starting point of examining the nature of the modern state in advanced capitalist societies cannot be other than an analysis of the transformation of post-war class structure corresponding to the significant changes in the composition of the work force brought about by the massive assimilation of industry and technology – the further separation of ownership and management, hence of owners and controllers; the expansion of the new middle class, the growth of a 'white-collar' stratum and a technical intelligentsia; the division between the working classes, and so on.[64] Renewed discussions in this area in the 1970s went far deeper and wider than the earlier 'classlessness' debate (see II.3) in two directions: the interaction between class struggles and national conflicts (notably Nairn, 1977b, ch. 1), and the shaping of class consciousness in the ways that further stabilise and legitimise capitalism (for example, Miliband, 1969, chs. 1 and 2).[65]

The Miliband/Poulantzas debate[66] opened after the publication of Miliband's *The State in Capitalist Society* (1969; which was basically a conventional Marxist statement) enriched British Marxism and also helped Marxist political analysis to advance. A simplified and sometimes confused division of arguments took place, between instrumentalist (Miliband) and structuralist (Poulantzas) and between the methodological empiricism of the former and the anti-empiricist 'abstractionism' of the latter.[67]

The first question that both sides must confront is the nature of the capitalist state. This involves answers based on two different but actually complementary approaches, that is, capitalist state as the state of capitalists, and as the state of capital. With the first approach, Miliband suggests a 'partnership' between those who control the state and those who own and control the means of production. The second approach, employed by Poulantzas, emphasises the determination of 'structural constraints'. According to him, Miliband is mistaken to reduce the relations between social classes and the state to 'inter-personal relations' of a 'plurality of elites', and therefore fails to comprehend the 'objective structures' of the political reality (1969, p. 242). Miliband strikes back by pointing out the danger of a 'super-determinism' which goes too far in disregarding the role of the rulers and thus is followed by an actual dismissal of the difference between, say, a state ruled by bourgeois constitutionists and one by fascists (1970b, pp. 32–3; 1973a, 38). Although Poulantzas cannot be charged with indifference to a gap as wide as that between these two kinds of bourgeois state (see especially his *Fascism and Dictatorship*, 1974), he does stress that Bonapartism was taken by Marx as 'characteristic of all forms of the capitalist state' (1969, p. 74). Consequently, the whole question of bourgeois democracy tends to be ignored in his theorisation. In strict logic he finds himself in a tight corner and suffers from what Anderson terms 'historical under-determination' (1977, pp. 36, 39).[68]

To define the state in terms of its function of cohesion, Poulantzas sees the 'ideological institutions' (the churches, political parties, unions, schools, mass media and, from a restricted point of view, the family) as being incorporated in the system of the state, because they contribute to social cohesion. While accepting the factual tendency of 'statisation' of these institutions, Miliband insists that they are not, in bourgeois democracies, part of the state. In rejecting the prevalent notion of 'state ideological apparatuses', he correctly distinguishes those non-state political systems to which some ideological institutions belong from those other institutions which indeed are consistent with the state monopolistic system of power (1969, pp. 183ff; 1970b, pp. 34–5). That is to say, the role of superstructures beside the state must be specified. Or, in the Gramscian rhetoric, the question is whether hegemony resides in the state or in civil society. In any case, it is clear that for the sake of both theoretical clarity and sensible strategy, it is essential to chart the boundaries of the state accurately.[69]

But there are also non-class factors affecting the nature of the state. In Miliband's view, Poulantzas fails to make the necessary distinction between class power and state power which results in a total deprival of any autonomy from the state and thus turns it into the merest instrument of a determinate class (1973a, pp. 40–3). Therefore, what this class power really is, how it operates (through what institutions, etc.), and what the relationship between the two powers is, remains unclear. Miliband himself is also vulnerable to the same charge, namely that he admits the autonomy of the state only in the extreme case of fascism (see Poulantzas, 1969, p. 74).[70] This means that during the debate, absolute instrumentalism, like determinism, falls into disfavour on both sides. It has become a common acknowledgement that Marx and Engels attribute to the state a considerable degree of independence not only in their analyses of Bonapartism or oriental despotism, but also in some concluding remarks which imply more general application. Serving the ruling class(es), yes; but at the same time the state is an institution in its own right, with its own interests and purposes.[71]

How far, then, is this state able to meet popular expectations? Is it open to reform, or must it be smashed? The question is sharpened in the western context in which modern democracy is the major form of capitalist regimes. Beside indicating a cultural domination, accompanied by a wide range of civil and political liberties, that is increasingly achieved by the state itself seeking legitimation, there is nothing new in the stress (by both Miliband and Poulantzas) on the combination of consent and coercion in the mechanisms of the bourgeois state.[72] The difficulty lies in its political transformation. Miliband's *Marxism and Politics*, published in 1977, was the first attempt in Britain systematically to reconstruct Marxist political theory and to tackle the question of bourgeois democracy.[73] He confirms the reformist function of the state in capitalist society and the possibility of 'dual power' in the transitional process. However, for him the classical Marxist proposition remains the truth that the working class cannot simply lay hold of the ready-made state apparatus and wield it for its own service (1977a, pp. 179–90).

In this connection Norman Geras's[74] discussion of Rosa Luxemburg (1976) contains interesting arguments.[75] Against Bernstein's optimism about evolutionary progress, a theme that pervaded Luxemburg's writings was the historical bankruptcy of bourgeois democracy and liberalism. However, Geras points out that there is an underestimation on her part of the vitality of this democracy and its role as an instrument for the self-emancipation of workers. 'She grasped earlier and better than anyone else' that the European working class had reached a historical turning point, that the epoch of peaceful growth and struggle in the context of capitalist stability lay behind it, while ahead there stretched a period of economic crisis and political conflict. But a revolutionary catastrophism limited her foresight and led her to fail to appreciate the potential support for democracy, not merely from the working class, but from the capitalist class itself in order to obtain popular consent. This had been said of course long ago by Bernstein, who saw democracy as the exclusive and natural political form for capitalist relations of production. Luxemburg rejected his view not only because it was false historically (capitalism had lived with other forms) but also because it mystified any perspective for the future. In defence of Luxemburg's revolutionary Marxism in opposition to both reformism and anarchism, Geras seems in retreat at this point from his critique of her underestimation of the dynamics and capability of bourgeois democracy (1976, pp. 198–200; 1978).[76] Like Anderson, he casts the 'normal mode' or 'mature form' of capitalist power as democratic. Yet they both deny the 'revisionist' legacies, despite the fact that apparently their 'normal' or 'mature' are not very far from Bernstein's 'natural'. Logically, they are saying that Bernstein was not all wrong, his idea has proved to be true in the higher stages of capitalist development. This is, indeed, still among the most crucial difficulties for Marxist political theory.

Attention was also paid to the nature of the socialist state. The common features of the communist regimes, as a conceptual challenge to Marxism, are the immense power they enjoy in an epoch supposed to be the beginning of the 'withering away' of the state, and the control of that power by one ruling party without either a genuine class base in the proletariat or an authentic democratic procedure of election. Marx and Engels, on the few occasions where they did claim the 'dictatorship of the proletariat', never defined in any specific way what that dictatorship would actually entail, or what the concrete exercise of socialist power would be like.[77] Beyond Trotsky's notion of a 'degenerate workers' state' (1937) and numerous other controversial conceptualisations of the post-revolutionary regimes,[78] the old question that Marx himself raised – 'what transformation will the state undergo in communist society?' (1875) – is yet to be answered.[79]

It has been long evident that the socialist revolution cannot itself resolve the problems posed by the idea of socialist democracy. Lenin seriously recognised only in his last years the tendency of bureaucratisation of the new regime and magnification of its repressive function. He never integrated his doctrine of the vanguard (an ultra-centralised, neo-Jacobin party) with his project of soviet democracy and popular participation.[80] The result, as Anderson sees it, was to permit an extremely swift reversion from the radical soviet democratism in his writings (especially *The State and Revolution*) to the radical party authoritarianism of the actual Russian state after the civil war (1976, p. 116). It was Luxemburg, among those who nevertheless sympathised with the October revolution, who most powerfully warned against the danger of Soviet decay in 1918. In light of the Luxemburg/SPD debate over strategies and the Luxemburg/Lenin polemic on nationalism and internationalism, Geras stresses Luxemburg's deep commitment to socialist democracy which was 'a momentous contribution but only for a future revolutionary generation' (1976, pp. 189, 192). Discussing her classical case, that she insisted on the need to break through the very framework of bourgeois-democratic institutions which both Bernstein and Kautsky wanted to preserve intact, Geras does not confront the hard core of the question: Bernstein's famous claim that 'democracy is at the same time means and end' and Kautsky's 'by the dictatorship of the proletariat we are unable to understand anything else than its rule on the basis of democracy' are certainly something that cannot be simply sniffed away, especially after all those bitter failures in the history of that later dictatorship which left the original motives far behind.

The question of what constitutes a socialist economy also centres on the role of the state. It is already common sense that it was mistaken to identify the state, even a 'state of the people', as it was assumed, with the 'social'. The very idea of nationalisation rests on the confusion over the state, on the wrong assumption that the nation-state is an unproblematic entity (Williams, 1979, p. 120). But just how a socially planned economy can be organised has not yet emerged either in theory or in experiments.[81]

Strategies

The incompleteness of historical materialism is marked, at bottom, by its very isolation as a revolutionary theory and by the absence of the bearers this theory assumed. The lack of strategic perspective on the left in relation to this incompleteness began to change in the 1970s because of the repercussions of the student movement, the Eurocommunist debate, and the rise of new social movements.

Against the tendency that often identifies the philosophical or economic writings of Marx and Engels as their crucial contribution to Marxism, Blackburn reminds his readers in an article published in NLR of what has been for him virtually forgotten by contemporary Marxists: the real focus of the work of the founders of historical materialism is political, as a revolutionary theory premissed upon the capacities of the modern workers' movement (1976, pp. 25, 62).[82] He does indicate a whole series of what he considers to be secondary characteristics – sex, religion, ethnic origin and so on – about members of the working class, but does not investigate what they mean to the struggle for socialism and human liberation at large. At this point, his view is representative of the British New Left which, though itself cross-class identified, had not been affected much by the prevailing disappointment with the western working class that characterised the idea and movement of the international New Left.

Conventional arguments over the path of political transformations are usually divided into two theoretical lineages, that is, revolutionary versus reformist.[83] For most of those who believe themselves to be Marxists, without a revolution socialism is not possible. To define revolution as such, however, does not entail an exclusion of social and economic reforms within the framework of the capitalist system. These reforms are actually expected, on a reasonable basis, to provide more favourable conditions for the organisational and educational work of socialist struggle. But to differentiate support for genuine reforms, as part of a greater revolutionary project, from that 'reformism' which had been a target of the New Left,[84] is not so easy and sometimes causes pointless disputes and more confusions.

Implicitly following Kautsky's argument in *The Road to Power* (1909), Miliband believes that the socialist strategy involves both a revolutionary and a reformist commitment, in so far as it also seeks reforms which could serve the revolutionary purpose. This Marxist reformism, using non-parliamentary methods of struggle such as strikes, demonstrations, campaigns, and other protest actions against repression by hegemonic conservatism (racial, sexual, and so on) and arbitrary power (governmental, etc.), leads to 'a very considerable transformation of the character of the state and of existing bourgeois democratic forms' (1977a, pp. 16, 158, 160–1, 164, 188–9; 1983, p. 307). He has thus preserved rather than renounced the Marxist proposition that the old state apparatus must be broken down. Between the two strategic models that traditionally divided the European socialist movement and were dubbed by Anderson the insurrectionary and the parliamentary (or constitutionalist) roads to socialism, Miliband's synthesis offers an alternative.

It promises an alternative especially because it is based on his assertion of the need for a socialist party-like organisation to carry out revolution and reforms. Given the specific British situation highlighted by the half-paralysed Labour Party, Miliband repeatedly argues that socialism in this country needs something new. A new party, in his supposition, is most likely to be at first some kind of federal form, a more or less loose alliance of groupings of people, and will have different factions working together in a state of 'permanent tension and argument'. Such a non-unitary character would be the price that a serious political formation as distinct from old vanguard or bureaucratic parties has to pay. But what the developed structure and type of a new party will be like is not attempted (1976; 1977b, pp. 47–50; cf. 1964b, pp. 83–4; 1979, pp. 25–7).[85] Can it function adequately and efficiently with endless internal splits? What should be the principal means of its struggle? In the absence of any mass movement for radical changes in reality, how might it organise political education and obtain popular support? These are questions related to the formulation of a feasible socialist programme in the first place, which are yet to be answered.[86]

One cannot avoid asking, even along with Miliband's non-parliamentary road via a 'dual power', how far it is possible to rely on an electoral majority for finally legislating socialism at regional and national levels. Geras discusses the limits of bourgeois democracy in the light of the Chilean experience of 1973, writing that 'it has been a central principle of revolutionary Marxism, supported by good evidence, that the road to socialism cannot bypass the preparation of the working class and its allies for armed self-defence and armed struggle' (1978, p. 311).[87] This was, as shown in Anderson's critique of Gramsci, a general *NLR* editorial stand.[88] Commenting on the same passage of Marx concerning the socialist transformation in such countries as America, England and probably Holland too, 'where the workers may attain their goal by peaceful means', Thompson, Anderson and Miliband, more or less representing the first New Left, the second

New Left and an 'integrated' New Left position respectively, contrast themselves
sharply with each other. In Anderson's view, because of a preoccupation with
militarist Bonapartism, Marx had 'tended to underestimate the repressive
capacity of the "pacifist" English, Dutch and American states' (1976a, p. 114).
For Miliband, Marx was willing to allow some isolated cases, but not the
common pattern, of socialist transition being achieved by non-violent means.
Referring to the Chilean tragedy, he draws the lesson on organised mobilisation
of popular forces (1977a, p. 79; 1970a). Being no longer a passionate revolutionary (see II.4), Thompson now challenges the very idea of revolution itself – 1789
and 1917 are the exceptions of history and the rule is made up by more confused
transitions. Leninism, he affirms, is 'irrelevant to this country and this time', and
'often entail[s] anti-libertarian premisses' (1978b, pp. 20, 22; cf. 1965, pp. 344–5;
1978a, p. 354).

What is most remarkable in the story of the New Left strategic debate is that,
running contrary to Thompson's path, Williams followed a personal evolution
from his 'reformist' to 'revolutionary' perspectives (to use his own terms). His earlier
uncertainty about the two roads to change (see II.4) had been replaced by a
conviction that 'the condition for the success of the long revolution in any real
terms is decisively a short revolution' and almost inevitably a violent one (1979, pp.
421; cf. pp. 410–24; 1975, pp. 68, 71–6). Writing in 1975, he honestly told us that:

> When I look at the history of the Chinese, the Cuban and the Vietnamese
> revolutions, I feel a basic solidarity not merely with their aims but with
> their methods and with the ways in which they came to power. If I found
> myself in Britain in any comparable social and political situation, I know
> where my loyalties would lie. ... I believe that it is not necessary to abandon
> a parliamentary perspective as a matter of principle, but as a matter of
> practice I am quite sure that we have to begin to look beyond it' (1975, pp.
> 73, 75).

This crossover of Williams and Thompson is always striking, exemplifying the
near impossibility of strategic thinking without an actual grounding in a socialist
movement.

Nationalism and Imperialism

Marx and Engels acknowledged the vitality of bourgeois nationalism (for
example, in the case of German and Italian unification) and internationalism
(exploiting new markets in the colonies) in the process of building capitalism. But
they failed to comprehend the global expansion of capitalism and hence the
complexity of the combined social formations in the backward continents and the
intensified uneven development of the world economy. This means that, limited
to the nineteenth-century scene, while firmly supporting the struggles for
independence of the Irish, the Poles and others, they missed the particular
historical importance of such national liberation movements and the conflicts
between the nation-states as well. There is no systematic theory or even a clear
line of positions ever established on these issues in their work. It was the second

generation of Marxists, including Lenin, Kautsky, Hilferding, Bauer and Luxemburg, that debated and developed theories of capital accumulation on a world scale, and a set of related questions (see Michael Löwy's survey, 1976). Luxemburg's preoccupation with nationalism as an absolutely anti-socialist force was symbolic of that strong but one-sided internationalist tradition among the first two Marxist generations. A historical turn after the First World War, as Anderson observes, was seen in internationalism being gradually replaced by nationalism in the mind and politics of the left.[89] For British socialists, violent conflicts in Northern Ireland in relation to Irish nationalism was a lasting reminder of this weakness in Marxist theory and the difficulty of regaining an internationalist spirit.

Pioneer New Left contributions within the Marxist tradition were Barratt Brown's *After Imperialism* (1963), a full-length study of the contemporary world economy, and Worsley's *The Third World* (1964), a sociological inquiry into the division between rich and poor peoples.[90] The significance of both books lies in these highly important themes, in spite of their rather minor influence.[91]

In examining Marxist concepts of the connection between capitalism and imperialism, Barratt Brown appreciates Lenin's (and Hobson's) theory especially in regard to Lenin's brilliant prophecy of the post-1918 situation: the outward impulse towards monopoly of great industrial corporations and the working of the 'law' of uneven development. Yet Lenin was wrong, in Barratt Brown's opinion, to see the British empire as created by the pressure of monopoly capital to invest overseas when profits fell at home. Moreover, the tribute from this investment was not the cause of 'moral corruption' of the British working class. A serious error in Marxist common sense is thus to focus on capital export: it was free trade rather than capital export that played an essential role in leading to an artificial world division of labour and an unequal relationship between developed and underdeveloped nations (1963b, pp. 11–14, 95–101, 453–4; 1972a, pp. 48–9; 1974b, pp. 69–70; cf. 1972b, part 1).[92] Moreover, the export of capital in fact provides a counter to the global polarising process. Barratt Brown's major concern here is the growth of transnational companies in relation to the power of modern nation state. For him, it would be confusing to refer to these giant companies as monopolies since it is their competition that creates anarchy in the world market. This must be properly addressed (1972a, pp. 50, 53, 56).

Case studies of imperialism centred on the United States. While American imperialism is analysed in political terms by Worsley as counter-revolutionary militarism (1964, pp. 304–5), Barratt Brown stresses its economic function: the fact that most transnational corporations were American gave the US government a special position in defending the general interest of capital. Military interventions, he argues, often contradicted this interest as they frustrated new and expanding markets (1972a, pp. 52–3). Contrasting US imperialism with European ones, Kiernan shows how little it makes sense to confine imperialism to direct colonial rule (1971). According to Stedman Jones, Marxist discussions have tended to concentrate too insistently upon imperialism as a global stage (the 'highest stage' in Leninist argument) of capitalist development, and neglect the distinction between the historical determinants of a social formation and the specific mode of domination engendered by it. The specificity of US imperialism, in his view, is its being 'an invisible empire' – its non-territorial nature, its formally anti-imperialist ideology, and the underlying continuity of American history in both forms (1969a, pp. 208, 211–13, 236). Nairn argued, however, that British imperialism's essential economic character was very close to the US model in terms of its more 'informal' structures after 1906 – the transition from empire to commonwealth, and an 'internationalist' ideology to cope with them (1972, p. 75). But his criticism of Miliband's theory of state for ignoring of the developmental uniqueness of, rather than fundamental similarities between, each particular state, and his claim for an 'advance on the terrain of differentiation and specific analysis' (1977b, pp. 14–15), turn out to be of the same line as the methodological emphasis of Stedman Jones.

The debate on the overall structure of the contemporary world economy and international relations in the frameworks of either the 'world-system approach' or the 'dependency theory', or otherwise, became a notable theme of NLR later on.[93] Yet this area remained a weak one among the fields that bore a New Left imprint. Thompson or Saville (as labour historians) made little contribution, nor did Hall (as a Caribbean) or Williams (as a sympathiser with the Welsh and Scottish nationalist movements). Early capitalist accumulation and later racial tensions and repressions were among topics of their work, but the whole question of imperialism and nationalism never really engaged them.[94] The younger NLR circle did hasten to publicise the condition of the exploited peoples and even provide some practical assistance to their liberation causes, but they too left theoretical questions largely unasked and unanswered.[95] Neither Blackburn nor Anderson, for example, ever worked on the subject of peasant (and in many cases armed) revolutions and their relationship to socialism. Only a very few New Left writers confronted the socio-economic structure of the newly independent nations and the nature of their 'socialist' or populist regimes, among them Worsley. He wrote on the 'lumpenproletariat' for SR in 1972, supporting Fanon's belief in the revolutionary potential of the peasantry and sub-proletariats, especially their racially discriminated sections. The key to the latent possibility of these classes becoming a directing and self-conscious force in political action is their leadership (this is true of the proletariat too). He made the point that Third World conditions also typified the life of the black sub-proletariat in, for instance, the United States. The notion of the 'Third World' therefore refers to a set of relationships rather than to countries (1972, pp. 207, 217–20, 223–7).

The other side of the question of nationalism concerns national identity in general which is, in the end, the question of the modern nation state and its socialist solution. Devoting himself to an investigation and critique of British nationalism – state, monarchy, regional/national conflicts – in a series of NLR articles published between 1970 and 1977, Nairn was the most influential thinker of the New Left in this respect.

The left in Britain had been bitterly divided since the early 1960s over the debate on entry to the Common Market, or a socialist attitude toward Europe. The issue manifested a profound dilemma of national identity, and 'a choice between Europe and the world' (Hall & Anderson, 1961, p. 1) had to be faced, especially by the Suez-preoccupied New Left. Barratt Brown and Hughes held that socialists should stay out of the Common Market because that would give a Labour government a chance to implement 'socialist planning'.[96] Thompson also sneered at any favourable consideration on entry all along (cf. 1978a, pp. 313–14, 334). MacIntyre was almost alone in supporting entry in the early 1960s (*Encounter*, February 1963, p. 65). The case of Williams is illuminating: after a few years of struggling with the confusion of opposing both the European Economic Community as a form of capitalist integration and 'modernisation', and the Conservative claim for national sovereignty, he at last (in 1975) chose a 'western European identity' against 'the economic nationalism of the Labour Left' (1976, p. 242; 1979, p. 381). This final reach must have surprised Nairn who thought that Williams, as being so much confined to the national culture, would be unable to do so (1972, pp. 139–43).

Nairn first concerned himself with British nationalism during the Labour Party's anti-Market campaign (1971), then developed a theoretical analysis of the issue a year later in 'The Left against Europe?' (1972). The latter, an uncompromising and 'predominantly negative' essay, was a restatement of his previously drawn profile of the Labour Party (see III.2 and 3), the profile of 'a lack, a failure, a missed opportunity' (1972, pp. x, xiv). In opposition to a 'national Labourist frenzy', Nairn saw the inevitability and a socialist strategic priority of capitalist European unity. The effects of moving British politics out on to the wider stage of Europe would provide a real battleground and better conditions of struggle for the left. And only so could and must proletarian internationalism become an integral part of class struggle in a new and immediate sense (see, esp. 1972, chs 8 and 9; 1977b, pp. 53–4). In neglecting the argument that a united Europe would also strengthen capitalist domination or imperialism, he was in an absolute minority of the left, old and new. But, in the course of events, before long socialists were to have to confront the reality of the European community.

With the EEC, as with Ulster, the left found itself enveloped in a nationalist atmosphere. The far reach of that very British political and cultural order of imperialist provincialism was already obvious and had reemerged frequently since the Suez crisis.[97] On the one hand, as Nairn noted, European socialism suffered from a contradiction in its world view: an over-identity with the globe (a Eurocentric commitment), or a universalism similar to the 'cosmopolitanism' which Gramsci saw as a persistent fault of the Italian intelligentsia (1972, pp. xvii–xviii). On the other hand, Deutscher could not be more correct in pointing out that the new waves of nationalism in the labour movements in the west were in a sense only a continuation of the same social-patriotism that came to the fore in 1914 (1971). By contrast, the world view of the bourgeoisie was to some extent genuinely internationalist. Even bourgeois politicians, remarked Deutscher, were beginning to sense that the nation state, at least in Europe, had 'become an anachronism' (1968). Miliband considered that in the process of capitalist inter-nationalisation in western Europe (sometimes in opposition to, but more often in conjunction with, American penetration), the EEC was an institutional expression of the attempt to overcome, within the framework of capitalism, the constantly more marked obsolescence of the nation state as the basic unit of international life. He had no doubt that the future of socialism in Britain was bound up with that future elsewhere (1969, p. 14; 1977b, pp. 38–9).

The complexity of a Marxist theory of nationalism lies in the ambivalent nature of the phenomenon itself: beside such things as fascism,[98] aggressive militarism, personality cults and dictatorship, and 'social imperialism' to which it can apply, there are also the populist, positive and historically just aspects or moments of the nationalist movements. In *The Break-up of Britain* (1977),[99] Nairn opened up new discussions of what he calls the 'twilight of the British state' indicated by the renewed armed conflict in Northern Ireland, the rise of Scottish and Welsh nationalism, and the increasing racial tensions that accompanied the increase in numbers of immigrant workers and their families. He seeks answers to two questions: one, why has the decline of the old British state system lasted so long, without catastrophe? Two, why does its breakdown begin to occur in the form of territorial disintegration rather than class war? (see 1977b, pp. 298–9, 310).[100]

On the matter of those 'English peculiarities' which were debated in 1964–6, Nairn focuses his arguments on the following points:

(1) Marxism's 'great historical failure' over the national question; yet from a theorisation of Lenin's 'pragmatic' position (the principles of self-determina-tion, the idea of possible conjunction between a national independent movement and a socialist revolution, etc.), a Marxist theory of nationalism could be developed (1977b, pp. 84–6, 329–31, 352).[101]

(2) The overall character of uneven capitalist development which alone provides an explanation of modern state formation and the origins of nationalism – the mobilisation of the masses against this 'uneven diffusion' and their own material backwardness (this is not confined to the poor countries) (*ibid.*, pp. 71–3, 89–90, 96, 101–2, 184, 220–1, 247, 250, 295).

(3) Nationalist revolts, instead of the struggle of the working class, as the grave-digger of the capitalist state in Britain. Nationalism is now seen not as false consciousness. It has played an even greater role than class consciousness in recent history. In other words, within certain contexts, the interests of the ruling class may coincide with those of the ruled, and any socialist movement today is likely to be intertwined with the dilemmas of nationalism. So the old assumption that national politics is in the final analysis a matter of class struggle and can only be settled through the struggle of the proletariat needs some radical amendment (pp. 43–4, 68–70, 89, 247).

(4) The contradiction between nationalism and internationalism in socialist thought and in current political movements that are basically carried out on

the national stage (pp. 78, 82–91, 354–5). This is most difficult, and paradoxical; to imagine that anyone could offer a strategic diagram and a neat formula for concrete internationalism, in the present situation, is 'to misunderstand that situation altogether' (1972, p. xi).

Nairn's attempt at a 'realistic' explanation of nationalism in the context of the dynamic of the uneven development of 20th century capitalism did not make many others feel more unrealistic in pursuing an internationalist perspective within the socialist tradition. International solidarity against the Vietnam War, for example, seemed to have exemplified something that might be a model for rebuilding genuine internationalism in the future (Halliday, 1971). Among Nairn's critics, from the classical Marxist point of view, Hobsbawm insists that 'neo-nationalism', as a by-product of the international concentration of capital, does not in itself require any change in, or any further theoretical elaboration of, Marxist analysis. Condemning any accommodation to nationalism on the left, he recalls that even toward those clearly progressive and emancipatory nationalist struggles, Lenin's attitude was 'Do not paint nationalism red' (1977b, pp. 8–10, 21–3). Hobsbawm's denial of the need for a more adequate and developed theory of nationalism obviously does no good to Marxism. As 'an impossible irony' (Eagleton, 1990, p. 23), there is no way to overcome nationalism unless all its rights and wrongs, confusions and dilemmas, causes and impacts be faced and worked through.[102]

The nationalist movements in Scotland and Wales have posed no real threat to the British state so far, nor even has the lasting upheaval in Northern Ireland. With a national decline observed and 'an Anglocentric nativism' (Nairn, 1988, p. 390) opposed, the capitalist state has much greater endurance and more ability to protect itself than it seemed to possess in the mid-1970s. In particular, the British state and political order proved to enjoy 'exceptional stability and continuity' (Stedman Jones, 1984a). Also, it is indeed arguable whether a break-up of the unitary state would benefit socialism in Britain. Nairn maintained that these new nationalist movements could result in a crisis of the Labour Party if they took away its traditional strongholds in the north and southwest. However, even if this split is to be the case, the decisive point for either the survival of the capitalist state or the future of socialism remains in England. As to Northern Ireland, despite all that had been said emotionally about its tragic predicament (for example, in the pages of *NLR* and *Seven Days*), the New Left did not propose any feasible policy suggestions for a democratic solution to the conflict and a political rearrangement of UK society.[103] Nor was there a clarified New Left position with sustained arguments along the line of self-determination or otherwise.

One of Anderson's open questions which he considers to constitute the central challenge to historical materialism reads, 'What is the meaning and position of the nation as a social unit, in a world divided by classes?' (1976, p. 103) It has become a commonplace Marxist acknowledgement that an all-embracing class analysis needs to be modified simply because the world is also divided by nations and other identities which are not primarily based on socio-economic relations. These identities are socially (more than ideologically and conceptually) constructed and often intercrossed. The priority of class interest and class struggle is now always problematic. Like the 'nation', class is only one, though an essential, particular form of human alienation and one contending force that competes with other collective identities in contemporary culture and politics.

Economics

The New Left contribution to Marxist political theory was not matched by a comparable discussion of economics. Indeed hardly any established theoretical progress in this area was made in Britain except for the achievements of the older Marxist generation of Maurice Dobb (1946; 1973), and more significantly, the Cambridge School of Piero Sraffa (1960) and Joan Robinson (1965, 1970).

For the Marxist British New Left, by the 1970s, it was clear that certain long-standing Marxian formulas were no longer scientifically appropriate, but the basic critique presented in *Capital* remained a key to the exposition of contemporary political economy. Mandel's *Late Capitalism* (1972) had been widely influential, which explained why even though this capitalism appeared to be still immensely powerful and fairly stable, it had lost its dynamic of innovation. According to the New Left economists, the prevailing theories of the market were unable to comprehend today's central economic issues because they lacked a sociological and historical insight such as Mandel's, namely a Marxist or Weberian focus on the class and power system which structured the economy (Nell, 1972; Meek, 1967a; Rowthorn, 1976). From this general position, there were a few studies of Marx's original writings and of important contemporary work produced by non-British Marxists or British non-Marxists. But the main concern was to find coherent arguments for an alternative economic strategy for Labour. Without close connection with the narrowly defined New Left, the controversial concepts and theories such as capital and value, the 'transformation problem', productive and unproductive labour, the laws and motion of capitalist development – the tendency of a falling rate of profit, the cyclicity of crises, the role of government, were largely pursued in the forum of CSE with its *Bulletin* after 1970.[104] The *NLR* (and NLB) and *SR* occupied only the fringe of these debates.[105]

Two old books that can be regarded as characteristically a New Left devotion to Marx's economics (in the sense that they seek to bridge the Marxist classics and modern criticisms of them) are Ronald Meek's[106] *Studies in the Labour Theory of Value* (1956, 1973) and *Economics and Ideology* (1967). The former is a defence of Marx's value theory;[107] the latter ranged more widely, with reflections on the development of economic thought in the present day (Sraffa, Keynes, Schumpeter, Robinson and Lange). Having become more and more critical of Marx since the publication of the later book and also in the new edition of the former, Meek not only casts doubt upon the application of the value theory to the determination of the value of labour-power, the 'falling tendency of the rate of profit' and the 'increasing misery' doctrine, but also shifts his focus from 'value' to 'distribution': some basic elements of Sraffa's conceptual framework could conceivably be adopted and used by Marxist economics (1973, pp. xvi–xvii, xxix–xxxii, xli–xlii; 1967b, pp. 142, 121, 127–8). Moreover, with 'something like a scientific basis' of Keynesian intervention, 'Keynes helped to pave the way for a new type of economic thinking which may well transcend all previous economic systems, including his own' (1967b, p. 195). In *Smith, Marx and After* (1977), published shortly before his death, Meek's last message was a sad scepticism about 'whether Marx's perspective and methodology are still worth our serious attention today' (1977, pp. 133, 145, 165).

In Barratt Brown's insufficiently expounded analysis of Marx's five principal theses and predictions, two are proven right (the centralisation of capital and the polarisation on a world scale of wealth and poverty), two wrong (the falling rate of profit, steady increase of the reserve army of labour) and one open (the cyclical crises of capitalism as an economic system). The reason for such a considerable degree of non-fulfilment and above all for the escape of capitalism from a final collapse in the foreseeable future must, in Barratt Brown's view, be found in the crucial role of state intervention which has no place in Marx's critique. He thus regards Keynesianism as a more advanced economic 'model' than Marx's (1972c, pp. 139–42). At this particular point, Anderson suggests that, in view of the new developments that confounded classical predictions of capitalist decay and breakdown, the 'very absence of any political theory proper in the late Marx' might be 'logically related to a latent catastrophism in his economic theory' (1976, pp. 46, 115–6). These are controversial judgements and no definite conclusions can yet be drawn.[108]

Among the younger New Left participants, Bob Rowthorn alone was actively involved in the theoretical debates on economics. He developed a new model to reveal how conflict over the distribution of income affects the general level of prices in advanced capitalist economies.[109] The model, because of its adoption of some monetarist arguments, was opposed by left-wing Keynesians. He also took issue with his non-Marxist colleagues on the prevailing economic thought of which the older New Left economists appeared to be much less critical.

Inspired by Sraffa's work, a strong trend among left wing economists was to seek a reconciliation of neo-Ricardianism with Marxist theory. Against this trend, Rowthorn first examines the bases of the system of conventional neo-classical economics and Sraffa's criticism of them. Then in an influential article on vulgar economy, he criticises the neo-Ricardian approach for its exclusive emphasis on the spheres of exchange and circulation, and its total ignorance of the social aspects, namely class relations, in the process of production (1974a). By the same token, he praises Mandel for his reassertion of production as the starting point which for many years had been rejected by dominant socialist and radical thinking in Britain (1976).[110] The weakness of Rowthorn's criticism, as two commentators point out, is that many neo-Ricardians did accept value analysis as a 'sociology of capitalist exploitation', though not an explanation of the motion of capitalism. To concentrate on this point is therefore to reduce Marxist economic theory from a science to a moral polemic (Fine and Harris, 1976, p. 151). Yet political and moral dimensions of economics are important, and so are institutional factors on which Rowthorn is right to place great emphasis (1980, pp. 95, 104–6, 115–6, 122–4).

Norman Geras's exploration of the concept of 'fetishism' in *Capital* is also (and bound to be) a political analysis of ideological mystification in the economic sphere. For him, one of Althusser's errors (in *For Marx* and *Reading Capital*) is to obliterate the historical specificity of capitalist opacity, and hence to dismiss the crucial task for socialists of developing an accurate theory of contemporary capitalism which should combine scientific aspirations and ethical commitment (1972b, pp. 285, 301–5).[111] Writing within the Marxist tradition, as Rowthorn and Geras do, Ian Steedman nevertheless takes neo-Ricardianism more seriously. His *Marx after Sraffa* (1977), a systematic re-evaluation of Marxian economics in the light of Sraffa's challenge, was the only full-length study in the subject ever published by NLB.

The New Left economists, especially those who had themselves constituted a fair part of the Labour Left, worked on an alternative to Conservative economic policies. After the failure of the so-called 'modernisation strategy' that expressed the post-war social democratic consensus, *Labour's Programme 1973* appeared to be the most left-wing statement the Party had adopted since 1945, with its radical proposals for increasing government intervention, workers' participation, and the power of organised labour based on the earlier 'social contract' between the unions and the party. The new programme was backed by those of the IWC group: Hughes, Barratt Brown, Coates and, not particularly identified with a New Left, Stuart Holland.[112] To withdraw from the EEC was advocated not only on the grounds of 'pure socialist principle' (Coates), but also because of the immediate need to reverse Britain's decline and to solve the current economic problems which were believed to have been aggravated by EEC membership. By loosening relations with the capitalist continent, they hoped that a Labour government might be able to introduce socialist measures and to plan the national economy.[113] Here a crucial question is, however, how and how far socialist domestic policies could be carried out within the surrounding capitalist European and world economy. The question was largely left behind, both by Nairn, in his arguments for entering the EEC, and by others who stood against entering it and now called for withdrawal.

Barratt Brown and Rowthorn paid special attention to the significance of transnational companies and their complex relationship to the capitalist nation states (Rowthorn, 1971a; 1971b; 1974b; Rowthorn and Hymer, 1970). Since the old socialist project of nationalising these companies became, at the least, more and more unrealistic, Barratt Brown suggested that short- and medium-term socialist programmes should begin by cutting into the power of the giant companies – through 'opening books' and increased public control – both at home and in their international operations. He developed a strategic thinking of transnational economic co-operation, a kind of international planning, ultimately for the rational use of resources for the needs of the people (1971, 2nd edn. of 1963b, p. xxxvi). This he once described as a 'long economic revolution', working beneath and interacting with the long cultural and political revolutions to which the New Left had long committed itself (1971, p. 209). Labour's abandonment of the alternative strategy in the 1980s and its creeping acceptance of Conservative economic policy foreclosed many of the questions debated in the 1970s, and so they simply ceased pressing political issues.[114]

The New Left's theoretical reconstruction of historical materialism was a response to the profound challenge to Marxism from overall new conditions of the contemporary world. But it was also an intellectual reflection of the rise and fall of the New Left movement itself, an attempt to answer political questions at the roots of grand theory with which most participants of the movement were preoccupied.

What is astonishing, however, is the near absence in this reconstructive process of the 1970s of any major and appropriate theoretical analysis of what happened in the late 1960s: of those epochal yet transitory events by which the worldwide 'New Left' gained its name; of the historical reasons or unreasons, the meaning and the impacts of that unprecedented period in which not only students, but also workers and other social strata and groups thought and acted so extraordinarily. The most creative ideas of the British New Left were actually formulated in that particular decade, such as those about culture, cultural revolution and cultural politics; about the peculiarities of the English; about the working classes, the minorities, youth, the intelligentsia; about emancipation, either in pursuing 'the liberation of desire' (or a 'Schillerian uprising', in Taylor's phrase, 1988, p. 113) and 'democratic participation' in the west, or in the liberation causes in the third world. Had all these ideas been developed further and deeper (and yet a few of them were) in relation to the reconsiderations of the classical Marxist heritage as well as the later development of that tradition, the work of the 1970s would have been much more interesting and fruitful.[115]

4. BEYOND THE CLASSICAL HERITAGE

'Cultural Materialism'

'Cultural materialism', a concept and theory founded around 1976 by Williams to define his recently reached position, was one of the few marked accomplishments that was deeply rooted in the experience of the New Left. As a result of his conscious effort to move beyond the 'eclecticism' of the early New Left, the formation of cultural materialism exemplified a 'much more general theoretical revision' of Marxism (1976b, pp. 243-4; Introduction to 1977). But it was a revision of very different sort, one within and based on the 'fundamental approach of historical materialism' (as Marx defined it) which Williams saw as 'profoundly true' (1975, p. 71). To materialise cultural processes, or to apply historical materialism to culture by seeing it and specific artists' practices as a material productive process, is something already 'latent within' the classical doctrine, namely, 'a way of understanding the diverse social and material production (necessarily often by individuals within actual relationships) of works to which the connected but also changing categories of art have been historically applied' (1983d, p. 273). This is a cultural theory that cannot exempt itself from a rigorous examination of its own social formations and historical situations and is therefore 'a theory of the specificities of material cultural and literary production within historical materialism' (1977, p. 5; 1986, p. 19).

Contemporary Marxism, rejecting the current once dominant within it of mechanical determinism and extending its scope to the wider area of culture – not only education and arts, but also feelings and imagination – is to achieve 'the real meanings of totality' and was a movement to which Williams found himself glad to belong (1975, p. 76). Thus Hall commented that cultural materialism was the 'most condensed and persuasive reflection on the strengths and limitations of the classical Marxist tradition' (1988a). Eagleton, on the other hand, considered that in Williams's invaluable concern to return cultural practices to their material reality, he nonetheless tended to dismiss the materialism/idealism opposition itself and the hypothesis of ultimate determination. Or, in other words, he still sought to preserve 'the primal reality of art' (1981, p. 76; 1976a, p. 22). This criticism is not generally justified as applied to Williams's arguments seen in their integrity.

Radically departing from the earlier outlook of *Culture and Society* and *The Long Revolution*, Williams developed his cultural theory and political thinking in *Modern Tragedy* (1966, 1979) to narrate the epic yet tragic revolution against imperialism in a critical realist tradition; in *Drama from Ibsen to Brecht* (1968) and *The English Novel from Dickens to Lawrence* (1970) to reveal historically active literary conventions, dramatic forms and practical criticisms or, in other words, the totalising context of 'text' and 'history'; in *Communications* (revised edns. 1968, 1976) and *Television: Technology and Cultural Form* (1974) to conceptualise the mode of cultural production and make his case for the social and democratic control of the media; in *Orwell* (1971) to recast socialism through portraying George Orwell's political difficulties and final defeat as a socialist; in *The Country and the City* (1973) to relate the variety of literature to a particular history of capitalist modernisation, to see that literature as part of the conditions of the means of production and hence the whole of social relationships; in *Keywords* (1976a) to pursue idea-category unity in a 'culture and society' vocabulary and inquire into its changes and developing meanings; in *Marxism and Literature* (1977) to work over the interactions between a Marxist aesthetic theory and other forms of literary thinking and writing, situating language as the means of political domination and ideological struggle. These works reflected, most creatively and richly, the historical conflicts and interplay of values, ideas, cultural and political trends in human life, British in the first place, but also that of the 'empire' and its international reach.

What he invented and steadily systematised, however, does not stray from the starting point of historical materialism that sets primary productive activities for the maintenance of human existence as the very basic condition for any development of civilisation. There is of course a hierarchy of different kinds of production with reference to social needs, which capitalism never got right for long. Williams, like many others, correctly stressed that this hierarchy must be historically relative and itself determined within a cultural order (1979, pp. 352–6). Yet he warned of the danger of reaching the point in which the epistemological wholly absorbs the ontological, a 'rabid idealism' that captured the intellectual left in the 1960s and the 1970s (*ibid.*, p. 167). In a moving introduction to a posthumous collection of essays in honour of Williams, Eagleton would finally and fairly write the following:

> He fought all his life against various left-wing reductions or displacements of these things, and believed that language and communication were where we lived, ... In this sense, he had held all along what some others on the left came gradually to discover sometimes later, through Gramsci or discourse theory or psychoanalysis or the 'politics of the subject'. And then, just when everyone else had caught up with him and was busy pressing this case to an idealist extreme, he turned on his heel and began to speak of material modes of cultural production.... . He had got there before us again. (ed. 1989, p. 9)[116]

The Country and the City was a key text in this stimulating process of Williams's search for materialism. In the two major forms of settlement which have grounded our civilisation, he seeks contrasts between rural and urban England in their historical realities (economies, communities, cultures, tensions and conflicts); finds changing interpretations of those realities in English literature which presents (or mispresents) images, 'structures of feelings', consciousnesses, and experiences of social relations. The constant background thesis for these investigations and reflections is the industrial revolution that took place earlier and thoroughly in England and later had transformed the world. 'The City and the World' (1973) thus looks at the ideas of country and city on the international stage, confronting the British heritage of imperialism and capitalism as a dominant mode of production far beyond where it arose. It is not so simple, Williams argues, that the pull of the image of the country is toward old, human and natural ways, while the pull of the image of the city is progress, modernisation, development. Surely the romantic elegy of a lost rural life is not a solution, but neither is the 'scientific' confidence in a 'metropolitan socialism' (1973c, pp. 81–3):

> The terrible irony has been that the real processes of absolute urban and industrial priority, and of the related priority of the advanced and civilised nations, worked through not only to damage the 'rural idiots' and the colonial 'barbarians and semi-barbarians', but to damage, at the heart, the urban proletarians themselves, and the advanced and civilised societies: over whom, in their turn, the priorities exercised their domination, in a strange dialectical twist. (p. 87)

He is here thinking of the real historical experience of the twentieth-century revolutions: the Chinese and the Cubans gained their ultimate strength in the countryside. In an epoch of national and social liberation movements, the exploited rural and colonial populations became the main sources of continued struggle. He is also very much referring to the environmental destruction resulting from blind industrialism, capitalist and communist alike. The revival of the Morrisian utopia of balanced communities and societies is therefore most welcome and relevant to his concern with overcoming the crisis of industrial society, the opposition of city and country, the division of labour and other forms of human alienation which the capitalist system continues to generate and sustain (pp. 86–9). Later in a discussion of the notion of an 'organic society', Williams tells us that:

> I am very powerfully moved by the early churches, by the great cathedrals, and yet if I don't see the enormous weight of them on man, I don't altogether know how to be a socialist in the area where I work. ... The nature of their power does not necessarily end, in the tidy way that the simplest kind of Marxism suggests, with its epoch. The cathedrals are not just monuments of faith, the country houses are not just buildings of elegance. They are constantly presented to us as 'our heritage', inducing a particular way of seeing and relating to the world, which must be critically registered along with our acknowledgement of their value.
> (1979, p. 309)

'Everything about the man', writes Hall, ' – his mind, his way of writing and speaking, his political intelligence – is in those few sentences' (1988a, p. 21).

Williams's lasting inspiration to the younger Marxist generation was matched by their persistent criticisms of him – Eagleton and *NLR* apart, from the CCCS, for example. The failure of some modern variants of Marxism to grasp changing social relations was particularly evident, as Williams saw it, in comparison with some other theories of communications and of art. But charges were made against his populism,[117] empiricism and intellectual parochialism, which also underlay the whole New Left divide (II.3, III.1 and III.4). It was a divide characterised by a set of contrasts, between a commitment to the moral and political strength of ordinary working people and a focus on the formation of a hegemonic socialist intelligentsia; between a refusal of any abstract reworking of cultural theory and the assertion that 'culture' as an ideological term must be thoroughly theorised; between an indigenous preference for the English critical thinking and the hunt after new methods and perspectives beyond the British Isles that would break the confines of the national tradition. These are important yet to some extent artificial antitheses. Williams had gradually turned to become a very highly appreciated thinker for many of his young opponents, and his writing an appealing subject matter.[118] From debating with and about Williams, an influential group of Marxist critics emerged (with Eagleton as its most prominent representative), who more assertively claimed the militant social function of criticism.[119]

The concept of culture had often been taken as encompassing the social and even the historical in a vigorous New Left tradition. Being critical of culturalism (a term invented by Richard Johnson), the CCCS played a notable part in both preserving this tradition and modifying it with different focuses and methods. The development of what came to be cross-disciplinary cultural studies, a field preoccupied with a left intellectual orientation, owed a lot to the fruitful work of the Centre.[120] It was not the concrete concern with actual trends or 'lived culture' in modern capitalist society (such as media, sub-cultures, youth culture, counter-culture, popular arts), but an interest in theory that marked the Centre's departure from its own path that had been associated with the names of Richard Hoggart and early Williams. This theoretical engagement surpassed the old Centre at such points as a recognition of the limits of English literary/social criticism; an active encounter with French structuralism, linguistic and discourse theories, and psychoanalysis (Saussure, Lévi-Strauss, Althusser, Foucault, Derrida, Lacan); conscious participation in the movement of a new social history (of women, ethnic minorities, dissident cultures, etc.); and a more recent move to political/ideological institution formations, thus attempting to approach cultural issues in the light of a thorough examination of the state. All these helped Hall, Richard Johnson (who succeeded Hall's directorship in 1979) and their colleagues both in the Centre and later in the Open University (for example, the Popular Culture course led by Anthony Barnett, who was also an editorial member of NLR) effectively to develop certain cultural themes.[121]

The Centre and cultural studies, in Hall's retrospect, experienced first a liberating break with previous conceptualisations of mainstream sociology (which had been under the shadow of hegemonic American sociological models and methodology) and then a complex impact of structuralism. The latter, through its theoretical anti-humanism, decentred cultural processes away from their intentional centre in man's project and therefore 'obliged us really to rethink the "cultural" as a set of practices: to think the material conditions of signification and its necessary determinateness'. This is another way of seeking a materialist definition of culture: culture is conditional and conditioned (1980). A comparison can be made here between Williams and Hall. There was in the former always a sense of the deepest reluctance to give up hope that cultural possibilities might effect great social changes (Ward, 1981, p. 71). The latter laid his hope on a more specific ideological struggle rather than culture, and stressed more those political elements and institutions (in contrast to Williams's concern with technology) for or against which socialists must fight or 'practice'.

Studies of culture and its historical varieties and changes also engaged many other individuals and quite a few research or publishing institutions. History Workshop and its journal and book series formed another major forum on cultural themes (see the final part of IV.4). These themes had been crucial for 'social history' in a body of work inspired by *Past and Present* (founded in 1952 mainly by a group of communist historians) and the New Left classics such as *The Making of the English Working Class*. An external push was given by those of the French *Annales*, whose concern with both historical totality and (in the post-

1968 era) the particular location of oppressed social groups, whose great interest in the cultural dimension of a particular period, whose approach to culture as a system of relations, all reinforced the culturalist tradition among British social historians, though to different degrees and even directions. Against traditional labour history, they claimed to shift attention from the leadership, elites and formal organisations, to the minds and lives of the majority of labouring people who were not, as so often assumed, culturally impoverished and lacking political consciousness. Debate over the themes of leisure (popular and working-class recreation) and social mobility mediated by *Past and Present* and the Society for the Study of Labour History;[122] Thompson's study of plebeian culture in eighteenth-century England (1974; 1971a); Stedman Jones's of 'outcast' Victorian Cockneys (1971b; 1974)[123] and later, Samuel's writings about the Workers' Theatre Movement, East End London underworld and labour community life (1981c; 1985a; 1975; with Bloomfield and Boanas, 1986) are some exemplary works. With a marked New Left trait in terms of an undogmatic yet distinctively Marxist understanding of history, these authors made their case of claiming culture as indispensable to any critical undertaking in historiography.

It had been a long journey – from early studies of how social and cultural changes affected public opinions in general and working-class attitudes in particular, with a sense of the passivity of that class (Hoggart, Williams), to the debate over the 'peculiarities' of the national culture with different emphases on either the negative notion of labourism (from Miliband/Barratt Brown to Anderson/Nairn) or the positive moral strength of the British working class (Williams, Thompson), both as integral cultural objects; from the discovery (Samuel, Stedman Jones) of non-coincidence or discontinuity between class ascription (economic position and politico-cultural inheritance) and class politics,[124] to the (much criticised) assertion of constructive and constitutive function of a 'language of class' in political mobilisation, or the articulation of the social through historically located discourse (Stedman Jones, Hall);[125] from a community approach to the media, communications and education, popular culture, counter culture and common culture (Williams, Taylor, Hall, Eagleton), to a 'new sociology' that in one way applies to sociological and technological explanations of the institutional changes and patterns of literary/artistic production (Williams, Hall, CCCS) and in another to sociologico-anthropological analyses of culture as an unevenly developed world system (Worsley); from a 'structure of feeling' (Williams) that interlinks social relations, cultural forms and conscious as well as unconscious subjectivities in their historical richness and variety – from all this to the extensive play of the Gramscian concept of hegemony (Hall, Anderson, Williams) defined as a dominant system of meanings and values that constitutes the experienced reality of our lives and actual conditions for ideological struggle.[126]

This seems to be a tortuous journey of search, not without difficulties, confusions and self-criticisms, to a generally recognisable cultural materialism, of one kind or another, formulated with different styles, emphases or interpretations. Indeed it was the New Left, but not only the New Left, who reinserted vital concerns with culture into Marxism while retaining the Marxist tradition vigorously.

What has been sketched in the present section cannot be more than a very brief outline. So will be the following two sections. It becomes inappropriate to continue a distinct 'New Left' history as one looks at the whole context of that background by the mid-1970s: not only that the New Left movement began to drift further away from the political scene, but also, intellectually, there developed a growing flow between and a flux of currents of ideas and thoughts which were not always identifiable or divisible into 'New Left' or 'non-New Left' categories. The earlier discussions, works and biographies by and of the New Left had themselves increasingly provided research subjects which mostly occupied people without a New Left origin. New and significant debates (like the one over structuralism), though frequently reflecting the old divisions among different New Left tendencies, more and more involved arguments and perspectives from others who, again, had not been associated with the New Left. It is also inadequate, on the other hand, to claim an end of the intellectual history of a movement in accordance with its disappearance from the political scene. Certainly there is no rupture, for example, between a 'New Left' and 'post-New Left' Williams in the integrated body of his late work (*The Country and the City*, 1973; *Marxism and Literature*, 1977; *Politics and Letters* (interviews with NLR), 1979; *Problems in Materialism and Culture*, 1980; *Culture*, 1981; *Towards 2000*, 1983). It is here that the project of reconstructing an intellectual history of the New Left can be challenged on the ground that what is dealt with in that history is not necessarily bound up with new leftism.[127] A simple but strong defence of such a project, however, is that it would be very doubtful whether the New Left people could ever have produced the *same* works without having experienced that deeply emotional movement.[128]

Science, Technology and Social Change

It is strikingly noticeable that the British New Left was almost completely without natural scientists among its participants and silent about the natural sciences in its intellectual discourse. Comparing this absence with the pre-war 'old left' that contained a remarkable generation of 'red scientists' (such mathematicians, biologists and physicists as Hyman Levy, J. B. S. Haldane, Lancelot Hogben, J. D. Bernal, Joseph Needham, Patrick Blackett, C. H. Waddington), we must note the negative aspect of the 'new' characteristics of the New Left. Not only did the English national culture not produce a classical sociology of the quality of that of Weber, Durkheim or Pareto, or western Marxism, as the second NLR editors so forcefully criticised, but also they, and their predecessors as well, never acknowledged explicitly or implicitly the missing link to science and its politics in their own culture.[129] Consequently, the Marxist New Left never found its way to meet the most recent challenges of theoretical anti-Marxism raised in the philosophy of science (for example Popper, 1957).

Not that nothing can be found to illuminate some feeble continuities between the tradition of the old scientific Left[130] and that of the overwhelmingly culturally preoccupied New Left. But there was rather a radical break which was so obvious that the latter's lack of interest in the original Marxist attention to the interaction between society and nature mediated by labour (and thus by technology), the knowledge of nature and the social relations involved in the knowing process, must be explained. In other words, the question of why the New Left project (unlike the CP or the Left Book Club in the 1920s and 1930s) was virtually unattractive to working scientists and other intellectuals such as philosophers, historians and sociologists of science needs an answer.

There were indeed scattered organisational connections, for instance, in the Reasoner initiative (with which Hyman Levy was at least a sympathiser), in the ULR circle (whose London Club had an autonomous section of left scientists), in the early CND and WEA where the New Left activists and others including some science and technical people (such as John Cox of CND's National Executive, Antoinette Pirie of its Scientists' Group,[131] Joseph Rotblat of the 'Pugwash movement',[132] Jerome Ravetz at Leeds,[133] and of course Bertrand Russell and Julian Huxley) worked together, and in the VSC whose broad reach to laboratories reminded one of the Cambridge Scientists' Anti-War Group of the 1930s. The institutional bases for discussion of and struggle for the unity of science and socialism, and socialist planning of science (see Bernal, 1939) was first provided by the Association of Scientific Workers (functioning around 1919–39) and decades later by the British Society for Social Responsibility in Science (BSSRS) which was established in 1969.[134] This new development made by young left scientists surprisingly bypassed the New Left who, for the most part of it, were busily debating political and cultural issues of the student revolution. It was surprising because what BSSRS claimed – public and democratic control of science in view of science increasingly coming to be a form of power – was absolutely central for any socialist programme and perfectly identical with the general New Left line of argument.

No matter who missed whom, the old cry of the Modern Quarterly (founded in 1938 and re-established for a decade or more after the war under John Lewis with CP sponsorship, with a list of editors and contributors full of famous 'red professors', Fellows of the Royal Society included) or the CP's Daily Worker (which had well-received regular science features) did find an echo, strangely weak and rather distorted though, in the New Left publishing enterprise. A few early pieces on the social control of science (Peter Russell, 1962; David Cooper, 1965; Martin Rossdale, 1965, 1966) aside, concerning the problem of scientific methodology, NLB published Alfred Schmidt's classic The Concept of Nature in Marx (1962, English trans. NLB, 1971), Herbert Marcuse's From Luther to Popper (1972), Paul Feyerabend's Against Method (1975; and later, his Science in a Free Society, 1978),[135] Goran Therborn's Science, Class and Society (1976), to list but a few. Apparently the taste and theoretical orientation of NLB were quite different from the Bernalist optimistic 'scientism' that dominated the two pioneer journals, but this will concern us later.

Intellectually, further fragmentary material could be gathered to construct a New Left concern with technology, if not really science: from Blackburn's (1965) or Barratt Brown's (1971) brief analyses of the economic (both productive and managerial) effects of the automation of the computer age, to Thompson's or Coates's extensive discussion of the notion of nuclear 'exterminism' (see Epilogue); from Hoggart (1957), Hall (1958) or Williams (1962, 1974) examining media manipulation in relation to the technological promotion of mass cultural consumption, to Barratt Brown (ed. 1976), Williams (1973a, 1983c) or NLR (for instance, the publication of Enzensberger on political ecology, 1974) becoming anxious about resources and ecology. The general attitude of the early New Left, at least ULR, according to Samuel, was 'sympathetic to the claims of science', implying that the gap between science and humanities should be closed (1989, p. 42). Yet the simple fact is that they did little in that direction. NLR did print some analyses of the relationship between the natural sciences and historical materialism which was believed to have founded a social science of Marxism, but was never an active participant in the current controversies around the question of science and ideology on the left in the 1970s. Valentino Gerratana published in NLR (1973) his 'Marx and Darwin', a sound discussion of Marx's view on science as based on an analogy between the evolution of the natural world and the development of human society. He was after all an Italian philosopher, and the editors of NLR though they liked the article, had said almost nothing for themselves.

The only New Left volume that was indeed devoted to the debate over the concepts of science, knowledge, subjectivity and their socially and historically constructed nature was CCCS's On Ideology (1977). The leading essay in the volume by Hall is entitled 'The Hinterland of Science', in which the complicated trajectory of the concept of ideology is traced back to its different settings in the English, the French and the German intellectual traditions. In contrast to European thought, Hall makes it clear that the concept plays no significant analytic role in Anglo-Saxon social theory. The three Marxist thinkers studied respectively in the volume by different research teams (collective collaboration was an admirable working style of the Centre) were Lukács, Gramsci, and Althusser, whose theories of ideology are examined, rare for the New Left, not only in relation to cultural politics but also to the sociology of knowledge.

It is still a curious matter whether and how the New Left, as individual critics, would take sides in the characteristic Snow-Leavis polemics on the 'two cultures'.[136] Even in Hall's close analysis of the 'struggle over method' among German intellectuals and the Weberian compromise of hermeneutic (interpretive) and causal ('scientific'/positivist) explanations (1977a, pp. 14–5), one can hardly tell where he himself stands. The fortunate or unfortunate literary/scientific disjunction was so evident in most of their work that it seems unlikely to be a mere accident. Also to be pointed out here is an obvious connection between these two weakest links of New Left scholarship or culture, namely, science and economics, which are in fact intimately intertwined: economic productive activity in industry, as Marx put it, is 'the *actual*, historical relationship of nature, and therefore of natural science, to man' (1844, pp. 142–3).

The case of Williams might be exceptional, despite the fact that even his work was very much confined to what he called cultural technologies and almost without any direct reference to the historical sociology, let alone philosophical and epistemological questions, of scientific knowledge. For Williams, a literary man by preoccupation but a conscious rebel against the existing specialisation and classification of the academic disciplines, what was 'absolutely' needed in the early 1960s (1961c, p. 20) was to develop a social theory of communications. This was a significant move, indicating a start toward a social science of technology.

Williams defines communications in terms of the massive information systems of transmission and reception (though not excluding the transport network). His theory deals with relations between culture and the technologies of media, between technology and its institutions, between technological progress and psychology, between technical inventions and society. Since, as he sees it, the institutional and material conditions for democratic participation in the process of creating meanings and values are becoming available, the central argument of his writings on the subject, from 'Communications and Common Culture' (1961c), *Communications* (1962) to *Television* (1974), has been always the essential need for public (and therefore democratically organised) ownership/control of the means of communications. This is an argument for transforming the whole technological apparatus, for 'communicative and *thus* social transformation' (1989a, p. 192). Such a transformation is bound to be a very difficult struggle of course, but it is also indispensable, because Williams (like Habermas) knows only too well why communications must be located in the power relationships of capitalism. Yet against a technological determinism (1974, pp. 9–31), he identifies the determinations, which are both economic and political, 'in a range quite beyond technology' (1989b, p. 123). Moreover, out of the 'long and bitter impasse of a once liberating modernism ... we could choose to develop the new technologies, by choosing a different kind of economy and society' (1989b, p. 139).

So it is not true or at least not accurate to describe the human condition as the insoluble choice between a necessary materialism and a necessary humanity. Making a distinction between techniques of production and their particular social form, the point is that it is not technology but the capitalist mode of production that has to be resisted. In view of deliberate and indifferent destructions in the history of industrialisation under capitalism and imperialism, 'I am ... [wrote Williams] convinced that resistance to capitalism is the decisive form of the necessary human defence' (1973c, pp. 78–9, 85). Here, Williams comes so very close to Bernal or Needham who had always believed that 'the natural sciences could only come to their most perfect fruition in a socialist society' (Needham, quoted in Werskey, 1978, p. 325).[137] But he would quickly add his objection to the confidence in an urban industrial future (which is also western 'chauvinist') held by the 'metropolitan progressives, many of them supposedly international-ists and socialists'. It is not all that simple that modernisation or a technological revolution will bring about socialism (1973c, p. 83). On the other hand, as already mentioned, cultural materialism is a theory of a physical or technical course of production of not only culture but politics as well (1977b, p. 93). Is it self-contradictory for Williams to claim both the neutrality (to avoid reactionary romanticism) of technology and its primary autonomy (as an institutional system) in producing and reproducing a certain social and political order? His radically culturalised and historicised conception of materialism contains deep insights (as we saw in the last section) but difficulties as well.

In any case, a possible explanation for the surprising New Left neglect of natural science might be found first in cultural materialism which presumably must include science as a productive force. Indeed many of the New Left ideas seem to take the scientific basis of socialism for granted and to ground themselves on a Marxism seen exclusively as a social theory. To develop a socialist approach to science is irrelevant because, in Anderson's opinion, 'the modern natural sciences are relatively (not, of course, absolutely) asocial in character'. In other words, they only 'forge concepts for the understanding of nature, not society'. It is the use of scientific discoveries that can be ideological, so the most dramatic case, which was 'politicising' Darwinism, is not a matter of science as such (1966, pp. 19–20, 5).[138] If Anderson is the worst case in this regard for his blindness to the social character and context of science, or the concepts of science as social concepts, Taylor might be the best in acknowledging that in Marxism, humanity cannot be studied without involving its natural environment.[139] But he too frames his own discussion only in terms of the relationship between individual and society, not nature and humanity (1966). Anderson and Taylor wrote at the time when the 'scientific spirit' prevailed, the aim of which was to establish a materialist theory of society modelled on the natural sciences.[140] Trying hard to be in balance, Stedman Jones, virtually presenting the NLR objection to the philosophy of western Marxism, stated that it was Marx's own belief that historical materialism was 'itself a real and responsible science'; yet one must not in the name of scientific Marxism import methodological procedures derived from physical science, or indeed from scientific ideologies (1971a, pp. 34, 57–60).

Marx himself cherished the future realisation of 'one science', a unitary science of nature and man resulting from the hitherto separate two sciences being 'incorporate[d] into one another', as natural science had already transformed human life through industry and technology, and prepared human liberation from intellectual mystification and material scarcity.[141] It is unclear what kind of response one can expect from the Marxist New Left to Marx's position, so well put and widely quoted as 'One basis for life and another basis for science is a priori a lie' (1844, p. 143).

Not criticising the British New Left who regrettably had no great respect for him until much later (see IV.2), Lukács wrote in 1967 that 'it is the materialist view of nature that brings about the really radical separation of the bourgeois and socialist outlooks'. His own failure to grasp this in 1923, he goes on, prevented the clear elaboration of the concept of praxis, and the methodological upgrading

of societal categories distorts their true epistemological functions (Preface to the
new edition of *History and Class Consciousness*, 1971, p. xvii). Gramsci, by contrast
a hero for the British Left (save Anderson), pointed out in his critical notes on
Bukharin's attempt at a popular presentation of Marxist sociology in the early
1930s (1957, pp. 90–117) how mistaken was the concept of dialectic (referring to
History and Class Consciousness) wherever it was confined only to the history of
mankind: 'if human history should be conceived also as the history of nature (also
through the history of science), how can the dialectic be separated from nature'
(1957, p. 109; Schmidt's discussion, 1971, pp. 165–96)? Lukács's self-criticism of
(and the implication of Gramsci's remark in regard to) an 'overriding subjectivism' happened to suit well the tendency of at least part of the New Left, in the
direction of what Lukács calls 'an abstract utopianism in the realm of cultural
politics' (1971, p. xii) or what Ernest Gellner rejects as illusory exaggeration of
the importance of 'culture' (as custom and credence rather than scientific
knowledge) in shaping the course of social changes (mentioned in Anderson,
1990, *NLR* 182, pp. 68–9).

   Also, the 'scientism' of the old left, a complete optimism about scientific
rationality, was suspected of being allied to economism which was precisely what
the New Left revolted against or what made the New Left new in its early days.[142]
This anti-determinist stance was keenly related to the later New Left attack on
positivism in general and British empiricism in particular. The publication of
Feyerabend's theory of knowledge by NLB, which was an epistemology against
method (the book was dedicated to his 'fellow anarchist', Imre Lakatos, Hungarian by origin and an immigrant in England), seemed to be a gesture paying
tribute to the open anti-dogmatism of anti-empiricist philosophies of science. But
Popper, one of Anderson's 'white émigrés' (along with half a dozen others who
contributed to, in *NLR*'s judgement, the valueless English national culture, cf.
III.4) had never been taken seriously in the New Left anti-positivist campaign.
On the one hand, his individualist methodological critique of 'holism', with its
political application known as 'piecemeal social engineering', was maybe too banal
a challenge for the revolutionary New Leftists who in different ways liked the
notion of totality a so-called 'holistic' view. On the other hand, the Popperian
contrast between open and closed societies and opposition to historicism, a fatalist
and teleological version of Marxism which the philosopher made a target (1945;
1957), actually fitted the New Left's own position in fighting Stalinism in both its
ideological (historical determinism) and political (communist totalitarianism)
forms.[143]

   This leads to another possible reason. Even though the response to the
Frankfurt tradition was not particularly warm in Britain (in fact, as discussed
before, criticisms of the 'romantic anti-scientific' tendency of mainstream western
Marxism from the second New Left were strong), the Marcusian/Habermasian
thesis that modern science is a form of domination still seemed irresistibly
inspiring. The critique of post-industrial-scientific civilisation and its blind
'technological spirit' (or 'technocratic consciousness') in *One-Dimensional Man*

(Marcuse, 1964; see also. 1969a) was powerful, and so was the revelation of repressive 'instrumental reason' in *Dialectic of Enlightenment* (Adorno and Horkheimer, 1947) and *Critical Theory* (Horkheimer, 1968), or *Toward a Rational Society* (Habermas, 1968a) and *Knowledge and Human Interests* (1968b). Before long, virtually without an involvement in the philosophy and politics of science and after a feverish but disappointing engagement in Althusserian structuralism, the British Marxist critics found the collapse of faith in science already overwhelming on the left, again first on the continent and then across the English Channel. Epistemologically idealist and relativist and politically pessimist, the new development went quite against the rationalist critical thinkers.

In addition, Labour's modernisation programme of the 1960s (see the Party document *Science and the Future of Britain*) might have also played a part.[144] The Wilson government was a major target of the New Left critique of labourism and Labour imperialism: if Wilson's propaganda around his proposal of 'a white-heat technological revolution' suffered from the overall distrust of his policies, it would not be a surprise. In a similar way, the long-held NLR position against communism and communist history seems to be also a background factor. The science tradition of 'red professors', almost only because it was associated with the CP, was dismissed altogether.

What is all the more paradoxical is that most New Left critics in Britain had for a definite moment turned to Althusserianism which claimed scientificity on the grounds of theoretical anti-humanism and anti-historicism. It is worth asking what the formulation of a position on the whole issue of interactions between nature and man, science and society would have brought about had the Marxist New Left been able to achieve one.

Methodology and Historiography

For the same reason that particularly 'New Left' lines of argument had become more and more indistinguishable in the 1970s (see IV.4, the first sub-section), the following can be no more than an outline of a nevertheless very significant aspect of Marxist scholarship in England, one which represented the search for a method by both the two New Left generations and other Marxist theorists, a search which in the most illuminating way dominated the field of historical inquiry.

Indeed, Marxism had its greatest success in the history profession in Britain where the historical school of British Marxism had been solidly established by the work of a remarkable generation of Communist historians (V. Gordon Childe, George Thompson, Dona Torr, Maurice Dobb, Christopher Hill, Rodney Hilton, Eric Hobsbawm, Victor Kiernan, Edward Thompson, John Saville and others), and sustained through its institutional bases such as the journal, *Past and Present* (which was however joined by non-Marxist editors like Lawrence Stone). The fact that it was the historians who first came out fighting against Stalinism within the CP around 1956 alone demonstrated the strength of this school, which had ever since inspired younger scholars associated with the New Left. However, discontinuity between traditional Marxist historiography and some new developments became evident above all in the 'structuralist turn' of not only the second New Left, but also a larger circle of left intellectuals after the mid-1960s. It was a momentary engagement, yet the major debates initiated at this conjunction between empiricist history and structuralist intervention had continuously contrived to produce important historical and theoretical discussions, and anticipated later arguments around post-structuralism.

Structuralist Marxism belonged to an intellectual tradition that was as foreign as other western Marxisms to the anti-metaphysical climate and language of conventional English social thought. It attracted those in Britain who were seeking a way to break down the dominance of indigenous empiricism and positivism (see III.4) and, politically, the growing 'eclecticism' of Eurocommunism and its liberal humanist/evolutionist notion of progress. This 'scientific Marxism' (as represented by Della Volpe and Colletti in Italy but mainly by Althusser and Balibar in France) was taken as a revolutionary response to both intellectual and political deficiencies of Hegelian Marxism and in Britain, a 'moralist' Marxist theory that had a particularly strong influence on the old New Left. However, in effect, the age of theoretical practice of the 1970s resulted, with its worst byproduct of theoretical sectarianism, in a further dislocation of Marxist discourse from real social life and concrete political struggles, and therefore from lively important questions of political economy. That was a crisis of Marxism as a science of working-class emancipation, which was deeply felt after 1968 and further intensified by an abstract 'theoreticism' to which the intellectual movement of the period somehow spontaneously led.

It began with *NLR*'s European project. Ben Brewster,[145] a major introducer and translator of the French literature of structuralist Marxism for the *Review* and NLB,[146] wrote in 1967 that:

> many socialists in England are still defending Marxist humanism against Stalinist dogmatism, without realising that this battle is largely won; ... To bring Marxist theory into line with contemporary conditions a completely new conception is needed. Althusser's work represents one approach to such a scientific Marxism. (1967, p. 14)

Excited by the displacement of the Marx of the 1844 Manuscripts by the Marx of *Capital* through the discovery of an 'epistemological break' between the two, Althusser's British followers found the Althusserian concepts, non-teleological, non-economic determinist, and anti-empiricist as they were, fruitful and inspiring: concepts of relative autonomy (different levels were interdependently autonomous; the economic level only determines in the last instance), overdetermination (structural causality or structural determinism), ideology (as immutable; and as a notion of representation with a stress on linguistics), theoretical practice (knowledge or science as production or as the effect, and a process of theoretical and discursive construction), and non-Hegelian totality of 'structure' (social formation, mode of production, etc.). The theoretical problematic involved in these concepts which were generated from a 'symptomatic reading' of Marx did significantly transform the nature of the questions and the forms in which they were posed and answered. The briefly flourishing Althusserian Marxism thus reshaped the intellectual wisdom of the British left.

However, doubts arose before long. In 1971, SR published Kolakowski's not very convincing yet sweeping attack on Althusserism (1971). Almost simultaneously, Geras's careful criticism of the methodological idealism of Althusser's conception of science and hence the inadequacy of his grasp of the relationship between theory and politics of the class struggle appeared in NLR (1972a). The Review also introduced André Glucksmann's critique of Althusser's close affinities with the pre-Marxist traditions of European philosophy (1972), expressing at least its own scepticism about the Althusserian scientific theory of knowledge in the following assessment: 'In fact, no Marxist epistemology as such yet exists' (NLR 72, p. 66). With the publication of Pre-Capitalist Modes of Production (1975) and Mode of Production and Social Formation (1977) by Barry Hindess and Paul Hirst, which represented an extreme version of the theoretical bias rooted in structuralist Marxism, the fever was calmed with a wave of wider resistance also from many who were previously devoted Althusserians.[147] 'There is no real object "history" ' but only 'representations' of 'texts' (not the 'past'), declared the two authors (1975, pp. 317, 309, 311). So 'the study of history is not only scientifically but also politically valueless' (p. 312). Their total rejection of epistemology and therefore of any 'objects' such as mode of production, or any correlation between what is supposed to be representable ('reality') and what takes the form of theoretical discourse ('knowledge') (1977) further caricatured Althusser's position. They were in fact pioneers in the lagging development of post-structuralism and discourse theory in England, which, almost because of the theoretical impasse of the very direction that their own work set out to demonstrate, never had an impact beyond the narrow reach, even among the academic left, of a few active but small journals like the early Radical Philosophy and Screen.[148]

Hindess and Hirst belonged to the post-1968 Marxist generation that had been heavily influenced by NLR led by Anderson and others. Both were editorial members of the short-lived journal Theoretical Practice (1971–3) and the surviving Economy and Society which carried on structuralist Marxist analyses. Brewster, formerly of NLR, became the editor of Screen in the high point of its activities between 1974 and 1976. Alerted to the danger of abandoning historical materialism, most of those from the New Left who were inspired by the Althusserian school, maintained a well-balanced attitude towards newer French trends of thinking, and indeed were criticised from time to time for not confronting themselves with the most advanced ideas of those trends or being dogmatic. Hall and the Birmingham Centre, under the influence of both Gramsci and Althusser (and Laclau as well), for example, were once made a target from the feminist perspective of Screen for intending to preserve 'limit-positions' within Marxism (Rosalind Coward, 1977, 1977–8; Hall et al., 1977–8).

Still the clash of arguments over structuralism and its implication in historiography among the New Left-oriented British Marxists was fierce and unpleasant. A specific instance of that clash centred on Thompson's self-proclaimed empiricism and his bitter attack on Althusser's work, and a more general case was the debate on history and theory. The privilege to human agency and 'experience' given in Thompson's analytic framework contrasts sharply with structuralist stress on an underlying organisation of complex relations and symbolic systems which position and 'project' the subject. The dismissal of scientific objectivity in the former approach is matched by the disappearance of creative subjectivity in the latter. One of the key notions of the controversy was experience. The notion was always of primary importance but vague in Thompson, from *The Making of the English Working Class* to *Whigs and Hunters*; from 'Patrician society' to 'Eighteenth-century English society' (III.2).[149] He tried to clarify it in his theoretical works including *The Poverty of Theory*, but never succeeded. Seeing experience, individual as well as collective or social, as the very basis for any historical reconstruction, he did not bother to ask questions such as how this raw experience as 'data' was already constituted or translated or recorded, and on the other hand, how unexpressed human feelings and trajectories might be grasped (the 'problem of silence'). His frequent confusion of experience with facts or evidence was also subject to criticism. His defence in general necessarily hinged on the superiority of historical process over static structure, and a dialectical interaction between conceptualisation and empirical investigation.[150]

Without any compromise on the basic polemical points, the Thompson debate at least allowed each side to elaborate its respective arguments and that elaboration greatly helped a reconsideration of Marxist thinking and historical writing in Britain. Hobsbawm was therefore not right to answer 'no' to the question whether interest in the work of Althusser had led to fruitful advances in Marxist history (1978b, pp. 37–8). He was, like Thompson, in opposition to the Althusserian 'bias against history'. But shouldn't 'pure' empiricist 'bias against theory' be equally opposed? It was precisely because the English tradition remained entrenched in an anti-theoretical stance that there would arise in 1978–9 a further and major debate over historical method. Lamentably, its tone fell to 'the worst standards of the cold war'.[151] It reawoke the old pains of the early division between the two generations of the first New Left as well as between the two New Lefts, spilled over into quite irrelevant personal preferences (notably by Thompson),[152] and exhibited at several points sad yet persistent sectarianism.

Mainly through the *History Workshop Journal* (the debate was opened by Richard Johnson in *HWJ* 6), the debaters divided themselves roughly into two contending camps known as 'in defence of theory' versus 'in defence of history'. The former position, though also rejecting any exclusively formalist and abstract way of operating theory or what Hall called the intellectual terrorism of vulgar Althusserianism, emphasised the genuine contribution of structuralist Marxism and, for British Marxists, the serious theoretical gains made from its intervention. These gains challenged 'the poverty of empiricism' (as expressed earlier by Stedman Jones, 1966) in some fundamental sense and paved the way for the more conscious construction of concepts capable of apprehending reality and thus theoretically informed historical analysis. The latter position, on the other hand, sought to defend the concrete and empirical mode of historiography which was seen as 'not only justifiable as social science', but also 'politically necessary to socialists' (G. Williams, 1979, p. 116). A dialogue between conceptual models and actuality, in Thompson's words, constituted the basis of the correct historical method – 'neither abstract, nor a-historical, nor transcendental, but contextual and materialist' (1981, p. 403).

The origin of the 'theory' side can be traced back to Stedman Jones's initial attack on empiricist and positivist approaches written more than a decade prior to the debate (1967; see also III.4). The essay, inspired by the *Annales* school that participated in structuralist history through its slogan of 'abolition of the subject', argued for the theoretical foundation of any history. The argument remained central in his 1976 article entitled 'From historical sociology to theoretical history'. Neither he, nor others who were on the same side, however, saw themselves as wholehearted structuralists.[153] Hall admitted that the CCCS was for a time over-preoccupied with theoretical and epistemological issues, yet efforts had been made to build its work on 'a substantially greater concrete and historical basis'. For the Centre, according to him, critique and rejections of structuralism were as significant as influences absorbed and positions affirmed (1980a, pp. 24–5, 29, 42–3; cf. R. Johnson, 1979b). What he called for now was 'the necessity of theory to put beside the poverty of theoreticism' (1981a, p. 377). Both Richard Johnson and Anderson considered traditional British Marxist historiography and the imported structuralist approach to be complementary and reconcilable. Johnson showed how history, theory and politics were combined in the 'best Marx' (1978; 1982; cf. McLennan, 1979a; 1979b). Anderson expected better practice of history based on a 'critical balance or synthesis' of the two traditions which should be mutually digestible (1980, p. 127; cf. Foreword to 1974a). His own work on the lineages of the absolutist state (see p. 165) was in a way a successful attempt at such a synthesis.

The 'history' side had its root in the empiricist inclination of the communist historians. The break between integral and mere cultural concerns that had taken place to separate the two generations within that tradition was studied by Johnson in his two influential essays (1978; 1979a). However controversial Johnson's discovery might be (see, for example, Kaye's theme of 'continuity', 1984, pp. 21–2), even Thompson himself admitted his 'weakness in economic theory' (1981, p. 404; cf. Hobsbawm's remark, 1978b, p. 39). Yet 'anti-theoretical' seems to be not the right label here. What was at issue was indeed not 'how much theory' but 'what kind of theory'. Thompson's argument against Althusserism, for example, was set up at the theoretical level because it was the only way to confront it (1976d; 1978a, pp. 332–3; 1972). Saville had always stressed the importance of fighting bourgeois thought at its most advanced points. He spoke of history as a totality in the Marxist conception and rejected 'the theoretical and methodological poverty' of new economic history (1974b, pp. 13, 16). Samuel, probably because of his earlier personal and intellectual connection with populist communists and certainly more because of his leading role in the unfolding History Workshop movement (see p. 165), fell prey to the camp of history. He offered, however, a well reasoned statement, acknowledging that structuralism forced historians to consider a more conceptually informed basis for historical representations. But theory-building for him had no privileged immunity from empirically grounded critiques (1978). As far as history was concerned, he maintained, the enemy was 'abstracted empiricism' (1981a, p. 411).

The similar challenge posed by structuralism to sociology was also appreciated by Samuel, Hall (1977a; 1979a; 1980a) and Johnson (1979c) among others (for example, Sklair, 1981). By contrast, although the sociologists of the old New Left were critical of the mainstream empiricist social sciences, they were not prepared to confront the unfortunate disturbance of Althusserism. Peter Worsley's powerful presidential address (1973) to the British Sociological Association focused on the great need for theory, yet he did not mention either Althusser's Marxism or structuralism at large except (as a marginal point) the 'ahistoric idealism' of Lévi-Strauss's anthropology and the 'historical irony' that French Marxists were so attracted to it (1973, pp. 7–8). It was not until later that he explained why structuralist theory was unacceptable: not only because of its anti-historical thrust, but also because the concept of culture was missing in its Marxist form (1980). Concerning the question of method, 'abstracted empiricism' and the 'grand theory' of history and humanity had been for him all along 'equally unrewarding temptations' (Foreword to 1964a).

The following passage from Stedman Jones's article on class struggle (1975), written before the history and theory debate, so strikingly different in both its language and content not only from the youthful NLR cultural revolution of the 1960s but also from the absolutist tone of some of the participants of the later debates, is a nice summary of where socialist history was heading in order to overcome its ambivalence to 'theory':

> Mainly as a reaction against the positivism dominant within social science, English social historians have tended to disguise sharp analytical distinctions. If their guiding lines have been Marxist, they have also drawn much from a native socialist tradition, a tradition which remembered *Capital* as much for its moral passion as [for] its theoretical achievement.

Moreover, their methods have by no means been inspired solely by Marxist sources. The less positivistic realms of sociology, traditional kinds of economic history, social anthropology and the 'history from below' approach, have all been drawn upon (1975, p. 35).[154]

In the practice of historical writing, the 1970s began to see the harvest of methodological concerns. In the area of labour history, a rethinking of the industrial revolution and the making (and remaking) of the English working class and, representatively, of Chartism became a popular topic. A major theoretical issue involved in this topic was the phenomenon and concept of labour aristocracy, relating questions of the model of the proletariat in Marxist theory and of the course of workers' movement in actual politics – how to explain the destiny and the shift in consciousness of the working class in the third quarter of the nineteenth century or the political stability of mid-Victorian England and their consequences.[155] In one direction, Gramsci's vision of an organic intelligent-sia was a focus of analysis (for example, Kiernan, 1972a, 1972b); in the other direction, Balibar's reading of the Marxian distinction between the 'formal' and 'real' subordination of labour to capital was highlighted (Stedman Jones, 1975), suggesting a return of attention from the political-ideological superstructure to the labour process itself.

Another noted area was the transition from feudalism to capitalism, and, by extension, not only the origins of capitalism, but also the origins and evolution of pre-capitalist modes of production and the development of the 'world system'. Work on these large themes resulted in fruitful historical and theoretical writings of a more traditional Marxist kind, which reworked the famous Dobb/Sweezy controversy (Hilton, ed. 1976) and inspired the 'Brenner debate' carried out mainly by *Past and Present* from 1976,[156] but also by *NLR* and, at one point, *HWJ* (which first published Hilton's introduction to ed. 1976). The most impressive New Left products in this area, published simultaneously in 1974, were Immanuel Wallerstein's *The Modern World System* in the United States and Perry Anderson's companion volume, *Lineages of the Absolutist State* and *Passages from Antiquity to Feudalism*, in Britain. They constituted part of an important body of work contributed earlier by Arghir Emmanuel (on unequal exchange, 1969), Andre Frank (on underdevelopment, 1969) and Samir Amin (on imperialism, 1973a, 1973b) among others. Anderson's condensed macroscopic history of European absolutism in relation to the rise of capitalism and to the transition of the ancient social formations was extraordinary, in the sense that it posed and answered general theoretical questions by way of historical investigation. It also made the sole contribution to the discussion of the 'Asiatic mode of production', which did not attract any other writers from the British New Left. Highly praised by many, the two volumes, 'written in the great tradition', as Miliband put it, offered long-term challenges to both the enemies and followers of the method of historical materialism (1975, pp. 51, 62).[157]

Socialist history in Britain had been nourished since 1966 also by the nation-wide History Workshop movement which was waged within the long tradition known as 'people's history' that involved more recently the CP Historians' Group (Schwarz, 1982) and the early New Left. The backbone of the movement was the Ruskin History Workshop led by Raphael Samuel and his friends including Stedman Jones. The personal trajectory of the latter from being among the most exclusivist *NLR* theorists to a leading populist but also theoretically European-oriented Workshop historian was a characteristic achievement that mirrored, on the one hand, the diverse paths of maturity of the second New Left, and, on the other hand, the great compatibility of the History Workshop community. Under the banner of 'history from below', by means of engaging professionals as well as ordinary people in producing oral and written histories of local, community, women's and trade union groups, the movement sought 'not only to relate forms of social thought and behavior to their material roots, but also to uncover the social meaning of lost or disappearing forms of struggle, ritual or myth and to reconstitute their coherence' (Stedman Jones, 1975, p. 36). This seminal movement manifested itself as a living heir of the original New Left in its non-sectarian orientation, non-university confined activities, adult education projects, links with the unions and workers (for example, the miners)[158] and, more, support for women's struggles. It also created a new type of political forum, through the Workshop annual conferences; frequent Ruskin meetings, self-managed local programmes, History Workshop series and pamphlets beside the journal *HWJ*, in which socialist intellectuals might not only integrate with, but also grow out of the culture and politics of working people themselves.[159]

However, there were from the very beginning strong suspicions about the dominant History Workshop approach concerning the problem of small-scale micro history: was it capable of grasping the general historical trends that also demanded looking at history from above? Criticisms, more or less justified, were made of the Workshop's tendency to separate 'social history' from economic history, of its 'quasi-empiricist' mode of research and lack of theory, its sentimental romanticisation of past political experience, and its partial emphasis on the earlier periods, with a sense of nostalgia, almost as an escape from more urgent current issues.[160] An even sharper charge was made by Stuart Hall for its peculiar populism:

> History Workshop's notion of 'people's history' – as if, simply to tell the story of past oppressions and struggles is to find the promise of socialism already there, fully constituted, only waiting to 'speak out'. ... But the whole record of socialism ... is against this too-simple populism. A non-reductive Marxist theory must entail facing up to all that is involved in saying that socialism has to be constructed by a real political practice, not merely 'rediscovered' in a recuperative historical reflection. (1981a, p. 384)

The core of the History Workshop historians seemed to be aware no less than Hall of the need for such an active political practice, yet the criticism remained substantial in its own right. More patiently, in Tom Nairn's long term perspective, the History Workshop movement was 'progressive' because its work was to supply the data and conviction for the future mass mobilisation for socialism. The central gravity of the whole enterprise lay in this future process in which it might serve as 'a cultural bond between sectarian Marxism and a wider popular movement' (1977b, pp. 303–5).

A quick summary of what has been mapped out in this chapter of the Marxism of the British New Left: some remarkably significant achievements in literary criticism, history, and widely defined 'cultural studies'; some advance in political and sociological analyses; but few gains in philosophy and economics. To compare this picture with the more balanced one of the old Marxist left in Britain, the former is strikingly uneven in terms of the polarising of its strengths and weaknesses. To compare, further, the entire landscape of British Marxism, old and new, with that of the twentieth-century Anglo-Saxon culture in general purely with regard to the division of intellectual labour, an obvious contrast appears, again, in the fields of philosophy and economics.

What is at issue is not how advanced or backward the theoretical work of the Marxist New Left was by any academic criterion, nor merely to acknowledge, positively, the regeneration of Marxist discussions with unprecedented openness and flexibility on the part of most of the New Left or, negatively, their poor presentation in philosophical questions and economic thought. But the latter negative factor does matter, of course, from the socialist point of view, even if only because of the need for a scientific critique of the present and a creative vision of the future. This failure must have contributed to the continuing absence of a sound New Left programme for an alternative political and economic management of society. Yet what concerns us most here is rather how far in theory as well as in reality, mainly through intellectual activities, the New Left had and could have grasped the leading trends and the fundamental problems of contemporary society, and intervened or potentially could make an effective intervention in the actual course of social changes.[161]

Looking back at all of those missed opportunities (a 'modernisation' project had easily been taken away from the hands of the left and carried out by the right, for example), there seems to be no guarantee that the pattern of losing battles on the left would be transformed. At the one-day conference on thirty years of the New Left held at Oxford on 14 November 1987, Samuel addressed his crowded audience thus:

> Whenever I feel gloomy about politics, I think of Marx's eleventh thesis on Feuerbach – the philosophers have only interpreted the world; the point is to change it – and then think also that one can have consolation from reversing it – if we can't actually change the world, at least we can do is to understand it.

These words of profound inner doubt represented an ironic reflection on the slogan of the first New Left, which was taken as the title of the conference organised by enthusiastic young socialist students: 'Out of Apathy'.

5. 'WOMEN: THE LONGEST REVOLUTION'

At the 1987 Oxford Conference, criticism was made of both the absence of women participants in the early New Left and a near silence in its writings on questions of gender identity, the family, sexuality, domestic labour and the relationship between these and politics. This criticism is justified in the sense that there was no conscious effort to establish an independent movement for women's liberation on the part of the New Leftists, though many of them, especially the ULR people, were sympathetic to what became later the feminist challenge.[162] Not only were there very few women on the platforms of NR and NLR (for example, Doris Lessing and Dorothy Thompson,[163] and from the younger generation, Juliet Mitchell)[164] and very few New Left publications promoting a feminist outlook, but it was also true that the Review in general and people like Edward

Thompson in particular, in different ways, took a rather orthodox defensive position against the new development that led to a significant contemporary feminism, transforming the landscape of late twentieth-century critical theories and radical politics.[165] A striking example is Lessing and *The Golden Notebook* (1962). Among her widely read and influential novels, this was an important work arguing for women's consciousness within the political context of the 1950s. The book was not taken seriously in its feminist dimension by the New Left, either her fellow ex-communists or younger Marxist theorists. Moreover, she herself did not think the issue of women was that significant in the age of 'cataclysms we are living through' (Introduction to the 1971 edition, pp. viii–ix).

We may admit the criticism, but there is nevertheless the fact that the New Left carried within itself the seeds of some future developments and fostered the most original and influential feminist thinkers. Any research into the British women's liberation movement cannot, after all, trace its embryonic stage without reference to the New Left movement. Thanks to this conjuncture, the mainstream women's movement in Britain has had a strong socialist commitment. This commitment was typically expressed by leading British feminists such as Sheila Rowbotham,[166] a member of the New Left *May Day Manifesto* group; Beatrix Campbell, a communist friend of the New Left; and Barbara Taylor, from the 1968 generation of the Marxist New Left.[167]

Historical connection between the New Left and the women's movement is found, above all, in those years marked by a youthful demand for total liberation: student militancy, sexual liberalisation, the civil rights movement, popular radicalism. Women activists were first organised in the Women's Liberation Workshop (1969), Lesbian Liberation (1970), Ruskin History Workshop on Women and Family (1971), Women's Liberation National Congress (1972), and through socialist-feminist journalism. Newly founded political papers, *Black Dwarf*, *Red Mole*, and *Seven Days*, all involving NLR people, were quite actively engaged in feminist discussions.[168] Later the participation of women historians in the History Workshop vigorously pushed both the feminist orientation of the journal itself and the women's history movement of the 1970s. Rowbotham, the author of *Hidden from History* (1973), a representative text of voicing the silenced, would identify herself with the Marxism and populist politics of the first New Left. Feminist issues were also taken into the CCCS publications and became required topics in the pages of NLR though more so after the New Left movement had virtually subsided.[169]

Intellectually, while the women's movement put into question the previous male-dominated socialist movement and the whole architecture of socialist thought including the forms of Marxism which underlay these movements, it also benefited from this critique to the extent that a rigorous analysis of the sexual division of labour, the oppression of women, the material base of patriarchalism, and of the alliance between feminism and socialism for a universal human emancipation, could be formulated. From Marx's sense that the degree of the attainment of human essence by the human species or the ultimate triumph of the human over animal essence in the human being is indicated in the quality of the relation of man to woman (see especially, 1844, p. 347),[170] to Engels's belief in the historical character of the enslavement of women (1884); from Fourier's utopia of free satisfaction of psychophysical needs (Riasanovsky, 1969) to Marcuse's sexual aesthetic of a new society (1955), and relevant theories of other social Freudians and Freudo-Marxists: Wilhelm Reich, Erich Fromm, Norman O. Brown;[171] from Bebel's *Women and Socialism* (1879) or Lenin's *Women and Society* (1913–21) to Trotsky's remarks on a meaningful revolution that must free women and children, or Adorno's and Deutscher's similar concern with the end of the bourgeois family and its lying ideology,[172] or Mao's observation that liberated woman (as well as man) does not yet exist (in China),[173] we see that while the socialist tradition is still far from sufficient, it has nevertheless been firmly and vitally necessary in the direction of women's liberation. Indeed, it is precisely the logic, the egalitarian and universalist promises of socialism that validates feminist arguments and struggle. This is why it can be said, however paradoxically, that the entire socialist movement and the New Left in particular well prepared socialist feminism in Britain.

In making the feminist case, Juliet Mitchell stands out. Her pioneering essay, 'Women: the Longest Revolution', was published in *NLR* in 1966, well before the existence of a women's movement.[174] Actively involved in the theoretical build-up and politics of the early second *NLR* in the 1960s and greatly influenced by both French existentialism and structuralism, she defined her position as Marxist-feminist. She turned to psychoanalytic theories in her later work, yet never reversed her political starting point. Writing in 1983, she recalled that it was Franz Fanon's argument from his Algerian experience that women who constituted a conservative force should be emancipated only after a revolution that provoked her indignation. She was then to write the essay, very much for her New Left friends and colleagues (1984, p. 17).

The essay was an inquiry into the current silence concerning women's condition within contemporary socialism and a critique of the classical socialist literature in which the question of women's liberation was inadequately presented and 'resolved'. Mitchell's own solution to what she called the economist impasse of the theoretical heritage that she briefly examined (Fourier, Bebel, Marx, Engels, Lenin, De Beauvoir) was a structuralist one: the concrete combination of the four key structures, production, reproduction, sex, and the socialisation of children, produces a specific, complex unity of the woman's position, which is always 'overdetermined'. Still she emphasises that the main thrust of any emancipation movement must concentrate on the economic element – the entry of women fully into production – because the labour situation prescribed women's situation within the men's world of transforming nature. Strategically, while economic demands are primary, they must be accompanied by a pro-gramme that affects all four structures. The exclusion of women from production and their confinement to a monolithic condensation of functions in the family is 'the root cause of the contemporary social definition of women as *natural* beings' (1966, in 1984, p. 51).

This is followed by an important recognition of the ideological dimension necessary for any feminist analysis. Both the woman and the family are cultural creations. 'It is the function of ideology to present these given social types as aspects of Nature itself' (*ibid*, p. 19). Mitchell's attraction to the Althusserian notion of 'immutable' ideology was a major strand that led her to her subsequent studies of psychoanalysis as a means to expose the work of ideology or of internalisation of social values and codes. After all, Althusser himself was strongly influenced by Freud: 'Ideology is eternal, exactly like the unconscious' (1971, p. 152). This overwhelming concern with ideology anticipated later feminist theses of ideologically framed discourse and of knowledge-production as a political process.

A few years later, Mitchell wrote *Women's Estate* (1971) during the high tide of student rebellions and the rise of the women's movement. This short book in many ways reflected the revolutionary mood and politics of the time. The theme of the failings of past socialist theory concerning women's position was developed in discussions of the relationship between class and sex differences or between middle-class reformism and working-class socialism within a broad women's movement. In Mitchell's view, 'at this stage' the common subordinate estate of women across class and race barriers was crucial (1971, pp. 13–14, 19–39, 72–4, 162–3). However, she argued that the struggle for women's liberation necessarily meant a struggle against the capitalist system that proclaimed the liberal values of freedom, equality and the individual rights but prevented, by its very definition, their realisation (pp. 66, 177). Ideology continued to be central here, especially in her analysis of 'the magnification of familial ideology as a social force' (pp. 145, 152–8); and was taken further as the antithesis of psychoanalysis itself described by her as a scientific discovery (pp. 163–72).

Acknowledging that there was not yet any theoretical scientific base from which the oppression of women could be understood (pp. 178–9), *Women's Estate* did not challenge the current women's liberationist concepts. Rather, it clarified and located the theoretical conflicts and difficulties that the women's movement must confront. Mitchell's thorough investigations of the nature of patriarchy, the meaning of feminism, the value of Freud and the relevance of Lacan (the Lacanian interpretation of Freud's work, which replaced its biological basis with language and thus cultural references, see Lacan, 1977, p. 106) all came later with her massively influential volume, *Psychoanalysis and Feminism* (1974), which centred psychoanalysis on the agenda of feminist arguments.

Mitchell's interest in psychoanalysis had a specific New Left imprint: psychological perspectives were introduced into politics at the beginning of the 1960s in Britain with the work of R. D. Laing and David Cooper, and the publication in NLR of Sartre, Marcuse and later, Lukács, the Frankfurt School and Lacan. Referring in particular to Marcuse's *Eros and Civilisation* (1955) which (together with *One-Dimensional Man* (1964) and other writings) would excite the whole generation of 1968 in the western world, she admitted the special impression on her of its 'psychoanalytic arguments [that] masked political' (1984,

p. 55). In a wider context there was the cultural trend of the New Left thought: Thompson (in history), Williams,[175] Hoggart and Hall (in literature and what became known as cultural studies).[176] Her intellectual inclination was largely identical with the new *NLR* in its hostility towards 'vulgar empiricism' (Mitchell, 1971, p. 164; Mitchell and Oakley, 1976, p. 10).

As a radical reassessment of Freud's theory, *Psychoanalysis and Feminism* challenges feminist critics (from Clara Zetkin to recent American feminists) who rejected Freud for his supposed biological determinism, what Mitchell would demonstrate to be mistaken. For the single reason that Freud's metapsychology of sexuality and the unconscious discovered the crucial importance of the social construction of feminity, and thereby could help conceptualise the practice of women's struggle, her appreciation of him was immense: 'to ignore Freud is like ignoring Marx ...' (1971, p. 168). In Freud, the subject is a construction in that the Oedipus complex functions as a psychic structure and as the internalised law of (patriarchal) human order; the unconscious, as the way mankind live their humanity, acquires and represents the inherited ideas of (patriarchal) society. It was this cultural (or bio-social universal) reading of Freud, this social stress on the formation of the self, of primary gender identity, of sexual difference, of the uncertainty of feminity (there was no essential category, 'women'), that signified Mitchell's work as a political undertaking in developing a critical theory of patriarchy.[177]

She took patriarchy to mean the law of the father, the power that was established as a result of the hypothesised pre-historical incest taboo, the role of the father and the exchange of women. Structural anthropology (Lévi-Strauss) and linguistics (from the Saussurean model of mutually defining signs to the Freudian 'language of the unconscious' and the Lacanian formation of subjectivity through symbolic systems) helped an analysis of how kinship structures were internalised or how the family was socially and ideologically reconstructed: 'It is ... on account of their cultural utilisation as exchange-objects (which involves an [economic] exploitation of their role as propagators) that women acquire their feminine definition' (1974, pp. 407–8). This exchange that so far defines human civilisation is reproduced in the patriarchal ideology of every form of society, which itself comes, however, to contradict its own bearer in bourgeois society, the so-called biological nuclear family. Here the earlier feminist concept of patriarchy as a 'universal mode of power relationships' (Kate Millett, *Sexual Politics*) was not taken over but modified with an emphasis on its ideological nature (pp. 379–81, 406–9, 413). Notably, Mitchell's Freud is not historically universal.[178] As the end of class conflict is visible within the contradictions of capitalism, patriarchal culture will be overthrown (pp. 409, 416).

The word 'overthrow' reflected Mitchell's ever optimistic perspective.[179] While admitting the difficulty of combating the persistent ideology, she nevertheless believed that the origin of women's oppression could be traced and its maintenance be understood and overcome. However, this optimism was somewhat at odds with her total acceptance of the Freudian eternal unconscious and her critique of Engels's historical account unfavourably contrasted with Freud's identification of entire human society with patriarchy, in his closed system of libido and anthropological myth. She did not show how it would be possible to argue within the story of Oedipus that women's subordination was not fatal, or at least enduringly unchangeable.[180] For her, the right questions that should be asked about patriarchy are not those of Engels such as 'why did it happen?' and 'historically when?', but in the first instance, 'how does it happen [in the present context] and when does it take place in our society'? By seeing the woman as the first slave, women the first oppressed class, in human history, Engels's quest for origins is confined to social-economic explanations. On the other hand, Freud's concern with the ideological dimension, with the precise developmental moments of the girl's acquisition of her inferior, feminine place in patriarchal culture, seemed to Mitchell to have told more about the historical situation as well as its persistence (1974, esp. pp. 364–9; 1971, p. 153). While Engels may be wrong to suppose, as a logical implication of his famous Morganian narrative, that women's liberation would be achieved along with the abolition of private property and class antagonism, Freud's theory for its part does not offer anything on the direction of change. Another important but more difficult question that Mitchell did not ask is how to end patriarchy or how to build a new civilisation.

The chapters devoted to Reich (on sexuality and political structure), Laing (on the family and the politics of experience) and radical feminists (on Freud) discuss the influence and limitations, theoretical as well as political, of their existential, psychological and sociological or empirical phenomenologies, in the context of the 'science' of Freud's psychoanalysis. Positively, *Psychoanalysis and Feminism* was one of the significant attempts to reconcile Marxism and psychoanalysis. Only such an attempt, according to the Lacan Study Group of which Mitchell was a member, would 'make possible the conceptualisation of feminist practice'.[181]

With Ann Oakley, Mitchell edited *The Rights and Wrongs of Women* in 1976. Sally Alexander of the History Workshop and Dorothy Thompson were among the contributors. Originally designed as an 'anti-text' – what the French would call deconstruction – against the orthodox ideology on the position of women, the editors found that because social thinking in general failed to see women as a distinct social group, the orthodox texts themselves did not exist. In her own essay, 'Women and equality', Mitchell explains this failure in terms of the power of bourgeois ideology and the limitations of the concept 'equality' attached to that ideology. Again it is the social and not a biological ('natural') distinction between men and women, the social structuring along sex lines, where the roots of sexual inequality can be revealed (see also the jointly written introduction, pp. 14–15). She did not go into the depth of the dilemma involved in her categories, namely the conflict between the feminist stress on 'difference' and the demand for 'equality', that would attract feminist studies in the 1980s.[182]

Mitchell's New Left preoccupation with Marxism and the third world made her specially interested in China. Admiring many significant achievements accomplished for and by Chinese women, she nevertheless insisted that the success of the socialist revolution had not brought about women's liberation there (nor in the Soviet Union). She was certainly right about this. Yet the following statement would be a surprise to her readers: 'It is only in the highly developed societies of the west that an authentic liberation of women can be envisaged today' (1966, in 1984, p. 45). Why? She did not say. It is perhaps more plausible to add 'men' together with women in her sentence. But even so the economic/technological determinist flavour of this observation is striking and very much in contradiction to her otherwise coherent arguments.

Mitchell belonged to the first intellectual generation in the British Isles seriously to encounter European thoughts and theories/ideas developed in other continents. Her exchange with American scholars was also mutually fruitful – a typical case which enriched Perry Anderson's nearly all-male 'Atlantic dimension' (1990). Post-1968 socialist feminism in England deserves a full-length historical study. It must include more recent developments which cannot be discussed here – only touched on in my 'Epilogue'.

NOTES

1. Thompson resigned from teaching at Warwick because he supported the students over this particular issue.
2. The IS group founded the Irish Civil Rights Solidarity Campaign in 1968.
3. It was estimated that 200 occupations occurred in the years 1969–70, and over 100 in 1971–74. The ones that had nationwide impact included the occupations of Upper Clyde shipbuilders and the Plessey factory in Scotland. See Young, 1971, pp. 438–9; Ali, 1978, pp. 139–44. About the return of class politics in general during that period, see Barnett, 1973, pp. 3–21, 29–32; Blackburn, 1971; Ali, 1978, pp. 139–60.
4. 280,000 miners struck for seven weeks and won. According to Glyn, Harrison and Sutcliffe, it was the biggest and most significant class battle in Britain since 1926 and it dealt a damaging blow to the capitalist ruling order (Glyn and Sutcliffe, 1972, Postscript; Glyn and Harrison, 1980, pp. 87–9). Compare a report on the start of the strike by John Hoyland in *Seven Days*, 9 Jan. 1972.
5. Splitting off from the *Black Dwarf* (which existed from June 1968 to Sept. 1970), the *Red Mole* was launched in March 1970. This was a split of IMG over the decision to create a Leninist youth organisation, the Spartacus League. The *Red Mole* changed to *Red Weekly* in 1973. See Hayter, 1971, pp. 128–9. About IMG or a 'New Left Trotskyism', see Shipley, 1976, pp. 105–25; Callaghan, 1987, pp. 113–60. CSE was formed in 1970 and soon had more than 1,000 members. 'We are committed to the development within the labour movement of a materialist critique of capitalism in the Marxist tradition' (CSE pamphlet, 1976). *Cambridge Journal of Economics* and *Capital and Class* were founded later in 1977.
6. The French intelligentsia was then in a process of what Fredric Jameson called 'full de-Marxification' (1990, p. 5).
7. There is also, according to Martin Jay, a theoretical totality, that is, a common commitment to 'Marxist holism' of these competing Marxisms. Cf. Jay, 1984.
8. Anderson himself of course acknowledges that 'both the Della Volpean and Althusserian schools have been distinguished by certain common features which set them off from other systems within Western Marxism' (1976a, p. 73).
9. For some references to the growing 'translation industry' and discussions in English around the newly available material in the period of 1965–72, see Robert Young, 1973, pp. 398–400. Another important journal that engaged itself in importing continental theories especially structuralism and post-structuralism was *Screen*. See Easthope, 1983; 1988.
10. *Selections from the Prison Notebooks of Antonio Gramsci*, published simultaneously

by Lawrence and Wishart (London) and International Publishers (New York). It was not the first adequate selection of Gramsci's notebooks in English, but the first with a good general introduction and a wealth of explanatory notes. Another translation done by *NLR* (Nairn) was Giuseppe Fiori's *Gramsci: Life of a Revolutionary* (1965; NLB, 1970).

11. There was a widespread borrowing of such a key Gramscian term as 'hegemony' within Anglo-Saxon political discourse in Marxist and non-Marxist analyses of politics and history. 'Gramsci has become part of our intellectual universe' (Hobsbawm, 1977, p. 206). Some examples representative of creative use of the concept are Williams, 1973b; Hobsbawm, 1975; Thompson, 1974, 1975a. See also John Merrington, 1968, a fine introduction to the Italian thinker; Kiernan, 1972a, an insightful yet cursory commentary; Hobsbawm, 1977, a defence of the Eurocommunist interpretation of Gramsci's thought. This thought, in Kiernan's words, is 'a treasure-trove for us to delve into, or a rediscovered missing link, a lost generation, in the evolution of Marxism' (1972a, p. 2). For the Gramsci studies in Britain before 1968, see *SR* 1968, p. 170.

12. Namely, his illusion of achieving economic power prior to the seizure of the national political power during the movement of factory occupations and councils in Turin. 'The absence of a theory of insurrection is, in fact, the missing link in the whole of Gramsci's early writings' (Anderson, 1968b, p. 26).

13. For Anderson, these can be seen especially in his theory of the state (1976b, pp. 12–3), of hegemony mediating state and civil society (pp. 18–26, 31–4), of coercion and consent (pp. 44–5).

14. Anderson's reconstruction of the three Gramscian versions are (1) predominance of hegemony (in civil society) over coercion (of the state) as the fundamental model of bourgeois power; (2) adjusting version 1 by adding the central ideological role of the state: a combination of force and consent in hegemony; (3) a correction of version 2: the state = political society + civil society. The consequences are, for 1, the illusion of left social-democracy that the cultural control of the ruling class essentially ensures the order of the capitalist rule; for 2, a conflation of juridical rules and conventional norms, and ignorance of the monopoly of legitimate violence of the capitalist state; and for 3, the lack of any comprehensive account of the history or structure of bourgeois democracy, and hence a comparison of this and fascism in the *Prison Notebooks*. See, 1976b, pp. 26–42.

15. Hall, for example, has written recently that the nature of power itself in the modern world is that it is also constructed in relation to political, moral, intellectual, cultural, ideological and sexual issues. 'The question of hegemony is always the question of a new cultural order' (1987, pp. 20–1). He acknowledges that Gramsci has 'really transformed my own way of thinking about politics' (p. 16).

16. In Portugal, Anderson argues, the infantry and artillery may not, but the commandos and airforce remained intact to suppress socialism. In Hobsbawm's view, on the contrary, the case of Portugal shows precisely the crucial role of hegemony – in the absence of hegemonic force even revolution can run into the sand. Other examples are Chile and Uruguay: beyond a certain point the use of coercion to maintain rule becomes frankly incompatible with the use of apparent consent, and the rulers have to choose between the two. Where they choose the former, the results have not usually been favourable to the working class movement (1977a, p. 211).

17. Note his explanation of dual power and the variable of external military intervention in 1976b, pp. 76–8. For him, one of the basic axioms of historical materialism is that secular struggle between classes is ultimately resolved at the political level of society, namely, at the level of construction and destruction of the state (p. 11). Here the barb that he 'moves away' from the emphasis on the question of class (cf. Kaye, 1984, pp. 58–9) obviously missed its target.

18. Ernest Mandel writes angrily that it is 'fraudulent' to invoke the heritage of Gramsci in defending the 'neo-reformist orientation upheld by the Eurocommunist leadership' (1978, p. 201). With Anderson he opposes reformism; against Anderson he cannot see the slightest evidence that Gramsci ever abandoned revolutionary

Marxist quintessence. For Miliband, Eurocommunism must be sharply distinguished, in theoretical and programmatic terms, from social democracy (1978). Critical commentaries on the ideas and movements of the Eurocommunist parties can be frequently found in *NLR*, written by Jon and Fred Halliday, Ronald Fraser, Blackburn and others. For the conceptual significance of 'hegemony' as a fundamental tool in socialist strategic thinking which Anderson failed to acknowledge, see Laclau and Mouffe, 1985.

19. Besides, Trotsky's analysis of Nazi Germany is 'the only developed theory of a modern capitalist State in classical Marxism', and of Stalinism the most coherent and advanced within the Marxist tradition (1976b, pp. 73, 75; 1983b, p. 49; 1976a, pp. 96–101, 118–21). Anderson speaks highly of such scholars known as Trotskyists, Isaac Deutscher, Roman Rosdolsky and Ernest Mandel.

20. Anderson was quite a fundamentalist of post-war leftist anti-communism. His strong hostility toward the Communist Parties and the 'bureaucratic' socialist states, and his disbelief in any possibility of reform of the latter, prevented him from understanding and anticipating some profoundly important developments in post-revolutionary societies.

21. Debate between Nicolas Krasso (a *NLR* editorial member) and Mandel in *NLR* over Trotsky's Marxism (nos. 43, 44, 47, 48, 56) was taken by Blackburn as a proof of *NLR*'s non-Trotskyist position (interview with Blackburn by the author, 26 Nov. 1987). Mandel claimed that Trotsky represented the principles of Soviet democracy and revolutionary internationalism. Krasso argued, while reviewing Deutscher's 'unfinished revolution', that for these 'utopian' principles Trotsky had become 'a romantic myth and symbol'. This seems to me to have no power to either prove or disprove the Trotskyist editorial politics of the *Review*. Later on, however, the 1983 split of its board was probably a result of serious disagreement with the Trotskyist orientation, that those who remained in *NLR* afterwards in some way confirmed.

22. *NLR* also published Löwy's essay on Lukács and Stalinism (*NLR* 91) and an interview with Lukács conducted by a *NLR* member in Budapest in late 1968 (*NLR* 68).

23. See Wohlfarth's earlier comment from a different point of view, 1967, p. 65.

24. *NLR* did an interview with Hedda Korsch in 1972; see *NLR* 76.

25. See Laing and Cooper, 1964, an abridged English translation of Sartre's later writings with a significant introduction.

26. Goran Therborn, a frequent Swedish contributor to *NLR*, offered a general evaluation of the Frankfurt School in political and sociological terms (1970). Norman Birnbaum's studies of the critical philosophers (1969; 1971) are non-Marxist in character. He was though actively involved in the making of the New Left in Britain, moved away in the early 1960s and has been no longer identifiable with the movement ever since.

27. See Wohlfarth, 1967; *NLR*, 'Presentation of Adorno-Benjamin' (1973); the English translations of *Minima Moralia* was published by NLB in 1974, *Dialectic of Enlightenment* in 1979, *In Search of Wagner* in 1981. *NLR* printed Marcuse's 'Industrialisation and Capitalism' (1965), 'Re-examination of the Concept of Revolution' (1969) and an interview with him in Cockburn & Blackburn, eds, 1969. *Studies in Critical Philosophy* was published by NLB in 1972. Two very brief comments on Marcuse's philosophy can be found in *NLR*: Laing's review of *One-Dimensional Man* (1964) and G. A. Cohen, 1969, which situates Marcuse's thought in its relation to the German philosophical traditions from which Marxism itself emerged. Martin Jay's *The Dialectical Imagination* (1973) or David Held's *Introduction to Critical Theory* (1980) were among the rare full-length English language treatments of the history and philosophies of the Frankfurt thinkers from a generally defined Marxist point of view before 1980. Both authors were without any affiliation with the British New Left.

28. They responded more to the writings of Benjamin and Goldmann than to Lukács, Adorno, Lefebvre, Brecht or Marcuse. *NLR* introduced the exchange between Benjamin and Adorno on the former's work and characterised the relationship of

the two men as a progress towards a more revolutionary Marxism under Brecht's influence on Benjamin, and in turn Benjamin's on Adorno (*NLR* 77, *NLR* 81, 1973). The first book-length English-language study of Benjamin ever produced by a British Marxist was Eagleton's *Walter Benjamin, or Towards a Revolutionary Criticism*, published later in 1981 by Verso.

29. See Eagleton, 1990, esp. chapters 8, 13, 14. Emerging from and turning out to be a major Marxist critic of the English 'culture and society' tradition, Eagleton in this splendid work in a way confirmed Anderson's point by 'politicising' aesthetics. He also observed that 'the characteristically idealist cast of German thought has proved a more hospitable medium for aesthetic enquiry than the rationalism of France or the empiricism of Britain' (p. 2).

30. In regard to political economy, Anderson mentioned Paul Baran and Paul Sweezy in a footnote (pp. 46–7) and referred at several points to, of course, Mandel and Michal Kalecki, but all were not considered to be in any way 'western Marxist'.

31. In his Afterword, Anderson criticises the 'central weakness' of this conclusion as it lacks an examination of 'the actual conditions or precise horizons' of the unity of theory and practice (p. 109).

32. Charles Taylor explains, 'at a purely intellectual level', why Marxism in general never found a congenial home in England in 'Marxism and Empiricism', 1966.

33. As a commentator remarks, the confrontation of 'history' and 'agency' does not do much to explain what is wrong with Stalinism (Ree, 1974, pp. 34–5). See II.2.

34. For example, it is a question as to what extent it is capable of confronting and resolving the problem of tragedy. With Taylor, Eagleton argues that in *Modern Tragedy* (1966), Williams's two humanist positions in relation to the idea and reality of tragedy (tragedy is common, local and personal yet it can be historically transcended) are mutually incompatible. 'The convergence in Williams's thinking of a Marxian historical perspective and a deeply-rooted personal humanism leads not only to enrichment: it leads also, at unavoidable points, to contradiction' (1970, pp. 110–12).

35. I am indebted to Nick Stargardt for this point.

36. According to Thompson (1979), in the mid-1950s, Hoggart's attitude to Marxism was one of explicit hostility, Williams's one of active critique, Hall's one of sceptical ambivalence; whereas the *Reasoner* group, with which was associated a number of Marxist historians – among them Saville, the Thompsons, Miliband, Barratt Brown, Worsley, Meek, Harrison, and less closely, Hill, Hilton and Hobsbawm – was attempting to defend, re-examine and extend the Marxist tradition at a time of political and theoretical disaster. Later, however, Williams and Hall had shown increasing respect for and confidence in the notion of a Marxism as a total and systematic theory, and, to the same degree, Thompson confessed that his own confidence in such systematisation had become less, and 'today I am very close indeed to Williams on critical points of theory' (pp. 397, 399).

37. Goldmann's standing as a Marxist theorist, because of his intellectual connections with the young Lukács and therefore with Kant and Hegel, and because he was in opposition to what he saw as dogmatic, one-sided structuralism, had by the time of his death in 1970 diminished in France during the upsurge of Althusserism. Goldmann defined his own approach as 'genetic structuralism' and stressed its historical dimension (1952; 1975). See Glucksmann, 1969; Mulhern, 1975b.

38. For their views on the role of socialist intellectuals, see the final section of Coates, 1971b and the last chapter of Barratt Brown, 1972b.

39. They discussed elsewhere the concrete steps towards and principles of workers' control, including union nomination at the workplace, report back and recall, participation in decision-making in nationalised as well as privately owned industries, and so on. See IWC pamphlet series and the publications cited in III.3.

40. See Fred Halliday's very brief comparison between Korsch's and Gramsci's writings on local councils in his introduction to Korsch, 1970, pp. 10–11.

41. It is worth mentioning here Michael Rustin's suggestion of 'the possibility of basing political organisations, of a broad and unsectarian kind, on the work place rather than on the residential community'. Writing in 1981, he was thinking of professional

work settings other than the factory. This strategic option, he commented, failed to be explored by the New Left (1981, pp. 82–3). But how would he relate his proposal to the idea and experience of workers' control? Can 'councils' be designed to and really play the role of political organisation? Concerning the organisational basis of 'control' and thinking quite the opposite to Rustin, Lawrence Daly believed in community control of industry simply because the worker's 'interest as a consumer has to be taken into account' (1989, p. 139).

42. While appreciating (as always) the work of Ernest Gellner (who came from Czechoslovakia), a rare case of 'genuine independent liberalism', Anderson now came to finally conclude what he had seen as 'the dominance of a White immigration' in the national culture (1990, *NLR* 180, p. 67).

43. See Thompson's angry confession reflecting on accusations of him by his 'younger feathered cousins' who were, with a rush of wind, 'off to Paris, to Rome, to California': 'I had thought of trying to join them ... but my wings grow no bigger. If I were to try I know very well that with my great bulk of romantic moralisms, my short-sighted empirical vision, and my stumpy idiomatic wings, I would fall – flop! – into the middle of the Channel' (1973, p. 319).

44. Note that Williams was also interested in the 'revisionist' theoretical work concerning cultural theory by the Soviet 'Vitebsk Group' of the 1920s: P. M. Medvedev, V. N. Volosinov and M. M. Bakhtin (cf. 1986, pp. 22–5).

45. Speaking of the recent achievements of Anglo-American philosophy, he lists 'the attempt to construct a systematic theory of meaning (Davidson, Dummett), the causal theory of names (Kripke, Putnam, Donnellan), and the associated revival of epistemological realism, the emergence of anti-empiricist philosophies of science (Lakatos, Feyerabend, Kuhn), the reconstruction of bourgeois political and legal philosophy (Rawls, Nozick, Dworkin, Raz), the debates provoked by Quine's critique of meaning and Chomsky's transformational grammar'. 'None of these developments', he continues, 'can be dismissed as trivial or pedantic' (pp. 4–5).

46. For example, Eagleton attacked French deconstructionism (1981, 1984); Anderson and his *NLR* had been consistently against post-structuralism presented by Barry Hindess and Paul Hirst (1975; 1977; Hirst, 1979) (cf. IV.4); Anderson saw Paris in the early 1980s as 'the capital of European intellectual reaction' that represented the 'historical local defeat of historical materialism' (1983a, p. 32) and talked about the 'emptiness' of postmodernism, featured by philosophical as well as historical relativism, with reference to art (1988).

47. See Williams: 'Once the central body of thinking was itself seen as active, developing, unfinished, and persistently contentious, ... my respect for the body of thinking as a whole ... significantly and decisively increased' (1977, p. 4). See also Gregor McLennan *et al.*, 1977, in which the question, by what criteria we may judge what constitutes the 'scientific' and what does not, is asked and discussed. Barratt Brown regards Marx's schema of social structure and development as a great 'Newtonian model' (1972c; cf. Shanin's comment, 1972, pp. 145–7).

48. See his suggestion concerning the three hallmarks that separate historical materialism from all other contributions to the culture of socialism: (1) its sheer scope as an intellectual system, (2) its character as a theory of historical development and (3) its radicalism as a political call to arms in the struggle against capitalism. But each of these traditional privileges is being challenged today (1983a, pp. 86–8).

49. It was not until later, in 1978, that he made his case against Marxism as a 'science' and, in particular, the 'mountainous inconsistency', the unverifiable laws and wrong predictions of *Capital* as a 'scientific' work (1978a, pp. 65, 162–72). See Daniel Little's critique of Thompson's 'unfounded' criticism, 1986, pp. 187–95.

50. These areas and questions include Marx's treatment of the capitalist state, his silence on the characteristics of the international system of the nation states and on nationalism; his economic theory and some controversial or wrong conclusions drawn from it; Lenin's contradiction between the Soviet democratism and the party authoritarianism in both theoretical and practical terms, his failure in continuing the strategic line of making distinction between the west and the east; Trotsky's inadequate generalisation of the notion of 'permanent revolution', his confusion of

different forms of the capitalist state, his economic catastrophism, and the concept of 'workers' state' (1976a, pp. 103–4, 113–21). See 1983a, which deals with a more widely defined pattern of development of Marxism in the west since the mid-1970s.

51. Later, in a reconsideration on utopian socialism, Stedman Jones somehow retreated from his earlier assessment, claiming the need for 'the removal of the teleological and reductionist presuppositions that characterised Engels's approach' (1981, p. 138).

52. See Maurice Dobb's classical contribution, 1946; 1963. Surely Lenin talked about social revolution as the precondition for the development of productive forces in the twentieth-century backward countries. So did Gramsci, who even put the transfer of cultural/political 'hegemony' prior to the change of the relations of production. Needless to say, Mao was clearly aware of this revisionist priority when he led the Red Army marching in the poor mountain areas of the Chinese countryside.

53. Or in Jameson's ironic remark, 'everything changes when you grasp base-and-superstructure not as a full-fledged theory in its own right, but rather as the name for a problem, whose solution is always a unique, ad hoc invention' (1990, p. 46).

54. Thompson argues mainly against the notion of structured 'levels' of a given social formation. But Anderson correctly points out a 'parallelism' between Thompsonian and Althusserian (e.g. Poulantzas) accounts of modern law: law can be empirically omnipresent in a society, as Thompson has shown, yet remains analytically a level of it, as Poulantzas maintains; and that level can indeed be elevated as a superstructure above the economic base, even while being indispensable to it, as G. A. Cohen demonstrates. 'There is no incompatibility between these successive propositions' (1980, pp. 71–3). See also Cohen's critique of Thompson's 'mistaken rejection' of the metaphor (1978, pp. 86–7).

55. Further, Williams writes: 'from my own work on the nineteenth century, I came to view it as eventually a bourgeois formula; more specifically, a central position of utilitarian thought' (1971, p. 10); cf. Eagleton. Williams noted that the base/superstructure thesis and the being/consciousness one make significantly different emphases: the latter is an ontological doctrine and the former historical (1989, pp. 172–3).

56. Conceptualisation of 'totality', of course, has been engaged in very different ways and on the whole it has not got rid of the 'determination difficulty'.

57. Worsley regards the base/superstructure model as incompatible with the idea of a dialectical science of society. Debates over it can never be at an end as long as it is retained, for the model constantly requires repair jobs (1982, p. 113). Indeed, in Saville's words, it 'led many into mechanical and dogmatic conclusions' (1974b, p. 9).

58. In this essay Hall examines how Marx's conception of base and superstructure shifted from the identity-correspondence position of *The German Ideology*, through 'an analytic break' inside the text of *The Eighteenth Brumaire*, to the developed theory of superstructure within the framework of 'determination in the last instance' in *Capital*.

59. Marx places stress on the 'effectivity' of certain aspects of superstructure: the political and the ideological may exert the dominant role in pre-capitalist societies. See Hall, 1977b, pp. 49–50; 1974.

60. See G. A. Cohen's functional explanation in 1978, pp. 231–4.

61. See Hall's more recent statement: 'I don't believe that economics is the primary definer in the sense of the first instance, or that the economy stitches up the results in the end' (1988c, pp. 63, 72–3).

62. Marcuse suggests a re-examination of the structural relations between 'corporate capitalism' and socialism, that is, of the qualitative difference of socialism as a definite negation of capitalism (1969a, pp. 28–9). It is quite commonly argued, in relation to the notions of 'post-scarcity' or 'post-industrial society', capitalism and socialism are different means, corresponding to the different material and political situations, for pursuing industrialisation. The mission of the working class is therefore to industrialise society rather than to make a socialist revolution

(cf. Oglesby, ed. 1969, pp. 18–19). For E. H. Carr, all modern revolutions made in the backward countries are essentially no more than the first stage of industrial revolution carried through 'from above' (1950). Blackburn also holds that socialist revolution triumphed in those countries where the failure of capitalist civilisation provoked popular resistance (Preface to ed. 1978, p. 13). See Dunn, 1972; Elster, 1984.

63. On the other hand, as Miliband noted, although a systematic theorisation of the state cannot be found in Marx's and Engels's work, they did constantly refer to the state in different circumstances in almost all of their important writings (1965). See also Jessop, 1978.

64. For a general observation, see Blackburn, 1976, pp. 38–41. Birnbaum discussed the British case in 1969a, pp. 7–26. See also his 1971, pp. 101–6.

65. The battle for consciousness waged in terms of traditions, communications, the work process (divisions of labour), and cultural elements including religions (cf. 1977a, ch.3).

66. See Miliband, 1969, 1970b, 1973a; Poulantzas, 1969, 1976. See Laclau's review on the debate, 1975.

67. See Miliband's note on his two exchanges with Poulantzas, 1983, p. 26; 1970b, *NLR* 59, pp. 27–30; 1973a, *NLR* 82, pp. 84–6. Poulantzas, 1969, pp. 240–3; 1976, pp. 65, 68, 72. According to Laclau, Poulantzas's *Political Power and Social Classes* (1968) and Miliband's *The State in Capitalist Society* (1969) are deeply contrasting studies within different systems of knowledge (1975).

68. Anderson was nevertheless an overall defender of Poulantzas. He remarks that *Fascism and Dictatorship* 'represents a rare example of theoretical and empirical synthesis in contemporary Marxist literature' (1977, p. 39). Jane Caplan, on the contrary, illustrates how in this work 'extreme theoretical precision is combined with crude empirical inaccuracy' (1977, p. 84).

69. Geras recommends Trotsky's writings on the struggle against fascism in Germany (1936), which is concerned precisely with different forms and methods of the bourgeois rule and the different social blocs they attempted to construct (1978, p. 309).

70. At least up to 1969, Miliband defined the state in capitalist society as the 'guardian' or 'protector' of class domination and exploitation, and as the coercive instrument of a ruling class. See, esp. 1969, pp. 265–6 and chapter 1 for detailed arguments.

71. It simultaneously confines and defends class rule, according to Miliband, in order to ensure 'law and order' which basically benefit the economically dominant class (cf. Bottomore *et al.* eds. 1983, p. 466).

72. See for example Trotsky: under a democratic regime, the bourgeoisie leans for support primarily upon the working class, and all bourgeois democracies rely on a combination of repression and concession (1971, pp. 158, 281).

73. See his later work, *Capitalist Democracy in Britain*, 1982.

74. Norman Geras, born in 1943 in Rhodesia, educated at Pembroke and Nuffield College, Oxford, and since 1967 a lecturer in politics and government at the University of Manchester, has been an editor of and frequent contributor to *NLR* since 1976.

75. See Löwy's warm review of the book in *NLR* 101–102, pp. 138–42.

76. He developed sound arguments on the relation between ends and means in chapter 4, 1976.

77. It has been argued that Marx's use of this phrase is a sociological description of the class character of political power rather than a definition of the forms of the government machinery. For Miliband, Marx refers to both, and precisely the nature of the political power guarantees its class character (1965, p. 17).

78. Anderson suggests the following for investigation in this area: (1) the political structure of a socialist democracy, (2) the pattern of an advanced socialist economy, (3) the socio-cultural pattern of a 'liberation levelling', and (4) the international relations between unevenly developed socialist countries (1983a, pp. 99–100; cf. 1983b). The first notable attempt made in area (4) was by Miliband, 1980. See Benedict Anderson's discussion of nationalism as the real, undeniable ground for 'inter-socialist' wars, 1983.

79. In principle, the whole concept of 'the dictatorship of the proletariat' had been rejected by almost all kinds of contemporary socialists including the New Left. The only notable exception was Balibar's *On the Dictatorship of the Proletariat* (NLB, 1977). See Coates's negative comment on the book, 1977.

80. Lenin conceded that the phenomenon of political bureaucracy was in fact to some extent inevitable because of the backwardness of the society where socialist revolution was made in a chosen 'historical opportunity'. He also accepted the situation of the dictatorship of one party as he believed that the Bolshevik Party 'has won for itself the position of vanguard of the whole factory and industrial proletariat' (quoted in Carr, 1950, p. 230). However, there is a fundamental discontinuity between Leninism and Stalinism as convincingly argued by Moshe Lewin, 1967. See also Colletti, 1969; Miliband, 1977a, pp. 144–8; Geras, 1976, pp. 192–3.

81. Within the Swedish model to which *NLR* paid special attention in the 1960s (Anderson, 1961) we may find some significant elements of a possible future socialist economy. On the questions concerning adjusting and pre-adjusting the market and relating central and local interests, see Barratt Brown's distinction between 'economic planning in a market economy' and the 'planned economy', 1970, pp. 257–71. Anderson (1983a, pp. 100–1) recommends Alec Nove's *Economics of Feasible Socialism* (1983) which is about and for socialism written from outside the Marxist tradition. More recently there have been extensive discussions of socialist planning and 'market socialism' since the Nove/Mandel debate in *NLR*.

82. He also argues for the richness and significance of the analyses of the state and strategy in Marx's and Engels's classics. Historical materialism, according to him, either discovered or thoroughly reworked every important political concept previously represented by such thinkers as Machiavelli, Montesquieu and Rousseau. For example, the concept of the dictatorship of the proletariat contains a transformed version of the Rousseauian concept of popular sovereignty (1976 pp. 25, 66). See his introduction to Debray, ed. 1970.

83. Revolution is, in the classical formulations, 'the overthrow of the existing ruling power and the dissolution of the old order' (Marx, quoted in Blackburn, 1976, p. 28); or that 'the transfer of state power from one class to another class is the first, the principal, the basic sign of a revolution, both in the strictly scientific and in the practical political meaning of the term' (Lenin, 1917, p. 33). Reformism, on the other hand, seeks reforms without claiming transformation of the political power.

84. In the British context, Blackburn sees reformists as those who 'identified socialism with nationalisation and welfare measures carried through by the capitalist state' (1976, p. 24). Much-criticised 'labourism' (see III.3) obviously falls into the same category. For Hall, reformism means the liberal and social democratic illusion of political change without political power. This reformism represents a strong indigenous tradition, as authentic a English working-class tradition as the revolutionary one. It is precisely here that the task of socialists makes sense (cf. 1982). See also Saville, 1973a.

85. With reference to my question, he wrote that 'there has not been much response to my saying that a new socialist party (not in place of the Labour Party, but parallel to it) is needed. Many people – in fact a lot of people – agree with me, but also believe, on various grounds, that the time is not ripe. ... My own view is quite firm that such a new formation is badly needed; but it cannot come into being until a lot of people in diverse parts of the labour movement come to believe that it is both feasible and desirable'. He mentioned the recent coming into being of the Socialist Conference, which was generated out of the Socialist Society: 'It is not a new party, of course, but it is worth following its evolution' (letter to the author dated 14 April 1989). One of the main obstacles in the way to a new socialist organisation, as Margot Heinemann reminded me, is that 'the British electoral system, combined with the power of the media, makes the formation of new political parties far more difficult than elsewhere in Europe' (letter to the author dated 27 Nov. 1987). For a critique of this electoral system, see John Peck, 1984 and Williams, 1979, pp. 381–2.

86. After the *May Day Manifesto*, there had been of course a number of valuable attempts on the part of the British New Left. See for example Rustin, 1985.

87. He denounces the CPGB programme, *The British Road to Socialism* (1968), in 1976, p. 167.
88. See also Fred Halliday's criticism of the 'rightward slippage' of the Eurocommunist parties, 1983, pp. 167–8.
89. For Anderson, one of the most striking and paradoxical features of western Marxism is its lack of internationalism. With the victory of 'socialism in one country' in the USSR, the tide of post-Second World War national independent movements, and the final nationalist perspectives adopted by European communism, the dominant framework of Marxist culture had undergone a fundamental change (1976a, pp. 68–9).
90. The authors, respectively, developed their arguments in a second editions of the books which were published around the 'hot time' of the student movement. Barratt Brown's *Essays on Imperialism* (1972) and *Economics of Imperialism* (1974) continued the line of his 1963 book. Worsley's *The Three Worlds* published later in 1984 was an extensive study of culture and world development. To the question 'Do you still consider yourself a Marxist?', Worsley's answer was 'Yes and no' (interview with the author, 19 May 1987). This ambiguity seems to have something to do with his long-term concern with the Third World questions which are sometimes in contradiction with or often omitted from traditional Marxist analysis.
91. In 1964, an attempt by Barratt Brown to call together a seminar of economists and historians to consider problems of imperialism led to a meeting of just four people (Barratt Brown, 1974b, p. 17). *After Imperialism* was reviewed by Mandel (1964) and Kiernan (1965) in *NLR*, and Alavi (1964) in *SR*. Mandel's criticism concerned trade, Alavi's investment. See Kiernan's review on studies of imperialism in Britain in general, 1964.
92. See esp. 'A critique of Marxist theories of imperialism' in 1972a and 'Marxist theories of imperialism' in 1974b. He looks at imperialism as a concept in Marxist political economy, the intellectual origins of it (Hobson and Schumpeter), the competing Marxist theories (Marx, Hilferding, Luxemburg, Lenin), 'neo-Marxist' explanations (Magdoff, Baran and Sweezy, Emmanuel), and main criticisms of them (classical liberal and Keynesian). Kautsky's and Bukharin's analyses are omitted in his examination. See Kiernan, 'The Marxist theory of imperialism and its historical formation' in 1974, which offered a brief but more comprehensive critique. The book is dedicated to Saville.
93. See for example the particularly interesting exchange between Bill Warren (1973; cf. his *Imperialism: Pioneer of Capitalism*, 1980) and Arghiri Emmanuel (1974) concerning whether or not, reversing the Leninist thesis, capitalist industrialisation resulted from imperialism; and between Mandel and Warren, the impending global recession and its possible consequences (*NLR* 87, *NLR* 88).
94. Later, Williams commented, within his own field, that the notion of the rise of a national literature, the definition of a nation through its literature, and the idea of literature as the moral essence or spirit of the nation, are supports of a specific political and social ideology (1979, p. 119). See some recent writings, mostly by the old participants of the New Left, on this subject in Samuel, ed. 1989, vol. 3, *National Fictions*.
95. See *NLR*, 'The Marxism of Regis Debray', *NLR* 45, pp. 8–12; in Blackburn, ed. 1975, Fred Halliday explores the causes and consequences of the Ceylonese insurrection, and Tariq Ali examines the nationalist movement in Pakistan and Bangladesh. Halliday also wrote about the tension in the Middle East, the Soviet power, China's foreign policy and revolutions made in Africa. Some good reports on and analyses of Third World issues can be found in the pages of *Seven Days*. Blackburn and Ali, as members of IMG, travelled to Vietnam (Ali alone), Cuba and Bolivia and, among other activities, took part in the international campaign to rescue Regis Debray. See Blackburn's introduction to Debray, 1970; Ali's 'In Lieu of an introduction' in 1978.
96. See Barratt Brown, 1961b. With Hughes and others, he also proposed a World Economic Conference to provide an alternative to the integration of capitalist Europe and its unequal relationship with underdeveloped countries.

97. And more recently in the Falklands war. See Samuel (ed.) *Patriotism: The Making and Remaking of British National Identity*, 1989. The volumes were born out of anger at the war and the recognition of the notion of 'nation' as remaining 'a powerful mobilising myth' (Introduction). See Nairn's explanation of 'patriotism' as a 'false consciousness': much political history is the story of how the national divisions of humanity (territorial, cultural, racial, etc.) have invariably been exploited to contain and repress its artificial divisions within societies (class, caste, etc.) (*Seven Days*, 24 Nov. 1971). Later (1977b), he changed this view. See also an interesting discussion of the 'nation', conservatism and internationalism between Hall and his commentators in Nelson and Grossberg (eds.) 1988, pp. 64–7.

98. For Nairn, 'Fascism is the archetype of nationalism' (1975, p. 17). See Kiernan's arguments against the claim that fascism originated 'in the outward pressures of monopoly capitalism' (1974, p. 150). Most visibly in Japan, fascism originated in those older tracts of national life and emotion that capitalism had only half assimilated (1964, p. 278).

99. This is a collection of Nairn's *NLR* essays on nationalism. See R. Johnson's comments on the book in 1980, pp. 67–70.

100. See his recent study of the importance of 'the crown' in preserving the stability of the British state, 1988.

101. For the 'deficiencies' of Marx's and Engels's view on the British state, see 1977b, pp. 18–19.

102. An African character, Akande, in Williams's novel, referring to the unequal trade between rich and poor countries, tells that 'nationalism, is in this sense like class. To have it, and to feel it, is the only way to end it. If you fail to claim it, or give it up too soon, you will merely be cheated, by other classes and other nations' (1964, p. 322). This is a profound but passing remark. Politically, Marxists since Comintern had been expected to (1) first 'settle matters with its own bourgeoisie' (*The Communist Manifesto*) and (2) support national independence and liberation movements on the condition that the 'hegemony' is sought in order to lead nationalist struggles to an eventual socialist advance. But within this basically instrumental scheme, many problems remain unsolved. See Sartre's introduction to Fanon's *The Wretched of the Earth*; Avineri's brief but fine commentary on a socialist theory of nationalism, 1990. See also Benedict Anderson's much-praised study of the origin and spread of nationalism as an ideology of what he calls 'imagined communities', 1983. He has a good discussion of the play of contemporary nationalism in the politics of socialist nation states; see, esp. pp. 140–7.

103. Otherwise there might be a chance for the Labour government to carry on some constitutional reforms and finally settle the problem. For impressive reports on and analysis of the question of Northern Ireland, see esp. *Seven Days*, 15 Dec. 1971; 12 Jan. 1972.

104. Young Marxist economists around CSE and/or the Labour Militant Tendency, such as Andrew Glyn, Bob Sutcliffe, Ben Fine, Lawrence Harris, John Harrison and Philip Armstrong, were impressive debators. Glyn and Sutcliffe's *British Capitalism, Workers and the Profits Squeeze* (1972), for example, was a powerful analysis and made a direct impact on Labour politics. See Glyn and Sutcliffe, 1972b; Fine and Harris, 1976, 1979; Armstrong and Glyn, 1980; Glyn and Harrison, 1980.

105. See Steedman, Sweezy *et al.* 1981 on the value controversy; Harcourt's useful guide to some major debates, 1972; 1986, part 3; a survey of the controversial issues in Marxist economic theory made by Fine and Harris, 1976. *NLR* printed some fragmentary commentaries, e.g., Dickinson, 1963; Gough, 1972; Therborn, 1974.

106. Ronald Meek was born in New Zealand in 1917, went to Cambridge in 1946 working for a Ph.D. under Piero Sraffa, moved to Glasgow in 1948 as a lecturer in political economy, was appointed to the Tyler Chair of Economics at the University of Leicester in 1963, and died in 1978. He was a communist dissident of the *NR* group in 1957 and an editor of the first *NLR* in 1960. See Bradley and Howard (eds) 1982, which contains a bibliography of Meek.

107. Meek and Robinson had a long period of correspondence discussing the question of the validity of the labour theory of value and gave each other up at last, which he regretted. For Robinson's arguments, see esp. 1965.

108. About Marx's law of the falling rate of profit, for example, Fine and Harris offered a different interpretation and argued for its validity (1976, pp. 160–7). Glyn and Sutcliffe demonstrated a profits squeeze (the rate of profit fell as the profit share declined) of British capitalism since 1950 and the impact of this falling profitability on economic life (1972a, pp. 54–69; appendices C, D, E). See also Glyn and Harrison, 1980, pp. 53–6, 175–80.

109. See earlier debate on incomes policy between him and Barratt Brown/Royden Harrison (*NLR* 34, *NLR* 37). See also Rowthorn, 1980, 1981.

110. See his review of *Late Capitalism*. His disagreement with Mandel concerns the organic composition of capital on which, in his view, Mandel placed undue emphasis. Following the argument of Glyn and Sutcliffe, Rowthorn shows that the decline of the rate of profit since the mid-1960s was caused by the fall of the share of profits in output or, in other words, by the resistance of the working class to additional surplus value (that is, wage demands in a period of full employment) rather than by the rise of the organic composition (1976).

111. See Meek on alienation and fetishism, referring to the chief importance of the *Grundrisse* and of the concept of 'alienation' as a link between the *1844 Manuscripts* and *Capital* (1973, pp. vii–xi).

112. For the background, see Gamble, 1981, pp. 181–4, 268; Glyn and Harrison, 1980, ch. 4; Coates and Hillard (eds) 1986, part 4. For the proposals, see Holland, 1974; Coates and Topham, 1972; Hughes's Fabian tracts, Spokesman and IWC pamphlets, esp. 1967, 1971, 1974, 1972 (with Eaton and Coates); Eaton, Barratt Brown and Coates, 1975. See Hughes and Pollins, (eds) 1973.

113. See Barratt Brown, 1974a. A pamphlet produced by a group of Cambridge economists, Ellman, Rowthorn, Smith and Wilkinson, proposed to alter Britain's external economic relations in order to 'loosen the hold of imperialism on the British economy, so as to give a hypothetical left-wing government the freedom to pursue radical internal policies' (1974).

114. See Elizabeth Durbin, 1985, in which the daughter of Evan Durbin offers a history of the development of the economics of 'democratic socialism' in Britain and its impact on the Labour Party's policies.

115. Compared to a series of articles led by Anderson's 'Origins of the Present Crisis' written in 1964 (see III.2 and 4), for example; years later, *NLR* in general appeared to be less novel, with less exciting publications, but more orthodox and unpleasantly abstract.

116. See Eagleton, 1984, p. 109, where he had already made a similar comment despite his criticism of Williams in the same volume.

117. See Williams on 'populism' with reference to his own political formation, 1976/7, pp. 239–43; Introduction to 1977.

118. There has been a massive literature on Williams's work since the mid-1970s. See Eagleton, 1976a; Waston, 1977; Merrill, 1978/9; Giddens, 1979; R. Johnson, 1979; L. Johnson, 1979; Clarke, Critcher and Johnson (eds), 1979; Green, 1975.

119. See Eagleton: 'Modern criticism was born of a struggle against the absolute state; unless its future is now defined as a struggle against the bourgeois state, it might have no future at all' (1984, p. 124). After his earlier Christian socialist period, Eagleton developed his Marxist aesthetic theory and cultural thinking in 1976b, 1976c, 1981, 1984, 1986 and 1990b. See an interesting exchange between him and Mulhern on the Lukácsian aesthetic tradition and ideology in *NLR* 91, 92, 108.

120. See Johnson's summary answer to the question 'what is cultural studies anyway?': The radical premises of cultural studies are (1) 'cultural processes are intimately connected with social relations, especially with class and class formations, with sexual divisions, with the racial structuring of social relations and with age oppressions as a form of dependency'; (2) 'culture involves power and helps to produce asymmetries in the abilities of individuals and social groups to define and realise their needs'; (3) 'culture is neither an autonomous nor an externally

determined field, but a site of social differences and struggles' (1983, p. 17). Explaining the vocation of cultural studies, Hall emphasises their concern with changing ways of communication and thus of life. The area of cultural studies is 'where power cuts across knowledge, or where cultural processes anticipate social change' (1992, p. 10).

121. About the work of the Centre, see above all Hall's introductory essay, 1980. See also the series of *Working Papers in Cultural Studies*, nos 1 – 11; Hall and Jefferson, (eds) 1975; Hall, Critcher, Jefferson, Clarke and Roberts, 1978; selected essays in CCCS, 1977; 1978; Hall, 1979a; 1979b; Clarke, Critcher and Johnson (eds) 1979; Johnson, 1979b; McLennan, 1979; Hall, Hobson, Lowe and Willis (eds) 1980; Johnson, McLennan, Schwartz and Sutton (eds) 1982; McLennan, Held and Hall (eds) 1984a; 1984b.

122. See Stedman Jones's critical review of the debate, 1977a; E. and S. Yeo, 1981.

123. Note that Stedman Jones's emphasis was placed on the specificity of class consciousness of twentieth-century English urban life which found expressions more in music halls, pubs, working men's clubs and distinctions of accent, residence and dress than in trade unionism or labour politics (1974).

124. See esp. Samuel and Stedman Jones, 1982b; Stedman Jones, 1984b. See E. M. Wood's systematic critique of this separation between the 'economic' and the 'political', 1986.

125. Stedman Jones, 1977a, 1982, 1983; Hall, 1982, 1988b, 1988c. See Laclau, 1977, chapter 3; Laclau and Mouffe, 1985, two influential books along this line of argument.

126. See Williams, hegemony, as 'a whole body of practices and expectations, over the whole of living: our senses and assignments of energy, our shaping perceptions of ourselves and our world', is 'in the strongest sense a "culture"'(1977, p. 110).

127. Lionel Elvin, whose suggestions and criticisms have been extremely valuable to this research, wrote that 'Hoggart ... has been influential in his own right, quite apart from any possible affinities with New Leftism. Similarly, Thompson owes his standing to his excellence as a historian, and Williams to his as a historian and student of British cultural history' (notes on my first draft, November 1987).

128. In the case of Williams, he told us how the New Left movement actually made him a Marxist (Introduction, 1977b).

129. Mervyn Jones was to comment, finally, at the 1987 Oxford Conference on the New Left in retrospect that 'if you scan through the twenty-odd names of people who are speaking at this conference, you won't find any scientists. I think this is a very serious matter for the left, because increasingly over the years some of the major issues which we have had to confront require a certain scientific understanding: nuclear weapons and power, pollution and other general environmental issues' (see Robin Archer *et al.*, (eds) 1989, p. 135). This was not only a problem of the New Left, but also, as he pointed out, to some extent of the post-war British left on the whole, which requires an explanation and serious self-questioning on the left. Earlier in 1981, Hall also admitted that an analysis of the scientific, technical, and political interconnections within the decision-making power structure was missing (1981b).

130. See Jonathan Ree's excellent discussion of 'Marxism and the Scientism' in 1984, pp. 79–105; Gary Werskey's collective biography, 1978; Branson and Heinemann's brief sketch, 1971, pp. 260–1. See also the second edition (1971) of *Science at the Cross Roads* (N. I. Bukharin *et al.*, 1931), proceedings of the Second International Congress of the History of Science and Technology held in London from 29 June to 3 July, 1931, for the Soviet influence on the thinking of left-wing British scientists.

131. For some activities of CND's scientists' group, see Duff, 1971, pp. 157–9. See also Werskey, 1978, pp. 219, 324–5.

132. Rotblat was one of the signatories of the Russell-Einstein Manifesto (London, 1955) and also one of the twenty-two scientists presented at the first Pugwash Conference in 1957. About the movement, see Rotblat, 1962; 1983; Epstein and Webster (eds) 1983, pp. 137–54.

133. For Ravetz's influential work on scientific knowledge and its problems which for him have changed from the epistemological to the social, and have been and still can be, against 'vulgar optimism' of the Enlightenment, profoundly tragic, see 1971; 1973.

134. BSSRS held its inaugural meeting at the Royal Society in London in April 1969. Bernal, Hogben, Levy and Needham were in the list of its founding members. The group that actually set up the organisation was composed of young scientists and sociologists of science, including Hilary Rose, Steven Rose, Robert Smith, David Butt, Jonathan Rosenhead and Leslie Sklair. See Rose and Rose, 1969, pp. 108–9.

135. *NLR* printed Roy Bhaskar's comparative discussion of Feyerabend and Bachelard, 1975.

136. See C. P. Snow, 1959; F. R. Leavis, 1962. Snow, a scientist by training and a novelist by vocation, saw science as the most powerful revolutionary force in modern times, emphasising reason and pragmatic practice. He was an advocate of bridging the hitherto uncommunicating 'literary culture' and 'scientific culture'. Leavis, on the other hand, resisted the danger of losing the humanist and imaginative content of life and art/literature in an 'external civilisation' determined by advancing science and technology. For him, the sharp boundaries between the two realms ought not be eliminated (cf. 1972). It is likely that most of our New Left figures had sympathy with Leavis, given their professional and intellectual preoccupations. But they rarely said anything on this and one cannot just speculate. Later (long after disconnecting himself from the British New Left) in his 1981 Delhi lectures, Taylor attacked the 'dangerous', 'destructive' and 'damaging' tendency in modern technological civilisations to assimilate human to natural science (1983).

137. As Bernal put it, 'in its endeavour, science is communism' (1939, p. 415).

138. See Robert Young's critical review of the Anderson-Thompson debate which, as a typical case of the New Left intellectual orientation, 'stop[s] short at the door of the scientific laboratory' (1973, pp. 421–7).

139. For Marx, man 'becomes human over history in forging his human nature, that is, the nature of a free being who can control [non-human] nature and himself'. This means the development of both technology and self-consciousness (1966, p. 242).

140. Later, the natural sciences came to be on the defensive in continuing to claim truth/knowledge and objectivity.

141. Compare Marx in the 1844 Manuscripts (natural science would one day become the 'basis of human science', p. 143) and in *Capital* (the danger of 'abstractly' modelling natural science in formulating a mechanical materialist conception of history, vol. 1, p. 372). He was, in any case, a persistent defender of the unity and interactions between the evolution of socio-economic formation and natural history, grounding human development in a changing relationship with nature and believing equation between 'fully developed naturalism' and 'fully developed humanism' (1844, p. 135). For a very condensed yet comprehensive sketch of Marx's view on science, see Cohen, 1978, pp. 403–17; see also Cohen's summary of Engels in the same volume, pp. 131–47.

142. This is not to suggest that the 'scientific utopia' of Bernalism had not been challenged before the New Left; indeed, the latter actually never bothered to confront itself with that tradition.

143. Taylor wrote about antagonism between the Marxist and empiricist conception of history in Popperian terms (1966, pp. 235–41, 244). MacIntyre commented in *NR* that Stalin and Popper nonetheless shared anti-theoretical empiricism (1958/9, *NR* 7, p. 95). This might be the single piece in the early New Left publications that did take the issue with Popper on 'historicism' but virtually without an impact (in contrast to Marcuse's influential essay on 'Popper and the problem of historical laws', 1959, in 1972c).

144. C. P. Snow was appointed Parliamentary Secretary in the new Ministry of Technology in the Wilson government. This had perhaps further discredited him

in the eyes of those among the New Left who would share more with F. R. Leavis in the debate over 'two cultures'.

145. Brewster was a LSE militant and a member of the *NLR* editorial board between 1966 and 1971.

146. The English introduction and translation of French Marxism were one-sidedly limited to certain schools and figures and neglected many others (e.g. Lucien Sève); and also often with major omission in the translated material. For a fairly comprehensive survey of modern French Marxism, see Michael Kelly, 1982. See also Ted Benton's useful book on the rise and fall of structuralist Marxism, 1984. Beside publishing Althusser and Balibar, *NLR* introduced Colletti to its English readers in 1969 (*NLR* 56), Della Volpe in 1970 (*NLR* 59) and, among other authors, Maurice Godelier in 1972 (on *Capital* in Blackburn (ed.) 1972; on Lévi-Strauss's structural anthropology, *NLR* 69).

147. *NLR* printed Althusser's 'Essays in self-criticism' in 1976 and some critiques of the political implications of Althusserism (e.g. *NLR* 101–102). Anderson offered his own critique of the theoretical one-sidedness of structuralist philosophy in 1980 and further in 1983a. For Stedman Jones, neither socialist humanism nor Althusserianism represented satisfactory attempt to transcend economism, 1979. CCCS published a number of volumes on the problems with structuralism; see for example Richard Johnson, 1979c. See also Anthony Giddens's critical account of structuralist Marxism in 1979b, chapter 1 and 1981, vol. 1; Simon Clarke *et al.*, 1980, a rejection of the fundamental tenets of Althusserian theory as 'one-dimensional Marxism'.

148. For *Screen* and other British journals that were engaged in theoretical discussions and translations of what came to be under the general label of 'post-modernism', see Easthope, 1983; 1988, esp. pp. 232–5.

149. For a bibliography of Thompson that covers the period of 1947 and 1988, see Kaye and McClelland (eds) 1990, pp. 276–80.

150. For criticisms of Thompson, see Anderson's systematic critique, 1980, which is also a critical assessment of Althusserian Marxism. See also Hall, 1981a, on the inadequacy of Thompson's usage of 'experience', pp. 383–5; Richard Johnson, 1978, 1979c; Kitching, 1983, chapter 3. For rejoinders, beside Palmer's (1981) and Kaye's (1984) overall defence, see Donnelly, 1976; Gray, 1979; McClelland, 1979. See also Ellen Wood's balanced commentary, 1982; a recent collection of critical reflections on Thompson's work edited by Kaye and McClelland, 1990.

151. Stedman Jones, 1979, p. 202; see Raphael Samuel, 1981a, pp. 376–8; report on the HW conference in *RHR* 25.

152. Thompson's style was fairly described by Johnson as 'absolutism'. See remarks gathered in Samuel (ed.) 1981a, pp. 386–96, 396–408, 402–3.

153. With Samuel, Stedman Jones would write for *HWJ* later in 1985 about their common 'defensive hostility' toward the attempt to sever the connection between Marxist theory and historical work, and their favourable confirmation of the 'very worth of empirical enquiry' (editorial, *HWJ* 20).

154. Being less confident in Marxism, later he sought to combine 'a non-empiricist approach to history and a sceptical relation to received social theory' (1983, p. 7).

155. Earlier major works in the area are Saville, 1952, 1969; Hobsbawm, 1964; Royden Harrison, 1965. The Anderson-Nairn theme of 'corporativism' (see III. 2) is certainly relevant. For the revival of the interest since the 1970s, see Dorothy Thompson, 1971, 1984; James Hinton, 1973, 1983; John Foster, 1974 (reviewed by Saville, 1974a; Stedman Jones, 1975); Hobsbawm, 1975 (reviewed by Stedman Jones, 1977b); Robert Gray, 1976; Samuel, 1977; Stedman Jones, 1974, 1982, 1983 (reviewed by James Cronin, 1986; Ellen Wood, 1986). For the debate over the labour aristocracy, see Moorhouse, 1978; Field, 1978/9 (cf. III. 2).

156. See Robert Brenner, 1976 (an American contribution to *Past and Present*, that reopened the debate), 1977, 1978. See Hans Medick's review, 1981.

157. From a different point of view, by way of concentrating on the laws, constitutions and political, religious and social institutions, Anderson's history 'from above' reproduced bourgeois historiography (cf. Scruton, 1985, pp. 137–8). Anderson

did adopt, for good reasons, some non-Marxist approaches such as neo-Malthusian demography and Weberian continuity between the classical world and the shaping of capitalist society.

158. See, for example, greetings from TGWU and NUM for the publication of *HWJ* in its first issue, Spring 1976.

159. The Oral History Society was founded in 1971 backed by the Workshop. Local workshops were organised in the Federation of History Workshops in 1980. The HW Centre for Social History was formed in 1983. For the history and significance of the History Workshop movement, see Samuel's long Preface and Afterword to ed. 1981a. See also Royden Harrison's review of *HWJ* 1, 1976.

160. Saville, for example, criticised the 'looseness of theoretical rigour' of the Workshop: the job of Marxist historians was, as Gramsci said, to confront the leading ideas of the time. But in a way of 'antiquarianism', 'we've allowed ourselves to become very soppy'. The Northern Marxist Historians' Group was organised in 1984, aiming 'to get away from the looseness of the History Workshop' (interview, 19 October 1987). Saville published his *1848: The State and the Chartist Movement* (1987), deliberately seeing history 'from above'. Hobsbawm had sympathy and solidarity for what he called 'the neo-populist historians' and 'neo-romantics' of the History Workshop type, but thought that they 'lack hard theoretical interests' (letter to the author, 3 May 1987). See Selbourne, 1980; Kitching, 1983, pp. 70, 72. Samuel replied to some of these criticisms in 1980.

161. There are things to celebrate: for instance, Williams's work attracted a very wide readership; Worsley's sociology textbooks became market leaders; Hall (and others) chaired some Open University's courses (e.g. on State and Society) that had an even broader audience, although all these had made little visible influence on immediate political struggles.

162. Compare Sheila Benson, who was a New Left Club organiser in London, 1989. She recalls that the ranks of the activists of the London Club were made up more or less equally of women and men, and the New Left still contrasted favourably with the Labour movement and the CP in its response to the 'women's question'. Yet Hall, in retrospect, talks about 'the almost totally hidden question of gender' about which the New Left preserved 'a profound unconsciousness' in its early days (1989, pp. 37–8). Compare also Dorothy Wedderburn, 1989. Professor at the Imperial College of Science and Technology and the Principal (until 1990) of Royal Holloway and Bedford New College, she was then a CND and Labour local organiser in Cambridge with an ex-communist background, and a contributor to *NR*, *SR*, and the New Left *May Day Manifesto*. She explains that the low number of women writing for the New Left journals was reflecting the sex structure in the universities at the time, given the fact that the women who did write were all academics. She also emphasises, from her own experience, the universal training for political activities, regardless of sex difference, that one got in the CP.

163. Dorothy Thompson was born in 1923, graduated in History from Girton College, Cambridge, and worked in adult education and sociological surveys from 1948. She began to teach in the University of Birmingham in 1968, was a member of the national executive of the Society for Study of Labour History and a Visiting Professor of several American universities. Together with Edward Thompson, she was a participant of the CP Historians' Group and the early New Left. Among her works, *Over Our Dead Bodies: Women Against the Bomb* (1983) connects the two themes of peace and women's liberation.

164. Juliet Mitchell was born in New Zealand in 1940, lived in London after 1944, read English at St Anne's College, Oxford, then lectured in English literature at the University of Leeds and Reading. She gave up her teaching post in 1970 and became a professional writer, lecturer and practising psychoanalyst. She was a *NLR* editorial member between 1962 and 1983.

165. *NLR* did not print any further discussion on women's liberation for several years after Mitchell's 'Women: the Longest Revolution' (*NLR* 40, 1966) except an exchange between Mitchell and Quintin Hoare (*NLR* 41). For Thompson's criticism of the tendency of breaking away from 'real political issues' within

feminist activism, the 'alternative culture' project and 'immobilism' of theoretical Marxism, see, for example, 1980b, pp. xi–xiii. See Joan Scott's critique of *The Making*... and of Thompson's preoccupation and identification with 'the (manly) political tradition' of what he called a 'rational' socialist movement, 1988, pp. 68–90.

166. Sheila Rowbotham was born in 1943, studied history at St Hilda's College, Oxford, then taught in colleges and schools, and worked for the WEA; lectured widely in Britain, America, Canada and Netherlands. She was a member of *Black Dwarf* editorial board and the *Red Rag* Collective, active in the LP Young Socialists, VSC and the IS, later an associate editor of *HWJ*.

167. The 'political settlement between men and women', wrote Campbell, 'produced a historical compromise with capital' which closed people's socialist imagination (1984, p. 229). Rowbotham declared that she was more concerned with the interconnection between socialism and feminism, and the organisation of working class women than with the feminist movement in isolation (1976, p. 56). Taylor had argued most forcefully for the case for 'feminist socialism', a utopian style of 'socialist endeavour which aims to transform the whole order of social life and in so doing transforms relations between the sexes' (1983, xviii), and a feminism that was taken as one of the 'key motivating impulses' of the socialist project (1981, p. 161).

168. Two other influential magazines were *Red Rag*, produced by a collective of women Marxists and ex-communists, and Nottingham-based *Socialist Women*. I read a document by chance which interested me: while *Seven Days*, with both its men and women editors, was committed to and seriously discussed the issue of women's liberation, there was a long statement protecting its 'male chauvinism' produced by its women staff just before the paper was about to close due to financial difficulties: 'Male comrades must realise that it is neither possible to abolish their own male chauvinism by giving verbal support to women's liberation, nor can a collective practice be spontaneously constructed where contradictions exist. Real problems cannot be wished away' (March 1972).

169. For a brief narrative of the early stage of the women's movement in Britain, see Rowbotham, 1970; 1979a; 1983, chs 1 and 2. See also Lambertz, 1978–9.

170. Marx: 'It is possible to judge from this relationship [of man to woman] the entire level of development of mankind. It follows from the character of this relationship how far man as a species-being, as man, has become himself and grasped himself; the relation of man to woman is the most natural relation of human being to human being. It therefore demonstrates the extent to which man's natural behavior has become human or the extent to which his human nature has become nature for him' (1844; 1975, p. 347).

171. For a well-researched sketch of these connections, see Frank and Fritzie Manuel, 1979, pp. 708–10, 794–6.

172. Some of these are cited in Geras, 1990, p. 5.

173. Mao: 'It isn't simply a question of replacing the Tsar with Khrushchev, one bourgeoisie with another, even if it's called communist. It's the same as with women. Of course it was necessary to give them legal equality to begin with! But from there on, everything still remains to be done. The thought, culture, and customs which brought China to where we found her must disappear, and the thought, culture and customs of proletarian China, which does not yet exist either, must appear. The Chinese woman doesn't exist yet either, among the masses; but she is beginning to want to exist. And then, to liberate women is not to manufacture washing machines – and to liberate their husbands is not to manufacture bicycles but to build the Moscow subway' (interview with André Malraux, 1967; in Malraux, 1970, p. 465).

174. The first national feminist conference held in Oxford in 1970 marked the founding of an independent women's movement in Britain. See 'Women – the Ruskin weekend', in *Red Mole*, no. 1, 17 March 1970.

175. Williams's writings referring to the 'system of nurture' (1961b) and marginalisation of women (1964; 1970b) seemed to have no particular influence on Mitchell. But

it is worth quoting Williams at some length from his conversation with Eagleton in 1987: in *The English Novel from Dickens to Lawrence*, 'I describe the Brontë sisters as representing interests and values marginalised by the male hegemony. Not only that, however, but representing human interests of a more general kind which showed up the limits of the extraordinary disabling notion of masculinity. ... I suppose I found it easier to explore that in more personal terms, in my novels. That's no real excuse; I ought to have been doing this in my other work too ...' (1987, p. 319).

176. See McRobbie's interview with Mitchell: Mitchell, 1988; 1984, pp. 128, 171, 195, 255.

177. Mitchell's presentation of Freud in her first two chapters, 'The Making of a Lady', can be read together with her essays and lectures reprinted in 1984, part II, on the process of growing up in nineteenth-century English novels.

178. The question of the scope and applicability of Freud's account of sexual development was left open in in *Psychoanalysis and Feminism*, but Mitchell suggested the 'universality' of its 'basic structure' (p. 363). See the concluding chapter.

179. Compare the tone of *Psychoanalysis* to either that of the title of her earlier essay, or of her later work on Lacan, *Feminine Sexuality* (with Jacqueline Rose, 1982). In her 1988 interview, she said that the problem was 'the great difficulty of psychic change'; after all, 'we couldn't change everything' (1988, pp. 87, 89).

180. See Nancy Fraser's critique of the 'determinism' of the narrative of 'the father's law' from a pragmatic standpoint (1989); Judith Butler's review of criticism of the Freudian (reproduced in Mitchell's work) 'stabilisation' of infantile development and hence of the constitution of gender identity (1990).

181. *NLR* 97 (May/June 1976), p. 112. Mitchell believed that where Marxist theory explained the historical and economic situation, psychoanalysis explained sexuality; and both are needed for understanding ideology (1971, p. 172; 1974, p. xx). However, these attempts seem to be not very satisfactory for the initiators themselves. A decade later, Mitchell would have stated not only that the link between psychoanalysis and anthropology was now felt to be 'mistaken', but also that she no longer hoped 'it would prove possible to use psychoanalysis as an incipient science of the ideology of patriarchy' (1984, pp. 77, 221). See a footnote referring to Mitchell's shifted position in Joan Scott, 1988, p. 207.

182. See, for example, Scott, 1988, chs 8 and 9. See Eagleton's essay on irony and commitment in nationalism and feminism, 1990a.

From the New Left
to the New Social Movements

The Demise of the New Left

Along with general retreat of socialist and left oppositions during the latter part of the 1970s which followed the economic recession of 1975–6 under the Callaghan Labour government (within the long-term structural decline of the British economy), the different New Left traditions further scattered, leaving hardly any identifiable strains as a common and distinctive position.

Politically, the rise of the radical New Right and the convergence of neo-conservatism and neo-liberalism (Levitas, ed. 1986; Barry, 1987, pp. 103–39), and the reform of the British state through its new legislation in both foreign and domestic affairs, had further stabilised the system. Meanwhile, a realignment of the political forces on the left also got under way: Labour split and the subsequent formation of the Social Democratic Party, the reorganisation of the Labour Left (including the ambiguous development of the Militant Tendency) and its intellectual alliance (notably the founding of the Socialist Society), the conflict between the CP *Morning Star* group and *Marxism Today* (the 'Eurocommunist' *MT* line was strongly disapproved by some old New Left people such as Saville, Worsley and Samuel, but attracted others like Hall and Stedman Jones), and above all, the emergence and rapid growth of the 'new social movements'. The mood of self-questioning amongst leftists was brought into focus by the widespread debate (see Jacques and Mulhern (eds) 1981) following Hobsbawm's Marx Memorial Lecture, 'The Forward March of Labour Halted?' (1978a), which called on the left to adjust its strategy to the novel situation, a situation in which the halt of the labour movement was soon to be settled by prolonged Thatcherism. And this was seen, at long last, as in more general terms a failure of the western industrial working class to realise its 'historically appointed role', which was also a recognition of the internal stratification and recomposition, conflicting interests, and non-unified political outlooks of that class itself (Hall, 1982).

Intellectually, it became necessary more than ever to appreciate the importance of non-Marxist sources for socialist discussion and of genuine theoretical engagement with Marxism by non-new left especially non-Marxist thinkers. Respect shown for the contributions of Anthony Giddens or Alec Nove beside Ernest Gellner in the pages of *NLR* was only one sign of a withdrawal from continental European Marxist currents. The decline of French Marxism (with the tragic personal crisis of Althusser, the death of Sartre, the cultural collapse of a Marxist generation and its replacement by 'post-Marxist' varieties) and indeed of Marxist influence throughout western Europe (save Germany because of Habermas and critical theory) coincided with the development of Anglo-American analytical Marxism that was first marked by the publication of G. A. Cohen's defence of historical materialism (1978). Cohen's 'old fashioned' but sustained way of approaching theoretical problems made a strong case for the 'precious heritage' of English lucidity against the 'Althusserian vogue' (p. x). As far as the method is concerned, the continental now gave way to the British, thus ending the impetuous rejection of the national culture by the second New Left. It was almost a 'negation of negation', a return, with qualifications, to the root values of the native ethos – clarity, logical rigour, soberness, scepticism and distrust of any dogmatic ideology, maybe even a utilitarian and individualist bent.

All these suggest the completion of a New Left passage from the old Left to the new oppositional social forces: new theories and forms of struggle of and for women, peace, anti-racism, ecology. The relationship between these new sources of popular resistance and 'workers' as an unproblematic classical category, and therefore between identity politics and class politics, focused the unfolding debates on the left in the 1980s (see contributions from the former New Left participants, e.g., Hall, 1982; Williams, 1983a, pp. 245–67; Anderson, 1983a, pp. 89–106; Stedman Jones, 1984b, 1985; Miliband, 1985). The end of the New Left, however, does not entail the defeat or invalidity of many of its ideas, nor its stream of 'community politics' characterised by locally based, self-organised, democratically participated and often 'single issue' centred protests against the system (as best seen in the Left Clubs, CND, the *May Day Manifesto* initiative and the History Workshop movement), which obviously had a close affinity with the more recent development (cf. Taylor and Ward, 1983). Keeping alive within newer political and intellectual activism, the original impulse of the New Left helped to bring about and carry forward the new social movements which, to be sure, had their independent roots. This displacement was expected to be the beginning of a long, confusing, difficult but more hopeful process of building a flourishing and liberated human civilisation, as analysed by Williams in *Towards 2000* (1983), a book that may well continue to influence generations to come.

The Legacy of the New Left

What concerns us here is strictly limited to what the new social movements had inherited and still can learn from the New Left. As early as in 1972, a group of New Leftists prepared to convene a seminar on 'problems of liberation and the environment' and the papers were published in a Spokesman collection, *Socialism and the Environment*. Two important institutional bases founded by the New Left in Britain were the International Liaison Committee for European Nuclear Disarmament (END; its programme, *Russell Appeal*, 1980) and the Socialist Environment and Resources Association (SERA, in conjunction with the IWC and CND among other organisations). Both were sponsored mainly by the Bertrand Russell Foundation with Ken Coates as one of its directors. Of the former, Thompson and Coates, in their respective ways, were the most active organisers and creative theorists (Thompson, 1980a, 1980c, 1982a, 1982b; Coates, 1982, 1984); of the latter, Barratt Brown was a founder and Williams served as vice-president, and both were among its most influential advocates (Barratt Brown *et al*, 1976; Williams, 1983c). These people exemplified in their personal careers the continuity from the New Left to the resurgent peace and emerging ecology movement.

More significantly, it was the New Left who gave initial impetus to the new process in which an emphasis on challenging the dominant system as a whole, even from local and specialised interest campaignings, had persisted. The linkage between the general and the particular has to be articulated, accompanying actual demands and changes that should not leave the main body of politics intact. Writing in 1973 about the evident risk to human survival caused by ecological damage and crises of resources in both capitalist and socialist countries, Williams reached the conclusion that the area of decision making was the central battleground and all the real decisions were about modes of social interest and control. 'The active powers of minority capital, in all its possible forms, are our most active enemies' which would 'have to be not just persuaded but defeated and superseded'. (Williams, 1973c, p. 84; cf. 1975 'Retrospect ...' to 1962, pp. 186–7; 1982). Precisely in the sense of combating the power relationship of capitalist society, various new social forces could be united in a broad socialist front as far as socialism itself might be redefined and its Marxist tenets reconsidered.

However, arguments developed in the writings of socialist feminists or socialist environmental and peace campaigners with a new left background had not always been grounded on premises of a scientific socialist kind. In the former case, it was because sexual inequality must be looked at in a historical and cultural range far beyond capitalism; and the inspiration for the women's movement was traced to pre-Marxian utopianism and non-socialist sources (see IV.5; also Barbara Taylor, 1981). In the latter case, addressing universal human interests, themes such as the logic of exterminism (Thompson, 1980c)[1] precluded the entire conventional vocabulary of the capitalism-socialism confrontation especially because existing socialism shared responsibility for much global destruction. *NLR*-mediated international debate on the issue was published in the Verso collection, *Exterminism and Cold War* (1982). Indeed problems associated with techno-industrial society in which the two systems competed seemed to be more profound than their political appearance. The terms 'Red' and 'Green', as they were used by Williams (1982) or *NLR* (interviews with Bahro, 1984), for example, thus referred not so much to the different attitudes toward socialism as to the different emphases on the problems representing themselves at these different levels.

Yet efforts had been made notably by the former participants of the New Left to advance socialist ideas in the light of the new social movements and, in turn, these ideas were intended to provide theoretical basis for the latter. In one way, socialism asserted itself by refusing the primacy accorded to the material productive process and hence simple and sole contests between capital and labour in the traditional sense, so a whole range of radical movements involving new agencies including mental labourers would bear the task of transforming capitalism (Stedman Jones, 1983b; 1984b). In another direction, socialism found an accurate expression in the thesis of self-governing or democratic control of human destiny, now in the form of non-state international co-operation for disarmament and development within an anti-militarist and anti-imperialist tradition (the Holland/Barratt Brown proposal, 1983). A third line of argument followed the powerful formula conveyed by Engels, recalled by Luxemburg, sophisticated by Fromm or Marcuse in terms of needs and freedom beyond necessity, and remembered by present-day protesters: socialism or barbarism (for example Coates, 1972)? Socialism, seen as the only alternative to a barbarous solution to the modern crises, in Williams's perhaps too optimistic analysis, was not only compatible with but actually required newly existing and immediately potential resources for new kinds of politics (1983a, 'Resources for a journey of hope'). In relating socialism to human liberation at large, Anderson was convinced that:

> Not every prospect of human emancipation coincides with the advent of socialism, which has no monopoly on utopian discourse today. Not every contribution to socialism as a body of thought coincides with the output of Marxism, which has no monopoly of critical theory on the Left either.
> (1983a, p. 105)

These words reflected both the scope and the limits of a New Left legacy that might and might not be ultimately surpassed by the mind and the course of unfolding new social movements.

Afterword

In 1958, in the very characteristic style of the 'moralism' of the first New Left, Raymond Williams had addressed intellectual socialists, drawing their attention to reforming education in Britain:

> I give myself three wishes, one for each of the swans I have just been watching on the lake. I ask for things that are part of the ethos of our working class movement. I ask that we may be strong and human enough to realise them. I ask, naturally, in my own fields of interests. ...the biggest difficulty is in accepting deep in our minds, the value... that the ordinary people should govern; that culture and education are ordinary; that there are no masses to save, to capture, or direct .... (reprinted in *Review Guardian*, 3 February 1989)

A true commitment to democracy in its common but most fundamental sense was touchingly expressed in this passage. Although he greatly changed his language and even his voice, that commitment remained the same.

Ten years later, in the historical moment of 1968, Perry Anderson explained, in a very different tone, why the second New Left would launch an all-out attack on the national culture:

> A coherent and militant student movement has not yet emerged in England. ... one of the main reasons for [this] lateness ... is precisely the lack of any revolutionary tradition within English culture. ... The chloroforming effects of such cultural configuration, its silent and constant underpinning of the social status quo, are deadly. (1968a, pp. 214, 276–7)

The failure to assess that culture in its comprehensive perspective and to acknowledge the need for a revival of moral concern and utopian thought that so much marked the early New Left had been at last admitted by Anderson and his *NLR* colleagues. Yet their uncompromising rejection of a parochial and reformist social thinking in its classical sense never shifted.

By 1978, the British New Left movement was over. Looking back, with a sense of isolation and bitterness for his polemics against part of the left rather than the right, Edward Thompson, whose distaste for the later stages of that movement was well known, wrote:

> We remained identified with the 'left' by common solidarities and common campaigns ... . But at the same time much of this left did not want our arguments and was developing ideas, attitudes and practices inimical to the rational, libertarian and egalitarian principles to which we were committed. (1978a, p. ii)

Being always inspired by an idealised Morrisian tradition and the spirit of heroic anti-fascist struggles (T. J. and E. P. Thompson, 1947), he called for bringing those inspirations back into the heart of the current movement, especially because the rationality and good faith of the socialist project itself were endangered by what he termed 'immobilism' of the tide of theoretical Marxism (1978a, p. 192; 1978b, p. 21).

Yet another decade passed quickly. What had quietly transformed the British scene in the past twenty years, as Robin Blackburn – the editor of *NLR* which was literally the last and the only surviving symbol of the New Left – put it, was a 'populist strain':

> the idea of controlling one's own life, which in 1968 was subsumed into hopes of a complete change of society, showed its negative side when it no longer appeared that society was going to change. Then Mrs Thatcher was able to give a neo-conservative twist to this radical individual appeal: instead of controlling your own place of work it became a question of owning your own house. Common to both was anti-statism. (Quoted in Fraser, 1988, pp. 325–6)

NLR found itself in the frontline confronting neither the morally and politically collapsed streams of the old Left nor the familiar ruling-class Right, but now a New Right.

It was exactly at this point that Stuart Hall, one of the most powerful spokesmen of independent socialists today hailing from the New Left, saw the nature, the difficulty and the vitality of the ideological struggle:

> The Right's success depends as much on its capacity to address precisely the contradictions that are already within the formations of the Left, to move effectively into positions that are contested. ... many positions on the Right are secured not by displacing but by disarticulating the discourse of the Left.

In other words, 'the right advances through occupying strategic territory within the terrain of the left' in the production of politico-politics (1988c, pp. 57–8). Speaking in the context of the triumph of 'authoritarian populism' of the New Right in the 1980s (1980b; Hall and Jaques, 1983),[2] Hall's point necessarily ran against what Williams (and indeed the entire libertarian-socialist wisdom) believed about ordinary people voluntarily expanding their lives in an emancipatory direction (1958a), emphasising instead the counter-hegemonic battle for socialist ideas on the basis of abandoning any teleological illusion as to the inevitability of socialism (1982).

Jonathan Ree, a left-wing philosopher, wrote about 1968 that 'the socialist intellectual youngsters occupy the buildings, while the socialist intellectual oldsters occupy the chairs' (1974, p. 33). What a circular model, as indicated by Eric Hobsbawm (1972, p. 283), that confined modern radicalism in the west to academia. It is easier to say something cynical, especially when it contains truth. It is harder, however, to explain why, let alone to change the situation.

NOTES

1. See Williams's critique of the theme for its 'technologically determined logic' and pessimism, 1980c. For the debate on disarmament and cold war, see NLB collection, 1982, contributed by Thompson, Williams, Fred Halliday, and Mike Davis among others; Clarke and Mowlem (eds) 1982; Halliday, 1983.
2. For a well-argued criticism of Hall's writings on Thatcherism, see Jessop et al. 1984. See also Levitas (ed.) 1986, a background survey of the New Right.

Bibliography

Abelove, H., Blackmar, B., Dimock, P. and Schneer, J. (eds 1976), *Visions of History*, Manchester: Manchester University Press.

Abrams, P. (ed. 1978), *Work, Urbanism and Inequality: UK Society Today*, London: Weidenfeld & Nicolson.

Abrams, P., Deem, R., Finch, J., and Rock, P. (eds 1981), *Practice and Progress: British Sociology 1950–1980*, London: Allen & Unwin.

Adorno, T. and Horkheimer, M. (1947), *Dialectic of Enlightenment*, London: Allen Lane.

Alavi, H. (1964), 'Imperialism old and new', *SR* 1964.

Alexander, K. (1958–9), 'Conviction', *NR* 7, Winter 1958–9.

—— (1960), 'Power at the base', in NLB, *Out of Apathy*, London: Stevens & Sons.

Ali, T. (ed. 1969), *The New Revolutionaries*, New York: William Morrow.

—— (1975), 'Pakistan and Bangladesh: results and prospects', in Blackburn (ed.), *Explosion in a Subcontinent*, Harmondsworth: Penguin.

—— (1972), *The Coming British Revolution*, London: Jonathan Cape.

—— (1978), *1968 and After*, London: Blond & Briggs.

Althusser, L. (1965), *For Marx*, Allen Lane, 1969.

—— (1971), *Lenin and Philosophy and Other Essays*, London: NLB.

Althusser, L. and Balibar, E. (1970), *Reading Capital*, London: NLB.

Amin, S. (1973a), *Unequal Development*, New York: Monthly Review Press, 1976.

—— (1973b), *Imperialism and Unequal Development*, New York: Monthly Review Press, 1977.

Anderson, B. (1983), *Imagined Communities: Reflections on the Origin and Spread of Nationalism*, London: Verso.

Anderson, L. (1957a), 'Free Cinema', *ULR* 2, Summer 1957.

—— (1957b), 'Get out and push!' in Maschler (ed.), *Declaration*, London: MacGibbon & Kee.

Anderson, P. (1961), 'The Swedish model', *NLR* 7, Jan./Feb. 1961, and *NLR* 9, May/June 1961.

—— (1964a), 'Origins of the present crisis', *NLR* 23, Jan./Feb. 1964, reprinted in NLB, *Towards Socialism*, London, 1965.

—— (1964b), 'Critique of Wilsonism', *NLR* 27, Sept./Oct. 1964.

—— (1965a), 'The Left in the '50s', *NLR* 29, Jan./Feb. 1965.

—— (1965b), 'Problems of socialist strategy', in NLB, *Towards Socialism*, London.

—— (1966), 'Socialism and pseudo-empiricism', *NLR* 35, Jan./Feb. 1966.

—— (1967), 'The limits and possibilities of trade union action', in Blackburn and Cockburn (eds), *The Incompatibles*, Harmondsworth: Penguin.

—— (1968a), 'Components of the national culture', *NLR* 50, July/Aug. 1968, reprinted in Cockburn and Blackburn (eds), *Student Power*, Harmondsworth: Penguin, 1969.

—— (1968b), 'Introduction to Gramsci 1919–1920', *NLR* 51, Sept./Oct. 1968.

—— (1974a), *Passages from Antiquity to Feudalism*, London: NLB.

—— (1974b), *Lineages of the Absolute State*, London: NLB.

—— (1976a), *Considerations on Western Marxism*, London: NLB.

—— (1976b), 'The antinomies of Antonio Gramsci', *NLR* 100, Nov./Dec. 1976.

—— (1980), *Arguments within English Marxism*, London: Verso.

—— (1981), 'Communist Party history', in Samuel (ed.), *People's History and Socialist Theory*, London: Routledge.

—— (1983a), *In the Tracks of Historical Materialism*, London: Verso.

—— (1983b), 'Trotsky's interpretation of Stalinism', *NLR* 139, May/June 1983.

—— (1987), 'The figures of descent', *NLR* 161, Jan./Feb. 1987.

—— (1988), 'Modernity and revolution', in Nelson and Grossberg (eds), *Marxism and the Interpretation of Culture*, Urbana/Chicago: University of Illinois Press.

—— (1990), 'A culture in contraflow', *NLR* 180, March/April 1990, and *NLR* 182, July/Aug. 1990.

Anderson, P. and Hall, S. (1961), 'Politics of the Common Market', *NLR* 10, July/Aug. 1961.

Archer, R., Bubeck, D., Glock, H., Jacobs, L., Moglen, S., Steinhouse, A. and Weinstock, D. (eds 1989), *Out of Apathy: Voices of the New Left, 30 Years On*, London: Verso.

Armstrong, P. and Glyn, A. (1980), 'The law of the falling rate of profit and oligopoly', *Cambridge Journal of Economics*, vol.III, no.1.

Arnold, G. L. (1962), 'Britain: the new reasoners', in Labedz (ed.), *Revisionism*, London: Allen & Unwin.

Aronson, R. (1977), 'The individualist social theory of Jean-Paul Sartre', in NLB, *Western Marxism*, London.

Atkinson, D. (1969), 'The academic situation', in Nagel (ed.), *Student Power*, Harmondsworth: Penguin.

Avineri, S. (1990), 'Toward a socialist theory of nationalism', *Dissent*, Fall 1990.

Bahro, R. (1984), *From Red to Green: Interviews with New Left Review*, London: Verso.

Baldick, C. (1983), *The Social Mission of English Criticism: 1848–1932*, Oxford: Clarendon Press.

Baran, P. and Sweezy, P. (1966), *Monopoly Capitalism*, New York: Monthly Review Press.

Barnett, A. 'A revolutionary student movement', *NLR* 53, Jan./Feb. 1969.

—— 'Class struggle and the Heath government', *NLR* 77, Jan./Feb. 1973.

—— 'Raymond Williams and Marxism: a rejoinder to Terry Eagleton', *NLR* 99, Sept./Oct. 1976.

Barnett, C. (1972), *The Collapse of British Power*, New York: Morrow.

Barratt Brown, M. (1958), 'A new foreign economic policy', *NR* 4, Spring 1958.

—— (1958–9), 'The controllers', *ULR* 5, Autumn 1958; *ULR* 6, Spring 1959; *ULR* 7, Autumn 1959.

—— (1960), 'Workers' control in a planned economy', *NLR* 2, March/April 1960.

—— (1961a), 'Do we need a new political basis?', *Peace News*, 20 Oct. 1961.

—— (1961b), 'Neutralism and the Common Market', *NLR* 12, Nov./Dec. 1961.

—— (1963a), 'Crosland's enemy: a reply', *NLR* 19, March/April 1963.

—— (1963b), *After Imperialism*, London: Heinemann.

—— (1964), 'Nationalization in Britain', *SR* 1964.

—— (1968a), Openning the Books, IWC pamphlet, no.4, Spokesman.

—— (1968b), 'The limits of the welfare state', in Coates (ed.), *Can the Workers Run Industry?*, IWC, Sphere Books.

—— (1969), *Adult Education for Industrial Workers: The Contribution of Sheffield University Extramural Department*, the National Institute for Adult Education, London.

—— (1970), *What Economics Is About: Worker, Consumer, Government and Corporation*, London: Weidenfeld & Nicolson.

—— (1971), 'The welfare state in Britain', *SR* 1971.

—— (1972a), *Essays on Imperialism*, Nottingham: Spokesman.

—— (1972b), *From Labourism to Socialism: The Political Economy of Labour in the 1970s*, Nottingham: Spokesman.

—— (1972c), 'Marx's economics as a Newtonian model', in Shanin (ed.), *The Rules of the Game*, London: Tavistock Publications.

—— (1974a), *Europe: Time to Leave – and How to Go*, Nottingham: Spokesman pamphlet, no.34.

—— (1974b), *The Economics of Imperialism*, Harmondsworth: Penguin.

—— (1984), *Models in Political Economy: A Guide to the Arguments*, Harmondsworth: Penguin.

—— (1988), 'Away with all the great arches: Anderson's history of British capitalism', *NLR* 167, Jan./Feb. 1988.

Barratt Brown, M. and Coates, K. (1969), *Accountability and Industrial Democracy*, IWC pamphlet, Nottingham: Spokesman.

Barratt Brown, M., Coates, K. and Topham, T. (1975), 'Workers' control versus "revolutionary" theory', *SR* 1975.

Barratt Brown, M., Emerson, T. and Stoneman, C. (eds 1976), *Resources and Environment: A Socialist Perspective*, Nottingham: Spokesman.
Barratt Brown, M. and Harrison, R. (1965), 'Labour's incomes policy', *Tribune*, 8 Jan. 1965.
Barratt Brown, M. and Holland, S. (1974), *Public Ownership and Democracy*, IWC pamphlet, no.38, Nottingham: Spokesman.
Barrett, M., Corrigan, P., Kuhn, A. and Wolff, J. (eds 1979), *Ideology and Cultural Production*, New York: St Martin's Press.
Barry, N. P. (1987), *The New Right*, London: Croom Helm.
Bebel, A. (1879), *Woman and Socialism*, H. W. Lovell, 1886.
Benewick, R., Berki, R.N. and Parekh, B. (eds 1973), *Knowledge and Belief in Politics: The Problem of Ideology*, London: Allen & Unwin.
Bensaid, D. *et al.*, (1970), 'Students and the vanguard', *Black Dwarf*, no.29, 20 Feb. 1970.
Benson, S. (1989), 'Experiences in the London New Left', in Archer, *et al* (eds), *Out of Apathy*, London: Verso.
Benton, T. (1984), *The Rise and Fall of Structural Marxism: Althusser and His Influence*, New York: St Martin's Press.
Berlin, I. (1963), *Karl Marx*, Oxford: Oxford University Press.
Bernal, J. D. (1939), *The Social Function of Science*, Cambridge, MA: MIT Press, 1967.
Bhaskar, R. (1975), 'Feyerabend and Bachelard: two philosophies of science', *NLR* 94, Nov./Dec. 1975.
Bicat, A. (1970), 'Fifties children, "sixties people"', in Bogdanor and Skidelsky (eds), *The Age of Affluence*, London: Macmillan.
Birnbaum, N. (1960), 'Foreword' to NLB, *Out of Apathy*.
—— (1969a), *The Crisis of Industrial Society*, Oxford: Oxford University Press.
—— (1969b), 'The staggering colossus', in Nagel (ed.), *Student Power*, London: Merlin.
—— (1971), *Towards a Critical Sociology*, Oxford: Oxford University Press.
Black Dwarf, London, June 1968–Sept. 1970.
Blackburn, R. (1963), 'Prologue to the Cuban revolution', *NLR* 21, Oct. 1963.
—— (1965), 'The new capitalism', in NLB, *Towards Socialism*.
—— (1967a), 'The unequal society', in Blackburn and Cockburn (eds), *The Incompatibles*, Harmondsworth: Penguin.
—— (1967b), 'Inequality and exploitation', *NLR* 42, March/April 1967.
—— (1969), 'A brief guide to bourgeois ideology', in Cockburn and Blackburn (eds), *Student Power*, Harmondsworth: Penguin.
—— (1970), 'Introduction' to Debray (ed.), *Strategy for Revolution*, New York: Monthly Review Press.
—— (1971), 'The Heath government', *NLR* 70, Nov./Dec. 1971.
—— (ed. 1972), *Ideology in Social Science: Readings in Critical Social Theory*, London: Fontana/Collins.
—— (ed. 1975), *Explosion in a Subcontinent: India, Pakistan, Bangladesh and Ceylon*, Harmondsworth: Penguin.
—— (1976), 'Marxism: theory of proletarian revolution', *NLR* 97, May/June 1976.
—— (ed. 1978), *Revolution and Class Struggle: A Reader in Marxist Politics*, Sussex: Harvester Press.
—— (1988), 'Raymond Williams and the politics of a new left', *NLR* 168, March/April 1988.
—— (1992), 'A brief history of *NLR* 1960–1990', in *NLR* , *Thirty Years of NLR*, Index.
Blackburn, R. and Cockburn, A. (eds 1967), *The Incompatibles: Trade Union Militancy and the Consensus*, Harmondsworth: Penguin.
Blackburn, R. and Mandel, E. (1970), 'Lenin/the New Left/spontaneism', *Red Mole*, no. 2, 1 April 1970.
Bloomfield, J. (ed. 1977), *Class, Hegemony and Party*, London: Lawrence & Wishart.
Bogdanor, V. (1970), 'The Labour Party in opposition', in (eds), *The Age of Affluence*, London: Macmillan.
Bogdanor, V. and Skidelsky, R. (eds 1970), *The Age of Affluence*, London: Macmillan.
Bondy, F. (1970), 'Jean-Paul Sartre', in Cranstone (ed.), *The New Left*, New York: Library Press.
Bottomore, T., Harris, L., Kiernan, V. G., and Miliband, R. (eds 1983), *A Dictionary of Marxist Thought*, Oxford: Basil Blackwell.
Boyers, R. and Orrill, R. (eds 1972), *R. D. Laing and Anti-Psychiatry*, New York: Harper & Row.

Bradley, I. and Howard, M. (eds 1982), *Classical and Marxian Political Economy: Essays in Honour of Ronald Meek*, New York: St Martin's Press.

Branson, N. (1985), *History of the Communist Party of Great Britain 1927-41*, London: Lawrence & Wishart.

Branson, N. and Heinemann, M. (1971), *Britain in the 1930s*, London: Weidenfeld & Nicolson.

Brenner, R. (1976), 'Agrarian class structure and economic development in pre-industrial Europe', *Past and Present*, Feb. 1976.

—— (1977), 'The origins of capitalist development: a critique of neo-Smithian Marxism', *NLR* 104, July/Aug. 1977.

—— (1978), 'Reply to Sweezy', *NLR* 108, March/April 1978.

Brewster, B. (1967), 'Presentation of Althusser', *NLR* 41, Jan./Feb. 1967.

Briggs, A. and Saville, J. (eds 1960), *Essays in Labour History: In Memory of G.D.H.Cole*, revised edn., London: Macmillan, 1967.

Burke, P. (1986), 'Revolution in popular culture', in Porter and Teich (eds), *Revolution in History*, Cambridge: Cambridge University Press.

Bukharin, N. I. *et al.*, (1931), *Science at the Cross Roads*, reprinted with a new Foreword and an Introduction, London: Cass, 1971.

Burnham, J. (1941), *The Managerial Revolution: What is Happening in the World*, 2nd edn. London: Greenwood Press, 1972.

Butler, J. (1990), 'Gender trouble, feminist theory, and psychoanalytic discourse', in Nicholson (ed.), *Feminism/Postmodernism*, London: Routledge.

Butt, D. (1960), 'Men and motors', *NLR* 3, May/June 1960.

—— (1961), 'Workers' control', *NLR* 10, July/Aug. 1961.

Byrne, P. (1988), *The Campaign for Nuclear Disarmament*, London: Routledge.

Callaghan, J. (1987), *The Far Left in British Politics*, Oxford: Basil Blackwell.

Callinicos, A. (1976), *Althusser's Marxism*, London: Pluto Press.

—— (1990), *Against Postmodernism: A Marxist Critique*, New York: St Martin's Press.

Campbell, B. (1984), *Wigan Pier Revisited: Poverty and Politics in the Eighties*, London: Verso.

Caplan, J. (1977), 'Theories of fascism: Nicos Poulantzas as historian', *HWJ* 3, Spring 1977.

Carr, E. H. (1950), *The Bolshevik Revolution 1917-1923*, London: Macmillan.

—— (1962), *What is History?*, New York: Knopf.

Carr, M. I. (1958), 'Mr Osborne and an indifferent society', *ULR* 4, Spring 1958.

Caute, D. (1988), *Sixty-Eight: The Year of the Barricades*, London: Hamish Hamilton.

CCCS (1977), *On Ideology*, London: Hutchinson.

Clark, G. (1960), '*ULR* club at Notting Hill', *NLR* 1, Jan./Feb. 1960.

Clark, M. and Mowlem, M. (eds 1982), *Debate on Disarmament*, London: Routledge.

Clark, S. (1985), 'The Annales historians', in Skinner (ed.), *The Return of Grand Theory*, Cambridge: Cambridge University Press.

Clarke, J., Critcher, C. and Johnson, R. (eds 1979), *Working Class Culture: Studies in History and Theory*, New York: St Martin's Press, 1980.

Clarke, S. (1979), 'Socialist humanism and the critique of economism', *HWJ* 8, Autumn 1979.

Clarke, S., Lovell, T., McDonnell, K., Robins, K. and Seidler, V. (1980), *One-Dimensional Marxism: Althusser and the Politics of Culture*, London: Allison & Busby.

Coates, D. (1984), *The Context of British Politics*, London: Dover.

Coates, D. and Hillard, J. (eds 1986), *The Economic Decline of Modern Britain: The Debate between Left and Right*, Sussex: Wheatsheaf Books.

Coates, D. and Johnson, G. (eds 1983), *Socialist Strategies*, Oxford: Martin Robertson.

Coates, K. (1965), 'Democracy and workers' control', in NLB, *Towards Socialism*, London.

—— (1967), 'Wages slaves', in Blackburn and Cockburn (eds), *The Incompatibles*, Harmondsworth: Penguin.

—— (ed. 1968a), *Can the Workers Run Industry?*, IWC, Sphere Books.

—— (1968b), *A Future for British Socialism*, Spokesman.

—— (1969), 'The student-worker alliance', *Black Dwarf*, no.10, 27 Jan. 1969.

—— (1971a), *The Crisis of British Socialism: Essays on the Rise of Harold Wilson and the Fall of the Labour Party*, Nottingham: Spokesman.

—— (1971b), *Essays on Industrial Democracy*, Nottingham: Spokesman.

—— (1972), 'Socialism and the environment', in (ed.) *Socialism and the Environment*, Nottingham: Spokesman.

—— (1973), 'Socialists and the Labour Party', *SR* 1973.

—— (1976), 'How not to reappraise the New Left', *SR* 1976.

—— (1977), 'Dictatorship, ancient and modern', *Tribune*, 28 Oct. 1977.

—— (1982), *Heresies: Resist Much, Obey Little*, Nottingham: Spokesman.

—— (1984), *The Most Dangerous Decade*, Nottingham: Spokesman.

Coates, K. and Topham, A. (1964), 'Workers' university', *NLR* 27, Sept./Oct. 1964.

Coates, K. and Topham, A. (eds 1968a), *Industrial Democracy inGreat Britain: A Book of Reading and Witness for Workers' Control*, London: MacGibbon & Kee.

Coates, K. and Topham, A. (1968b), 'Participation or control?', in Coates (ed.), *Can the Workers Run Industry?*, IWC, Sphere Books.

Coates, K. and Topham, A. (1969), 'Workers' control', *MT*, Jan. 1969.

Coates, K. and Topham, A. (1972), *The New Unionism: The Case for Workers' Control*, London: Owen.

Coates, K. and Topham, A. (1986), *Trade Unions and Politics*, Oxford: Basil Blackwell.

Coates, K. and Williams, W. (1969), *How and Why Industry must be Democratised*, IWC pamphlet, Nottingham.

Coates, K. and Silburn, R. (1970), *Poverty: The Forgotten Englishmen*, Harmondsworth: Penguin.

Cockburn, A. (1969), 'Introduction' to Cockburn and Blackburn (eds), *Student Power*, Harmondsworth: Penguin.

Cockburn, A. and Blackburn, R. (1969), *Student Power*, Harmondsworth: Penguin.

Coe, T. (1982), 'Hobsbawm and jazz', in Samuel and Stedman Jones (eds), *Culture, Ideology and Politics*, London: Routledge.

Cohen, G. A. (1969), 'Critical theory: the philosophy of Marcuse', *NLR* 57, Sept./Oct. 1969.

—— (1978), *Karl Marx's Theory of History: A Defence*, Oxford: Oxford University Press.

Cohen, J. (1982), 'Review of *Karl Marx's Theory of History: A Defence*, *Journal of Philosophy*, vol. 79, no. 5.

Cohen, R.S. (1978), 'Marx' and 'Engels', in the *Dictionary of Scientific Biography*, vol. 15, Supplement 1, New York: Charles Scribner's Sons.

Cole, M. (1961), *The Story of Fabian Socialism*, Stanford: Stanford University Press.

Colletti, L. (1969a), 'Lenin's State and Revolution', reprinted in Oglesby (ed.), *The New Left Reader*, New York: Grove Press.

—— (1969b), *From Rousseau to Lenin*, London: NLB, 1972.

Collins, H. and Abramsky, C. (1965), *Karl Marx and the British Labour Movement: Years of the First International*, London: Macmillan.

Comninel, G. C. (1987), *Rethinking the French Revolution: Marxism and the Revisionist Challenge*, London: Verso.

Cooper, D. (1965), 'Two types of rationality', *NLR* 29, Jan./Feb. 1965.

Cooper, D. E. (1970), 'Looking back on anger', in Bogdanor and Skidelsky (eds), *The Age of Affluence*, London: Macmillan.

Cornforth, M. (ed. 1978), *Rebels and Their Causes: Essays in Honour of A.L.Morton*, Atlantic Highlands, NJ: Humanities Press.

Coward, R. (1977), 'Class, "culture" and the social formation', *Screen*, vol. 18, no. 1, Spring 1977.

—— (1977/8), 'Response', vol. 18, no. 4, Winter, 1977/8.

CPEC (the Communist Party Executive Committee), 'Statement on *The Reasoner*' (13 Sept. 1956), *World News*, 22 Sept. 1956.

Cranston, M. (ed. 1970), *The New Left: Six Critical Essays*, New York: Library Press.

Crick, B. (1962), *In Defence of Politics*, Harmondsworth: Penguin.

Crick, B. and Porter, A. (eds 1978), *Political Education and Political Literacy*, London: Longman.

Crick, B. and Robson, W. A. (eds 1970), *Protest and Discontent*, Harmondsworth: Penguin.

Cronin, J. E. (1986), 'Language, politics and the critique of social history', *Journal of Social History*, Fall, 1986.

Crosland, C. A. R. (1952), 'The transition from capitalism', in Crossman (ed.), *New Fabian Essays*, London: Fabian Society, 1970.

—— (1956), *The Future of Socialism*, London: Jonathan Cape.

—— (1962), *The Conservative Enemy: A Programme of Radical Reform for the 1960s*, London: Jonathan Cape.

Crossman, R. S. H. (1960), *Labour in the Affluent Society*, London: Fabian Society.

—— (ed. 1970), *New Fabian Essays*, London: Fabian Society.

CSE (1976), *On the Political Economy of Women*, CSE pamphlet, no. 2, 1976.

Curran, J. (ed. 1984), *The Future of the Left*, Cambridge: Polity Press.

Daly, L. (1960), 'The Fife Socialist League', *NLR* 4, July/Aug. 1960.

Dawley, A. (1978/9), 'E. P. Thompson and the peculiarities of the Americans', *RHR* 19, Winter, 1978/9.

Debray, R. (1967), *Revolution in Revolution: Armed Struggle and Political Struggle in Latin America*, New York: Monthly Review Press.

—— (1970), *Strategy for Revolution* (ed. and intro. by Blackburn), New York: Monthly Review Press.

Deutscher, I. (1968), 'Germany and Marxism', *NLR* 47, Jan./Feb. 1968.

—— (1971), 'On Internationals and internationalism', in *Marxism in Our Time*, London: Jonathan Cape.

Dickinson, H. D. (1963), 'Contemporary Marxist economics', *NLR* 21, Oct. 1963.

Dobb, M. H. (1946), *Studies in the Development of Capitalism*, 2nd edn., London: Routledge, 1963.

—— (1948), *Soviet Economic Development since 1917*, 6th edn., New York: International Publishers, 1967.

—— (1973), *Theories of Value and Distribution since Adam Smith*, Cambridge: Cambridge University Press.

Donald. J. and Hall, S. (ed. 1986), *Politics and Ideology*, Milton Keynes: Open University Press.

Donnelly, F. K. (1976), 'Ideology and early English working-class history: Thompson and his critics', *Social History*, no. 2, May 1976.

Duff, P. (1971), *Left, Left, Left: A Personal Account of Six Protest Campaigns 1945–65*, London: Allison & Busby.

Dunn, J. (1972), *Modern Revolution: An Introduction to the Analysis of a Political Phenomenon*, Cambridge: Cambridge University Press.

Durbin, E. (1985), *New Jerusalems: The Labour Party and the Economics of Democratic Socialism*, London: Routledge.

Dutschke, R. (1969), 'On anti-authoritarianism', in Oglesby (ed.), *The New Left Reader*, New York: Grove Press.

Eagleton, T. (1970), *The Body as Language: Outline of a 'New Left' Theology*, London: Sheed & Ward.

—— (1976a), 'Criticism and politics: the work of Raymond Williams', *NLR* 95, Jan./Feb. 1976.

—— (1976b), *Criticism and Ideology: A Study in Marxist Literary Theory*, London: NLB.

—— (1976c), *Marxism and Literary Criticism*, Berkeley: University of California Press.

—— (1981), *Walter Benjamin, or Towards a Revolutionary Criticism*, London: NLB.

—— (1984), *The Function of Criticism: From the Spectator to Post-Structuralism*, London: Verso.

—— (ed. 1989), *Raymond Williams: Critical Perspectives*, Boston: Northeastern University Press.

—— (ed. 1989), 'Base and superstructure in Raymond Williams', in (ed.), *Raymond Williams*, Boston: Northeastern University Press.

—— (1990a), 'Nationalism: irony and commitment', in Eagleton, Jameson and Said, *Nationalism, Colonialism, and Literature*, Minneapolis: University of Minnesota Press.

—— (1990b), *The Ideology of the Aesthetic*, Oxford: Basil Blackwell.

Eagleton, T. and Wicker, B. (eds 1968), *From Culture to Revolution*, London: Sheed & Ward.

Easthope, A. (1983), 'The trajectory of *Screen*', in Barker, Hulme, Iversen and Loxley (eds), The Politics of Theory, Essex: University of Essex Press.

—— (1988), *British Post-Structuralism since 1968*, London: Routledge.

Eaton, J., Barratt Brown, M. and Coates, K. (1975), *Economic Strategy for the Labour Movement: An Alternative*, Nottingham: Spokesman pamphlet, no.47.

Eaton, J., Hughes, J. and Coates, K. (1972), *UCS: Workers' Control – the Real Defence Against employment is Attack!*, IWC pamphlet, no. 25, Nottingham.

Ellman, M., Rowthorn, B., Smith, R. and Wilkinson, F. (1974), *Britain's Economic Crisis*, Nottingham: Spokesman.

Elster, J. (1982), 'Belief, bias and ideology', in Hollis and Lukes (eds), *Rationality and Relativism*, Cambridge, MA: MIT Press.

—— (1984), 'Historical materialism and economic backwardness', in Ball and Farr (eds), *After Marx*, Cambridge: Cambridge University Press.

Emmanuel, A. (1969), *Unequal Exchange: A Study of the Imperialism of Trade*, London: NLB, 1972.

—— (1974), 'Myths of development versus myths of underdevelopment', *NLR* 85, May/June, 1974.

END (1980), *Russell Appeal*, Nottingham: Spokesman.

Engels, F. (1878), *Anti-Duhring*, The Progress Publishers, Moscow, 1962.

—— (1884), *The Origins of the Family, Private Property and the State*, London: Lawrence & Wishart, 1942.

Ensor, P. C. K. (ed. 1904), *Modern Socialism*, London/New York: Harper & Brothers, 1910.

Enzensberger, H. M. (1974), 'A critique of political ecology', *NLR* 84, March/April 1974.

Epstein, J. and Thompson, D. (eds 1982), *The Chartist Experience: Studies in Working Class Radicalism and Culture 1830–60*, London: Macmillan.

Epstein, W. and Webster, L. (eds 1983), *We Can Avert a Nuclear War*, Cambridge, MA: Oelgeschlager, Gunn & Hain.

Fanon, F. (1961), *The Wretched of the Earth*, New York: Grove Press, 1964.

Feyerabend, P. (1975), *Against Method: Outline of an Anarchistic Theory of Knowledge*, London: NLB.

Field, J. (1978/9), 'British historians and the concept of the labour aristocracy', *RHR* 19, Winter 1978–9.

Fine, B. and Harris, L. (1976), 'Controversial issues in Marxist economic theory', *SR* 1976.

Fine, B. and Harris, L. (1979), *Rereading 'Capital'*, London: Macmillan.

Foster, J. (1974), *Class Struggle and the Industrial Revolution*, London: Weidenfeld & Nicolson.

Frank, A. G. (1969), *Capitalism and Underdevelopment in Latin America*, New York: Monthly Review Press.

Fraser, N. (1989), 'The uses and abuses of French discourse theories for feminist politics', unpublished paper, Jan. 1989.

Fraser, R. (ed. 1968), *Work: Twenty Personal Accounts*, Harmondsworth: Penguin, 2 vols.

—— (1988), *1968: A Student Generation in Revolt*, London: Chatto & Windus.

Gaitskell, H. (1956), *Socialism and Nationalization*, Fabian Tract, no. 300, London: Fabian Society.

Galbraith, J. K. (1958), *The Affluent Society*, Harmondsworth: Penguin.

Gamble, A. (1981), *Britain in Decline*, London: Macmillan.

Gardner, L. (1976), 'A comrade's point of departure', New Statesman, 29 Oct. 1976.

Gellner, E. (1958), 'Logical positivism and the spurious fox', *ULR* 3, Autumn 1957.

—— (1959), *Words and Things: A Critical Account of Linguistic Philosophy and a Study in Ideology*, London: Gollancz.

—— (1970), 'Myth, ideology and revolution', in Crick and Robson (eds), *Protest and Discontent*, Harmondsworth: Penguin.

Geras, N. (1972a), 'Althusser's Marxism: an account and assessment', *NLR* 71, Jan./Feb. 1972.

—— (1972b), 'Marx and the critique of political economy', in Blackburn (ed.), *Ideology in Social Science*, London: Fontana.

—— (1976), *The Legacy of Rosa Luxemburg*, London: NLB.

—— (1978), 'Luxemburg and Trotsky on the contradictions of bourgeois democracy', in Blackburn (ed.), *Revolution and Class Struggle*, Sussex: Harvester.

—— (1990), 'Seven types of obloquy: travesties of Marxism', *SR* 1990.

Gerratana, V. (1973), 'Marx and Darwin', *NLR* 82, Nov./Dec. 1973.

Giddens, A. (1979a), 'Raymond Williams's long revolution', *Times Higher Educational Supplement*, 14 Dec. 1979.

—— (1979b), *Central Problems in Social Theory: Action, Structure, and Contradiction in Social Analysis*, Berkeley: University of California Press.

—— (1981), *A Contemporary Critique of Historical Materialism*, London: Macmillan.

Gluksmann, A. (1972), 'A ventriloquist structuralism', *NLR* 72, March/April 1972.

Gluksmann, M. (1969), 'Lucien Goldmann: humanist or Marxist?', *NLR* 56, July/Aug. 1969.

Glyn, A. and Harrison, J. (1980), *The British Economic Disaster*, London: Pluto Press.

Glyn, A. and Sutcliffe, B. (1972a), *British Capitalism, Workers and the Profits Squeeze*, Harmondsworth: Penguin.

Glyn, A. and Sutcliffe, B. (1972b), 'Labour record', *NLR* 76, Nov./Dec. 1972.

Goddard, D. (1969), 'Limits of British anthropology', *NLR* 58, Nov./Dec. 1969.

Goldmann, L. (1952), *The Human Sciences and Philosophy*, London: Jonathan Cape, 1969.

—— (1975), 'Dialectical materialism and literary history', *NLR* 92, July/Aug. 1975.

Goodman, G. (1979), *The Awkward Warrior – Frank Cousins: His Life and Times*, Nottingham: Spokesman, 1984.

Gorz, A. (1966), 'Sartre and Marx', *NLR* 37, May/June 1966).

Gott, R. (1983), 'The difficult years', in Minnion and Bolsover (eds), *The CND Story*, London: Allison & Busby.

Gough, I. (1972), 'Productive and unproductive labour in Marx', *NLR* 76, Nov./Dec. 1972.

Gramsci, A. (1957), *The Modern Prince and Other Writings*, London: Lawrence & Wishart.

—— (1971), *Selections from the Prison Notebooks of Antonio Gramsci*, (trans. and introduced by Hoare and Nowell-Smith), London: Lawrence & Wishart.

Gray, R. Q. (1976), *The Labour Aristocracy in Victorian Edinburgh*, Oxford: Clarendon Press, published in 1980.

—— (1979), 'E.P.Thompson, history and Communist politics', *MT*, June 1979.

Green, M. (1975), 'Williams and cultural studies', *Cultural Studies*, CCCS working papers, no. 6.

Greenwood, E. (1978), *F.R.Leavis*, Harlow: Longman.

Gross, J. (1969), *The Rise and Fall of the Man of Letters: Aspects of English Literary Life since 1880*, Harmondsworth: Penguin.

Habermas, J. (1968a), *Towards a Rational Society*, London: Heinemann.

—— (1968b), *Knowledge and Human Interests*, London: Heinemann.

—— (1973), *Legitimation Crisis*, Boston: Beacon Press, 1975.

Hall, S. (1958), 'A sense of classlessness', *ULR* 5, Autumn 1958.

—— (1960), 'The supply of demand', in NLB, *Out of Apathy*, London: Stevens & Sons.

—— (1961a), 'Student journals', *NLR* 7, Jan./Feb. 1961.

—— (1961b), 'The Cuban revolution', *NLR* 7, Jan./Feb. 1961; *NLR* 9, May/June 1961.

—— (1963), *Steps Towards Peace*, London.

—— (1968a), *The Young Englanders*, London: National Committee for Commonweath Immigrants.

—— (1968b), 'The new revolutionaries', in Eagleton and Wicker (eds), *From Culture to Revolution*, London: Sheed & Ward.

—— (1969), 'The hippies: an American "moment" ', in Nagel (ed.), *Student Power*, London: Merlin.

—— (1971), 'Deviancy, politics and the media', CCCS working papers, no.11.

—— (1973), 'The "structural communication" of events', CCCS working papers, no.5.

—— (1974), 'Marx's notes on method: a reading of the "1857 Introduction"', *Cultural Studies*, no. 5, Autumn 1974.

—— (1977a), 'Hinterland of science: The sociology of knowledge', in CCCS, *On Ideology*, London: Hutchinson.

—— (1977b), 'Rethinking the "base-and-superstructure" metaphor', in Bloomfield (ed.), *Class, Hegemony and Party*, London: Lawrence & Wishart.

—— (1979a), 'Cultural studies: two paradigms', in *Media, Culture and Society*, London: Academic Press.

—— (1979b), *Drifting into a Law and Order Society*, The Cobden Trust Human Rights Day Lecture, 1979.

—— (1980a), 'Cultural studies and the Centre', in Hall *et al.*, (eds), *Culture, Media, Language*, London: Hutchinson.

—— (1980b), 'Popular-democratic vs. authoritarian populism: two ways of talking democracy seriously', in Hall, 1988b.

—— (1981a), 'In defence of theory', in Samuel (ed.), *People's History*, London: Routledge.

—— (1981b), 'CND revisited', a talk given at the History Workshop seminar, 1 June 1981.

—— (1982), 'The battle for socialist ideas in the 1980s', *SR* 1982.

—— (1987), 'Gramsci and us', *MT*, June 1987.

—— (1988a), 'Only connection: the life of Raymond Williams', *New Statesman*, 5 Feb. 1988.

—— (1988b), *The Hard Road to Renewal: Thatcherism and the Crisis of the Left*, London: Verso.

—— (1988c), 'The toad in the garden: Thatcherism among the theorists', in Nelson and Grossberg, (eds), *Marxism and the Interpretation of Culture*, Urbana/Chicago: University of Illinois Press.

—— (1989a), 'The first New Left', in Archer *et al.*, (eds), *Out of Apathy*, London: Verso.

—— (1989b), 'Politics and letters', in Eagleton (ed.), *Raymond Williams*, Boston: Northeastern University Press.

—— (1992), 'Race, culture and communications: looking backward and forward at cultural studies', *Rethinking Marxism*, Spring 1992.

Hall, S., Chambers, I., Clarke, J., Connell, I., Curti, L. and Jefferson, T. (1977/8), 'Marxism and culture', *Screen* 18, no. 4, Winter 1977/8.

Hall, S., Critcher, C., Jefferson, T., Clarke, J. and Roberts, B. (1978), *Policing the Crisis: Mugging, the State, and Law and Order*, London: Macmillan.

Hall, S., Hobson, D., Lowe, A., Willis, P. (eds 1980), *Culture, Media, Language: Working Papers in Cultural Studies, 1972–9*, London: Hutchinson.

Hall, S. and Jaques, M. (eds 1983), *The Politics of Thatcherism*, London: Lawrence & Wishart.

Hall, S. and Jefferson, T. (1975), *Resistance through Rituals: Youth Subcultures in Post-War Britain*, London: Hutchinson.

Hall, S. and Whannel, P. (1964), *The Popular Arts*, New York: Pantheon.

Halliday, F. (1969), 'Students of the world unite', in Cockburn and Blackburn (eds), *Student Power*, Harmondsworth: Penguin.

—— (1970), 'Introduction' to Karl Korsch, *Marxism and Philosophy*, London: NLB.

—— (1971), 'Internationalism', *Seven Days*, 1 Dec. 1971.

—— (1972), 'Enniskillen voice in the clouds', *Seven Days*, no. 16, Feb. 1972.

—— (1975), 'The Ceylonese insurrection', in Blackburn (ed.), *Explosion in a Subcontinent*, Harmondsworth: Penguin.

—— (1979), *Iran: Dictatorship and Development*, Harmondsworth: Penguin.

—— (1983), *The Making of the Second Cold War*, London: Verso.

Hanson, H. (1957), 'An open letter to Thompson', *NR* 2, 1957.

—— (1960), 'Socialism and affluence', *NLR* 5, Sept./Oct. 1960.

Harcourt, G. C. (1972), *Some Cambridge Controversies in the Theory of Capital*, Cambridge: Cambridge University Press.

—— (1986), *Controversies in Political Economy: Selected Essays by G. C. Harcourt* (ed. by O. F. Hamouda), New York: New York University Press.

Harman, C., Clark, D., Sayers, A., Kuper R. and Shaw, M. (1968), 'Education, capitalism and the student revolt', *IS* 34, 1968.

Harrison, J. F. C. (1961), *Learning and Living: 1870–1960 – A Study in the History of the English Adult Education Movement*, London: Routledge.

Harrison, R. (1960), 'Retreat from industrial democracy', *NLR* 4, July/Aug. 1960.

—— (1965), *Before the Socialists: Studies in Labour and Politics 1861–1881*, London: Routledge.

—— (1976), 'Putting history in the hands of the workers', *Times Higher Education Supplement*, 23 July 1976.

Haseler, S. (1969), *The Gaitskellites: Revisionism in the British Labour Party 1951–64*, London: Macmillan.

Hayter, T. (1971), *Hayter of the Bourgeoisie*, London: Sidgwick & Jackson.

Heinemann, M. (1976), '1956 and the Communist Party', *SR* 1976.

Held, D. (1980), *Introduction to Critical Theory: Horkheimer to Habermas*, London: Hutchinson.

Hibbin, S. (ed. 1978), *Politics, Ideology and the State: Papers from the Communist University of London*, London: Lawrence & Wishart.

Hill, C. *et al.*, (1957), 'The minority report on party democracy', the 25th (special) Congress of the CPGB, April 1957.

Hilton, R. (1976), 'Feudalism and the origins of capitalism', *HWJ* 1, Spring, 1976.

—— (ed. 1976), *The Transition from Feudalism to Capitalism*, London: NLB.

Hindess, B. and Hirst, P. (1975), *Pre-Capitalist Modes of Production*, London: Routledge.

Hindess, B. and Hirst, P. (1977), *Mode of Production and Social Formation: An Autocritique*, London: Macmillan.

Hinton, J. (1965), 'The labour aristocracy', *NLR* 32, July/Aug. 1965.

—— (1969), *Unions and Strikes*, London: Sheed & Ward.

—— (1973), *The First Shop Stewards Movement*, London: Allen & Unwin.

—— (1983), *Labour and Socialism: A History of the British Labour Movement*, Amherst, MA: University of Massachusetts Press.

—— (1989), *Protest Visions: Peace Politics in 20th Century Britain*, London: Hutchinson Radius.

Hinton, J. and Hyman, R. (1975), *Trade Unions and Revolution: The Industrial Politics of the Early British Communist Party*, London: Pluto Press.

Hirst, P. (1979), *Law and Ideology*, London: Macmillan.

Hoare, Q. (1965), 'Education: programmes and men', *NLR* 32, July/Aug. 1965.
—— 'On "Women: the longest revolution"', *NLR* 41, Jan./Feb. 1967.
Hobsbawm, E. (1954), 'The labour aristocracy in 19th-century Britain', in Saville (ed.), *Democracy and the Labour Movement*, London: Lawrence & Wishart.
—— (1978), 'The Historians' Group of the Communist Party', in Cornforth (ed.), *Rebels and Their Causes*, Atlantic Highlands, NJ: Humanities Press.
—— (as Newton, F. 1959,) *The Jazz Scene*, New York: Monthly Review Press, 1960.
—— (1961), 'Parliamentary cretinism?', *NLR* 12, Nov./Dec. 1961.
—— (1964), *Labouring Men: Studies in the History of Labour*, London: Weidenfeld & Nicolson.
—— (1968), 'French May', *Black Dwarf*, 1 June 1968.
—— (1969), 'May 1968', in Hobsbawm, 1973.
—— (1972), 'Karl Marx's contribution to historiography', in Blackburn (ed.), *Ideology in Social Science*, London: Fontana.
—— (1973), *Revolutionaries: Contemporary Essays*, London: Weidenfeld & Nicolson.
—— (1975), *The Age of Capital 1848–1875*, New York: Scribner.
—— (1977a), 'Gramsci and political theory', *MT*, July 1977.
—— (1977b), 'Some reflections on "The break-up of Britain"', *NLR* 105, Sept./Oct. 1977.
—— (1978a), 'The forward march of labour halted?', in Jacques and Mulhern (eds), *The Forward March of Labour Halted*, London: Verso.
—— (1978b), 'Interview', in Abelove *et al.*, (eds), *Visions of History*: Manchester: Manchester University Press.
—— (1978c), '1968 – a retrospect', *MT*, May 1978.
—— (1986), '1956', *MT*, Nov. 1986.
—— (1989), *Politics for a Rational Left*, London: Verso.
—— (1990), *Nations and Nationalism since 1780: Programme, Myth, Reality*, Cambridge: Cambridge University Press.
Hoggart, R. (1957), *The Uses of Literacy: Aspects of Working Class Life, with Special Reference to Publications and Entertainments*, London: Chatto & Windus.
—— (1958), 'Speaking to each other', in Mackenzie (ed.), *Conviction*, London: MacGibbon & Kee.
—— (1960), 'Working-class attitudes' (a discussion with Williams), *NLR* 1, Jan./Feb. 1960.
Holden, D. R. (1976), 'The first New Left in Britain: 1956–62', Ph.D. dissertation, University of Wisconsin Madison.
Holland, S. (1974), *The Socialist Challenge*, London: Quartet Books.
—— (ed. 1983), *Out of Crisis: A Project for European Recovery*, Nottingham: Spokesman.
Horkheimer, M. (1968), *Critical Theory*, New York: Herder & Herder, 1972.
Horowitz, I. L. (ed. 1964), *The New Sociology: Essays in Social Science and Social Theory in Honour of C. Wright Mills*, Oxford: Oxford University Press.
Howarth-Williams, M. (1977), *R. D. Laing: His Work and Its Relevance for Sociology*, London: Routledge.
Howe, I. (ed. 1970), *Beyond the New Left*, New York: McCall Publishing Co.
Hoyland, J. (1972), 'Miners: week one', *Seven Days*, 9 Jan. 1972.
Hughes, J. (1957), 'Steel nationalization and political power', *NR* 2, Autumn 1957.
—— (1960a), *Nationalized Industries in the Mixed Economy*, Fabian Tract 328, London: Fabian Society.
—— (1960b), 'The commanding heights: the mixed economy', *NLR* 4, July/Aug. 1960.
—— (1963), 'The British economy: crisis and structural change', *NLR* 21, Oct. 1963.
—— (1964), 'An economic policy for Labour', *NLR* 24, Jan./Feb. 1964.
—— (1967), *An Economic Strategy for Labour*, Fabian Tract, no. 372, London: Fabian Society.
—— (1971), *Behind the Dole Queue*, Nottingham: Spokesman.
—— (1974), *Profit Trends and Price Control*, Nottingham: Spokesman pamphlet.
—— (1989), 'New Left economic policy', in Archer *et al.*, (eds), *Out of Apathy*, London: Verso.
Hughes, J., Eaton, J. and Coates, K. (1972), *Workers' Control: The Real Defence Against Unemployment Is Attack*, IWC pamphlet, Nottingham.
Hughes, J. and Pollins, H. (eds 1973), *Trade Unions in Great Britain*, Newton Abbot: David & Charles.
Hyman, R. (1974), 'Workers' control and revolutionary theory', *SR* 1974.
Ingham, G. (1988), 'Commercial capital and British development: a reply to Michael Barratt Brown', *NLR* 172, Nov./Dec. 1988.

International Socialism, Journal for Socialist Theory, Editorial, no. 35, Winter 1968–9; no. 36, 1969.

IWC (1968), *Declaration of the Sixth National Conference on Workers' Control*, Nottingham, 31 March 1968.

Jacques, M. and Mulhern, F. (eds 1981), *The Forward March of Labour Halted*, London: Verso.

Jameson, F. (1990), *Late Marxism*, London: Verso.

Jay, M. (1973), *The Dialectical Imagination: A History of the Frankfurt School and the Institute of Social Research 1923–1950*, Boston: Little Brown.

—— (1984), *Marxism and Totality: The Adventures of a Concept from Lukacs to Habermas*, Berkley: University of California Press.

Jenkins, R. (1959), *The Labour Case*, Harmondsworth: Penguin.

Jessop, B. (1978), 'Marx and Engels on the state', in Shibbin (ed.), *Politics, Ideology and the State*, London: Lawrence & Wishart.

Jessop, B., Bonnett, K., Bromley, S. and Ling, T. (1984), 'Authoritarian populism, two nations, and Thatcherism', *NLR* 147, Sept./Oct. 1984.

Johnson, L. (1979), *The cultural Critics: From Matthew Arnold to Raymond Williams*, London: Routledge.

Johnson, R. (1978), 'Edward Thompson, Eugene Genovese, and socialist-humanist history', *HWJ* 6, Autumn, 1978.

—— (1979a), 'Culture and the historians', in Clarke *et al.*, (eds), *Working Class Culture*, New York: St Martin's Press, 1980.

—— (1979b), 'Histories of culture/theories of ideology', in Barrett *et al.*, (eds), *Ideology and Cultural Production*, New York: St. Martin's Press.

—— (1979c), 'Three problematics: elements of a theory of working class culture', in Clarkes *et al.* (eds), *Working Class Culture*, New York: St Martin's Press.

—— (1980), 'Barrington Moore, Perry Anderson and English social development', in Hall *et al.*, (eds), *Culture, Media, Language*, London: Hutchinson.

—— (1981), 'Against absolutism', in Samuel (ed.), *People's History*, London: Routledge.

—— (1982), 'Reading for the best Marx: history-writing and historical abstraction', in Johnson *et al.*, (eds), *Making Histories*, London: Hutchinson.

—— (1983), 'What is cultural studies anyway?', occasional paper, no. 74, CCCS, Sept. 1983.

Johnson, R., McLennan, G., Schwarz, B. and Sutton, D. (eds), (1982) *Making Histories: Studies in History-Writing and Politics*, London: Hutchinson.

Jones, M. (1958), 'The time is short', in Mackenzie (ed.), *Conviction*, London: MacGibbon & Kee.

—— (1976), 'Days of tragedy and force', *SR* 1976.

Katsiaficas, G. (1987), *The Imagination of the New Left: A Global Analysis of 1968*, Boston: South End Press.

Kautsky, K. (1909), *The Road to Power*, (trans. A. M. Simon) Chicago: S. A. Bloch.

Kaye, H. J. (1979), 'Totality: its application to historical and social analysis by Wallerstein and Genovese', *Historical Reflections*, Winter, 1979.

—— (1984), *The British Marxist Historians: An Introductory Analysis*, Cambridge: Polity Press.

Kaye, H. J. and McClelland, K. (eds 1990), *E. P. Thompson: Critical Perspectives*, Philadelphia: Temple University Press.

Kaye, M. (1960), 'The New Drama', *NLR* 5, Sept./Oct. 1960.

Kelly, M. (1982), *Modern French Marxism*, Oxford: Basil Blackwell.

Kelly, T. (1970), *A History of Adult Education in Great Britain*, Liverpool: Liverpool University Press.

Kettle, A. (1958), 'Rebels and causes', *MT*, March 1958.

—— (1960), 'On the "New Left"', *MT*, June 1960.

Kiernan, V. G. (1954), 'Wordsworth and the people', in Saville (ed.), *Democracy and the Labour Movement*, London: Lawrence & Wishart.

—— (1959), 'Culture and society', *NR* 9, Summer 1959.

—— (1964), 'Farewells to empire: some recent studies of imperialism', *SR* 1964.

—— (1965), 'The new nation-states', *NLR* 30, March/April 1965.

—— (1968), 'Notes on Marxism in 1968', *SR* 1968.

—— (1969), 'Notes on the intelligentsia', *SR* 1969.

—— (1971), 'Imperialism, American and European', *SR* 1971.

—— (1972a), 'Gramsci and Marxism', *SR* 1972.

—— (1972b), 'Victorian London: unending purgatory', *NLR* 76, Nov./Dec. 1972.

—— (1974), *Marxism and Imperialism*, London: Edward Arnold.

Kirsner, D. (1976), *The Schizoid World of Jean-Paul Sartre and R.D.Laing*, Queensland: University of Queensland Press.

Kitching, G. (1983), *Rethinking Socialism: A Theory for a Better Practice*, London/New York: Methuen.

Klugmann, J. (1969), 'The revolutionary ideas of Marx and the current revolt', *MT*, June 1969.

Koelble, T. A. (1991), *The Left Unraveled: Social Democracy and the New Left Challenge in Britain and West Germany*, Duke University Press.

Kolakowski, L. (1971), 'Althusser's Marx', *SR* 1971.

—— (1981), *Main Currents of Marxism*, vol. III, Oxford: Oxford University Press.

Korsch, K. (1970), *Marxism and Philosophy*, (trans. and introduced by F. Halliday), London: NLB.

Krasso, N. (1967), 'Trotsky's Marxism', *NLR* 44, July/Aug. 1967.

—— (1968), 'Reply to Ernest Mandel', *NLR* 48, March/April 1968.

Labedz, L. (ed. 1962), *Revisionism: Essays on the History of Marxist Ideas*, London: Allen & Unwin.

The LP National Executive Committee (1957), *Industry and Society: Labour's Policy on Future Public Ownership*, London.

Lacan, J. (1966), *Ecrits: A Selection*, London: Tavistock, 1977.

Laclau, E. (1975), 'The specificity of the political: the Poulantzas-Miliband debate', *Economy and Society*, 5, no. 1, Feb. 1975.

—— (1977), *Politics and Ideology in Marxist Theory: Capitalism – Fascism – Populism*, London: Verso.

Laclau, E. and Mouffe, C. (1985), *Hegemony and Socialist Strategy: Towards a Radical Democratic Politics*, (trans. by Moore and Cammack) London: Verso.

Laing, R. D. (1964), 'One-dimensional man', *NLR* 26, July/Aug. 1964.

Laing, R. D. and Cooper, D.G. (1964), *Reason and Violence: A Decade of Sartre's Philosophy 1950–1960*, London: Tavistock Publications.

Lambertz, J. (1978/9), 'Feminist history in Britain', *RHR* 19, Winter, 1978-9.

Leavis, F. R. (1943), *Education and the University: A Sketch for an 'English School'*, Cambridge: Cambridge University Press, 1979.

—— (1962), *Two Cultures? The Significance of C. P. Snow*, London: Chatto & Windus.

—— (1972), *Nor Shall My Sword: Discussions on Pluralism, Compassion and Social Hope*, New York: Barnes & Noble.

Lenin, V. (1917), *The State and Revolution, Collected Works* (45 vols.), vol. 25, Moscow: Foreign Language Publishing House, 1969.

Lessing, D. (1957), 'The small personal voice', in Maschler (ed.), *Declaration*, London: MacGibbon & Kee.

—— (1962), *The Golden Notebook*, London: Michael Joseph, 1973.

Levitas, R. (1986), *The Ideology of the New Right*, Cambridge: Polity Press.

Lewin, M. (1967), *Lenin's Last Struggle*, London: Faber & Faber.

Lewis, G. U. (1957), 'Candy flossing the celtic fringe', *ULR* 2, Summer 1957.

Lipton, M. (1966), 'The mythology of affluence', *NLR* 35, Jan./Feb. 1966.

Little, D. (1986), *The Scientific Marx*, Minneapolis: University of Minnesota Press.

Lovell, A. (1957), 'The scholarship boy', *ULR* 2, Summer 1957.

—— (1961), 'Film chronicle', *NLR* 7, Jan./Feb. 1961; *NLR* 8, March/April 1961.

Löwy, M. (1975), 'Lukács and Stalinism', *NLR* 91, May/June 1975.

—— (1976a), *Lukács: From Romanticism to Bolshevism*, London: NLB.

—— (1976b), 'Marxism and the national question', *NLR* 96, March/April 1976.

—— (1977), 'Rosa Luxemburg: a new evaluation', *NLR* 101-2, Feb./April 1977.

Lukács, G. (1923), *History and Class Consciousness*, London: Merlin, 1971.

—— (1968), 'Lukács on his life and work', *NLR* 68, May/June 1971.

—— (1970), 'The twin crises', *NLR* 60, March/April 1970.

Luxemburg, R. (1913), *The Accumulation of Capital*, London: Routledge, 1951.

Lvasheva, V. (1958/9), 'Revisionism of Marxism in Britain', October, Moscow; English trans. *NR* 7, Winter 1958-9.

McCallum, P. (1983), *Literature and Method: Towards a Critique of I. A. Richards, T. S. Eliot and F. R. Leavis*, London: Gill & Macmillan.

McClelland, K. (1979), 'Some comments on Richard Johnson, "Thompson, Genovese, and socialist-humanist history"', *HWJ* 7, Spring, 1979.

McCrinelle, J. and Rowbotham, S. (eds 1977), *Dutiful Daughters: Women Talk about Their Lives*, London: Harmondsworth: Penguin.

MacEwen, M. (1976), 'The day the Party had to stop', *SR* 1976.

McInnes, N. (1972), 'Lukács: the restoration of idealism', in McInnes, *The Western Marxists*, New York: Library Press.

MacIntyre, A. (1958/9), 'Notes from the moral wilderness', *NR* 7, Winter 1958/9; *NR* 8, Spring 1959.

Mackenzie, N. (ed. 1958), *Conviction*, London: MacGibbon & Kee.

Mckenzie, R. and Silver, A. (1962), 'Conservatism and the working-class Tory in England', in Worsley (ed.), *Problems of Modern Society*, Harmondsworth: Penguin.

McLellan, D. (1972), 'The *Grundrisse* in the context of Marx's work as a whole', in Walton and Hall (eds), *Situating Marx*, London: Human Context Books.

—— (1986), *Ideology*, Minneapolis: University of Minnesota Press.

McLennan, G. (1979a), 'Richard Johnson and his critics: towards a constructive debate', *HWJ* 8, Autumn 1979.

—— (1979b), 'Philosophy and history: some issues in recent Marxist theory', *HWJ*, Autumn 1979.

—— (1982), 'Thompson and the discipline of historical context', in Johnson *et al.*, (eds), *Making Histories*, London: Hutchinson.

McLennan, G., Held, D. and Hall, S. (eds 1984a), *The Idea of the Modern State*, Milton Keynes: Open University Press.

McLennan, G., Held, D. and Hall. S. (eds 1984b), *State and Society in Contemporary Britain: A Critical Introduction*, Cambridge: Polity Press.

McLennan, G., Molina, V. and Peters, R. (1977), 'Althusser's theory of ideology', in CCCS, *On Ideology*, London: Hutchinson.

Magri, L. (1969), 'The May events and revolution in the West', *SR* 1969.

Malraux, A. (1967), *Anti-Memoirs*, New York: Bantam Books, 1970.

Mandel, E. (1964), 'After imperialism', *NLR* 25, May/June 1964.

—— (1968a), 'Trotsky's Marxism: an anti-critique', *NLR* 47, Jan./Feb. 1968.

—— (1968b), 'Lessons of May', *NLR* 52, Nov./Dec. 1968.

—— (1969), 'The new vanguard', in Ali (ed.), *The New Revolutionaries*, New York: William Morrow.

—— (1971), *The Revolutionary Student Movement: Theory and Practice*, New York: Pathfinder.

—— (1975), *Late Capitalism*, London: NLB.

—— (1978), *From Stalinism to Eurocommunism: The Bitter Fruits of 'Socialism in One Country'*, London: NLB.

—— (1986), 'In defence of socialist planning', *NLR* 159, Sept./Oct. 1986.

Mandel, E. and Warren, B. (1974), 'Recession and its consequences', *NLR* 87-88, Sept./Dec. 1974.

'Manifesto of the London Women's Liberation Workshop' (1970), *Black Dwarf*, no. 37, 5 Sept. 1970.

Manuel, F. E. and Manuel, F. P. (1979), *Utopian Thought in the Western World*, Cambridge, MA: Harvard University Press.

Marcuse, H. (1955), *Eros and Civilization: A Philosophical Inquiry into Freud*, Boston: Beacon.

—— (1964), *One-Dimensional Man: Studies in the Ideology of Advanced Industrial Society*, London: Routledge.

—— (1965), 'Industrialization and capitalism', *NLR* 30, March/April 1965.

—— (1968), 'Interview with Herbert Marcuse', *Guardian*, 23 Nov. 1968.

—— (1969a), 'Re-examination of the concept of revolution', *NLR* 56, July/Aug. 1969.

—— (1969b), 'On revolution', in Cockburn and Blackburn (eds), *Student Power*, Harmondsworth: Penguin.

—— (1969c), 'Repressive tolerance', in Wolff, Moore and Marcuse, *A Critique of Pure Tolerance*, Boston: Beacon.

—— (1970a), 'The problem of violence and the radical opposition', in *Five Lectures: Psychoanalysis, Politics and Utopian*, Boston: Beacon.

—— (1970b), 'On the New Left', in Teodori (ed.), *The New Left*, London: Jonathan Cape.

—— (1972), *Counterrevolution and Revolt*, Boston: Beacon.

—— (1972b), *Studies in Critical Philosophy*, London:.

—— (1972c), *From Luther to Popper*, London: NLB.

Markovic, M. and Cohen, R. S. (1975), *Yogoslavia: The Rise and Fall of Socialist Humanism: A History of the Praxis Group* (intro. by K.Coates), Nottingham: Spokesman.
Martin, D.E. (1970), 'R. D. Laing', in Cranston (ed.) *The New Left*, London: The Bodley Head.
Martin, D. E. and Rubinstein, D. (1979), *Ideology and the Labour Movement: Essays Presented to John Saville*, London: Croom Helm.
Martin, G. (1959), 'A look back at Osborne', *ULR* 7, Autumn 1959.
Marx, K. (1843), 'Letter to A. Ruge' (Sept. 1843), in *Karl Marx, Early Writings* (ed. Colletti), New York: Vintage Books, 1975.
—— (1844), 'Economic and philosophical manuscripts', in *Early Writings* (ed. Colletti), New York: Vintage Books, 1975.
—— (1847), *The Poverty of Philosophy*, New York: International Publishers, 1971.
—— (1850), 'A review of Guizot's book', in *Marx and Engels on Britain*, Moscow: Progress Publishers, 1953.
—— (1859), *Grundrisse*, New York: Harper & Row, 1973.
—— (1867), *Capital*, vol. I, Moscow: Foreign Language Publishing House, 1961.
—— (1875), *Critique of the Gotha Programme*, in Selected Works, vol. II, Moscow: Foreign Language Publishing House, 1950.
—— (1956), *Karl Marx: Selected Writings in Sociology and Social Philosophy* (eds by Bottomore and Rubel), London: Watts.
—— (1969), *Essential Writings of Karl Marx* (intro. by D.Caute), London: MacGibbon & Kee.
Marx, K. and Engels, F. (1845), *The German Ideology*, Moscow: Progress Publishers, 1976.
Marx, K. and Engels, F. (1953), *Marx and Engels on Britain*, Moscow: Progress Publishers, 1953.
Marx, K., Engels, F., Lenin, V. I. and Stalin, J. (1951), *The Woman Question: Selections from the Writings of Marx, Engels, Lenin, Stalin*, New York: International Publishers, 1951.
Maschler, T. (ed. 1957), *Declaration*, London: MacGibbon & Kee.
Mayer, A. J. (1981), *The Persistence of the Old Regime: Europe to the Great War*, New York: Pantheon Books.
Medick, H. (1981), 'The transition from feudalism to capitalism: renewal of the debate', in Samuel (ed.), *People's History*, London: Routledge.
Meek, R. L. (1956), *Studies in the Labour Theory of Value*, London: Lawrence & Wishart, 1973.
—— (1959), 'Mr. Strachey's economics', *NR* 8, Spring 1959.
—— (1967), 'Karl Marx's economic method', in Meek, *Economics and Ideology and Other Essays: Studies in the Development of Economic Thought*, London: Chapman & Hall.
—— (1977), *Smith, Marx, and After: Ten Essays in the Development of Economic Thought*, London: Chapman & Hall.
Merrill, M. (1978/9), 'Raymond Williams and the theory of English Marxism', *RHR* 19, Winter, 1978-9.
Merrington, J. (1968), 'Theory and practice in Gramsci's Marxism', *SR* 1968.
Meszaros, I. (ed. 1971), *Aspects of History and Class Consciousness*, London: Routledge.
—— (1975), 'Jean-Paul Sartre: a critical tribute', *SR* 1975.
—— (1986), *Philosophy, Ideology and Social Science*, New York: St Martin's Press.
Mezan, P. (1972), 'After Freud and Jung, now comes R. D. Laing', *Esquire*, 1 Jan. 1972.
Middleton, N. (1970), 'Return to Leninism', *Red Mole*, no. 2, 1 April 1970.
Miliband, R. (1958a), 'The politics of contemporary capitalism', *NR* 5, Summer 1958.
—— (1958b), 'The transition to the transition', *NR* 6, Autumn 1958.
—— (1961a), *Parliamentary Socialism: A Study in the Politics of Labour*, 2nd edn. London: Allen & Unwin, 1973.
—— (1961b), 'Footnote to labourism', *NLR* 8, March/April 1961.
—— (1962), 'C. Wright Mills', *NLR* 15, May/June 1962.
—— (1964a), 'Socialism and the myth of the golden past', *SR* 1964.
—— (1964b), 'Mills and politics', in Horowitz (ed.), *The New Sociology*, Oxford: Oxford University Press.
—— (1965), 'Marx and the state', *SR* 1965, reprinted in Miliband, 1983.
—— (1966), 'The Labour government and beyond', *SR* 1966.
—— (1968), 'Professor Galbraith and American capitalism', *SR* 1968.
—— (1969), *The State in Capitalist Society*, New York: Basic Books.
—— (1970a), 'State and revolution', *SR* 1970.
—— (1970b), 'Reply to Nicos Poulantzas', *NLR* 59, Jan./Feb. 1970; reprinted in Miliband, 1983.

—— (1973a), 'Poulantzas and the capitalist state', *NLR* 82, Nov./Dec. 1973; reprinted in Miliband, *Class Power*, London: 1983.
—— (1973b), 'Stalin and after', *SR* 1973.
—— (1975), 'Political forms and historical materialism', *SR* 1975.
—— (1976), 'Moving on', *SR* 1976.
—— (1977a), *Marxism and Politics*, Oxford: Oxford University Press.
—— (1977b), 'The future of socialism in England', *SR* 1977.
—— (1978), 'Constitutionalism and revolution', *SR* 1978.
—— (1979), 'John Saville: a representation', in Martin and Rubinstein (eds), *Ideology and the Labour Movement*, London: Croom Helm.
—— (1980), 'Military intervention and socialist internationalism', *SR* 1980.
—— (1982), *Capitalist Democracy in Britain*, Oxford: Oxford University Press.
—— (1983), *Class Power and State Power*, London: Verso.
—— (1985), 'The new revisionism in Britain', *NLR* 150, March/April 1985.
Miliband, R. and Panitch, L. (1987), 'Socialists and the "new conservatism"', *SR* 1987.
Miliband, R. and Saville, J. (1964), 'Labour policy and the Labour Left', *SR* 1964.
Mills, C.W. (1951), *The American Middle Classes*, Oxford: Oxford University Press.
—— (1956), *The Power Elite*, Oxford: Oxford University Press.
—— (1958), *The Causes of World War Three*, London: Secker & Warburg.
—— (1959), *The Sociological Imagination*, Oxford: Oxford University Press.
—— (1960), 'Letter to the New Left', *NLR* 5, Sept./Oct. 1960.
—— (1962), *The Marxists*, Harmondsworth: Penguin.
—— (1963), *Power, Politics and People: The Collected Essays of C. Wright Mills* (ed. by Horowitz), Oxford: Oxford University Press.
Minnion, J. and Bolsover, P. (eds 1983), *The CND Story: The First 25 Years of CND in the Words of the People Involved*, London: Allison & Busby.
Mitchell, J. (1964), 'Women's education', *NLR* 28, Nov./Dec. 1964.
—— (1967), 'Reply to Quintin Hoare', *NLR* 44, Jan./Feb. 1967.
—— (1971), *Women's Estate*, Harmondsworth: Penguin.
—— (1974), *Psychoanalysis and Feminism*, London: Allen Lane.
—— (1984), *Women: The Longest Revolution – Essays in Feminism, Literature and Psychoanalysis*, London: Virago Press.
—— (1988), 'An interview with Juliet Mitchell', *NLR* 170, July/Aug. 1988.
Mitchell, J. and Oakley, A. (eds 1976), *The Rights and Wrong of Women*, Harmondsworth: Penguin.
Mitchell, J. and Rose, J. (1982), *Feminine Sexuality: Jacques Lacan and the Ecole Freudienne*, London: W. W. Norton.
Mitchell, S. (1973), 'Introduction to Benjamin and Brecht', *NLR* 77, Jan./Feb. 1973.
Monds, J. (1976), 'Workers' control and the historians: a new economism', *NLR* 97, May/June 1976.
Moorhouse, H. F. (1978), 'The Marxist theory of the labour aristocracy', *Social History*, vol. III, no. 1, Jan. 1978.
Mulhern, F. (1975a), 'Comments on Eagleton's "Ideology and literary form"', *NLR* 91, May/June 1975.
—— (1975b), 'Introduction to Goldmann', *NLR* 92, July/Aug. 1975.
—— (1978), 'Marxism in literary criticism', *NLR* 108, March/April 1978.
—— (1979), *The Moment of 'Scrutiny'*, London: NLB.
Murdoch, I. (1958), 'A house of theory', in Mackenzie (ed.), *Conviction*, London: MacGibbon & Kee.
Murdoch, G. and McCron, R. (1975), 'Consciousness of class and consciousness of generations', in Hall and Jefferson (eds), *Resistance through Rituals*, London: Hutchinson.
Nagel, J. (ed. 1969), *Student Power*, London: Merlin.
Nairn, T. (1962), 'Crowds and critics', *NLR* 17, Winter 1962.
—— (1963), 'Landed England', *NLR* 20, Summer 1963.
—— (1964a), 'The nature of the Labour Party', *NLR* 27, Sept./Oct. 1964; *NLR* 28, Nov./Dec. 1964.
—— (1964b), 'The English working class', *NLR* 24, March/April 1964.
—— (1964c), 'The British political elite', *NLR* 23, Jan./Feb. 1964.
—— (1965), 'Labour imperialism', *NLR* 32, July/Aug. 1965.

—— (1970), 'The fateful meridian', *NLR* 60, March/April 1970.
—— (1971), 'British nationalism and the EEC', *NLR* 69, Sept./Oct. 1971.
—— (1972), 'The left against Europe', *NLR* 75, Sept./Oct. 1972; reprinted by Pelican Books, 1973.
—— (1975), 'The modern Janus', *NLR* 94, Nov./Dec. 1975.
—— (1977a), 'The twilight of the British state', *NLR* 101-102, Feb./April 1977.
—— (1977b), *The Break-up of Britain: Crisis and Neo-Nationalism*, London: NLB.
—— (1988), *The Enchanted Glass: Britain and Its Monarchy*, London: Radius.
Nell, E. (1972), 'Economics: the revival of political economy', in Blackburn (ed.), *Ideology in Social Science*, London: Fontana.
Nelson, C. and Grossberg, L. (eds 1988), *Marxism and the Interpretation of Culture*, Urbana/Chicago: University of Illinois Press.
Newman, J. (1969), 'Education and politics in Britain', in Nagel (ed.), *Student Power*, London: Merlin.
NLB (1960), *Out of Apathy*, London: Stevens & Sons.
—— (1965), *Towards Socialism*, London.
—— (1977), *Western Marxism: A Critical Reader*, London.
—— (1982), *Exterminism and Cold War*, London: Verso.
NLR (1960a), *Searchlight: A New Left Industrial Bulletin*, 4 issues, 1960.
—— *This Week: A NLR Daily*, Oct. 1960.
NLR editorial (1961a), 'The learning revolution', *NLR* 11, Sept./Oct. 1961.
—— (1961b), 'Notes for readers', *NLR* 12, Nov./Dec. 1961.
—— (1964), 'To our readers', *NLR* 24, March/April 1964.
—— (1965), 'Themes', *NLR* 32, July/Aug. 1965.
—— (1967), 'The Marxism of Regis Debray', *NLR* 45, Sept./Oct. 1967.
—— (1968a), 'Themes' on the student movement, *NLR* 50, July/Aug. 1968.
—— (1968b), 'Themes' on workers' councils and soviets, *NLR* 51, Sept./Oct. 1968.
—— (1968c), 'Introduction to 1968', *NLR* 52, Nov./Dec. 1968.
—— (1972a), 'Introduction to Gluksmann's 'A ventriloquist structuralism', *NLR* 72, Mar.-Apr. 1972.
—— (1972b), 'Interview with Hedda Korsch', *NLR* 76, Nov./Dec. 1972.
—— (1973a), 'Presentation of Adorno-Benjamin', *NLR* 77, Jan./Feb. 1973.
—— (1973b), 'Introduction to Adorno', *NLR* 81, Sept./Oct. 1973.
—— (1977), 'Introduction to Sartre', *NLR* 100, Nov./Dec. 1976 – Jan. 1977.
Nove, A. (1983), *Economics of Feasible Socialism*, London: George Allen & Unwin.
Nutting, A. (1958), *I Saw for Myself: The Aftermath of Suez*, London: Hollis & Carter.
—— (1967), *No End of a Lesson: The Story of Suez*, London: Constable.
Oglesby, C. (ed. 1969), *The New Left Reader*, New York: Grove Press.
Open University (1978), *Popular Culture*, course unit U203, Milton Keynes.
Osborne, J. (1981), *A Better Class of Person*, London: Faber & Faber.
Palmer, B. D. (1981), *The Making of E. P. Thompson: Marxism, Humanism and History*, Toronto: New Hogtown.
Parkin, F. (1968), *Middle Class Radicalism: The Social Bases of the British Campaign for Nuclear Disarmament*, Manchester: Manchester University Press.
Peck, J. (1984), *Proportional Representation*, CP pamphlet, London, Feb. 1984.
Popper, K. (1945), *The Open Society and Its Enemies*, vol. II, London: Routledge.
—— (1957), *The Poverty of Historicism*, London: Routledge.
Porter, R. and Teich, M. (1986), *Revolution in History*, Cambridge: Cambridge University Press.
Poster, M. (1989), *Critical Theory and Poststructuralism: In Search of a Context*, New York: Cornell University Press.
Potter, D. (1960), *The Glittering Coffin*, London: Victor Gollancz.
Poulantzas, N. (1967), 'Marxist political theory in Great Britain', *NLR* 43, May/June 1967.
—— (1968), *Political Power and Social classes*, London: NLB, 1973.
—— (1969), 'The problem of the capitalist state', *NLR* 58, Nov./Dec.1969; reprinted in Blackburn (ed.), *Ideology in Social Science*, Fontana, 1972.
—— (1974), *Fascism and Dictatorship*, London: NLB.
—— (1976), 'The capitalist state: a reply to Miliband and Laclau', *NLR* 95, Jan./Feb. 1976.
Pribicevic, B. (1959), *The Shop Stewards' Movement and Workers' Control, 1910–1922*, Oxford: Basil Blackwell.

Priscott, D. (1974), 'The Communist Party and the Labour Party', *MT*, Jan. 1974.
Quattrocchi, A. and Nairn, T. (1968), *The Beginning of the End: France, May 1968*, New York: Panther Books.
Ravetz, J. R. (1971), *Scientific Knowledge and Its Social Problems*, Oxford: Clarendon Press.
—— (1973), 'Tragedy in the history of science', in Teich and Young (eds), *Changing Perspectives in the History of Science*, Dordrecht: D. Reidel Publishing Co.
Red Mole, London, 1970–73.
—— (1970), 'Women: the Ruskin weekend', no. 1, 17 March 1970.
—— (1973), 'On our difference with the Communist Party and International Socialists', no. 32.
Ree, J. (1974), 'Socialist humanism', *Radical Philosophy*, Winter 1974.
—— (1984), *Proletarian Philosophers: Problem in Socialist Culture in Britain 1900–1940*, Oxford: Oxford University Press.
Reid, B. (1970), *Ultra-Leftism in Britain*, CP pamphlet, London, 1970.
Rex, J. (1960), *Britain Without Bomb*, CND pamphlet, London.
—— (1961), *NATO*, CND pamphlet, London.
—— (1970), *Race Relations in Sociological Theory*, New York: Schocken Books.
—— (1986), *Race and Ethnicity*, Milton Keynes: Open University Press.
RHR (1978/9), 'Editorial' (an introduction to British socialist historians), no. 19, Winter 1978-9.
—— (1981), report on the HW conference on 'People's history and socialist theory', no. 25, 1981.
Riasanovsky, N. V. (1969), *The Teaching of Charles Fourier*, Berkeley: Berkeley University Press.
Rieff, P. (ed. 1969), *On Intellectuals: Theoretical Studies/Case Studies*, New York: Doubleday.
Robinson, J. (1942), *An Essay on Marxian Economics*, London: Macmillan.
—— (1964), *Collected Economic Papers*, Oxford: Basil Blackwell.
—— (1970), *Freedom and Necessity: An Introduction to the Study of Society*, London: George Allen & Unwin.
Rock, P. and Cohen, S. (1970), 'The teddy boy', in Bogdanor and Skidelsky (eds), *The Age of Affluence*, London: Macmillan.
Roemer, J. (ed. 1986), *Analytical Marxism*, Cambridge: Cambridge University Press.
Rogow, A. and Shore, P. (1955), *The Labour Government and British Industry, 1945–51*, New York: Cornell University Press.
Rose, H. and Rose, S. (1969), 'Knowledge and power', *New Scientist* (London), vol. 42, 17 April 1969.
Ross, E. and Wilentz, S. (1981), 'Britain: the History Workshop Movement', *RHR* 25, 1981.
Ross, P. (1960), 'Manchester Left Club on youth', *NLR* 1, Jan./Feb. 1960.
Rossanda, R. (1975), 'Sartre's political practice', *SR* 1975.
Rossdale, M. (1965), 'Health in a sick society', *NLR* 34, Nov./Dec. 1965.
—— (1966), 'Socialist health service?', *NLR* 36, March/April 1966.
Rotblat, J. (1962), *Science and World Affairs: History of the Pugwash Conferences*, London: Dawsons of Pall Mall.
—— (1983), 'The purpose of Pugwash', in Epstein and Webster (eds), *We Can Avert a Nuclear War*, Cambridge, MA: Oelgeschlager, Gunn & Hain.
Rowbotham, S. (1970), 'Cinderella organizes buttons', in 'Year of the militant women', *Black Dwarf*, 5 Sept. 1970.
—— (1972), *Women's Liberation and the New Politics*, Nottingham: Spokesman pamphlet.
—— (1973a), *Woman's Consciousness, Man's World*, Harmondsworth: Penguin.
—— (1973b), *Hidden From History: Rediscovering Women in History from the 17th Century to the Present*, New York: Pantheon.
—— (1976), 'Interview', in Abelove *et al.*, (eds), *Visions of History*, Manchester: Manchester University Press.
—— (1979), 'The women's movement and organizing for socialism', in Rowbotham, Segal and Wainwright, *Beyond the Fragments*, London: Merlin.
—— (1981), 'Travellers in a strange country: responses of working class students to the university extension movement – 1830–1910', *HWJ* 12, Autumn 1981.
—— (1983), *Dreams and Dilemmas: Collected Writings*, London: Virago Press.
Rowbotham, S., Segal, L. and Wainwright, H. (1979), *Beyond the Fragments: Feminism and the Making of Socialism*, London: Merlin.
Rowntree, J. and Rowntree, M. (1970), 'Youth as a class', in Teodori (ed.), *The New Left*, London: Jonathan Cape.

Rowthorn, B. (1965), 'The trap of an incomes policy', *NLR* 34, Nov./Dec. 1965.
—— (1966), 'Capitalism and the modernizers', *NLR* 37, May/June 1966.
—— (1967), 'Unions and the economy', in Blackburn and Cockburn (eds), *The Incompatibles*, Harmondsworth: Penguin.
—— (1971a), 'Imperialism in the 1970s: unity or rivalry?', *NLR* 69, Sept./Oct. 1971.
—— (1971b), *International Big Business 1957–67: A Study of Comparative Growth*, Cambridge: Cambridge University Press.
—— (1974a), 'Vulgar economy', *CSE Bulletin*, vol. II, no. 5; reprinted as 'Neo-classicism, neo-Ricardianism and Marxism', *NLR* 86, July/Aug. 1974.
—— (1974b), 'Britain and the world economy', in Cambridge Political Economy Group, *Britain's Economic Crisis*, Nottingham: Spokesman Pamphlet, no. 44.
—— (1976), 'Late capitalism', *NLR* 98, July/Aug. 1976.
—— (1977a), 'Conflict, inflation and money', *Cambridge Journal of Economics*, vol. I, no. 3, 1977.
—— (1977b), 'Inflation and crisis', *MT*, Nov. 1977.
—— (1980), *Capitalism, Conflict and Inflation: Essays in Political Economy*, London: Lawrence & Wishart.
Rowthorn, B. and Hymer, S. (1970), 'The multinational corporation', in Kindleberger (ed.), *The International Corporation*, Cambridge, MA: MIT Press.
RSSF (the Revolutionary Socialist Students' Federation, 1969) Manifesto, *NLR* 55, May/June 1969.
Russell, P. (1962), 'The social control of science', *NLR* 16, July/Aug. 1962.
Rustin, M. (1961), 'Young socialists', *NLR* 9, May/June 1961.
—— (1981), 'The New Left and the present crisis', *NLR* 121, May/June 1981.
—— (1985), *For a Pluralist Socialism*, London: Verso.
Ryan, A. (ed. 1979), *The Idea of Freedom: Essays in Honour of Isaiah Berlin*, Oxford: Oxford University Press.
Samuel, R. (1958), 'New authoritarianism – New Left', *ULR* 5, Autumn 1958.
—— (1959), 'Class and classlessness', *ULR* 6, Spring 1959.
—— (1960), '"Bastard" capitalism', in NLB, *Out of Apathy*, London: Stevens & Sons.
—— (ed. 1975), *Village Life and Labour*, London: Routledge.
—— (1977), 'Workshop of the world: steam power and hand technology in mid-Victorian Britain', *HWJ* 3, Spring 1977.
—— (1978), 'History and theory', *HWJ* 6, Autumn 1978; reprinted in Samuel (ed.), 1981a.
—— (1980), 'On the methods of the History Workshop: a reply', *HWJ* 9, Spring 1980.
—— (ed. 1981a), *People's History and Socialist Theory*, London: Routledge.
—— (1981b), 'History Workshop: 1966–80', in Samuel (ed.), 1981a.
—— (1981c), *East End Underworld: Chapters in the Life of Arthur Harding*, London: Routledge.
—— (1985a), *Theatres of the Left 1880–1935: Workers' Theatre Movement in Britain and America*, London: Routledge.
—— (1985b), 'The lost world of British communism', *NLR* 154, Nov./Dec. 1985; *NLR* 156, March/April 1986.
—— (ed. 1989), *Patriotism: The Making and Unmaking of British National Identity*, 3 vols, London: Routledge.
—— (1989), 'Born-again Socialism', in Archer *et al.* (eds), Out of Apathy, London: Verso.
Samuel, R., Bloomfield, B. and Boanas, G. (eds 1986), *The Enemy Within Pit Villages and the Miners' Strike of 1984–5*, London: Routledge.
Samuel, R. and Stedman Jones, G. (eds 1982a), *Culture, Ideology and Politics: Essays for Eric Hobsbawm*, London: Routledge.
Samuel, R. and Stedman Jones, G. (1982b), 'The Labour Party and social democracy', in Samuel and Stedman Jones (eds), 1982a.
Samuel, R. and Stedman Jones, G. (1985), 'Ten years after', *HWJ* 20, Autumn 1985.
Samuels, S. (1969), 'English intellectuals and politics in the 1930s', in Rieff (ed.), *On Intellectuals*, New York: Doubleday.
Sartre, J. P. (1972), *Between Existentialism and Marxism*, London: NLB.
—— (1976), 'Socialism in one country', *NLR* 100, Nov./Dec. 1976.
Saville, J. (1954), *Democracy and the Labour Movement: Essays in Honour of Dona Torr*, London: Lawrence & Wishart.
—— (1956), 'Letter to the *World News*, *World News*, 19 May 1956.

—— (1957), 'Labour movement historiography', *ULR* 3, Autumn 1957.
—— (1959), 'A note on West Fife', *NR* 10, late Autumn 1959.
—— (1960), 'Apathy into politics', *NLR* 4, July/Aug. 1960.
—— (1964), 'The politics of Encounter', *SR* 1964.
—— (1965), 'Labour and income redistribution', *SR* 1965.
—— (1969), 'Primitive accumulation and early industrialization', *SR* 1969.
—— (1970), 'Britain: prospects for the 1970s', *SR* 1970.
—— (1973a), 'The ideology of labourism', in Benewick *et al.*, (eds), *Knowledge and Belief in Politics*, London: Allen & Unwin.
—— (1973b), 'Introduction' to *Working Conditions in the Victorian Age: Debates on the Issue from 19th Century Critical Journals*, London: Gregg International Publishers.
—— (1974a), 'Class struggle and the industrial revolution', *SR* 1974.
—— (1974b), *Marxism and History*, Hull: University of Hull.
—— (1976), 'The 20th Congress and the British CP', *SR* 1976.
—— (1987), *1848: The State and the Chartist Movement*, Cambridge: Cambridge University Press.
—— (1991), 'The Communist experience: a personal appraisal', *SR* 1991.
Schmidt, A. (1962), *The Concept of Nature in Marx*, London: NLB, 1971.
Schwarz, B. (1982), '"The people" in history: the CP Historians Group, 1946–56', in Johnson, *et al.*, (eds), *Making Histories*, London: Hutchinson.
Scott, J. (1988), *Gender and the Politics of History*, New York: Columbia University Press.
Scruton, R. (1985), *Thinkers of the New Left*, Harlow: Longman.
Sedgwick, P. (1970), 'Varieties of socialist thought', in Crick and Robson (eds), *Protest and Discontent*, Harmondsworth: Penguin.
—— (1976), 'The two New Lefts', in Widgery (ed.), *The Left in Britain*, Harmondsworth: Penguin.
Selbourne, D. (1980), 'On the method of the History Workshop', *HWJ* 9, Spring 1980.
Seven Days, London, Nov. 1971–May 1972.
—— (1971), 'Patriotism', 24 Nov. 1971.
—— (1972), 'Editorial', 22 March 1972.
Shanin, T. (ed. 1972), *The Rules of the Game: Cross-Disciplinary Essays on Methods*, London: Tavistock Publications.
Shipley, P. (1976), *Revolutionaries in Modern Britain*, London: The Bodley Head.
Skidelsky, R. (1970), 'Lessons of Suez', in Bogdanor and Skidelsky (eds), *The Age of Affluence*, London: Macmillan.
Skinner, Q. (ed. 1985), *The Return of Grand Theory*, Cambridge: Cambridge University Press.
Sklair, L. (1981), 'Sociologies and Marxisms: the odd couples', in Arams *et al.*, (eds), *Practice and Progress*, London: Allen & Unwin.
Snow, C. P. (1959), *The Two Cultures and the Scientific Revolution*, Cambridge: Cambridge University Press.
Sraffa, P. (1960), *The Production of Commodities by Means of Commodities*, Cambridge: Cambridge University Press.
Stedman Jones, G. (1965), 'London and the revolutionaries', *NLR* 31, May/June 1965.
—— (1967), 'The pathology of English history', *NLR* 46, Nov./Dec. 1967; reprinted as 'History; the poverty of empiricism' in Blackburn (ed.), *Ideology in Social Science*, London: Fontana.
—— (1969), 'The meaning of the student revolt', in Cockburn and Blackburn (eds), *Student Power*, Harmondsworth: Penguin.
—— (1970), 'The specificity of US imperialism', *NLR* 60, March/April 1970; reprinted in Blackburn (ed.), *Ideology in Social Science*, London: Fontana.
—— (1971a), 'The Marxism of the early Lukács: an evaluation', *NLR* 70, Nov./Dec. 1971; reprinted in NLB, *Western Marxism*.
—— (1971b), *Outcast London: A Study in the Relationship between Classes in Victorian Society*, Harmondsworth: Penguin.
—— (1972), 'The road to revolution', Seven Days, no. 19, 8–14 March 1972.
—— (1973), 'Engels and the end of classical German philosophy', *NLR* 79, May/June 1973.
—— (1974), 'Working-class culture and working-class politics in London', *Journal of Social History*, Summer 1974.
—— (1975), 'Class struggle and the industrial revolution', *NLR* 90, March/April 1975.

—— (1976), 'From historical sociology to theoretical history', *British Journal of Sociology*, vol. 27, no. 3, Sept. 1976.

—— (1977a), 'Class expression versus social control?', *HWJ* 4, Autumn 1977.

—— (1977b), 'Society and politics at the beginning of the world economy', *Cambridge Journal of Economics*, vol. I, no. 1, 1977.

—— (1977c), 'Engels and the genesis of Marxism', *NLR* 106, Nov./Dec. 1977; reprinted in Hobsbawm (ed.), *The History of Marxism*, vol. I, Brighton: Harvester, 1982.

—— (1979), 'Letter to *HWJ*', *HWJ* 8, Autumn 1979.

—— (1981), 'Utopian socialism reconsidered', in Samuel (ed.), *People's History*, London: Routledge.

—— (1982), 'The language of Chartism', in Epstein and Thompson (eds), *The Chartist Experience*, London: Macmillan.

—— (1983a), *Language of Class: Studies in English Working-class History 1832–1982*, Cambridge: Cambridge University Press.

—— (1983b), 'Why is the Labour Party in a mess?', in Stedman Jones, 1983a.

—— (1984a), 'Tawneyism is not enough', *New Statesman*, 21/28 Dec. 1984.

—— (1984b), 'Marching into history', in Curran (ed.), *The Future of the Left*, Cambridge: Polity Press.

—— (1985), 'Parternalism revisited', *MT*, July 1985.

Steedman, I. (1977), *Marx After Sraffa*, London: NLB.

—— (1979a), *Trade Amongst Growing Economics*, Cambridge: Cambridge University Press.

—— (1979b), *Foundamental Issues in Trade Theory*, London: Macmillan.

Steedman, I. and Sweezy, P. *et al.*, (1981), *The Value Controversy*, London: Verso.

Strachey, J. (1956), *Contemporary Capitalism*, London: Victor Gollancz.

—— (1959), *The End of Empire*, London: Victor Gollancz.

Sweezy, P. (1978), 'Comment on Brenner', *NLR* 108, March/April 1978.

Taylor, B. (1981), 'Socialist feminism: utopian or scientific?', in Samuel (ed.), *People's History*, London: Routledge.

—— (1983), *Eve and the New Jerusalem: Socialism and Feminism in the Nineteenth Century*, New York: Pantheon Books.

Taylor, C. (1957), 'Marxism and humanism', *NR* 2, Autumn 1957.

—— (1960a), 'What's wrong with capitalism?', *NLR* 3, May/June 1960.

—— (1960b), 'Comments on revolution', *NLR* 4, July/Aug. 1960.

—— (1966), 'Marxism and empiricism', in Williams and Montefiore (eds), *British Analytical Philosophy*, London: Routledge.

—— (1968), 'From Marxism to the dialogue society', in Eagleton and Wicker (eds), *From Culture to Revolution*, London: Sheed & Ward.

—— (1983), *Social Theory as Practice*, Oxford: Oxford University Press.

—— (1985), *Human Agency and Language*, Cambridge: Cambridge University Press.

—— (1988), 'Logics of disintegration', *NLR* 170, July/Aug. 1988.

Taylor, J. R. (ed. 1968), *John Osborne: Look Back in Anger*, London: Macmillan.

Taylor, R. (1970), 'The CND', in Bogdanor and Skidelsky (eds), *The Age of Affluence*, London: Macmillan.

Taylor, R. and Pritchard, C. (1980), *The Protest Makers: The British Nuclear Disamament Movement of 1958–65, Twenty Years On*, Oxford: Pergamon.

Taylor, R. and Ward, K. (1983), 'Community politics and direct action: the non-aligned left', in Coates and Johnston (eds), *Socialist Strategies*, Oxford: Martin Robertson.

Teich, M. and Young, R. (eds 1973), *Changing Perspectives in the History of Science: Essays in Honour of Joseph Needham*, Dordrecht: D. Reidel Publishing Co.

Teodori, M. (ed. 1970), *The New Left: A Documentary History*, London: Jonathan Cape.

Therborn, G. (1970), 'The Frankfurt school', *NLR* 63, Sept./Oct. 1970.

—— (1974), 'The theorists of capitalism', *NLR* 87-88, Sept./Dec. 1974.

—— (1976), *Science, Class and Society: On the Formation of Sociology and Historical Materialism*, London: NLB.

Thompson, D. (1960), 'Farewell to the welfare state', *NLR* 4, July/Aug. 1960.

—— (1971), *The Early Chartists*, Columbia: University of South Carolina Press.

—— (1983), *Over Our Dead Bodies: Women Against the Bomb*, London: Virago.

—— (1984), *The Chartists: Popular Politics in the IndustrialRevolution*, New York: Pantheon.

Thompson, E. P. (1955), *William Morris: Romantic to Revolutionary*, London: Lawrence & Wishart; rev. edn. (1976c), New York: Pantheon, 1976.
—— (1956a), 'Through the smoke of Budapest', *The Reasoner*, no. 3.
—— (1956b), 'Winter wheat in Omsk', *World News*, 30 June 1956.
—— (1957a), 'Socialism and the intellectuals', *ULR* 1, Spring 1957.
—— (1957b), 'A reply', *ULR* 2, Autumn 1957.
—— (1957c), 'Socialist humanism', *NR* 1, Summer 1957.
—— (1958a), 'Nato, neutralism and survival', *ULR* 4, Spring 1958.
—— (1958b), 'Agency and choice', *NR* 5, Summer 1958.
—— (1959a), 'The New Left', *NR* 9, Summer 1959.
—— (1959b), 'Apsessay in Ephology', *NR* 10, late Autumn 1959.
—— (1959c), 'Commitment in politics', *ULR* 6, Spring 1959.
—— (1959d), *The Communism of William Morris* (a lecture given in May 1959), London: The William Morris Society, 1965.
—— (1960a), 'Outside the whale', in NLB, *Out of Apathy*.
—— (1960b), 'Revolution', in NLB, *Out of Apathy*.
—— (1960c), 'Revolution again!', *NLR* 6, Nov./Dec. 1960.
—— (1960d), 'At a point of decay', in NLB, *Out of Apathy*.
—— (1961a; 1961b), 'The long revolution', *NLR* 9, May/June 1961; *NLR* 10, July/Aug. 1961.
—— (1961c), 'The segregation of dissent', *New University*, May 1961.
—— (1963a), *The Making of the English Working Class*, London: Victor Gollancz; 2nd edn. Harmondsworth: Penguin, 1968.
—— (1963b), 'C. Wright Mills', *Peace News*, 29 Nov. 1963.
—— (1965), 'The peculiarities of the English', *SR* 1965.
—— (1967), 'Preface' to Lynd, *Class Conflict, Slavery, and the United States Constitution*, Indianapolis: Bobbs–Merrill.
—— (1971a), 'The moral economy of the English crowd in the 18th century', *Past and Present*, no. 50, 1971.
—— (1971b), 'Class consciousness in history', in Meszaros (ed.), *Aspects of History and Class Consciousness*, London: Routledge.
—— (1972), 'Anthropology and the discipline of historical context', *Midland History*, vol. I, no. 3, Spring 1972.
—— (1973), 'An open letter to Leszek Kolakowski', *SR* 1973; reprinted in Thompson, 1978a.
—— (1974), 'Patrician society, plebeian culture', *Journal of Social History*, Summer 1974.
—— (1975a), *Whigs and Hunters: The Origin of the Black Act*, Harmondsworth: Penguin.
—— (1975b), 'A nice place to visit', *New York Review of Books*, 6 Feb. 1975.
—— (1976a), 'Romanticism, moralism and utopianism', *NLR* 99, Sept./Oct. 1976.
—— (1976b), 'Interview', Abelove *et al.*, (eds), *Visions of History*, Manchester: Manchester University Press.
—— (1976d), 'On history, sociology and historical relevance', *British Journal of Sociology*, vol. 27, no. 3, 1976.
—— (1978a), *The Poverty of Theory and Other Essays*, London: Merlin.
—— (1978b), 'E. P. Thompson: recovering the libertarian tradition', *The Leveller*, no. 22, Jan. 1978.
—— (1978c), 'Eighteenth-century English society: class struggle without class?', *Social History*, no. 3, May 1978.
—— (1980a), *Protest and Survive*, CND pamphlet, Nottingham.
—— (1980b), *Writings by Candlelight*, London: Merlin.
—— (1981), 'The politics of theory', in Samuel (ed.), *People's History*, London: Routledge.
—— (1980c), 'Notes on exterminism, the last stage of civilization', *NLR* 121, May/June 1980.
—— (1982a), *Zero Option*, London: Merlin.
—— (1982b), *Beyond the Cold War*, New York: Pantheon.
Thompson, E. P. and Saville, J. (1956), 'Taking stock', *The Reasoner*, no. 1.
Thompson, E. P. and Smith, D. (eds 1980), *Protest and Survive*, Harmondsworth: Penguin.
Thompson, E. P. and Thompson, T. J. (eds 1947), *There is a Spirit in Europe: A Memoir of Frank Thompson*, London: Victor Gollancz.
Thompson, J. and Held, D. (eds 1982), *Habermas: Critical Debate*, Cambridge, MA: MIT Press.
Tinkham, L. (1969), 'Learning one's lesson', in Cockburn and Blackburn (eds), *Student Power*, Harmondsworth: Penguin.

Titmuss, R. (1964), 'The limits of the welfare state', *NLR* 27, Sept./Oct. 1964.
Topham, A. (1964), 'Shop stewards and workers' control', *NLR* 25, May/June 1964.
—— (1965), 'Incomes policy', *SR* 1965.
Trotsky, L. (1937), *The Revolution Betrayed: What is the Soviet Union and Where is it Going?*, London: New Park, 1957.
—— (1971), *The Struggle Against Fascism in Germany*, New York: Pathfinder.
Wallerstein, I. (1974), *The Modern World System*, New York: Academic Press.
—— (1984), *The Politics of the World Economy: The State, the Movements, and the Civilizations*, Cambridge: Cambridge University Press.
Walton, P. and Hall, S. (eds 1972), *Situating Marx: Evaluations and Departures*, London: Human Context Books.
Walzer, M. (1980), *Radical Principles: Reflections of an Unreconstructed Democrat*, New York: Basic Books.
Ward, J. P. (1981), *Raymond Williams*, Cardiff: University of Wales Press.
Warren, B. (1973), 'Imperialism and capitalist industrialization', *NLR* 81, Sept./Oct. 1973.
—— (1980), *Imperialism: Pioneer of Capitalism*, London: NLB.
Waston, G. (1977), 'The significance of Raymond Williams', *New University Quarterly*, Summer 1977.
Wedderburn, D. (1962), 'Poverty in Britain today', *Sociological Review*, no. 3, 1962.
—— (1964), 'Pensions, equality and socialism', *NLR* 24, March/April 1964.
—— (1965), 'Facts and theories of the welfare state', *SR* 1965.
—— (1989), 'Activism of the New Left', in Archer *et al.*, (eds), *Out of Apathy*, London: Verso.
Werskey, G. (1978), *The Visible College: The Collective Biography of British Scientific Socialists of the 1930s*, New York: Holt, Rinehart & Winston.
Westergaard, J. H. (1964), 'Capitalism without classes?', *NLR* 26, July/Aug. 1964.
—— (1965), 'The withering away of class', in NLB, *Towards Socialism*.
Widgery, D. (1976), *The Left in Britain 1956–68*, Harmondsworth: Penguin.
Wiener, M. J. (1981), *English Culture and the Decline of the Industrial Spirit 1850–1980*, Cambridge: Cambridge University Press.
Williams, B. and Montefiore, A. (eds 1966), *British Analytical Philosophy*, London: Routledge.
Williams, G. (1979), 'In defence of history', *HWJ* 7, Spring 1979.
Williams, R. (1957a), 'Fiction and the writing public', in Williams, 1989a.
—— (1957b), 'Working-class culture', *ULR* 2, Summer 1957.
—— (1958a), 'Culture is ordinary', *Review Guardian*, 3 Feb. 1989.
—— (1958b), 'Our debt to Dr Leavis', *The Critical Quarterly*, Autumn 1958.
—— (1960a), 'Class and voting in Britain', *Monthly Review*, Jan. 1960.
—— (1960b), 'Working-class attitudes' (discussion with Hoggart), *NLR* 1, Jan./Feb. 1960.
—— (1961a), *Culture and Society 1780–1950*, London: Chatto & Windus, 1958; Harmondsworth: Penguin, 1961.
—— (1961b), *The Long Revolution*, London: Pelican Books.
—— (1961c), 'Communications and community', in Williams, 1989c.
—— (1962), *Communications*, 3rd edn. Harmondsworth: Penguin, 1976.
—— (1964), *Second Generation*, London: Chatto & Windus.
—— (1965), 'The British Left', *NLR* 30, March/April 1965.
—— (1966), *Modern Tragedy*, rev. edn. London: Verso, 1979.
—— (ed. 1967), *May Day Manifesto*, Harmondsworth: Penguin, 1968.
—— (1968a), 'Culture and revolution: a response', in Eagleton and Wicker (eds), *From Culture to Revolution*, London: Sheed & Ward.
—— (1968b), 'Seeing the connections', in Coates (ed.), *A Future for British Socialism*, Nottingham: Spokesman.
—— (1970a), 'An experimental tendency', *The Listener*, no. 3, Dec. 1970.
—— (1970b), *The English Novel from Dickens to Lawrence*, London: Chatto & Windus.
—— (1971), 'Literature and sociology: in memory of Lucien Goldmann', *NLR* 67, May/June 1971.
—— (1972), 'On Solzhenitsyn', in Williams, 1989a.
—— (1973a), *The Country and the City*, London: Chatto & Windus.
—— (1973b), 'Base and superstructure', *NLR* 82, Nov./Dec. 1973.
—— (1973c), 'The city and the world', in Williams, 1989a.

—— (1974), *Television: Technology and Cultural Form*, London: Fontana.
—— (1975), 'You're a Marxist, aren't you?', in Williams, 1989c.
—— (1976a), *Keywords: A Vocabulary of Culture and Society*, Oxford: Oxford University Press.
—— (1976b), 'Notes on Marxism in Britain since 1945', *NLR* 100, Nov./Dec. 1976; reprinted in Williams, *Problems in Materialism and Culture*, London: Verso, 1980.
—— (1977), *Marxism and Literature*, Oxford: Oxford University Press.
—— (1979), *Politics and Letters* (interviews with *NLR*), London: Verso.
—— (1980a), *Problems in Materialism and Culture: Selected Essays*, London: Verso.
—— (1980b), 'The Bloomsbury fraction', in Williams, 1980a.
—— (1980c), 'The politics of nuclear disarmament', *NLR* 124, Nov./Dec. 1980.
—— (ed. 1981), *Contact: Human Communication and Its History*, London: Thames & Hudson.
—— (1981), *Culture*, London: Fontana.
—— (1982), 'The red and the green', in Williams, 1989a.
—— (1983a), *Towards 2000*, London: Chatto & Windus.
—— (1983b), 'Marx on culture', in Williams, 1989a.
—— (1983c), *Socialism and Ecology*, SERA (the Socialist Environment and Resources Association) pamphlet, London.
—— (1983d), 'Lukács: A man without frustration', in Williams, 1989a.
—— (1984), *Writing in Society*, London: Verso.
—— (1986), 'The uses of cultural theory', *NLR* 158, July/Aug. 1986.
—— (1988), 'The politics of hope' (interview with Eagleton), in Eagleton (ed.), *Raymond Williams*, Boston: Northeastern University Press.
—— (1989a), *What I Came to Say* (ed. by Mulhern), London: Hutchinson Radius.
—— (1989b), *The Politics of Modernism: Against the New Conformists* (ed. by Pinkney), London: Verso.
—— (1989c), *Resources of Hope* (ed. Gable), London: Verso.
Wohlfarth, I. (1967), 'Presentation of Adorno', *NLR* 46, Nov./Dec. 1967.
Wollen, P. (1969), *Signs and Meaning in the Cinema*, London: Thames & Hudson.
Wollheim, R. (1961), 'Culture and socialism', Fabian Tract, no. 331, London: Fabian Society.
—— (1975), 'Psychoanalysis and feminism', *NLR* 93, Sept./Oct. 1975.
Wood, E. M. (1982), 'The politics of theory and the concept of class: E. P. Thompson and his critics', *Studies in Political Economy*, Fall 1982.
—— (1986), *The Retreat from Class: A New 'True' Socialism*, London: Verso.
—— (1990), 'Falling through the cracks: E.P.Thompson and the debate on base and superstructure', in Kaye and McClelland (eds), *E. P. Thompson: Critical Perspectives*, Philadelphia: Temple University Press.
Wood, N. (1959), *Communism and British Intellectuals*, New York: Columbia University Press.
Worsley, P. (1960), 'Imperial retreat', in NLB, *Out of Apathy*.
—— (1961), 'Revolution of the Third World', *NLR* 12, Nov./Dec. 1961.
—— (1964a), *The Third World*, London: Weidenfeld & Nicolson.
—— (1964b), 'Bureaucracy and decolonization: democracy from the top', in Horowitz (ed.), *The New Sociology*, Oxford: Oxford University Press.
—— (ed. 1970), *Modern Sociology: Introductory Readings*, Harmondsworth: Penguin.
—— (ed. 1972), *Problems of Modern Society: A Sociological Perspective*, Harmondsworth: Penguin.
—— (1972), 'Fanon and the "lumpenproletariat"', *SR* 1972.
—— (1973), 'The state of theory and the status of theory', *Sociology*, vol. 8, no. 1, 1973.
—— (1980), 'Marxism and culture: the missing concept', *Occasional Paper*, no. 4, University of Manchester.
—— (1982), *Marx and Marxism*, London: Ellis Horwood & Tavistock Publication.
—— (1984), *The Three Worlds: Culture and World Development*, London: Weidenfeld & Nicolson.
—— (1989), 'Non-alignment and the New Left', in Archer *et al.*, (eds), *Out of Apathy*, London: Verso.
Wright, E. O. (1978), *Class, Crisis and the State*, London: NLB.
—— (1983), 'Giddens's critique of Marxism', *NLR* 138, March/April 1983.
Yeo, E. and Yeo, S. (eds 1981), *Popular Culture and Class Conflict*, Sussex: Harvester.
Young, N. (1977), *An Infantile Disorder? – The Crisis and Decline of the New Left*, London: Routledge.

Young, R. (1973), 'The historiography and ideological contexts of the 19th-century debate on man's place in nature', in Teich and Young (eds), *Changing Perspectives in the History of Science*, Boston: D. Reidel Publishing Co.

Zaretsky, E. and Chodorow, N. (1976), 'Psychoanalysis and feminism: rejoinder to Wollheim', *NLR* 96, March/April 1976 and *NLR* 97, May/June 1976.

Index